Maturation:
The <u>Adult</u> Paradigm

Maturation:
The <u>Adult</u> Paradigm

To: Colina
from Dr. Skipi ! Keep
up your interest in
    Psychological Maturity

Skipi Lundquist Smoot, PhD

To order additional copies of this book, contact:
Xlibris Corporation
1-888-795-4274
www.Xlibris.com
Orders@Xlibris.com
94102

TABLE OF CONTENTS

PART I—THE UNIVERSAL ENVIRONMENT

The "Path" to Eternity (Spiritual & Human Development)
RUNS THROUGH THE FABRIC OF THE UNIVERSE
(Map of Reality) and is Paved with Laws of Cause and Effect

- Diagram of **Seed of Human Potential**
- The **Music of the Universe** "Who Can Hear the Music? "What Questions does it ask?"
- The **Evolving Dancer**—Opportunities for Discovering Unique Potential
- A Philosophical Diagram—The **Fabric** and **Music of the Universe**
- The Seed of **Unique Potential Human Realm** Underlying Connections Spirit Realm.

PART II—INTRODUCTION TO ADULT

PSYCHOLOGICAL MATURATION
The "Missing Link" for Resolution of Anxiety
DIMENSIONS OF ADULT EGO & COGNITIVE DEVELOPMENT

The Four Tasks of Maturation

"Don't leave me"

"I'm Afraid to be alone.

PART III—"DANCING" TO THE MUSIC OF THE UNIVERSE.

The Fabric of the Universe is paved with Objective Laws of Cause & Effect

The Five Lessons of Life

PART IV—THE EVOLVING DANCER—

Essence of the Human Spirit

FORWARD

WHO WILL BE INTERESTED IN THIS BOOK

PROBLEMS THIS BOOK ADDRESSES

I believe the contents of this book will be of special interest to those searching for methods to develop: 1) **resistance to psychological pain**, (Resilience) (2) **more Independent** (critical) **thought processes**, 3) **resolution of excessive emotional attachment to others**, 4) **resolution of conflicting role expectations**, and 5**) more successful personal relationships**. It will be especially helpful for those searching for wisdom concerning issues of 6) **Aging**, 7) the **Meaning of Life**, and 8) **methods for enduring Grief**.

PSYCHOLOGICAL MATURATION, THE "MISSING LINK FOR FUNCTIONAL RESOLUTION OF ANXIETY.

Although human dysfunction has traditionally been classified as Pathology, my own professional experience indicates a majority of adult distress is the result of Psychological Immaturity rather than mental illness. **Psychological Maturation,** on the **Continuum of Human Development, is the** usually **disregarded but essential "Missing Link for attainment of functional Resolution of Anxiety.** The traits representative of **Mature Human Development <u>can</u>** lead to healthy psychological and spiritual growth. <u>Educational Methods </u>for its achievement can be learned to help arrive at more successful life choices.

Maturation: **The <u>Adult</u> Paradigm** is an Ego & Cognitive Model of Psychological Development. **Functional Resolution of Anxiety** is presented as one of the most central characteristics of **Mature Ego** Development. **Development of Human** Maturity allows greater toleration of anxiety and growth of personal potential as well as more satisfying interpersonal relationships.

A specific **criteria** for objective problem solving is presented. Potential Life decisions can be evaluated against an easily understood, realistic criteria. While it is true that certain Psychological Disorders may be the result of a chemical imbalance or biological predisposition to mental illness, most anxiety, depression, family or relationship problems can be greatly helped or alleviated by 1) a clear understanding of the stages of human development and then 2) purposefully working toward more mature responses to stressful situations. Symptoms traditionally perceived as neurosis may instead be understood as dysfunctional immaturity

Why the Problem Exists— How we contribute to our own problems

Treating clients in my capacity of Clinical Psychologist has taught me that most personal and relationship problems fall on a continuum ranging between Immaturity/Maturity vs one of Pathology and Wellness. At the Core of Psychological Immaturity is the inability to resolve feelings of inadequqcy, feel emotionally separate and behave as a unique, independent person.

Modern Research in **Cognitive Therapy**[1] indicates a majority of people with Psychological Dysfunction or problems in living can be helped simply by learning to "perceive" their problems differently. A more realistic understanding of **"Why"** Life's difficulties may occur and **"How"** we may be contributing to our own problems are necessary first steps for initiating change and working toward more mature responses to stressful situations. **However, it is absolutely necessary to have a clear understanding of issues concerning methods for functional resolution of Anxiety. Most Clients do not.**

Humans Beings are born with a "seed" of Unique Potential and many differences. Socialization, parenting, temperament and belief systems lead to construction of "Personalized Roadmaps" from which attempts to make sense of the world are made. Narrowly focused perceptions of Reality seldom provide desired outcomes for personal and relationship happiness. People turn to Therapy as a last resort to answer such Questions as "What is normal?", "Why don't you change?" and/or "Shouldn't those who love each other agree?" Behavior is critically effected by personal levels of 1) Ego

---

[1]   Albert Ellis, William Glasser, etc

Development, 2) inborn temperament, 3) self esteem and 4) ability to delay gratification & tolerate frustration.

Few Therapists discuss **Psychological Maturity** with clients as 1) a developmental goal, 2) a significant factor in adaptive <u>Adult</u> Psychological Functioning, 3) a characteristic of successful interpersonal interaction or 4) **its** <u>lack</u> as a root cause of Emotional Dysfunction. Instead, emotional pain is usually defined as symptomatic of pathology, irrational beliefs, chemical imbalances, the result of dysfunctional parents and/or family relationships, etc.

I am convinced that **unawareness of the absolute** necessity for independent <u>critical thinking</u> continues to be a major factor in the failure of many to identify and resolve basic causes of emotional pain and inappropriate behaviors. I believe that a realistic, well thought out philosophy of life <u>can</u> lead to acceptance of personal responsibility, ability to accept reality and development of both psychological and spiritual growth. My Definition of Psychological Maturation is emotional and cognitive independence combined with the ability to face reality and accept the truth. I believe that this Developmental Stage provides the "**Missing Link**" for accurate understanding of Human thought processes and behaviors on a continuum of Immaturity vs Maturity.

Development of MY <u>Professional</u> Ideology

I have been a Licensed Clinical Psychologist and Marriage & Family therapist in Private Practice for over 20 years. I received my Education on the Christopher Newport Campus of William & Mary in Williamsburg, Va and Pepperdine & the California School of Professional Psychology in California. I am a former Owner-Operator of 3 successful McDonald's Restaurants in California and Virginia.

My Doctoral Research investigated influences of gender and psychological Characteristics on Successful Business management skills within McDonald's Corporation and Franchise Personnel. This Research identified Initiative, Career Ambition, and Sensitivity as the most important predictors, with Verbal Communication, Leadership, and Organization Skills also high on the list.

My early professional career (1975-1994) included providing Psychodynamic[2] & Cognitive Psychotherapy, Psychological Assessment[3] and Treatment planning for Private Practice Clients, Employee Assistance Programs (EAP), Private schools, Group Home residents and families, teen age gang members in Residential Programs and County Jail inmates. I have developed Indivual Education Plans (IEP's) for clients of County Social Workers and supervised numerous MFT and PhD level Interns. **Populations** worked with has **included child molesters, murderers and the** seriously mentally ill.

During those early Clinical encounters Clients Symptoms consistently revealed Emotional Enmeshment and lack of autonomous, rational, objective thought processes to be major sources of pain and dysfunction. At that time, I believed the General Public's apprehension and frustration surrounding the relevance of psychological treatment were consequences of 1) misperception of Psychotherapy as **"Psychobabble"**, 2) fear of being labeled "**Abnormal**" and/or 3) difficulty receiving referrals for adequate care due to Managed Care's confusing definitions of "medical necessity" as a result of their focus on "<u>bottom line</u>" Business (vs Policy Holders) Health.

Continuum of Human Maturity/Immaturity vs Normal/Abnormal Thought and Behavior.

My intense interest in Psychological Theory, Research, Psychological Assessment and Client disclosures in Psychotherapy **quickly lead me to realize** that not only clients but much of the medical community as well, were in the dark or in disagreement concerning what constituted **"Normal"** behavior.

Gradually I came to realize that a <u>specific</u> set of **attitudes and behaviors** were the <u>deterministic</u> **basis** for attainment of what I considered to be a mature Level of <u>Psychological Development.</u> I

---

2   Transference (redirection of feelings)

3   WAIS-R, WISC-R, WIAT, Rorshach, MMPI, DAP, TAT, etc. Wisc, iaat, wais, ksnap, conners adhd, barkley scales adhd, browns scales for adhd, LD, Neuropsych screening, Lddi, Bender, VMI, Tomal, Bnce, Qnst, Dtrroit for LD, Rorshach, Mmpi, Piers Harris, Taylor Johnson, TAT, CAT Beck anxiety and dep, TECD, Beck suicide, MSE, Neuropsych MSE, Holland, Strong, Manson addictive, Leadership style, Forer Workplace Attitude---

named this **Stage of Development, Psychological Maturation**[4]. I believed the characteristics of this Developmental Stage to represent a "Missing Link" **on the continuum of Human Maturity/ Immaturity rather than the commonly assumed Continuum between Normal vs Abnormal thought and behavior.**

Without a broad understanding of both normal and abnormal human attitudes and behavior, society will continue to 1) misidentify normal, dysfunctional but immature mental processes and 2) punish symptoms of mental illness and dysfunctional immaturity rather than address it with the education and treatment necessary for the potential growth of the human being who manifests it.

Convinced of the necessity and urgency for sharing my diagnostic findings and beliefs concerning essential diagnostic and treatment criteria I developed Brochures, Client Handouts and Business Seminars. I shared my Theories of Human Development and Methods of Treatment in supervision of interns, Professional Seminars and presentations to other professionals. I began writing a book. Psychological Maturation: The Adult Paradigm and Psychological Test, Test of Ego and Cognitive Development based on the underlying premise of Psychological Maturation as a Human Developmental Stage resulting from the ability to **Face** (objective) **Reality** and **Accept the Truth** of Cause & Effect.

Coping with Tragedy— Essence of Spirit on the Road of Life

Then in 1994 I was faced with personal tragedy of such magnitude that I was forced to recognize **Spiritual Philosophy** to be of equal importance to Psychological Maturation for human development. The murder of my 24 year old son, Blake became the catalyst for my personal search for spirit. For over a year, I frantically searched for answers concerning "where" he went, how life can be vibrant one minute and disappear the next and whether or not I could live with the pain of his loss.

---

[4]   The Self Actualization (Maslow) and/or Moral development (Kohlberg) theories were the closest I could come to what I came to define as Psychological Maturation: The Adult Paradigm.

During that year, my frenzied search for the spirit of my son, answers concerning Life's meaning and some type of evidence for validation of a spiritual realm consumed my existence. Because I am a scientist, needing some type of proof, a search for possible scientific hypotheses concerning the elements of a spiritual realm became my daily reason for living.

I found some clarification & possible answers to my frantic questions in the categories of my own independent cognitive conclusions, the scientific hypotheses of Quantum Mechanics and personal spiritual experiences (serendipity, synchronicity, dreams, etc). At the end of that year, I had no doubt that an independently arrived at, clearly thought out, objective philosophy of life was an essential aspect of successful human development. I knew it, because without the ability to face reality and search for as much objective truth as I could find, I could never have survived.

During the past 5 years, continued unbearable personal tragedy has presented itself on my path through life. In **2003**, two months after the heartbreaking loss of my adored 96 year old father, I was once again forced to face the necessity to say the dreaded words . . . "Goodbye for a little while" . . . to the living presence of a second son who had also entered Eternity without warning. Frantically calling out "Wake up Kurt . . . Wake Up," to the body lying silent and still in the warm summer afternoon . . . dazedly Dialing 911 . . . mechanically responding to instructions to touch his body in a search for life . . . I realized in numbness that his arm was ice cold and that his closed eyes would never again open in life. My heart cried out in so much pain . . . I honestly didn't believe I could live through it . . . again. But as a Psychologist . . . continually attempting to encourage clients to face reality and accept the truth, I knew I could not possibly demand less of myself.

In 2004, the overwhelming nightmare . . . too terrible to believe . . . impossible to understand continued. Turning toward sounds of a loud reverberating crash, moments after leaving a vibrant conversation with a living son, I found myself staring dumbfounded into the sightless dead eyes of yet a 3rd son . . . lying motionless on the floor before me. Horrifying memories of frantic screams . . . "Mark's dead, Mark's dead, . . .""Call 911" dwell in my heart. Mentally crouching in terror, trying to hide from the Paramedics dreaded words "he's gone" . . . I found myself once again forced to ask the unthinkable question

"How can I possibly live through this agony again?" But as before . . . drifting toward me on wisps of pain, the reality of its objective answer slowly settled over me . . ."Because I have no choice"

Why is this Book an Answer to many of life problems?

Most of us have asked such questions as **"Why was I born?"**, "Is there a purpose to life?" and "If there is a Purpose . . . What is my Mission in the world?" These questions, unique to each of us, can only be answered by asking the additional question "Where is the Real Me?" Topics set forth in this book include techniques for developing "unique personal potential", 4 essential tasks of Mature Human development and 5 Necessary Lessons for attaining Personal Strength, Success and Happiness.

Maturation: **The Adult Paradigm** is a New Self Help Model for Psychological Maturation. It teaches a clear logical, method for resolving conflict, coping with stress and making successful decisions based on critical evaluation of cause and effect underlying objective reality. It is an ideal accompaniment to Traditional Psychotherapy, Group, Family or Marital Therapy. Every effect has a cause. The Map describes methods for functional resolution of anxiety on a Continuum of Human Ego Development. A specific problem solving criteria is presented leading to functional resolution of anxiety and psychological growth. Psychological Maturation includes achievement of 1) **Objective critical thinking,** 2) **Resolution of Emotional Symbiotic Attachment,** 3) **Resolution of Narcissism** and 4) **an Objective—Philosophy of Life.**

The following points of view presented in this book are a culmination of my Personal and Professional experiences combined with Educational and Professional knowledge. I am convinced that

1. **Psychological Maturation** is a Human **Developmental Stage** resulting from the ability to **Face** (objective) **Reality, Accept the Truth** of Cause & Effect.
2. I perceive **Human Life** to be a multifaceted arena of **Instructional Opportunities** within **Human Relationships**, **Life Situations**, and **Universal Connections** (serendipity,

dreams, synchronicity, intuition, meditation, dreams) for development of both human and spiritual potential.

3. I believe the **Path to Eternity (Spiritual Maturation)** runs thru the **Fabric of the Universe** (Map of Human Reality) and is paved with Realistic **Laws of Cause & Effect**.

4. And I have become **convinced** as a result of my **readings and personal experiences that Scientific Research** (Quantum Mechanics, Hypnosis, Parapsychology, etc.) will eventually discover a method for **validation** of the existence of the Spiritual Realm.

You may ask "Why should any Professional assume to know the answers to the myriad of problems surrounding the lives of other Human Beings?" After all Psychologists are just people too . . . like everyone else". I agree that Answers to Life's meaning is Unique to each of us. But I also know from long personal and professional experience that answers to Human Problems lie in the areas of acceptance of Objective Reality and Critical thought processes. This book has been written as an Educational, Self Help Experience. Reading it will be like enrolling in a course of Psychological Theory.

I hope the words in this book will be of comfort to those searching for answers and resolution of personal and interpersonal pain, uncertainty concerning Meaning of Life and questions concerning Death and Dying . . . Answers to such questions reside in commonalities central to the concepts underlying Human Development and the buoyancy and hardiness of Spiritual Growth.

We are born at the beginning of our potential path into Eternity. By our attitudes and behaviors we choose to explore it . . . or . . . not.

PREFACE

Who I Am and Why I wrote this Book

I grew up in a logging Camp in Washington State in close proximity with owls, foxes, wild bears and wolves. My Father and Grandfather both worked in the Logging Industry. Our families lived in cabins in the woods across the train tracks from each other.

When I was 6, we moved to town so I could go to school. he depression in the 30's was a terrible economical burden to logging families, leading my parents to the necessity of living with my paternal grandparents until I married at 18 years of age. I was not encouraged to be educated. Neither my father nor mother finished high school. My father was an extremely intelligent man who hated the logging industry and worked as an Insurance Agent until he retired from Prudential Insurance Co. In 1964 after retirement, he bought the first of 5 McDonald's Unit in Lomita, Cal and ran them successfully until he died at 96 years of age. His License plates bore the legend MR MAC D

I am a Psychologist because of my Mother's mental illness. When I was young I believed she was the most beautiful woman in the world. At 44 years of age, after the death of her identical Twin Sister, my mother was diagnosed with Paranoid Schizophrenia. One of a set of identical twin girls she had 4 older brothers who doted on their darling little sisters. My mother was always quite self centered. As an adult she worked in a dress shop and modeled clothes in fashion presentations. After her world came to an end (when her sister died), she listened to voices of Communists over the Loud speakers in airports, heard voices discussing her through solid walls and was the recipient of shock treatment in Napa Hospital in Cal during the 1940's. After Neuroleptics were discovered she was able to baby sit or work at Good Will when she took her medication. When she refused, she lived in Board & Care Homes. She died at 76 "waiting for her life to begin".

My mother came to live with me, my husband and our two little boys after the death of her sister. The fear that I too might become mentally ill leads me at 35 years of age to enter both Psychotherapy and Community College to study Psychology. I was fascinated with the subject of Psychology and relieved to learn that although Schizophrenia does run in families it does so a negative gene, doesn't effect everyone in the family and those with a strong tolerance for stress are less often effected. Today I am positive her Dx was in error. Major Depression with Psychotic Symptoms would be a more accurate Diagnosis.

Moving to California after my father's sister, Jane married Ray Kroc, the founder of McDonald's restaurants, turned out to be the most **synchronistic** event in my life. For 13 years I owned and operated 3 McDonald's in California and Virginia. As a result of the sale of these Units I was able to finance 10 years of College.

My own Psychotherapy illustrated the fact that I didn't have to be a Victim. As a result of that knowledge I was able to take charge of my own life, finish College, Graduate school and earn a PhD in Clinical Psychology. My Doctoral Dissertation examined Psychological Characteristics of successful McDonald's Business Managers. I thank God and bow to Chicago every day at 5PM in honor of the absolutely wonderful **Serendipitous, Synchronistic** events that lead me (**from a poor small town, uneducated family**) to reading encyclopedia's about Schizophrenia, moving to California after my Aunt married Ray Kroc, to earning a PhD in Psychology. I raised my 4 sons in Virginia and California. I have been happily remarried for 32 years to a man who on a scale of 1-10 is a 10 husband.

My work is one of the most joyful experiences of my life. I tell my clients that if they can make a living doing something they would love to do for nothing, they have hit the jack pot. That is the way I feel about my profession. I enjoyed owning and running 3 McDonald's units, but I did not love it. I have never been sorry for selling them. But I am eternally grateful for the opportunity to have had them. They provided me with the assets necessary to go to College for 10 years, raise my 4 sons and do the research for my Doctoral Dissertations. I am absolutely convinced that we come to this world (the Earth School) to learn lessons from each other. I believe in **serendipity, synchronicity** and other types of **spiritual experiences** because the events in my life and the lives of my family members have been affected repeatedly as a result of many experiences of "Luck", Chance meetings, Fate and other instances of **serendipity** and **synchronicity.**

Development of Maturation Theory
-Early Professional experience-

After I received my PhD and began private practice, I realized that although students are taught numerous different methods of Psychotherapy, from Psychoanalytic to Behavioral to Cognitive to . . . etc . . . we are not taught **how** to do therapy. As a result I began keeping notes concerning my client's main issues and found them to fall into 5 categories of emotional and/or cognitive difficulty: 1) attempts to control others or external situations, 2) Did not take personal Responsibility (or too much for others, 3) Distorted Reality 4) inability to delay gratification or control frustration and/or 5) were always in a state of crisis. I began consideration of what might be the result of clients' perception of their areas of concern from the realistic frame work of Cause and Effect. I soon realized that if they were to do so, they would learn to face reality and accept the truth concerning their situation. They would also become more comfortable thinking for themselves, being emotionally separate, interdependent with others who were interdependent and arriving at their own objective realistic philosophy of life. Over a length of time, I came to the realization that such emotional and cognitive dysfunction were symptomatic of Psychological Immaturity resulting from issues of **ADULT SEPARATION ANXIETY** (Inability to feel and behave as a separate person).

Applying theory underlying concepts presented in my book, I have written a Psychological Test Instrument, **The Test of Ego & Cognitive Development (TECD).** This test has 10 scales 43 subscales. A Pilot Study in in Process. It can be used for Clinicians, Hospitals, Drug Addiction and Impulse control problems. It Identifies which maturation Task(s) or Lesson(s) is or is not deficient.

WHAT I LEARNED FROM MY CLIENTS:

During the early years of working with Clients, I saw that only about 20% of clients have a chemical imbalance or severe mental disorder. The other 80% although often anxious and/or depressed were not mentally ill. They were found to be unable to successfully & comfortably resolve Personal and Interpersonal conflict, cope with anxiety and stress or make confident successful decisions due to thought processes resulting from cultural, social, religious or familial expectations that don't mesh with those of marital partners, lovers, good friends, etc.

I realized that many of my clients had phenomenal results working with AA Sponsors in spite of fact such persons rarely have formal training in Psychotherapy. I decided that one of the most important reasons for their success was the fact that "they have been there done that". I realized that many Clients didn't like working with Single Therapists for Marital Issues or young therapists for problems related to mid life, aging, etc.

Because I believed clients could be helped more quickly and with less anxiety if therapeutic emphasis was placed on a Human Development Model of Strengths and Weaknesses vs the Medical Model of Pathology and Mental Illness, I theorized the average person would benefit in therapy from an Educational Model of Normality and Human Maturation.

I searched for a way to develop 1) a clear, simple Model for helping clients identify and understand their current level of Ego and Cognitive Maturity and 2) a clear, simple method (Realistic Attitudes and Behavioral Processes) for developing the highest possible level of Human Maturity the Client was capable of. As a result of my personal experiences, Professional Work with patients, and Doctoral Research with McDonald's Corporation Management Personnel during the years between 1985-1994, I integrated a model of Ego and Cognitive Maturation. The basic premise of this Philosophy is that personal Growth and Mature Relationships can occur as a result of Developing a Set of Attitudes and Behaviors in accord with the Universal process of cause and effect underlying Human behavior and Communication.

WHAT I TELL MY CLIENTS

- I tell my clients that Therapy with me is like taking a course in Psychological theory.
- I encourage my clients to see me an equal person who has "Been there/Done That" and Psychotherapy as an educational experience.
- I will help my clients work on the problems they believe are important.
- I will not tell clients what to do. I will give my opinion when and if asked. I will share what I did under similar circumstances if they request such information. I will critique possible scenarios. 0
- I encourage my clients to perceive the 5 Categories of emotional and behavioral symptoms as areas of negative energy ("Quick Sand") out of line with the reality of Cause & Effect. I encouraged them to

"float free" from the Negative energy, into the "Positive Energy of "Reality" and learn to walk on their own path.
- I help them realize that people who love each other do not always agree and that opposites do not always attract.
- I encourage them to realize that although Chemical attraction is very important in a new marriage, understanding what issues their own Non-Negotiable Values consists of is absolutely necessary for continued marital happiness.
- I have few expectations for clients individual Philosophy of Life except that it fit with their own well thought out values based on as much objective Reality as possible during the time of our existence in the world.

Defining an Objective personal Philosophy of Life is imperative for happiness. Marital partners rarely walk down the same Philosophical Path of life. However, it is important that individual paths would be close enough to hold hands as they walk through life together. Human beings have lessons to learn from each other. Those we choose to engage in Relationships with are not chosen by accident. We can choose to learn from them . . . or hide from them . . . as we see fit.

Maturation: The Adult Paradigm
Dancing to the Music of the Universe

Psychological maturation results from an Observing Ego sufficiently developed to face Reality and accept truth. Ego Boundaries must be strong enough to resolve excessive emotional dependency on others and develop unique personal identity & potential. Both my book & workbook have questionnaires and worksheets to assess and advance a readers' present level of personal maturation.

As a result of both professional and personal experience I believe that two categories of human development, **Psychological** & Spiritual, are the most important contributors to personal ability to cope with stress, resolve conflict, make successful confident decisions, set realistic goals and develop a well thought out personal philosophy of life. **Follow The Map (Lessons of Life) and learn to dance to the "Music" of the Universe (Cause & Effect),**

Personal Philosophy of Life—
"Fit" in the Universe

We are each born with a seed of Unique Human Potential. We may choose to explore it or not. **Development of Human potential** demands **Psychological Maturation**. And only by resolving the problems that deter us from psychological maturation are we free to explore our mission in the Universe.

Personal **Choices** are presented to each of us in the form of personal decisions, serendipity, synchronicity and problem solving with other people. The ability to face reality and make choices based on cause and effect allows The Human Developmental Stage of Maturation to occur.

I visualize **Cause and Effect** as a Force of Positive Energy (, Love, Reality, Respect) floating above the negative energy (quicksand of fear, resentment, unrealistic perceptions and expectations,) trapping our potential mature development within the confines of dysfunction. To break free from our self imposed bonds, allowing ourselves to bathe in the positive energy of love and respect for ourselves and others, we must face reality and accept the truth about ourselves and our environment. Only then are we free as human beings to explore our human and spiritual missions in the universe.

Psychological Maturation is the doorway leading to a more complete understanding of our unique potential and "fit" in the Universe. Although I believe "God" created the Universe including the spiritual Realm —it is unclear to me "what" God is. However, I believe that the "God" who created the Spiritual Realm also created the Universe in a manner that would allow the **evolution** of Life through animals, humans, etc. universe

Scientific Research indicates that Animals are ruled by their Limbic systems (**emotion**). Human Beings have evolved into similar but different creatures as a result of having been endowed with a **Cortex. The Cortex and Ego structure of human beings are separate from each other. This physiological separation allows Human beings to think about**

feelings and (providing that some level of Psychological Maturation has occurred) to choose to respond to feelings or not and devise methods of solving our problems in ways that allow human, moral and spiritual growth.

I believe Sexuality has been bestowed by our creator is a gift for perpetuating Life. The fact that it is enjoyable is an added plus, making the perpetuation of life forms more reliable. Sexuality is the animal part of human beings. A main difference between Animals and Human beings is our Cortex. I believe God has allowed Evolution to result in a cortex. I believe God expects Human Beings to to think for and help themselves. We have been given the Evolution tools necessary for and Human and Spiritual Development.

I perceive Human Life as a training ground for learning the lessons necessary for Psychological Maturation and spiritual evolution.

I believe that Science is a gift from Our Creator that will eventually lead to a method for development of scientific proof of the existence of the spiritual realm. I believe spiritual growth may be a result of the Lessons we learn on earth. I believe the Human Spirit evolves as a result of human development and underlying connections (spirituality, serendipity, dreams, etc.) in the Universe.

I believe there is a spiritual realm, that the **spiritual realm** is **Real** (Non Local) but we just can't see it. <u>Nonlocal</u> (Invisible but also real). This is either because its properties are too small to be seen (subtle matter) or are constructed from aspects of energy that have not been identified.

I believe the Soul comes from the Implicate Order and resides in human form (Explicate Order) while on Earth. Because the Soul comes from the spiritual Realm it can connect instantaneously with Human consciousness. The soul is composed of consciousness at different levels and accessible through different stages (sleep, hypnosis, dreams, obe's etc.). I believe in ESP, Out of Body, Underlying connections, communication with spirits, etc. I believe in Soul Mates. I believe our relationships with others are no accident because we have lessons to learn from each other.

I believe that at any moment in life our life is the direct result of our past choices. I believe that Mistakes are God's method of teaching us what works and what doesn't. Reincarnation makes more sense to me than any other type of spiritual theory. I am not a proponent of any type of Organized religion. However, I am very spiritual.

I believe the Purpose of Life and Human Mission is to grow, learn lessons for human and spiritual development. I believe the Purpose of Life and our Human Mission is to grow and learn lessons for human and spiritual development. I believe there is a Real Scientific Explanation for the Spiritual Realm, the Soul and Consciousness. I have had personal experience with dreams, Out of Body Experiences and  unexplained frequency realm type phenomena. I am also convinced that science will eventually be able to prove the existence of the spiritual realm, underlying connections and the reality of a multidimensional Universe.

INTRODUCTION

The "Map"

Maturation: ↑ the <u>Adult</u> Paradigm[1]
THEORY OF THE "Missing link"

<u>Normal/Abnormal</u>
Development of Human Cognition

Coming to Terms with Life—Why Life is so Hard
The average person searches in vain for an illusive something called **"Happiness"** not realizing answers lie in mature decisions based on ability to face objective (vs subjective) reality, accept truths concerning our past and present situations and willingness to recognize the difference.

Most people enter Therapy because their life isn't working, they don't understand why and they're willing "try anything" to feel better (including consulting a "Shrink" for help). Even in our modern educated society, many misperceptions concerning Psychotherapy exist. Some of the most erroneous conclusions include the beliefs that only a truly Mentally Ill person could benefit from consulting a Therapist, Adults "Should" be able to solve their own problems, that Psychotherapy is "Psychobabble", personal problems "should" be private, consulting a therapist is an admission of weakness or that a person who seeks help will be negatively judged by others.

Many of these barriers to solving or alleviating life's problems exist as a result of cultural, traditional or ideas learned in our families of origin. Most reflect an underlying disagreement concerning characteristics

---

[1] Copy right—Skipi Lundquist Smoot, PhD 1994

of normal human attitudes and conduct as well as the conviction that their own definition of Normal is correct.

The Search for Normal

To date there are no professionally or scientifically agreed upon definitions of Normal vs Abnormal Human attitudes and Behaviors. Depending on the theorist, Definitions of Normal behavior may include Typical (Socially conforming—Responsible—average—adhering to a pattern) and/or functional2 (inferred from successful use of high level defenses, displayed in socially appropriate attitudes and behaviors). Abnormal behavior **(departing from the Normal)** may include—dysfunctional3 mental processes traditionally perceived as learned patterns of Defensive pathological attitudes & behaviors. These defenses protect from both internal and external stressors.

Professionals generally agree upon criteria for diagnoses of Psychosis **(loss of contact with reality)** and Anxiety **(a state of distress lacking an unambiguous cause)**. And although definitions of Neurosis continue to change over the years, **broad usage** defines it as **any** of various **Functional** Disorders **(without organic lesion or change)** of mind/emotion involving anxiety, **phobia, or** abnormal symptoms in an otherwise intact **Reality Base of Personality.**

Modern Research in Cognitive Therapy[4] indicates a majority of people with Psychological Dysfunction or problems in living can be helped simply by learning to "perceive" their problems differently. Lacking a fundamental understanding of the scientific and research foundation on which Theories of Psychotherapy are based, many derisively brand it as an absurd milieu in which personal problems are discussed in terms of an undecipherable "jargon" labeled as "psychobabble". Few are willing to admit to or be treated for dysfunction when dysfunctional mental processes are identified as mental Illnesses, immorality or criminal processes rather than symptomatic of the immature processes it often represents. Even those who realize psychology has "something" of value to offer may not understand

---

[2] without apparent organic or structural impairment

[3] unable to functioning normally as result of disease or impairment

[4] Albert Ellis, William Glasser, etc

that law and Morality are only two legs of a triad that *must* include a comprehensive understanding of the science of human ego and cognitive development to be effective.

A clear understanding of the Stages of Human Ego Development will help lead to more mature responses to stressful life situations. Educational Methods for achievement of higher levels of Psychological Maturity can be learned to help arrive at more successful life choices.

Without a broad knowledge of **Normal/Abnormal** human attitudes and behavior, society will continue to 1) misidentify **normal, dysfunctional but** immature mental processes and 2) punish symptoms of **mental illness** and **dysfunctional immaturity** rather than address it with the education and treatment necessary for the potential growth of the human being who manifests it.

Public Need for Knowledge—
Consequences of Exploitation

Every day tragic **instances of extreme** Exploitation of the General Public's lack of knowledge concerning **Adult Psychological Maturation** is presented to audiences by **TV Talk show Hosts** as examples of "electrifying drama", a means of vicarious thrill seeking, or an aid to increase television ratings. Some of the poor unfortunate souls who willingly allow themselves to be exploited on National Television do so as a means to continue seeking the attention they so desperately have searched for all their lives. Others, immaturely perceiving themselves to be the center of the universe, feel right at home on National TV.

In addition, extremist Radio Talk Show Hosts "Blame the Victim" by presenting examples of Dysfunctional Adult Immature behavior and encourage us to "crack down on", "throw the book at", or quit helping "Lazy Freeloaders". As a result of too narrowly focused viewpoints, punishment as a method for dealing with immaturity is incorrectly perceived as many as reasonable.

The Reason? Ignorance of the big gap between behaviors which demonstrate refusal to behave responsibly and *psychological* ability to behave responsibility. That "gap" is often the result of a lack of knowledge concerning aspects of Psychological Maturation, education concerning how to develop it and knowledge of Scientific research in Human Development.

EXPLOITATION Of The Mentally Ill. Unfortunately, these misperceptions results in many unfortunate outcomes in Society that effect us all. For example although Research in Punishment vs treatment proves that Punishment doesn't work, we are still mandating the truly mentally ill to Death Row[5] and Punishing (jailing vs mandating treatment) drug addiction [6].

EXPLOITATION BY Business However, what does work (for Big Business Interests) is the fact that Jailing as many people as possible results in Big profits for the Corporate Prison System, construction companies and others who do business with the Prison System. The Prison system a big business. High Salaries for Prison System employees, high levels of money flowing into the coffers of Construction (building Prisons), etc. California has one of the largest % of population being jailed for everything under the sun.

EXPLOITATION by Insurance Carriers interesting It is to note that most Insurance Carriers will not authorize treatment of those diagnosed as Personality Disorder[7] because of the long often futile attempt to change cognitive and behavior traits. Recently many Insurance Carriers have begun new divisions called "Carve Outs". Clients who buy what appears to be a relatively inexpensive policy for Health Insurance from one company have no idea that it may be sent to one or more companies for payment.

---

[5] based on the Legal vs Psychological Definition of knowledge of right from wrong

[6] Scientific Research in Behavior Modification indicates that Punishment (Negative-Reinforcement of undesired behaviors) as a method of changing behavior does not always result in the desired outcome.

[7] Personality Disorder—DSM-IV (page 460) identifies personality disorders as collections of traits that have become rigid and work to individual disadvantage, to the point that they impair functioning or cause distress.

Few policy holders have ever heard of the term "ordinary and customary". This is a term that pays Dr's what each insurance company has decided is the amount a Dr should be paid. This amount is generally based on the Fee others Dr in the geographical area receive. If a Dr objects, the Insurance Co may likely stop referring clients or take the Dr off the insurance co's Panel. A panel of Dr's are expected to follow the Ins Co Guidelines for Treatment. Many Ins Co's hire Gatekeepers who decide whether treatment or continued treatment is "medically necessary". Medical Necessity is a subjective term drafted individually by Ins Carriers to meet their own criteria. However, a general rule of thumb of the term suggests it is a stage of improvement that should keep the patient functional (temporarily stable although not necessarily well). Ins Co's say these Gatekeepers are trained at the same level as the Dr. however, this is often untrue. For example in Psychotherapy treatment many Gatekeepers trained at a Masters Level critique and decide whether the Treatment designed by a PhD or MD will receive authorization or not. In addition, Gatekeepers seldom have personal interaction with the patient.

In addition, although Psychological Evaluations have been of great value in many areas of Psychological treatment, few Insurance company's will authorize them. Those that do will authorize only about 6 hrs for an Evaluation which usually takes at least 5 hrs to administer and an additional 6 hours to interpret and write a Report.

In the past Schools Systems have relied heavily on Psychologists to provide IEP's for providing necessary treatment for Children with LD's or other issues getting in the way of successful schooling. Now, although Schools still provide some Testing, it takes longer and longer for authorization and evaluation. Many Educational PhD's have quit working in the school system due to this problem.

In Orange Co eligible MediCal Clients may only receive treatment from Therapists who work at one of several Orange County Mental Health Agencies. The course of treatment for MediCal clients in Orange County is currently set at 6 visits with another 6 visits authorized if deemed necessary.

And while some public agencies and businesses now Mandate Psychological Evaluation from those seeking employment glaring exceptions occur. It is my opinion that a requirement for a complete Psychological Evaluation for those seeking Public Office[8] would save our Country billions of dollars in hearings, special elections, etc. As most of us are aware, election of persons with extremely high level of dysfunctional perceptions and behavior[9] into National Public Office over many years has lead to disastrous consequences.

CORPORATE EXPLOITATION Twenty years ago advertising a Medical Practice was deemed unethical. Today, "educating" the public in a Corporate subjective point of view has become a daily happening. In the last several years many of us, have become extremely irritated at what is seen as Pharmaceutical Co's attempts to cash in on the trust of the general public. The nauseating marketing of "Miracle Cures" for syndromes from post nasal drip, sweaty palms, restless leg syndrome, irritable bowel syndrome, etc has become a national disgrace. By encouraging the public to "ask your Dr" about the safety of their "correct" medications as well as numerous potential side effects for the dreaded syndrome (even those undiscovered before turning on the TV) Pharmaceutical Company's appear to have taken themselves out of the direct line of fire for legal retaliation.

Recently instances of Professionals taking fee's, gifts or performing research for Drug Companies with a vested financial interest in the outcome have come to light. As a result, many of us are convinced that necessary research is either not authorized, frequently bypassed or put "on the back burner" because financial resources are needed for continuation of currently popular "Miracle Cure" agenda.

Research in Human Development

Scientific theories of Human **Biological** Development, from infancy, childhood, adolescence, middle age through old age, are taught in High Schools and Colleges all over the world. Research. in the categories of

---

[8]   Psychological Testing would have identified many elected to public office with serious dysfunction including categories of Mental illness, Psychosis, Personality Disorders, etc.

[9]   Nixon and Bush as examples of the most glaring types symptoms

Human biology, neurology, cognition, intelligence, etc show general agreement concerning classification and standardization of functioning.

Studies in Childhood Development10 indicate that the mental processes of Cognition (knowing, recognizing and understanding) takes on many forms and grows at different rates during a life time. According to Piaget and Brunner Early childhood development is similar from one child to another, with each passing through the same sequence of irreversible and qualitatively different periods.

A characteristic of Adolescent cognitive change (*Formal operational stage:*[11]) is development of abstract thinking and ability to reason with alternative hypotheses. **In addition to biological** maturation (physical, sexual, intellectual, etc.) Adolescent Development can be seen as a time for consolidation and integration of personality and experience especially in the areas of personal identity and values. However, research cites evidence that many remain dependent upon external values and peer pressures throughout their lives.

Most theorists agree that the goal of **Human** Cognitive **Development** is 1) independence of the adult from automatically responding to learned internal or external cues, 2) confidently directing personal behavior after considering impending urges, and possibilities and then 3) choosing the most successful possibility. **As Biological** maturation fades in importance as a consistent developmental factor in adulthood, individual Cognitive differences are heightened by various types of divergent **experiences.** Social and Cultural ideology as well as Perceptual abilities are all important aspects of differing experiences. Although, there are wide variations in perceptual abilities people tend to follow a similar developmental pattern. If perceptual development (IQ, cognitive rigidity, brain damage, distortions of focusing, etc.) is impaired other cognitive processes will not develop completely.

The **Humanistic Movement** was led by American psychologists Carl Rogers and Abraham Maslow. According to Rogers, all humans are

---

10   Kohlberg, Lawrence (1958). "The Development of Modes of Thinking and Choices in Years 10 to 16". *Ph.D. dissertation, University of Chicago.*

11   Piaget's developmental theory,

born with a drive to <u>achieve their full capacity</u> and to <u>behave in ways</u> that are consistent with their true selves. **Rogers,** a psychotherapist, developed *person-centered therapy,* a nonjudgmental, nondirective approach that helped clients clarify their sense of who they are in an effort to facilitate their own healing process. At about the same time, **Maslow**[12] theorized that all people are motivated to fulfill a hierarchy of needs. At the bottom of the hierarchy are basic physiological needs, such as hunger, thirst, and sleep. Further up the hierarchy are needs for safety and security, needs for belonging and love, and esteem-related needs for status and achievement. Once these needs are met, **Maslow believed, people strive for** *self-actualization,* the ultimate state of personal fulfillment. As Maslow put it, "A musician must make music, an artist must paint, a poet must write, if he is ultimately to be at peace with himself. What a man *can* be, he *must* be."

Lawrence Kohlberg's[13] Theory Of Moral Development consisted of **Six stages** (planes of moral adequacy) to explain the development of moral reasoning (See Appendix 1). Created while studying psychology at the University of Chicago, Kohlberg's theory was inspired by the work of Jean Piaget. Kohlberg is said to have been fascinated with children's reactions to moral dilemmas.[1] He wrote his doctoral dissertation at the university in 1958,[2] outlining what are now known as his stages of moral development.

This theory holds that moral reasoning, which is the basis for ethical behavior, has six identifiable developmental stages. He followed the development of moral judgment beyond the ages originally studied by Piaget,[3] who claimed that logic and morality develop through constructive stages.[4] Kohlberg expanded considerably on this

---

[12] Maslow, M (1975) Hierarchy of Needs Motivation and Personality (2nd Ed) New York: Harper & Rowe

[13] Kohlberg, L (1971) The development of children's orientations toward a moral order. I. sequence in the development of moral thought Vita Humana 6, 11-33 (S. Karger Basel, 1963. Born in Bronxville, New York (October 25, 1927-January 19, 1987) he served as a professor at the University of Chicago & Harvard University. The development of children's orientations toward a moral order. I. sequence in the development of moral thought Vita Humana 6, 11-33 (S. Karger Basel, 1963

groundwork, determining that the process of moral development was principally concerned with justice and that its development continued throughout the lifespan,[2] even spawning dialogue of philosophical implications of his research.[5][6]

Kohlberg used stories about moral dilemmas in his studies, and was interested in how people would justify their actions if they were put in a similar moral crux. He would then categorize and classify evoked responses into one of six distinct stages. These six stages are broken into three levels: pre-conventional, conventional and post-conventional.[7][8][9] His theory is based on constructive developmental stages; each stage and level is more adequate at responding to moral dilemmas than the last.

Level 1—Premoral—External Locus of Control
Stage 1—Punishment and obedience orientation (obeys to avoid punishment. **Stage 2**—Naïve instrumental hedonism (Conforms to obtain rewards, and have favors returned)

Level 2—Morality or Conventional Role Conformity
Stage 3—Conforms to avoid disapproval and dislike by others. Stage 4—Conforms to avoid censure by legitimate authorities with resultant guilt Most people are here.

Level 3—Morality of Self Accepted Moral principles Internal Locus of Control—
Stage 5—Conforms to maintain respect of the impartial spectator judging in terms of community welfare Martin Luther King (Example). Stage 6—Conforms to avoid self-condemnation—Intrinsic internal morals.

Overview of Research in Human Development

Biological
- All Human beings follow a similar biological & Cognitive sequence of Patterns Piaget, Jean, Swiss psychologist, best known for his pioneering work on the development of intelligence in children **(1896-1980)**

Cognitive

- **Child is** ruled by the **Id** (instincts and feelings) because the **Secondary processes (Ego)** have not developed yet. Freud, Sigmund (1856-1939) Austrian physician, neurologist, and founder of psychoanalysis
- **Cognitive Development** progresses though 4 Major stages: 1) **Sensorimotor Stage** (0-2), objects permanence, 2) **Preoperational Stage** (2-7), egocentric (little awareness of perspective of others), language and rudimentary numbers develops, 3) **Concrete Stage** (7-12), thinking based on concepts such as categorization, reverse and conservation and 4) **Formal Operations** (12 & beyond) ability to consider alternatives.
- **Formal Operations** includes abstract reasoning, deduction, hypothesize and moral reasoning. Many adults remain dependent on external values and the philosophies of admired others due to not having developed the full capacity of reliance on personal abstracting reasoning and problem solving. Piaget did not believe possible to hurry through stages. Passage through stages is balanced by Assimilation (incorporation of new information into existing cognitive structures) and Accommodation (New info that doesn't fit into already existing cognitive structures is used to create new cognitive structures). Piaget Jean **(1896-1980),**
- Cognition takes many forms and grows at different rates. (IQ, Brain damage, etc.), Developmental Stages are universal and their sequence is invariant. Children of all cultures develop moral reasoning in the same way. **Lawrence Kohlberg's** Theories of Childhood Reasoning and Moral Development follows closely the work of Jean Piaget's theory of cognitive development, and perhaps even extends his predecessor's work. Kohlberg, Lawrence (1927-1987

Ego

- **Id**, component of the personality that contains the instinctual, biological drives that supply the psyche with its basic energy. Freud defined it as the most primitive component of the personality, located in the deepest level of the unconscious: it has no inner organization and operates in obedience to the pleasure principle. The infants life is dominated by the desire for immediate gratification of instincts, such as hunger and sex, until the **Ego** begins to develop and operate in accordance with reality. **Classical Freudian Theory**

- **Ego** operates by the rules of the Superego **(conscience). Conscience is formed from input of** parents and prohibitions of society, which determine personal standards and aspiration. The Superego Forms at Unconscious Level thru identification with parents and later admired others. Superego develops out of the Id from demands of reality. **Classical Freudian Theory.**
- **Ego** is agent of the personality working by Reality Principle **American Psychological Association**
- **Ego** 1) arises from ID due to Frustrations of reality. 2) Ability to adapt to life's changing requirements is limited. 3) Limitation is index of pathology and 4) Level of development is due to Techniques used to manage Anxiety. **Psychodynamic Theory, Freud & Others**
- All born with drive to achieve Full capacity in ways consistent with true Self Rogers, Carl
- All people are motivated to fulfill Hierarch of Needs (basic, safety, security, belonging, love, status and achievement).—Strive for Self Actualization **Maslow, A**
- Moral development is basis of ethical behavior and consists of 3 levels & 6 stages—external Locus of control, Role conformity and self Accepted Moral principles Kohlberg, L
- ABC Model of Cognitive Therapy— Albert Ellis believed "It's not what happens that causes your problems, its your belief about what happened. He believed that the ability to deal with Objective Reality resulted in development of Frustration Tolerance, Ellis, A
- Similar to Ellis in belief that Facing Reality leads to ability to Tolerate Frustration. **Glasser, W** Father of Reality Therapy

Psychological Components of Resilence

The most significant aspects of the "New Thinking" presented at the recent Psychotherapy Conference in Irvine fell into 3 categories of concern 1) the over use of Medication, 2) the hazy, confusing definitions of Normality vs Mental Illness and 3) the concept of **Resilience** as a technique for successful living.

The concept of Resilience **is seen by well respected professionals as a long overdue area of need for attention. In an APA Article—Road to Resilience**—Resilience—PTSD—Trauma Developing resilience is discussed as a personal journey in which people do not all react the same to traumatic and stressful life events. **Resilience is discussed as a p**rocess of adapting well in the face of adversity and "bouncing back" from difficult experiences. Research shows resilience to be ordinary rather than extraordinary. The article goes on to say "This doesn't mean that a person will not experience difficulty or distress". Emotional pain and sadness are common in people who have suffered major adversity or trauma in their lives. **Resilience** is not a trait that people either have or do not have. It involves behaviors, thoughts, and actions that can be learned and developed.

My Own Point of View concerning the new focus on **Resilience** can be stated in three words . . . **"It's about time"**. I have been gathering material, writing this book for over 10 years and teaching my clients the concepts of Resilience for over 20 years. The only difference is that I have been referring to the concept now called Resilience as a **Coping Mechanism**[14] and an **essential aspect of "Psychological Maturation"**.

The "Missing Link"-

As I mentioned in the Forward and Preface in my Book: **Maturation: The Adult Paradigm** . . . I have learned from personal experience that the ability to Accept the Truth of Objective reality is the result of accepting the fact that I do not have a choice. I can refuse to acknowledge a fact (because I don't want it to be true), cry about a fact (making myself and everyone else around me miserable) or learn to walk through the pain of emotion, come out the other side and live with the reality by accepting the truth.

Psychotherapy has given me the tools (Education and Cognitive Strength) to 1) "Face Reality & Accept the Truth" 2) Think about my

---

[14]   See Appendix 1

feelings and choose to respond to them or not, 3) Think for myself and 4) develop my own Objective Philosophy of life. This Philosophy includes the belief that it is my obligation to be a good Role Model to my children, my family and clients and that I don't have the right to waste the life that God has given me.

My own personal perception of issues surrounding resilience include the observation that there is an essential need for **Personal Responsibility, Facing Reality** about ourselves and our strengths and weaknesses, as well as **accepting the reality that some people really "**Can't**" help** themselves and need treatment, education, and not punishment. We need to demonstrate acceptance of our strengths and weakness by attempting to live up to our realistic potential as much as possible. However, chemical imbalances of some types do produce some types of FSP's (Psychosis). It is well known that Methamphetamine taken to excess can cause an excess of Dopamine in the Brain (the cause of Schizophrenia) and result in Symptoms of Psychosis.

Many respected Professionals (Kenneth Ring, MD, Michael Newton, MD, and Kuebler Ross, MD among others) have put forth their own beliefs that some persons presenting with symptoms of psychosis (false sensory perceptions) may not be psychotic—just closer to the spiritual realm than most of us. Other professionals, point to animals and children who seem to "perceive" things" others do not as possible examples of such characteristics.

Maturation: **The Adult Paradigm—A Guide for Psychological Development** presents a new model of Human Ego Development and Behavior that conceptualizes a majority of Adult Emotional Distress on a continuum of immaturity/maturity rather than pathology and wellness. The continuum of Ego and Cognitive Development is a usually disregarded but essential "Missing Link" for attainment of functional (vs dysfunctional) **resolution of** Anxiety.

Many search vainly for solutions to problems in living not realizing answers lie in realistic mature choices based on the ability to Face Objective Reality and Accept the Truth. The Map provides educational and self-help methods for attainment of Psychological Maturation leading to higher levels of frustration tolerance, functional coping skills, personal responsibility and successful relationships.

The Map Defines Psychological Maturation as a necessary Level of Ego Development for functional comfort with **both** emotional and cognitive independence. Such independence must include independent Objective Critical Thinking characterized by ability to think about feelings and choose whether to respond to them or not based on what is best for the self and others in the "long run" vs emotional "fixes" in the "here and now".

It is a hard, cold fact that much **of the Adult Population is unable to Successfully** 1) cope with Stress 2) resolve Personal/Interpersonal Conflict, 3) Make Confident Decisions, 4) understand and set realistic personal goals, or 5) develop a well thought out emotionally satisfying Philosophy for making sense of their lives.

The concept of Human Psychological Immaturity as a basic reason for personal or interpersonal conflict is seldom (if ever) taught in schools or in church's. Few Parents discuss it with their children. Instead, most parents perceive the results of their child's immaturity in terms of deliberate disobedience, cause for great alarm or an example of a "chip off the old block". Even parents who do understand the concept of childhood immaturity usually don't clearly understand how to help their child grow toward healthy realistic unique independence with the ability to understand a purpose in their lives.

Equally unknown to most adults is the realization that repressed dependency (need for approval, sensitivity, fear of rejection, abandonment, feelings of insignificance, etc) underlie most consciously experienced symptoms of Adult Separation Anxiety15 such as anxiety, indecisiveness, depression, frustration, anger, resentment, guilt/remorse.

Adult Psychological immaturity is a main factor behind high levels of stress, inability to resolve personal and interpersonal conflict, inefficient decision making and inability to derive pleasure from life.

---

15   Symbiosis—Differentiation—M, Bowen, Differentiation, M, Mahler

Many of us have little understanding of the characteristic attitudes & behaviors of Psychological Maturity nor how lack of those characteristics may effects our ability to successfully cope with life.

The necessity of understanding the concept of Psychological Immaturity in order to resolve the disabling symptoms of Separation Anxiety is almost never considered by the average adult when searching for reasons to explain their own unhappiness and frustrations. However, at the core of Immaturity, is an emotionally disabling inability to feel and behave as a unique, independent and emotionally separate person.

Understanding the importance of Scientific Research is especially helpful for understanding Human Development. For example, one of the **basic differences between** human beings **and** animals is the Cortex **of the Human** brain's. Research indicates the Cortex and the Ego develop separately allowing Human Beings to learn to think about their feelings and choose wheter to respond to them or not. Animals (who don't outgrow it) and small children (who do outgrow it) respond excessively to emotion (a characteristic of Immaturity). **Immature Adults** also may continue to over respond to Emotions.

I define **Psychological Maturation** as a Human Developmental Stage (emotional and cognitive) resulting from the ability to face objective reality and accept the truth. **I perceive Human life to be a multifaceted arena of opportunities within human relationships and life situations for development of both human and spiritual potential. I view** Anxiety as a Signal from the Unconscious Mind that an underlying ambiguous conflict is present and needs to be taken care of for Psychological Maturation (Adult Development) to continue successfully.

Therapy with Me

As a result of the many misperceptions concerning Psychotherapy, I encourage my clients to consider their professional relationship with me as between **two equal adults seeking answers to a client's unresolved problems**. I assure my clients that all human beings have problems and areas of issues that seem insurmountable at the time.

I assure clients that 80% of those seeking therapy have problems in living rather than "mental Illness or Psychosis. I explain that the definition of Neurosis is hazy and no one really can "prove" what it is. I suggest that most of us could be diagnosed with some type of **Neurosis** at some time in our lives. I attempt to clarify my hypothesis that **Neurosis** is just a term for symptoms underlying anxiety.

I often begin Treatment, by joking that Psychotherapy with me is similar to "taking a course in Psychology". I summarize, as clearly as possible the indispensable Theoretical Basis underlying Cognitive and Psychodynamic theories. I explains my use of Genograms (drawings of family relationships), in the context of the Psychodynamic theory as a technique for laying the foundation for the various Techniques I deem helpful for improving specific problematic situations.

I present Psychotherapy to my clients as an opportunity to investigate unresolved personal problems from a Cognitive exploration of Roles & Rules learned in Family of Origin. I emphasize the view that Anxiety is a Sign of distress lacking an unambiguous (clear) cause.

I Define the concept of Defense mechanisms (used by all of us) and discuss possible Symptoms that may result. These Symptoms (cognitions and behaviors) may have been defined by some as Neurosis because they appear in an otherwise intact Base of Personality

I perceive Anxiety as a Signal from the Unconscious Mind that an underlying conflict is present and needs to be taken care of for Psychological Maturation (Adult Development) to continue successfully. I present my Philosophy of **Adult Development** in an Educational format "similar to taking a course in Psychology" that investigates areas of concern in a clients family of Origin or situation in which childhood and/or adolescence was experienced. Using Cognitive Techniques I help clients examine personal problems in the context of Scientifically recognized Psychological Theory. I explain the theoretical rationale behind such concepts as

- **Fa**mily of Origin,
- **Transference** (responding to something happening in the Here and Now that brings up feelings similar to feelings to

something that happened in the There and then). An example of Transference may be a situation in which we instantly like or don't like a person on sight.

- **Research** in Adult Psychological Development,
- **Anxiety** as a signal of underlying conflict,
- Methods of <u>responding</u> to **Underlying conflict (Defenses)**,
- High and Low **Levels of Defenses** used which may result in Symptoms (Anxiety),
- Identification of <u>opportunities</u> and **Techniques** for Resolving personal issues and problems of living.

I emphasize the importance of **Transference** in working through issues in therapy. I discuss this in terms of **Homeostasis** (a state of equilibrium, or a tendency to reach equilibrium), roles we learned to play in the family, Reasons for playing the Roles we do, the Unconscious Aspects of Life our First memories often reveal, Family faces, etc.

I always use the **Genogram** (Family Map) in conjunction with Psychodynamic, Cognitive and Behavioral techniques to investigate the issues underlying the Anxiety that signals the presence of an unconscious or unresolved conflict. I use <u>Self Help</u> techniques such as understanding the Rules and Roles we learned in our families of origin. I discuss <u>Anxiety</u> as a major source of information concerning what is needed for growth to occur. I emphasize the importance of identifying "What I am afraid of, why I am afraid of it, etc." I present my visualization that instead of swimming in a Sea Of Emotion, I must get into the **Life Boat Of Cognition**.

<u>I recommend the use of a Work book</u> for identification of and working through many issues. I discuss the importance of all <u>Relationships</u> (Marriage, friendships, parenting, etc) as methods for understanding ways of problem solving and the importance of identification of negotiable vs nonnegotiable values. I offer Psychological Testing such as the MMPI and a Test of I written—The Test of Ego & Cognitive Development to clarify both emotional and cognitive understanding of our values, unconscious mind, etc. I also offer the Rorschach as an especially important method to identify unconscious issues that may be effecting personal and relationships anxieties.

I suggest that the Path to Personal Maturation is made up of both positive and negative energy in which immature Attitudes and Behaviors (illogical, distorted, controlling, manipulative, punitive, etc) can be seen as similar to a field of quicksand. The negative energy surrounds areas that we can't get out of, until we let go and float free into the positive energy of Cause &Effect (Reality). I believe that Psychological Development is necessary for our Spiritual lessons to be learned. I realize that everyone is not interested in examining Spiritual Issues (not religious issues) and do not pursue this line of investigation unless a client asks for techniques that may be helpful.

I have written numerous and often use **Vignettes** (stories) for Visualization of Psychological concepts. Two categories of Vignettes have proven especially useful in working with Psychotherapy Clients. I have designed one Type of Vignette to illustrate the **Psychological Concept** (and person inflicted) underlying a diagnostic (Denial, Obsessive Compulsive, Symbiosis, etc.) category. I have designed another type of Vignette to illustrate helpful **Coping Techniques** (anger, fear, emotional over responsiveness, etc.).

Maturation: **The Adult Paradigm** is an educational/self exploration type of therapy leading to increased levels of Frustration Tolerance, ability to face objective reality, accept the truth and psychological maturation. It teaches a clear logical educational model for resolving conflicts, coping with stress and making successful decisions. Personal growth and mature relationships (**4 Tasks of Psychological Maturation**) can occur as a result of adhering to a set of five universal principles (Laws of Cause & Effect) that underlie all human behavior and communication. These **5 Lessons of Life** identify situations over which we do or do not have control, teach appropriate responsibility for self and others, encourage facing reality and accepting truth, teach a method for making cognitive rather than emotional decisions and teaches a method for a crisis free lifestyle of moderation and balance.

The Path to Eternity—The Essence of the Human Spirit
Using Personal and Professional experiences combined with Educational and Professional Knowledge, I Define Psychological Maturation as a Human Developmental Stage resulting from the ability to **Face** (objective) **Reality** and **Accept the Truth** of Cause & Effect. **Missing Link—4 Tasks.** I Discuss Human Life on Earth—**as a** multifaceted arena of Instructional Opportunities **within Human Relationships, Life Situations, and Universal Connections (serendipity, dreams, synchronicity, intuition, meditation, dreams) for development of both human and spiritual potential. (The Evolving Dancer). I Present my Philosophy that the Path to Eternity (Spiritual Maturation) runs thru the Fabric of the universe (Map of reality) and is paved with Realistic Laws of Cause and Effect. 5 Lessons of Life. I** Present my conviction that Scientific Research **(Quantum Mechanics, etc.) will eventually devise a method for validation of the existence of the Spiritual Realm**

WHO WILL BENEFIT FROM THIS TYPE OF THERAPY?

Those seeking relief from Psychological Pain and Relationship Problems

- **Psychotherapy Clients** Who can't afford long term therapy, who went to therapy but didn't feel as though it worked for them
- **Those who are looking for answers to personal `or relationship problems**
- **Those Searching for the Answers to Psychological Pain**

Those seeking Answers to Questions concerning Meaning of Life

- **Those who like to make sense of their life and make their own decisions.**
- **Searching for the methods to arrive at their own personal Answers concerning m**eaning of Life
- Those faced with a pressing need to arrive at a personal philosophy of life as a result of severe trauma
- Those at Mid-Lif, Life Crisis or Trauma
- **Those who Life isn't working**

Those seeking help answering Questions concerning Death and Dying

- Scientific exploration for spiritual "fit" in Universe
- **Clients who have experienced significant Trauma, such as death of a loved one**
- **Those who have experienced Devastating Trauma such as rape, murder of a loved one, death of several family members**
- Those suffering from severe, even terminal illness

PART 1

The Universal Environment

The Path To Eternity Runs Through The Fabric Of The Universe And Is Paved With Laws Of Cause And Effect

Essence of Me—A Child who spoke with Stars
"Where would I be if I weren't alive?"

Prologue—The Question of Meaning
"Fellow Travelers who walked with me on the Road of Life for too short a time"

PROLOGUE

The Question of Meaning

"Fellow Travelers who walked with me on the Road of Life
for too short a time"

This book is dedicated to the Memories and Spirits of my three Sons and Father—Fellow Travelers and Soulmates who walked with me on the Road of Life for too short a time . . .

Blake Donald Lundquist,
Kurt Richard Lundquist
Mark David Lundquist
Warren Duncan Dobbins

"Good-bye for a little while . . ." "I remember you for love, love of others and love of life. Thank you for the gift you shared with me . . . Your lives. I will love you for Eternity and join you there" "Walk with God"

MEMORIES OF Blake—
Born 5/29/1970 Died 9/29/1994

Remembrances of Blake Donald Lundquist shared by his Mother,
Skipi Lundquist Smoot, at his Funeral, October 6, 1994.

On September 29, 1994, the most terrible day in my memory, our lives changed forever. I can only imagine what final thoughts went through Blake's mind as he stared into the gun that moments later sent his spirit into the embrace of God and his life's blood splashing from his right temple. He died without regaining consciousness, watching his daughter grow up, being married, visiting Hawaii, finishing college, sitting at the death bed of a parent, or . . . living the rest of his life.

On the hot, Thursday afternoon of September 29, 1994, my son, Blake, was murdered by plain clothed undercover police while driving his pickup truck on a quiet cul-de-sac in Placentia, California. He was 24 years, 4 months and 0 days old. An eyewitness reported that two men jumped from a White Isuzu truck waving guns and screaming, "Get out of your truck" just moments before one of their bullets ripped through his brain silencing it forever. He had been drinking a soda with his windows rolled up and his stereo playing loudly. He was shot through the closed drivers side window, left thumb and head (just above and behind his left ear). Apparently his hands had been raised in the traditional gesture of surrender or as an ineffectual shield to protect himself from harm. He was unarmed.

On October 6, 1994 the tall strong body of my 24 year old son came home for the last time . . . to lie on smooth satin . . . inside a bronze colored box, beneath a green hillside overlooking the Pacific ocean . . . a few blocks from where he was born. His spirit no longer residing in the world he loved, had entered Eternity . . . a victim of such intolerable tragedy I could hardly permit its pain to enter my mind . . . Nor can I keep its memory from torturing my existence.

Rising from tormented sleep, I tried to continue hiding from knowledge of his loss. 'Where are you?' I cried out in my mind as I listened to the quiet house. Turning toward the open door, that leads into the silent hall, I strained to hear his sound. 'Blake, are you there in the shadows?' I whispered into the darkness but Silence was my only answer. I sense his presence just out of reach in the hall's darkness. Since last Thursday Afternoon, at night, lying sleepless in bed, I continue to wait for him to come and tell me he's all right. But Now, each night, I search for the spirit rather than the living presence of the man who was son. Did he accomplish his mission in the world.? Or was he forced to "go" before he found his answers? I remember him for love. Love of others and love of life. I remember his curiosity, his independence, his stubbornness. I cry for the pain and the happiness that was his life. I love you, Blake and thank you for the gift you shared with me for 24 years . . . your life. I will never forget you. You're life was truly a gift from God.

My Father, Warren—Born 11/11/1906-Died 4/24/2003
Portions of Memories shared at Memorial Services in April 2003

How can I possibly say "good-bye to you, Daddy ? . . . when you're 1/2 of my essence as a human being, . . . A soul mate to my spirit? . . . when I can't even imagine a world without you in it? . . . I don't remember a time when the fact of your existence . . . and my love for you was not the **Cornerstone** that held my world together. **I can't imagine a way to tell you Goodbye** . . . **I've tried** . . . Last Friday night . . . as you began your journey into Eternity I touched your still warm hand . . . covered your thin shoulder, smoothed your beautiful white hair . . . kissed your sweet face . . . for a last time. **I can't imagine a way to tell you Goodbye . . . or an existence without you in it**, . . . because although the Humanness that is part of your existence reverts to dust . . . your spiritual essence will live in Eternity . . . as you join the wind over the Rose Garden . . . in joyous haste to greet your loved ones . . . waiting eagerly for your safe return . . . home. **I can never tell you goodbye** . . . because . . . I know that when my Spirit is ready to travel on the wind to join you . . . there . . . you will be waiting for me and greet me with open arms, in the company of those from whom we have learned our lessons, benefited from their love and loved in our life. Warren Duncan Dobbins, my father and soul mate, fly with the wind. I will love you for Eternity and join you there.

MEMORIES OF KURT—
My Son, Kurt—Born 5/21/1952 Died on or about 6/30/2003
Remembrances of Kurt Richard Lundquist shared by his Mother, Skipi Lundquist Smoot, at his Memories Services July, 11, 2003

On July 3, 2003 I again found myself trying to accept both the reality and necessity to once again say the dreaded words . . . "Goodbye for a little while" . . . to a beloved son as I frantically called "Kurt, Kurt, wake up Kurt" . . . to the lifeless body lying peacefully in his bed . . . Frantically calling 911 . . . mechanically responding to instructions to touch his body in a search for life . . . I realized in numb horror that his arm was ice cold . . . that his closed eyes would never again open in life.

As I tried to organize my thoughts . . . memories and emotions in preparation for yet . . . another . . . memorial service . . . I realized I was unconsciously trying to block the dreaded words "Goodbye for a little while" from entering my consciousness. I felt my heart cry out in so much pain . . . I honestly didn't believe I could go through it again.

"My darling son, how can I . . . <u>also</u> . . . tell **you** goodbye?" . . . "when I don't really believe you're gone?" Searching for proof that the reality of your death is fantasy . . . I frantically search the street in front of my house for your car parked by the roses . . . I search for your living presence on the couch in my little upstairs office at home . . . half expecting to find you sitting there, laughingly saying "Wake up, Mom, it was just a bad dream". **But . . . you don't materialize.** And as the fantasy settles into Reality . . . I am left with the devastation and agony that slowly, relentlessly, settled over me since that terrible Thursday evening.

"How can this be happening again?" I asked myself . . . Just <u>eight years</u> ago, **after** the murder of my 24 year old son, Blake . . . I had been forced to find a way to say "Goodbye for a little while" to my youngest son. In April, just <u>two months</u> before Kurt's death, I had been forced to deal with the earthly loss of my sweet darling father. "Isn't that enough?" I cried out in agony and pain . . . "Why am I being forced to find a way to live with this pain again?". Why so soon? . . . <u>Why</u>?. I whisper over and over into the black hole that has become my self" . . . And the answer drifts back to me on wisps of objective silence . . . "Because . . . I must . . . because its reality . . . and objective reality demands it".

As a psychologist, I continually attempt to help my clients face reality and accept the truth. How can I possibly demand less of myself? Especially when I know, without a doubt that "goodbyes" are both the most difficult but important aspects of human relationships . . . <u>because</u> without the benefit of closure, it is impossible to complete the primary obligation of all Human Beings . . . growth and development of the Soul as we interact with each other.

MEMORIES OF Mark—
My Son, Mark—Born 12/8/1954 Died on 12/8/06 on his 50th Birthday
Remembrances of Mark David Lundquist shared by his Mother at his Memories Services—
Memories of Mark—determination of the human spirit . . . Even against heavy odds . . . my second born son's motivation toward Successful

attainment of personal goals was the major, most defining characteristic of his life.

I walked on the **Road of Life** with Mark for 50 often extremely difficult, always loving years. We learned so much from each other. We have truly been Fellow Travelers on the Road of Life.

The horrifying circumstances surrounding Mark's death is a continuation of an overwhelming nightmare . . . too terrible to believe . . . Impossible to understand . . . The horror of carrying on a conversation with a living son one minute and staring dumbfounded into his dead eyes the next . . . is a situation of such agony I can barely allow it's memory to remain in my consciousness.

For the last few days I have forced myself to face the fact that a 3rd son of mine has vanished with no warning . . . Blake murdered 10 years ago . . . Last year Kurt closing his eyes to a refreshing afternoon nap from which he never awoke. And now Mark dying in front of my eyes on his Birthday.

The terrible pain of contradictory emotions . . . numbness, grief, guilt and even a certain sense of relief. overwhelms me. Again I found myself asking the question "How can I possibly live through this agony again?" But as before the facts are clear . . . because I have no choice. My child is dead. And I am still alive. I really don't know why, but I truly believe there is reason in the Universe. We all have lessons to learn from each other. Mark and I shared 50 years of lessons . . .

Mark, my soul mate and son, I can't believe you are gone. Our road through life has been wonderful, loving and filled with terror. But through it all, we never stopped loving each other. Through my tears, I can truthfully say, that after over 20 years of pain and failure Mark had successfully been on the Road of Sobriety. And because he had been able to maintain sobriety for 3 long years, he left this world as he came in . . . "A Winner".

The Child who spoke with Stars

The <u>Essence</u> of "Me"—
Where would <u>I</u> be if I weren't alive?

Waiting for sleep the 8-year-old child lay contemplating the night sky through a small window above the foot of her bed. Infinite space and the darkness of Eternity reflected light from twinkling stars . . ."Did I used to live in the sky before I was born?" thought the Child . . . "Is that where heaven is?", . . ."Does God live there?". the Child's mind called out to the brightest star.

Slowly, stealthily, . . . "Loneliness" entered the room and settled over the suddenly tremulous child. Carefully the intellect of the child formulated the next fearful query. Timidly but determinedly the frightening question was whispered toward Eternity . . ."Where would I be, if I weren't alive?" Struggling to hear the answer, the Child thought she heard Eternity whisper back from the darkness **. . . you would cease to exist"**. Swiftly, feelings of insignificance overtook her. The thought of a nonexistent "me" so terrified and overwhelmed her that she snuggled deep into soft blankets in an attempt to hide from its' desolation.

The Loneliness experienced by the Child appears to be Universal. Remembrances of this type of experience can almost always be vividly re-experienced by human beings of all ages. The subject of a Spiritual

Meaning of Existence is a broad and complex one. Many, overwhelmed by the concept, blindly accept Traditional answers. Some reject the possibility of the soul's separate existence as unlikely due to the inability of Science to prove it. Others, just give up thinking about it until at the death of a loved one, are forced once again to search for answers.

We are born at the beginning of our potential path into Eternity. by our attitudes and behaviors we choose to explore it . . . or . . . not!

CHAPTER 1

The Universal Environment

<u>The Path to Eternity</u>

- Human Adult Ego & Cognitive Development
- Psychological Maturation—The "Missing Link"

Maturation:
The <u>Adult</u> Paradigm

The Path to Psychological Maturity runs through the Fabric of the Universe and is Paved with Realistic Laws of Cause and Effect

<u>PSYCHOLOGY'S BEST KEPT SECRET</u>
DIGNITY AND DEVELOPMENT OF THE HUMAN SPIRIT

<u>We are born with a mission</u>—to explore our own path. Most of us begin our Journey "dancing" with abandon to intense emotional rhythms. Only later, . . . often in great pain, do some of us recognize the outstretched hand of Reality —and learn to dance to the Music of the Universe.

Human beings are relatively free to identify innate potential, goals and personal mission in life. Many search vainly for the 1) secret of life 2) the "right way to live, or 3) an illusive "something" called happiness not realizing the only secret is learning to make choices based on the "processes" of Cause and Effect underling Reality At the core of Immaturity lies disabling inability to feel and behave separately due to feelings of inadequacy, anxiety and fears of rejection and abandonment[1].

Contrary to popular opinion, a majority of human dysfunction falls in the category of Psychological Immaturity rather than Mental Illness. While certain psychological dysfunction may be the result of chemical or biological predisposition, most anxiety, depression, family or relationship problems can be greatly helped or eliminated by learning to think about our problems differently.

The Map is a Model for Ego & Cognitive Development. Psychological Maturation leads to higher levels of frustration tolerance, functional coping skills, personal responsibility and successful relationships.

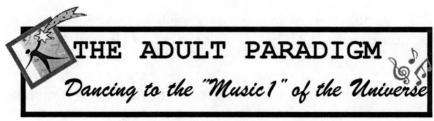

THE ADULT PARADIGM

Dancing to the "Music 1" of the Universe

Psychological Maturity:

The essential (but usually disregarded) **"Missing Link" to Human Happiness.**

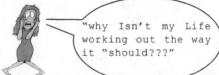

"why Isn't my Life working out the way it "should???"

THE UNIVERSAL QUESTION

Most People go to Therapy between age 30-40 (Mid Life) because **their life isn't working, they've tried everything to "fix" it, nothing is working and they're willing "try anything" to feel better.**

Contrary to popular opinion, a majority of human dysfunction falls in the category of Psychological Immaturity rather than Mental Illness. While certain psychological dysfunction may be the result of chemical or biological predisposition, most anxiety, depression, family or relationship problems can be greatly helped or eliminated by learning to think about our problems differently Psychological Maturation develops from Hearing and dancing to the Music of the universe. C&E.

Psychological Maturation and Educational Methods for its achievement can be learned to help arrive at more successful life choices.

Most of us have asked questions such as 1) "Why was I born?", "Why am I here?", "Is there a purpose to being alive?" and "If there is a Purpose . . . What is my Mission in the world?" These questions, unique to each of us, can only be answered by asking the additional question "Where is the REAL Me?" Answers to these questions are unique to each of us.

It is uncontroversial that we are each born with a seed of Unique Human Potential. **Development of Human potential** demands **Psychological Maturation**. And Only by resolving the problems that deter us from psychological maturation are we free to explore our mission in the Universe. Personal Choices are presented to each of us on our Path through the Universe in the form of choices, serendipity, synchronicity and problem solving with other people.

The ability to face reality and make choices based on cause and effect allows Human maturation to develop. Let go of the quicksand (negative energy) of unrealistic choices and behaviors and float free into the positive energy of cause and effect (Reality) allows development of psychological maturation. Only then are we free as human beings to explore our human and spiritual missions in the universe. **Psychological Maturation** is the doorway leading to a more complete understanding of our <u>unique potential</u> and "fit" in the Universe.

WHERE IS THE "Real" ME?

Examine Your Path   <u>CLOSELY</u> for Clues

The Search for
"NORMAL"—MENTAL PROCESSES

The "Search for Normal"—Traditional Definitions of Functional/ Dysfunctional vs Normal/Abnormal Mental Processes

Dysfunctional mental processes[1] are traditionally perceived as learned patterns of pathological defenses involving deviance & distress protecting from internal and external stressors[2]. Wellness is inferred from successful use of high level defenses displayed in socially appropriate attitudes and behaviors providing relief from interpsychic pain. Successful use of both high and low level of defenses may protect from anxiety. Neither act as internal or external change agents. Contrary to popular opinion the line between abnormal and normal mental processes is blurry and arbitrary. with no absolute symptoms of mental disorders. All dysfunctional symptoms appear in those identified as both normal and abnormal. Why is this?

Attempts to differentiate between the many shadings of Normal and Abnormal attitudes and behaviors has been an obscure assignment, avoided by most writers and theorists. **Traditional Definitions** of abnormal (departing from the Normal) behavior may include—**dysfunctional**[3] mental processes tradionally perceived as learned patterns of Defensive pathological attitudes and behaviors. Such defenses protect from both internal and external stressors.

---

[1] **DSM-IV MADE EASY, JAMES MORRISON** (PAGE 8-9)—Def of Mental disorder paraphrased, is "Mental disorder is a clinically important collection of syumptoms (behavioral or psychological) that causes an individual distress, disability or increased risk of suffering pain, disability, death, or the loss of freedom" He addes that Mental disorder describe disease not people, there is no sharp boundary between disorders or any disorder and normality.

[2] [2]ideology A cohesive set of beliefs, ideas, and symbols through which persons interpret the world and their place within it. The term was coined in late eighteenth-century France in reference to a projected science of ideas, but soon came to refer to a view of the world based on irrational beliefs as opposed to objective knowledge.

[3] Unable to function normally as result ofdisease or impairment

Traditional Definitions of <u>Normal</u> behavior include

- <u>Typical,</u> common behavior of a majority of people
- <u>Social conformity</u> (effects of culture on personality emphasized by Fromm) to <u>currently approved</u> behaviors
- Ability to <u>manifest</u> characteristics of a **responsible, realistic, appropriately assertive, socially, internally fulfilled attitudes and behaviors of an** "<u>Authentic</u>" self.

Important disparities quickly become apparent among these definitions and the necessary characteristics of those who manifest them. Responsible, realistic high functioning people often do not exhibit, typical, common, average or even currently socially approved attitudes and behaviors. History reveals numerous instances of behavior both socially approved and typical of the majority that were abnormal, dysfunctional and even amoral. Clearly

- typical average behavior is not always normal
- Social conformity may be both normal and low functioning
- socially disapproved behavior is not always dysfunctional
- high functioning independent, responsible behavior is not always typical or socially conforming conduct.
- responsible behavior sometimes requires socially nonconforming, atypical behavior, responsible people may not exhibit typical or currently socially approved attitudes and behaviors

*What **NECESSARY** aspect of human functioning is being **OVERLOOKED** in such typical definitions of **Normality**?*A <u>majority </u>of human dysfunction falls on two Continuums of Psychological functioning 1)<u>Immaturity/</u><u>Maturity </u>and 2) <u>Pathology/</u><u>Wellness.</u> Certain necessary aspects of human functioning are frequently ignored when perceived in current paradigms of Normality All dysfunctional symptoms appear in individuals identified as both normal and abnormal (Encarta).

Stages & ages of
human Biological development

Childhood ━━━━━━━━━━━━━━━━━━━━▶ Adulthood

Research concerning Human Biological Development

All Human beings follow a similar **Biological** & **Cognitive** sequence of Patterns. Biological and Mental Processes of Cognition (knowing, recognizing and understanding) takes on many forms and grows at different rates during a life time.

In adolescence Biological maturation (physical, sexual, intellectual, etc.) abstract thinking and ability to reason with alternative hypothesis develops[4].

The child grows faster in infancy than at any later time. The brain grows significantly in size and complexity in infancy. Although most of the brain's neurons (nerve cells) develop prenatally, organization and interconnection of these neurons depends significantly on experiences after birth. Infants who are deprived of normal stimulation and care are at risk of impaired brain development.

Normal physical development in infancy requires a nutritionally adequate diet, immunizations to guard against infectious diseases, and protections from environmental hazards[5]

---

[4] **Piaget, Jean, Swiss Psychologist (1896-1980)** best known for his pioneering work on the development of intelligence in children **Encarta Encyclopedia Child Development**

[5]

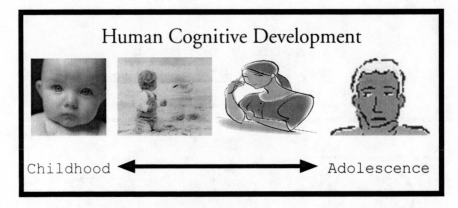

Human Cognitive Development

Childhood ◀━━━━━━━━━━▶ Adolescence

- **Child is** ruled by the <u>Id</u> (instincts and feelings) because the **Secondary processes (Ego)** have not developed yet. <u>Freud, Sigmund</u> (1856-1939) Austrian physician, neurologist, and founder of psychoanalysis
- <u>Cognition</u> takes many forms and grows at different rates. (IQ, Brain damage, etc.), <u>Developmental</u> Stages are universal and their sequence is invariant. Children of all culutres develop moral reasoning in the same way. **Lawrence Kohlberg's** Theories of Childhood Reasoning and Moral Develoment follows closely the work of Jean Piaget's theory of cognitive development
- **Cognitive Development** progresses though 4 Major stages: 1) **Sensorimotor Stage** (0-2), objects permanence, 2) **Preoperationsal Stage** (2-7), egocentric (little awarenss of perspective of others), language and rudimentary numbers develops, 3) **Concrete Stage** (7-12), thinking based on concepts such as catagorize, reverse and conservation and 4) **Formal Operations** (12 & beyond) ability to consider alternatives.
- **Formal Operations** includes abstract reasoning, deduction, hypothesize and moral reasoning. <u>Many adults</u> remain dependent on external values and the philosopies of admired others due to not having developed the full capacity of reliance on personal abstracting reasoning and problem solving. Piaget did not believe possible to hurry through stages. Passage through stages is balanced by <u>Assimilation</u> (incorporation of new information into existing cognitive stgructures) and <u>Accomodation</u> (New info that doesn't fit into already existing cognitive structes is used to create new cognitive structures). <u>Piaget Jean</u> **(1896-1980),**

- Kohlberg's Theories of Childhood Reasoning and Moral Development follows closely the work of Jean Piaget's Theory of Cognitive Development and perhaps even extends his predecessor's work. Kohlberg, Lawrence (1927-1987

Aspects of Adult functioning

Psychological, Moral and Ego Development

Psychological Development

IT may come as a surprise to most adults that a clear **Boundary** between <u>adolescent</u> and <u>adult</u> development has not been identified. There are legal definitions and other informal social definitions such as being employed, financially independent or generally considered mature by most others. Many psychological <u>characteristics</u> are <u>usually associated with maturity:</u> such as psychological independence, autonomy, independent decision making, stability, wisdom, reliability, integrity and compassion. In addition, different cultural demands and responsibilities result in many different and often contrary expectations for Adult attitudes and behaviors (Bischof, 1969). Freud defined Maturity as the ability to work and love,. However, at this time there is no clear age demarcation for its occurrence. A main reason for this is because psychologists have only recently recognized that adults "grow" too. (Human Development—Grace J Craig Prentice-Hall, Inc. 1976)

Although it is generally understood that adolescents "go with the Crowd" it is less well known that many adults also remain dependent on external values and the philosophies of admired others. This is due to not having developed the full capacity of reliance on personal abstract reasoning and problem solving. Several theories concerning characteristics that might define mature Adult Psychological development are present below.

Psychodynamic Theory (Freud, S & various early authors) includes Concepts that 1) The Ego arises out of the ID in response to the frustrations and demands (conflict) of reality on the organism, 2) the ability of an individual to adapt to life's changing requirements is limited, 3) the degree of limitation is the index of psychopathology and 4) Levels of ego development is the result of techniques used to manage anxiety.

The **Humanistic Movement** was led by American psychologists Carl Rogers and Abraham Maslow. According to Rogers, all humans are born with a drive to achieve their full capacity and to behave in ways that are consistent with their true selves. **Rogers,** a psychotherapist, developed *person-centered therapy,* a nonjudgmental, nondirective approach that helped clients clarify their sense of who they are, in an effort to facilitate their own healing process.

At about the same time, **Maslow** theorized that all people are motivated to fulfill a **hierarchy of needs.** At the bottom of the hierarchy are basic physiological needs, such as hunger, thirst, and sleep. Further up the hierarchy are needs for safety, security, belonging, love, status and achievement. Once these needs are met, **Maslow believed, people strive for *self-actualization,*** the ultimate state of personal fulfillment. As Maslow put it, "A musician must make music, an artist must paint, a poet must write, if he is ultimately to be at peace with himself. What a man *can* be, he *must* be."

Lawrence Kohlberg's 6 **stages of moral development** (planes of moral adequacy) were envisioned while studying psychology at the University of Chicago to explain the development of moral reasoning. This theory (inspired by the work of Jean Piaget) hypotheses that moral reasoning (the basis for ethical behavior) has six identifiable developmental stages (See Appendix 1) Kohlberg's work followed the development of moral judgment beyond the ages originally studied by Piaget, who claimed that logic and morality develop through constructive stages Kohlberg, determined that the process of moral development was principally concerned with justice and that its development continued throughout the lifespan, even spawning dialogue of philosophical implications of his research.

Kohlberg believed . . . and was able to demonstrate through studies . . . that people progressed in their moral reasoning (i.e., in their bases for ethical behavior) through a series of six identifiable stages which could be more generally classified into three levels. Kohlberg believed that individuals could only progress through these stages one stage at a time, coming to comprehension of a moral rationale one stage above their own. Therefore, it was important to present moral dilemmas for discussion which would help them to see the reasonableness of a "higher stage" morality and encourage development in that direction. Kohlberg saw this as one of the ways in which moral development can be promoted through formal education. He believed, as did Piaget, that most moral development occurs through social interaction. The discussion approach is based on the insight that individuals develop as a result of cognitive conflicts at their current stage.

Murray Bowen[6]—Father of Family Therapy in his Differentiation of Self Scale classifies levels of human functioning from the lowest (0) to the highest (100) with only a small percentage of society scoring above 60. The scale attempts to classify human functioning on the single dimension of "Who I am". The Self Scale assesses the level of "Self" in a person on the basis of whether decisions are based more on Thinking (High Scores) or Feelings (Low Scores).

Murray Bowen's Research indicates that "A person with a well-differentiated "self" recognizes realistic dependence on others, but can thoughtfully assess facts from being clouded by emotionality.". "People with a poorly differentiated "self" depend so heavily on the acceptance and approval of others they either quickly adjust to please others or dogmatically proclaim what others should be like and pressure them to conform. An extreme rebel is a poorly differentiated person who pretends to be a "self" by routinely opposing the positions of others[7].

---

[6]   Murray Bowen, MD—Family Therapy in Clinical Practice—Copyright 1978 Jason Aronson

[7]   Reprinted from Website of **Bowen Center for the Study of the Family** on Murray Bowen's research on Differentiation.

Helmuth Kaiser cited A citation from psychological literature[8] states "The struggle against seeing oneself as an individual is the core of every <u>Neurosis</u>" and "the universal defense (emotional fusion) against individuality is a Delusion". "The true conflict" resides in the fact of one's aloneness and our need to avoid and deny it".

Peck, R.C (1969)—Psychological Development in the second half of life. Believed Erickson stressed stages1-6 (1-25 years of age) too much. Peck agreed with Erickson's theory that trust, autonomy, initiative, industry, identity and intimacy are all important conflicts to resolve but believed the last 40-60 years of life were equally important to understand and plan for. His stages of Development He hypothesized that Aging and Growing old takes accommodation. None of Pecks stages are confined to middle or old age. The decisions made early act as building blocks for solutions of the adult and old age years. Research (Peck and Berkowitz, 1964) suggested that ages 50-60 are critical for making adjustments which will determine the way an individual lives out the rest of life. Coming to terms with Mortality

Jane Loevinger (B-1918—D-1982) a Developmental Psychologist developed a theory of Personality emphasizing gradual internalization of social rules with development of maturing conscience for the origin of personal decisions. Loevinger Stages of Ego Development (childhood to old age) Early stages reflect social codes with the latter a rational balance. It is similar to Theory of Humanistic Development

Maslow, Abraham —(1954)—Theory of Human Motivation Growth is "becoming" Motivation and Personality—Toward a Psychology of Being—Theory of Human Motivation—Developed as reaction against Freud and Skinner (Operant Conditioning). Mans need to develop his own potential. Self Actualization

Carl Rogers—(1902-1987) **developed a model for psychotherapy** <u>**(1940-1950)**</u> **which** approaches man's attempts to become fully functioning from the stance of realization of Personal Potential In Rogers's view, every person possesses a drive toward *self-actualization,*

---

[8]   **Hellmuth Kaiser (Effective Psychotherapy, 1965)**

the fulfillment of one's greatest potential. Mental illness develops when circumstances in a person's environment block this drive. The existential perspective sees emotional disturbances as the result of a person's failure to act authentically—that is, to behave in accordance with one's own goals and values, rather than the goals and values of others.

A summary of these theoretical Concepts might include the following:

- The human Ego arises out of the **Primary Process**[9] of the **ID** (needs and wants) and is ruled by the Pleasure Principle.
- **Secondary Process**[10] **(**Freudian —Reality Principle) is the ability to stand far enough away from emotions to tolerate frustration and delay gratification.
- **Henry Hartman's,**[11] Concept that Cognition develops independently from the Ego
- **Observing Ego**12 has potential to resolve Conflicts between Primary and Secondary Processes has the potential to resolve conflicts between wants, needs and objective reality.
- A Psychologically Mature "Self" is able to FACE OBJECTIVE REALITY AND ACCEPT THE TRUTH. Skipi Lundquist Smoot, PhD
- Anxiety is a Normal human emotion which signals the need for conflict resolution. Anxiety is related to the specific conflict. Neurosis is the Symptoms surround the underlying Conflict

---

[9] Psychoanalytic Concept of Primary Process thinking—basic tendency toward immediate gratification

[10] Mature Obsercing Ego—Psychoanalytic Theory—Secondary process thinking—Freud Reality Principle

[11] (1970) Father of Ego Psychology—Hartman, H

[12] **Immature Observing Ego**—Campbill, R Psychiatric Dictionary (1981) Psychoanalytic Concept of primary Process thinking—Basic tendency toward immediate gratification. **Mature Observing Ego**—Psychoanalytic Theory—Secondary process thinking—Freud Reality Principle

PERSONALITY "Masks of Anxiety"

Defending the "Self" from Fear
(Mature/Immature vs Normal/Abnormal)

Personality can be defined as attitudes and behaviors unconsciously designed to avoid anxiety, fear of abandonment and emotional independence. **"Masks" of Anxiety** (Personality) are unconsciously donned in attempts to settle both internal and external conflict without resolving issues that interfere with attaining emotional independence.

Maturation: The Adult Paradigm—A Guide for Psychological Development[13] discusses 1) Human Behavior on the continuum of Human Ego Development (Immaturity/ Maturity) as well as Pathology/Wellness and 2) Psychological Maturation as a usually disregarded but essential "Missing Link" for attainment of functional (vs dysfunctional) resolution of Anxiety.

At the heart of Psychological **Immaturity** lies excessive dependency, fear of rejection and feelings of personal inadequacy. Fearing emotional independence, **"Masks of Anxiety"** are donned in attempts to resolve relationship conflicts and avoid the twin realities of human differences and the necessity for healthy emotional separation. Anxiety is the result of both physical and psychological aspects of our personal situations. The physical side of anxiety often shows itself in symptoms of anxiety attacks such as racing heart, unreasonable fear of places or situations, sweating, breathing difficulties or even symptoms resembling heart attacks. The Psychological characteristics of anxiety are often composed of feelings of powerlessness, terrible danger, inability to relax, obsessive and compulsive thoughts (or

---

[13]   **Maturation: Adult Paradigm** (The Map) adapted from Psychological Theory underlying **FINDING THE "REAL" ME**-Learning to Walk on Your Own Path (Unpublished Book). **Skipi Lundquist Smoot, PhD** Copyright@ 1995-Psychological Theory underlying **FINDING THE "REAL ME"**-Learning to Walk on Your Own Path based on Scientific Theory, Data and Research.

behaviors) and irresolvable self doubt about decisions (provided we can make decisions at all). Sometimes we may find ourselves completely unable to make decisions or any type of progress toward our goals because of disabling unrealistic obstacles. A good definition of anxiety is feelings of unrest that occur when something in our subconscious can't be solved or ignored.

My definition of "personality" is that it presents the attitudes and behaviors (patterns of behaviors) we have chosen to cope with anxiety in our life. Some of us have personalities that hide our underlying anxieties (sometimes even from ourselves). This type of personality may be seen by others as overly relaxed, unwilling to pay attention to realistic concerns or sometimes even unable to see a problem exists. Other personalities may fall in the opposite direction. We are all acquainted with personalities of this type who react to every situation as though it were a dire emergency. Some personalities attempt to hide (consciously or sometimes unconsciously) problems from themselves or others by drinking, taking drugs, excessive sleeping, etc. Others attempt to withdraw from anxiety by associating only with people who cause no problems. When a friend or spouse wants to discuss a realistic concern with this type of person, anger, tensions, withdrawal or even divorce can be the result. Patterns of Personality are numerous. However, my point here is simply to explain that the result of our characteristic mode of "coping with our conflicts" (no matter what it is) can be defined as our Personality.

Continuum of Ego/Cognitive Development **The Signal of unresolved conflict—**		
Emotion Immaturity Child (Normal) **Adult** (Dysfunctional) Inconsistency, Contradiction, Unpredictability, Incongruity, Paradox, Illogicality	**Anxiety** A formless state of Unease due to inability to arrive at a functional state of closure.	**Emotional/ Cognitive Maturity** Acceptance, Enlightenment, Face Reality Accept Truth, Acknowledgment, Recognition_ Actuality **Highest Level—Self Actualization_**
Psychological Immaturity	**Anxiety**	**Psychological Maturity**
At the core of **Adult** Immaturity, is an emotionally disabling inability to feel and behave as a unique, independent and/or emotionally separte person.	**Anxiety** is a signal of unresolved subconscious issues to be solved for the process of Psychological development to successfully continue	**Psychological Maturity** can be defined in terms of **Secondary Process,** as well as Frustration Tolerance, Ability to Delay Gratification, Face Objective Reality and accept the truth.

I perceive Human Anxiety often defined as Symptoms of Neurosis to be a Normal Generator of Ego Development by signaling the presence of an unresolved underlying conflict necessary for development of Psychological Maturation.

I perceive Human Anxiety, a trigger of dysfunctional responses (Symptoms of the underlying problem) often defined as a Neurosis to be a generator of Ego Development by signaling the presence of unresolved conflicts. I believe that Neurosis (symptoms) are areas of specific conflicts and symptomatic of Lower Levels of Psychological Maturation.

I believe that 1) Anxiety (a Normal Human Response) designed to signal the presence of 2) unresolved internal conflict 3) Often resulting in dysfunctional Symptoms (defined as Neurosis). 4) Understanding reasons for and Resolution of these areas of

conflict is necessary for attainment of higher levels of Psychological Maturation. 5) Few human beings are ever entirely free of such symptoms.

- ANXIETY can be defined as a state of distress lacking an unambiguous cause An emotional reaction signaling presence of an Underlying Conflict. It may be perceived as a generator of potential psychological development and Maturation.
- NEUROSIS can be defined as Dysfunctional symptoms (anxiety, depression, phobia, etc) in otherwise intact Reality Base of Personality. surrounding Specific underlying conflict. Various functional disorders without organic lesion or change. Dysfunctional Emotional Behavior.

The Continuum of Ego/Cognitive Development defines Psychological Maturation as a necessary "missing link" for a broad comprehensive understanding of human mental processes. Without such in-depth consideration of both abnormal processes leading to mental disorders and normal but immature levels of psychological maturation this has often been a confusing task.

Psychological Maturation is the usually disregarded but essential, "Missing" Link for functional resolution of Anxiety on the Continuum of Human Ego Development. The continuum of Ego/Cognitve Development provides a necessary although frequently *Missing Link* for conceptualizing an inclusive paradigm of normal and abnormal processes. The interpsychic attributes of typical, average, socially conforming individuals are more understandable when categories of mental processes include immaturity in addition to normal and abnormal. Levels of psychological maturation identify a more complete rationale for instances of dysfunctional behaviors often erroneously identified in today's social environment as antisocial, immoral or mental illness.

As a result, independent, responsible refusal to behave in typical, average but **dysfunctional** fashion or conform to personally repugnant social expectations may be realistically identified as normal mature conduct. An in-depth consideration of both **abnormal** mental disorders processes and **immature** but normal **dysfunction** is possible when characteristics of psychological development are identified.

A major source of Adult psychological dysfunction are defenses (Masks of Anxiety) unconsciously assumed to avoid rejection, abandonment and physical and/or emotional independence due to fears of inadequacy The Immature goals of defiance, excessive dependency, substance abuse or emotional distortion are attempts to control the self and/or the environment. Clearly psychological maturation identifies an essential aspect of <u>adult</u> and <u>adolescent</u> **psychological dysfunctional** often **misidentified** as mental illness, antisocial or immoral behavior in today's social environment. **As a result, too few unhappy persons have been willing to admit to or be treated for dysfunction when to do so puts their mental processes at risk for diagnosis as mental illnesses, immorality or criminal behavior. However, without such a broad understanding of both normal and abnormal human attitudes and behavior society will continue to 1) misidentify** <u>normal, dysfunctional but immature mental processes</u> **and 2) punish symptoms of mental illness and dysfunctional immaturity rather than address it with the education and treatment necessary for the potential growth of the human being who manifests it. Differences between normal and abnormal mental processes often become evident when characteristics of** Psychological Development **are identified.**

Chapter 1
The Path to Eternity

The "MAP"

Maturation: Adult Paradigm

The Disregarded but Essential Missing Link
for functional resolutionof Anxiety of Human Anxiety

Face Reality—Accept Truth

There is no clear age demarcation for the occurrence or definition of Psychological Maturation. While Medical experts generally agrees upon criteria for diagnosis of <u>Psychosis</u> *(loss of contact with reality)* and <u>Anxiety</u> *(a state of distress lacking an unambiguous cause)*, definitions of <u>Neurosis</u> continue to change over the years. Broad usage defines <u>Neurosis</u> as **any** of various **Functional** Disorders *(without organic lesion or change)* of mind/emotion involving **anxiety, phobia, or** <u>abnormal</u> symptoms in an otherwise intact Reality Base of Personality.

Questions concerning whether **Anxiety** (a state of distress, unease, dread, fear, uncertainty, helplessness, etc) is a result of some aspect of **Neurosis, Pathology or Mental Illness** or due to **Normal vs Abnormal** mental process have been major sources of disagreement within professional, legal and general populations for decades. Over the years, many ambiguous, conflicting definitions of <u>"Anxiety"</u> have evolved. <u>Freud</u> classified Anxiety as **Unconscious Neurotic Conflict** while <u>Rollo May</u> referred to it as an often **Normal** formless state of unease due to realistic causes. Other authors have attributed it to unresolved **Dependency Needs (Horney),** Security Needs **(Sullivan)** and even a need For Power **(Adler).** However, definitions **of Anxiety appear to** share **the commonality of:** Troubled states of mind lacking unambiguous causes.

According to <u>Donald W Goodwin, MD in his book "Anxiety"</u>[14] all theories share the **common element** of "anxiety concerning the **presence of a problem** that needs to be solved but cannot because the person who has it is **unaware of its nature**". Scientific **Research**

---

[14]　Goodwin, Donald W, MD Anxiety

supporting the hypothesis that bringing the problem into conscious awareness is the answer to the problem **remains uncertain.**

Definitions of **"Neurosis"** have also changed over the years. While broad usage vaguely identifies it as a disorder of nerves, other definitions classify it more precisely as

- Various functional disorders of mind/emotion without organic lesion or change (involving anxiety, phobia),
- Abnormal symptoms of behavior or
- Areas of Dysfunction in an otherwise **intact Reality Base** of Personality.)

Neither do definitions of **"Pathology"**[15] (any condition that deviates from the normal Encarta Dictionary), **Normal** (Average, Conforming, adhering to pattern, typical, the standard or Socially Acceptable behavior American Heritage Dictionary)[16] or **"Abnormal"** (departing from the normal) shed much light on Resolution of Anxiety. Decisions concerning whether definitions of **"Mental Illness?"** (lunacy, psychosis, insanity) **or "Psychosis?"** (Fixations, hang-ups, neurosis, phobia, obsession) provide additional clarification on resolution of Anxiety appear to point out heavy-handed overstatement in these categories.

My own professional clinical experiences indicate that only about 20% of clients fall into the categories of Chemical imbalance, classical definitions of Mental Illness, Psychosis or other diagnosis of serious dysfunction. However, current understanding of Human Dysfunction presented in the definitions above reveal information concerning why traditional methods for resolution of anxiety is often unsuccessful.

As a result, I believe identification of methods for successful resolution of emotional pain and anxiety is of paramount importance to our profession. Whether Scientific Research will eventually find causes of emotional pain and anxiety (presented in the past) to objectively reside in verifiable categories such as neurosis, unconscious conflicts or other areas of dysfunction or pain is at this time unclear. However, current

---

[15]   (Encarta Dictionary)

[16]   (American Heritage Dictionary)

inconsistencies in definitions of mental processes underlying anxiety clearly point to the existence of a "Missing Link" for understanding methods of increasing <u>functional</u> resolution of anxiety.

THREE QUESTIONS

1. **"What crucial aspect of human functioning is being overlooked in such typical but incongruous definitions of Neurosis, Pathology or Mental Illnesses' as those presented above?**
2. **What necessary aspects of human development are being overlooked in the search for Functional Resolution of Anxiety?**
3. **What is the usually Disregarded but Essential "Missing Link" for functional resolution of Anxiety?**

"Masks" of Anxiety (Personality) are donned in attempts to settle both internal and external conflict without resolving issues that interfere with attaining emotional independence. attitudes and behaviors unconsciously designed to avoid anxiety, fear of abandonment & emotional independence.

Maturation: The_ADULT paradigm—*A Guide to Psychological Development* presents a clear, logical, educational model for resolving conflicts, coping with stress and making successful decisions. Personal growth and mature relationships (4 Tasks of Psychological Maturation) can occur as a result of behaving in accordance with a Universal set of Principles (Cause & Effect) underlying all human behavior and relationship communication. These Principles (5 Lessons of Life) identify situations over which we do or do not have control, teach appropriate responsibility for self and others, encourage facing the truth and accepting objective reality, teach methods for arriving at cognitive rather than emotional decisions and instructs readers in a method for developing as crisis free lifestyle as possible.

Psychological Immaturity as the <u>major cause of emotional distress</u> is seldom (if ever) discussed or considered by professionals, families, schools or legal institutions. Most of us put aside contemplation of the meaning of life until faced with a serious problem, mid life crisis, death of a loved one or intolerable tragedy. Few therapists identify lack of Psychological Maturation as a cause of <u>Adult</u> Emotional Dysfunction. Instead, Psychotherapy clients are usually counseled to perceive their pain as the result of psychological pathology, irrational beliefs, chemical imbalances, dysfunctional parents and families, etc.

Equally unknown to most adults is the knowledge that aspects of <u>repressed</u> dependency (need for approval, sensitivity, fear of rejection, abandonment, feelings of insignificance, etc) underlie most <u>consciously experienced symptoms</u> of <u>Separation Anxiety</u> (anxiety, indecisiveness, depression, frustration, anger, resentment, guilt/ remorse). The necessity of understanding the concept of Psychological Immaturity in order to resolve the disabling symptoms of Symbiotic Attachment [17] is almost never considered by the average adult when searching for reasons to explain their unhappiness and frustrations.

However, at the core of Psychological Immaturity, is an emotionally disabling inability to feel and behave as a unique, independent and emotionally separate person. Psychological immaturity is a main factor behind high levels of stress, inability to resolve personal and interpersonal conflict, inefficient decision making and inability to derive pleasure from life. Many of us have little understanding of the characteristic attitudes & behaviors of Psychological Maturity nor how lack of those characteristics may effects our ability to successfully cope with life.

<u>The Reason?</u> Ignorance of the big gap between behaviors which demonstrate *refusal* to behave responsibly and *psychological* <u>in</u>*ability* to behave responsibility. That "gap" is often the result of a lack of Psychological Maturation and Education concerning how to develop it. Few people realize that development of psychological maturity

---

[17] "The Struggle against seeing oneself as an individual is the core of every neurosis" wrote Hellmuth Kaiser. He spoke of the "universal defense" against individuality, fusion, as a delusion. He saw the conflict to be between recognizing one's aloneness and need to deny it. Contribution of Hellmuth Kaiser from Effective Psychoerapy (1965) by Fierman, Louis.

is an extremely effective method for successful conflict resolution, stress reduction, and problem solving.

This sad state of affairs is at least partially due to the fact that society often defines Maturity in Legal or Social rather than Psychological terms. In fact, many people perceive <u>a Psychological definition of Maturity as pure PsychoBabble—a type of explanation deemed to excuse or "coddle" persons who behave in an undisciplined, immoral, or childlike manner.</u> In addition, a common misperception of immature behavior is that it can be changed anytime the undisciplined person chooses to live responsibly. However, pressed for an explanation of what responsible behavior consists of, these people almost always define it in ways that fit their own perceptions of how others "should" live.

<u>Legal Maturity</u> **is defined** as having been reached at the age of 16 years of age (for driving), 18 (for voting) and 21 (for drinking). Some disagreement is found, however, among those who do not believe a person is Mature enough to run for congress until age 30 or President of the United States until 35. Age seems to be a major criteria for legal maturation.

There is even less consistency concerning realistic logic among **Social Definitions of Maturity**. A person is informally identified as being socially mature when employed, financially independent or having demonstrated biological maturity by becoming a parent. Some girls have attained biological Maturity (Parenthood) at 11 or 12 and boys at 12 or 13. However, these criteria hardly seem a logical method of defining responsible Mature behavior due to lack of a consistent criteria.

Psychological Definitions of Maturity, however, do shed some light on why Psychologically Maturity characteristics may be a major contributor to the ability of a Human Being to function successfully or unsuccessfully. Characteristics (identified by the Scientific research of Psychology) as being associated with Human Psychological Maturity are among others Personal Independence, Autonomy, Independent Decision Making, and some degree of stability, wisdom, reliability, integrity, and compassion. All of these characteristics are correlated with Psychologically Mature attitudes and behaviors such as the ability to face reality, control emotional and behavioral impulsiveness, accept the truth, and take appropriate responsibility for the self and others.

The Map Defines **Psychological Maturation** as a Level of **Ego Development** necessary for independent Objective, Critical Thinking, ability to Face Objective Reality and Accept the Truth and attainment of comfort with appropriate emotional and cognitive independence. Methods for Psychological Growth and functional resolution of Anxiety are considered on a Continuum of Human Ego Development rather than Pathology/Wellness when appropriate.

The average person searches vainly for a "secret" of Happiness not realizing answers reside in thoughtful choices based on a "Process" (Universal Principles of Cause And Effect) underlying **Psychological Maturation and Ego & Cognitive Development. This is due to the inability Of Much of the Adult Population To Successfully** 1) cope with Stress 2) resolve Personal/Interpersonal Conflict, 3) Make Confident Decisions, 4) understand and set realistic personal goals, or 5) develop a well thought out emotionally satisfying Philosophy for making sense of their lives.

It is the Message of this book that the problems identified above are often symptomatic of Psychological Immaturity and reflect difficulty resolving separation anxiety, feeling Psychologically mature, comfortable demonstrating unique, independent behavior. Solutions can be searched for and found in attaining higher levels of Psychologically Mature Ego and Cognitive Development. **Psychological Immaturity** as a major cause of Adult Psychological Dysfunction is a fact that is almost never discussed as a cause of emotional or interpersonal problems. At the core of Immaturity is the inability to feel and behave as a unique, independent and emotionally separate person able to face objective reality and accept the truth.

- **80%** of human pain and dysfunction falls on a continuum of Immaturity/Maturity rather then Pathology/Wellness
- **Psychological Maturation** is a usually disregarded but essential "Missing Link" to Human Happiness.

- Personal growth and mature relationships (Psychological Maturation) can occur by adhering to a set of Universal Principles (Laws of Cause and Effect) based on "<u>processes</u>" underlying Objective Reality.
- Facing objective (vs subjective) reality, accepting the truth, cognitive well thought out vs emotional decisions that face reality and accept the truth.
- Think about your feelings and choose whether to respond too them or not.

```
"Me-" Thinking  about
My Feelings behaviors
```

CHAPTER 2
THE UNIVERSAL ENVIRONMENT

THE DANCES OF LIFE

WE ARE BORN WITH A. MISSION . . .

. . . TO EXPLORE OUR OWN PATH

The Dance we choose may not lead down our own Path
Potential Influences of others (parents, siblings, teachers,
authorities) and Events exert significant influence over our lives.

Where does your *Present* path "Really" Lead?

THE <u>DANCES</u> OF LIFE

Defending the Self from Fear

Are you Dancing to the rhythms of 1) Intense emotion or 2) rational thought ? Do you know the difference?

The Emotional Dances can be recognized by the rhythms of impulse or intense emotion accompanying them. These Subjective often-illogical Dances are easily identified. Their behavioral dance steps often reflect rigid attitudes or distortions based on personal opinions insistent on "shoulds", "Oughts", generalizations, Black and white thinking, etc. Other Dances of Emotion result from **Anxiety** related to fear of rejection, low self esteem, feelings of entitlement or other areas of unresolved conflict.

At the heart of **Psychological Immaturity** lies excessive dependency, fear of rejection and feelings of personal inadequacy. <u>Fearing abandonment by others,</u> **"Masks of Anxiety"** (Behavioral and Attitudinal Symptoms of Immaturity) are unconsciously donned in attempts to resolve relationship conflicts and avoid the twin realities of human differences and the necessity for healthy emotional separation.

Anxiety is the result of both physical and psychological aspects of our personal situations. The **physical side of anxiety** often shows itself in symptoms of anxiety attacks such as racing heart, unreasonable fear of places or situations, sweating, breathing difficulties or even symptoms resembling heart attacks. The **Psychological characteristics of anxiety** are often composed of feelings of powerlessness, terrible danger, inability to relax, obsessive and compulsive thoughts (or behaviors) and irresolvable self doubt about decisions (provided we can make decisions at all). Sometimes we may find ourselves completely unable to make decisions or any type of progress toward our goals because of disabling unrealistic obstacles. A good definition of **ANXIETY** is feelings of unrest that occur when something in our subconscious can't be solved or ignored.

My definition of **"PERSONALITY"** is that it presents the attitudes and behaviors (patterns of behaviors) we have chosen to cope with anxiety in our life. Some of us have personalities that hide our underlying anxieties (sometimes even from ourselves). This type of personality may be seen by others as overly relaxed, unwilling to pay attention to realistic concerns or sometimes even unable to see a problem exists. Other personalities may fall in the opposite direction. We are all acquainted with personalities of this type who react to every situation as though it were a dire emergency. Some personalities attempt to hide (consciously or sometimes unconsciously) problems from themselves or others by drinking, taking drugs, excessive sleeping, etc. Others attempt to withdraw from anxiety by associating only with people who cause no problems. When a friend or spouse wants to discuss a realistic concern with this type of person, anger, tensions, withdrawal or even divorce can be the result. Patterns of Personality are numerous. However, my point here is simply to explain that the result of our characteristic mode of "coping with our conflicts" (no matter what it is) can be defined as our Personality.

The
ROCK & ROLL

Dancing to the Music of Emotion

DYSFUNCTIONAL BEHAVIORS

Dancing to the "Music" of Emotion

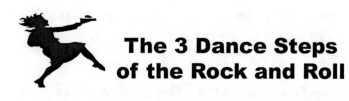

The 3 Dance Steps of the Rock and Roll

At the core of psychological immaturity lies excessive dependency, feelings of inadequacy and fear of rejection. Fearing abandonment by others **"Masks" of Anxiety** (Behavioral & Attitudinal Symptoms of Immaturity) are unconsciously donned in an effort to control anxiety and avoid emotional independence. underlying them

The Dance Steps underlying our chosen **"Mask" of Anxiety** are learned in relationships with parents, families, authorities, teachers etc. to protect our self from pain. **The 3 Dance Steps** of the **Rock and Roll** (arranged in almost endless variations) include attempts to control things over which there is no control, conforming to outside situations or the wishes of others and withdrawing from ourselves or others. All of us yearn to reside within loving accepting relationships. We all want to see ourselves as competent, successful, loved and loving people. The three Steps of the Rock & Roll are danced as attempts to resolve or hide from personal or relationship conflict and anxiety.

Many of us are taught that certain beliefs and behaviors are either right or wrong and as a result must be always or never done. Such a belief systems encourages a black and white philosophy of life that encourages numerous irrational and/or illogical conclusions. When presented with the objective truth that fact is usually "grey" [1], those convinced of the correctness of their Black/White, Right/Wrong ideologies often steadfastly and even angrily refuse to consider the possibility of error in their thinking processes.

Perceiving the Objective ideology of *Shades of Grey* as the **Blaring Trumpets** of a call to war, the Subjective *black/white thinkers*

---

[1] Albert Ellis—RET—Irrational, Illogical thinking processes—1950's Glasser—Reality Therapy— What behaviors caused the problem.-1960

don their chosen **"Mask" of Anxiety** and head for the **Dance Hall** where they to gyrate to the emotional rhythms underlying their chosen steps of the **ROCK & ROLL.**

Depending upon which Variation of the **Rock & Roll** we have chosen, we kick up our heels, bow to our partner, shove other dancers, grab others to help them perform "correctly", pout, stomp away or angrily shout denunciations when others don't want to dance the steps we have chosen for them. The Emotional Rhythms of the 3 fast slick side steps of the **Rock and Roll** (with variations) are exhausting. They all lead to pain and some to illness. They are dances of immaturity learned in a world of fantasy.

DANCE STEPS OF
THE ROCK & ROLL

STEP 1

CONTROL

- Open attempts to control attitudes and behaviors of others (Bossy or Know it all).
- Manipulative attempts to control attitudes & behaviors of Others (Passive or Sneaky).

STEP 2
CONFORM

- Conforms to Attitudes and Desires of Others

STEP 3
WITHDRAWAL

- Withdraws from the Self into Sleep, Drugs, Alcohol, Eating, etc.
- Withdraws from Others into Anger, Indifference, Divorce, Emotional Distance, Etc.

THE ROCK & ROLL

Emotional Rhythms Of The 3 Fast, Slick Sidesteps
(with variations)

THE <u>MINUET</u>

Dancing to the "Music" of the Universe

THE UNIVERSAL LAWS OF CAUSE & EFFECT

DANCING TO THE "MUSIC" OF THE Universe

The 5 Dance Steps of the Minuet

The **Path To Psychological Maturity** runs through the **Fabric Of The Universe** and is paved with **Universal Laws** of **Cause And Effect** based on "Processes" underlying objective reality.

Respect for human competence allows innate personal potential to develop. **Psychological Maturation** results from an **Observing Ego**[2] sufficiently developed to face Reality and accept the truth. **Ego Boundaries**[3] must be strong enough to resolve emotional dependency on others and develop unique personal potential.

The **Laws of Cause & Effect** underlying **Reality** assist Maturation by teaching which of our attitudes and behaviors reflect objective truth. Taking many forms (experiences, events, interactions with others, patterns of reoccurring behaviors, etc) the **"Music" of the Universe** (Cause & Effect) teaches **5 Lessons of Life** that underlie the success or failure of our experiences as well as which of our attitudes and Behaviors do or do not reflect reality. Listening closely, some recognize the balanced rhythms of Reality

---

[2] Hartmann, H—Father of Ego Psychology—Concept that thought develops independently from the Ego Berne, E—Adult Ego State—Transactional Analysis—Think about feelings and choose to disregard them

[3] Hartsman, H-Father of Ego Psychology. The Cognitive (thinking) processes develop separately from the Ego Ego Psychology—Emotional structure). Impulse Control-Delay of Gratification—Ego Boundaries—Codependency Beattym M

(cause and effect) and learn to dance to the **"Music" Of The Universe.**

LESSON 1—We have no "real" **control over** anyone or anything but ourselves.

LESSON 2A Acceptance of **PERSONAL RESPONSIBILITY** leads to the greatest possible development of Unique Individual Potential

LESSON 2B Attempts to take inappropriate **RESPONSIBILITY FOR OTHERS** lead to our becoming a crutch and their possible crippling

LESSON 3 Recognition of Objective **Reality (what "IS") vs Subjective Perceptions** (what we want, mistakenly believe is or feel "should" be) allows accepting the truth about ourselves and our relationships

LESSON 4 Well thought out COGNITIVE SOLUTIONS based on what's best for us and others in the long term vs Short Term **Emotional** "Fixes". lead to more successful personal & Relationship decisions

LESSON 5 A life dedicated to **BALANCE AND MODERATION** allows the most successful development of as many aspects within ourselves, our situations and our relationships as possib

THE DANCE STEPS
OF THE MINUET

STEP 1

CONTROL

- You Can only Control Yourself

STEP 2

RESPONSIBILITY

- You Must take Responsibility for your self
- You cannot assume Responsibility for others

STEP 3

REALITY

- Face reality & accept the truth

STEP 4

DECISION MAKING

- Make well thought out long term decisions vs. short term emotional "fixes"

STEP 5

MODERATION & BALANCE

- Live an Organized, Planned Life style vs one of Crisis & impulse

THE MINUET

5 Thoughtfully Balanced Dance Steps

CHAPTER 3

THE UNIVERSAL ENVIRONMENT

FINDING THE *"Real"* ME?

**Opportunities along the Road of Life can lead to both
Psychological & Spiritual Development**

Where _is_ the "Real" Me?

Examine Your Path CLOSELY   for Clues

We are born with a Mission—to explore our own path

Dancing to the "Music" of the Universe

1. The **Fabric Of The Universe** presents opportunities for both Human and Spiritual Growth. The **Fabric** (physical environment, events, people, etc.) is reflected in the tangible parts of the Universe (Persons, Opportunities, Choices).

2. The **Music Of The Universe** (a "force" of **positive energy** residing in the environment) is an intangible, invisible process underlying events and relationships providing opportunities for both Psychological & Spiritual Development. The **Music** presents opportunities for growth within **Human Relationships** and/or **Life Situations** based on the C&E of Reality **as well as opportunities for communication** between the Spiritual and Physical Realm) through **Universal Connections** (serendipity, dreams, synchronicity, intuition)

3. **Path to Eternity** (Human & Spiritual Growth) runs thru the **FABRIC** of the Universe (**Map of Reality**) and is paved with Realistic **Laws of C & E.**

4. **Psychological Maturation** is a Human **Developmental Stage** resulting from the ability to **Face** (objective) **Reality** and **Accept the Truth** of Cause & Effect. **4 TASKS**

5. **Human Life** is a multifaceted arena of **Instructional Opportunities** within Human Relationships, Life Situations, and Universal Connections (serendipity, dreams, synchronicity, intuition), meditation, dreams). for development of both human and spiritual potential. **EARTH SCHOOL**

The "Map"

MATURATION: ∧ THE <u>ADULT</u> PARADIGM

*The Map of Reality
Runs through the Fabric of the Universe
and is paved with Universal Laws Of Cause And Effect.*

Personal growth, mature relationships and development of Unique Potential (Psychological Maturation) can occur by Learning to recognize the underlying "Processes" of Reality.

At the core of psychological immaturity lies excessive dependency, feelings of inadequacy and fear of rejection. Fearing abandonment by others "Masks" of Anxiety (Behavioral & Attitudinal Symptoms of Immaturity) are unconsciously donned in an effort to control anxiety and avoid emotional independence.

The Fabric & Music Of The Universe Teaches Life Lessons Necessary To Resolve Emotional Dependency On Others & Achieve Psychological Maturation

*Follow The "Map" & Learn to Dance
to the "Music" of the Universe*

Finding THE "Real" ME?

Human Life is the training ground for evolution of Psychological Maturity and Spiritual Development. The "Real" Me appears as a result of realistic interaction between the "seed" of human potential and components within the Universe. Goals of the Fabric and Music of the universe are to resolve interpersonal dependency, develop maturity and explore unique potential.

The Music of the Universe is a "force" of positive energy residing in the environment. It floats above the negative energy produced as a result of unrealistic perceptions and expectations held for ourselves and others. The negative energies of anger, frustration, hate, fear or resentment within ourselves and our relationships trap our potential mature development within the confines of dysfunction. In order to break free from from self imposed bonds, allowing ourselves to bathe in the positive energy of love and respect for oursleves and others we must face reality and accept the truth about ourselves and our environment.

The Fabric (physical environment, events, people, etc.) is reflected in the tangible parts of the Universe. The Music (a "force" of positive energy residing in the environment) is an intangible, invisible 'process' underlying events and relationships. The Music teaches the realistic lessons of life. Residing both outside ourselves and within our unconscious mind it has the potential to free and assist development of Psychological and Spiritual maturation.

WHAT IS THE MUSIC OF THE UNIVERSE, HOW DOES IT WORK ... and HOW CAN WE RECOGNIZE THE MUSIC?

The Music, invisible & intangible resides in the opportunities and choices that present themselves in our lives. We may "hear" it in interaction between people or the opportunities that present themselves within the events in our lives. When choices are made in line with reality positive energy propels us toward successful outcomes. When choices are made in opposition to reality negative energy is the environment and relationships leads to outcomes that seldom develop our unique self. Negative emotions stuck in pathology. Lessons unlearned go back to relearn them.

WHO CAN HEAR THE MUSIC?

Those who are developed Psychologically and Spiritually enough to take advantage of it opportunities. The Music becomes louder as we learn to make our choices based on realistic cause and effec. It becomes fainter as we make choices based on unrealistic criteria such as unrealistic expectations about control, ignoring reality, making choices based on emotions vs realistic thoughts and living a life filled of impulse.

WHAT QUESTIONS DOES IT ASK?

It provides us with situations in which we must ask ourselves whether or lives are working or not? It encourages us to ask ourself why or why not our personal lives and relationships mature and fullfilling. If our answer is No, life leads to symptoms, neurosis, dysfunctional relationships, personal immaturity, etc. If Yes, It prods us to identify which of the lessons we have have learned and which do we need to keep learning? The more lessons learned the more ability we have to develop the 4 Tasks of Human Maturation.

HOW DOES IT PRESENT INFORMATION?

The Music transmits messages throughout our lifetimes whether or not we are able to 'hear' them. Message can be heard in relationships with certain people or Events. When events of a similar kind keep happening a pattern appears. In positive events we know we are doing something right or wrong when the pattern is negative. For Instance a woman continues to get involved with men who take advantage of her. A **"pattern of abuse"** is a clear message she needs to address. Ask Which of Our Relationships do or do not work. Why or why not?. Many times an Insight about our life dawns on us. This type of experience happens frequently in psychotherapy therapy. A sort of "Aha, experiences" it appears because the right questions have been asked. It has the potential to give information about the type of lessons we need to learn.

Synchronicity is a group of Lucky temporal events seeming to happen by chance. Whether it is really chance has been the subject of many books. Synchronicity happens often in lives and making the choice to take advantage of these opportunities may lead to growth. Another type of experience that may seem strange to many people are **Premonitions. These experiences** allow us to "Know" certain things. They may present themsselves in a dream or while awake as intuitive knowledge or a hunch. Some people are very suseptible to the information premonition offers while others are not.

Serendipity is Chance (?) Events that allow us to make choices Leading to Positive Results. Scott Peck says "Spiritual Growth is inseperable from the process of Human Maturation" "We choose and are chosen by serendipity". He quotes "Budha found enlightment only when he stopped looking for it, when he let it come to him"[1] "It may not have come to him if he had not tried to find it". **Dreams are a method of** Learning what our unconscious knows and wants to tell us. Dreams are the language of the unconsicous mind. In **Psychotherapy** much can be uncovered that resides in the unconscious mind. It is also a method of learning new ways to live that may prove more successful than our old ones. Many of us **intuitively** understand parts of our life but don't know how we know it. Children are often in touch with inner knowledge, but loose it as we become socialized out of paying attention to our intuitive knowledge. The **Unconscious Mind** can often tell us much. We must but listen closely for our inner knowledge.

DIMENSIONS OF MATURITY

Embedded in the Fabric of the Universe, the Music has the potential to teach 5 realistic lessons (Laws) of life that if followed allow psychological maturity to develop. Making choices based on these Laws help resolve dependency (separation anxiety), achieve psychological maturity and allow the evolution of the human spirit. Human maturation evolves along a continuum of maturity. Symptoms of adult separation anxiety include anxiety, indecisiveness, depression, frustration, anger, grief, resentment guilt and remorse. These feelings are the result of fear of personal inadequacy, abandonment, need for approval, dependency and oversensitivity. Learning to walk on our own path and being ourselves without guilt, take personal responsibility

---

[1]   Peck, s Road Less Traveled Serendipity Pgs 305, 308 Synchronicity Pg 308

for our choices, face reality and accept the truth is the best method of stress reduction and conflict resoltuion. Psychological Maturation allows us to think independently, feel emotionally separate, problem solve with others and develop our own independent unique personal philosophy of where we 'fit' in the world. When we are mature we have the ability to face reality and accept the truth.

THE EVOLVING DANCER

The **'Real'** Me enters the world as a 'seed' of potential with the possibility to unfold in a continual "process" of psychological and spiritual maturation. This 'seed' of potential assisted along its development path as a result of ability to 'hear' informational possibilities presented in many different ways (the Music). Authors & readers of Psychology, Parapsychology, Eastern Religions, and Spirituality have long been intrigued with the concept of Serendipity and speak of it often in attempts to clarify difficult to explain happenings. It is also defined as "an inherent power or ability". Apparently not everyone is able to make use of such a personal characteristic that has the potential to lead to making fortunate and unexpected discoveries by accident.

What exactly is Serendipity? Why do some of us have the ability to take advantage of it while other do not? What is it good for, anyway? It has been spoken of as a type of Spiritual Grace[2], Fate, or Karma[3] by which we are given the opportunity to explore alternative life experiences.

Serendipity is defined in the New College Edition of the American Heritage Dictionary as "the faculty to make fortunate and unexpected discoveries by accident". The term was coined by Horace Walpole after the characters in the Fairy Tale "The 3 Princes of Serendipity" who are described there as having the faculty to make such discoveries.

For the past 10 years, while thinking about personal development, I have investigated the idea of Serendipity as it relates to Human Maturation. It appears to be available to some and not to others. It

---

[2] "The Road Less Traveled" by Scott Peck, MD Chapter 1V, the Miracle of Serendipity (pg 253).

[3] Karma (Hinduism & Buddhism) is the sum and consequences of a person's actions during the successive phase of his existence, regarded as determining his destinly. "New College Edition of the American Heritage Dictionary"

appears to be the result of personal awareness. Often connected to Intuition or Spirituality It is entirely possible that it is always there and if we learn to recognize and take advantage of it, our lives have the opportunity for enrichment. However, since it is a Spiritual concept, it will in all like hood remain in the category of concepts resistant to Scientific Proof.

At the present time, Psychological Scientific Literature contains research on such Spiritual Concepts as Astral Projection (Ring, K. 1980), Life After Death Experiences (Moody, R. 1975-1979) and Out of Body Experiences (Monroe, R.1971,1985, 1993), The Holographic Universe (Talbot, M 1991), God and the New Physics (Davies, P 1981)

An Author of a Popular Psychological Self Help Book for Codependent Parents [4] describes a relationship process, she calls "The Mirror Channel" to have the capacity for development of Human Growth. She describes this process to be a result of attraction to others with complementary psychological dysfunctions of those we possess. Our own problems, "mirrored" in the behavior of the other, can be used as a method of viewing and changing our dysfunctions.

I arrived at the conclusion that Mental Health is a process of Ego and Cognitive Development along a continuum of Maturity as a result of my work with Clients in Individual & Family Psychotherapy, Psychiatric Hospitals, Strangers in Group Therapy Sessions, Business Executives in Seminars, Inmates in Jail, and countless Psychological Test Batteries administered to children, adolescents, and adults in both inpatient and outpatient settings.

Psychological theory has traditionally explained most Psychological Disorders as anxiety covering deeply buried "conflicts" within the "subconscious" mind of the Patient in analysis. Many patients spend years gaining "insight" and "working through" their "transferences" in the offices of their Doctors.

Modern research in Cognitive Psychology indicates that most people with Psychological Disorders or Problems in Living can be helped simply by learning to change the way they "see" the problem. Depression and Anxiety Disorders are often solved by learning to "think about the situation" differently. Cognitive Therapy tells us "it is not what happens to us that causes anxiety and depression, it is "our beliefs" about what happens to us that leads to our behaviors and emotional reactions.

---

[4]   Jacequelin Costeau

The **Behavioral and Ego Developmental Model** of Mental Health explains Psychological Problems on a continuum of Human Development ranging from immaturity to maturity rather than illness and/or pathology. While it is true that certain psychological disorders may be the result of a chemical imbalance or a biological predisposition, most anxiety, depression, family or relationship problems can be greatly helped (or elevated) by understanding the meaning of Human change and growth and the stages of Adult Development.

As mentioned in the First Part of this Section, many people spend years searching for 1) the "secret" of life, 2) the "right" way to live, or 3) an illusive "something" called "Happiness", without realizing the only 'secret' is learning to make choices taking the Process of Maturation into account. This process is mainly concerned with 1) Learning to choose whether or not to respond to emotions and 2) understanding and accepting Reality.

I often use Psychological testing as a means to identify personal strengths, weaknesses, immaturities, characteristics defenses, and develop Treatment Plans. My Clients are instructed in the concepts of working through less mature stages of development on their way to more mature stages of Self knowledge, Personal Growth and Harmonious relationships with others.

How does Serendipity fit into the Development of Human Maturation? There appears to be two "forces" in Human Life, one that "pulls" toward relationships and the other towards growth as an Independent person[5]. The Concept of Serendipity provides a rationale for situations presented as opportunities for growth in both Human and Spiritual Development.

Lessons of Life
are based on
Laws of "Cause & Effect

Universal Laws
of "Cause & Effect"
run through the
Fabric of the Universe

---

[5]   Kerr, MD—Family Evaluation—Dr. Kerr presents the theories of Eric Berne as they relate to the processes of Differentiation and Emotional Separation.

INTRODUCTION TO PART II

Psychological Maturation

The "*Missing*" link

For Resolution Of Anxiety

Dimensions of Adult
Ego & Cognitive Development.

Respect for human competence allows innate personal potential to develop. Psychological maturation results from an Observing Ego sufficiently developed to face Reality and accept truth. Ego Boundaries must be strong enough to resolve excessive emotional dependency on others and develop unique personal identity & potential.

WHERE IS THE `Real" ME?"

Examine Your Path CLOSELY for Clues

Human Ego & Cognitive Development
4 Tasks of Maturation

TASK 1
UNIQUE INDEPENDENCE

Unique Personal Identity is a result of Positive Self Esteem, Feelings of Self Worth, ability to face objective reality and the necessary self confidence to develop personal potential. Unique Personal Identity develops from a functional Observing Ego and realistic Self Worth and Esteem

TASK 2
EMOTIONAL SEPARATION

Resolution of excessive Emotional Dependency on Others. Symbiotic Attachment evolves from Ego Boundaries [2] strong enough to resolve Symbiotic Attachment [3]

TASK 3
Interdependence

Interdependent perception of the needs of self and others as equally important. **Interdependence** [4] requires 2 "Mature Selves" equally committed to needs of both.

TASK 4
Personal Philosophy of Life

ndependent, thoughtfully arrived at broadly focused Objective Philosophy of Life.

Dimensions & Constructs Of Psychological Maturation

 **"Don't leave me"
. . . "I'm Afraid to
be alone.**

At the core of Psychological immaturity lies excessive dependency and fear of rejection due to feelings of inadequacy. The goal of immature behavior is reduction of anxiety. **"Masks" of Anxiety** are donned in attempts to resolve relationship conflicts and avoid the twin realities of human differences and the necessity for healthy emotional separation.

Psychological Maturation occurs as a result of learning to make choices based on an instructional "process" of Cause and Effect underlying personal Ego Development and communication within Relationships.

Four tasks of Human Development (Independent thought emotional separation, interdependence and a personal Philosophy) lead to adaptive functioning, personal responsibility and Psychological Maturation.

Five lessons of Life (the Process) teach control, responsibility, reality, cognitive decision making and moderation.

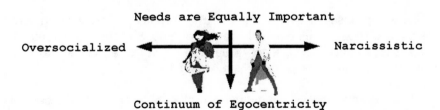

Needs are Equally Important

Oversocialized ←————————→ Narcissistic

Continuum of Egocentricity

4 **Tasks** of Ego & Cognitive Development
Psychological & Spiritual Essence

Respect for human competence allows innate personal potential to develop. Maturation results from an Observing Ego sufficiently developed to face Reality and accept the truth. Ego Boundaries must be strong enough to resolve emotional dependency on others and develop unique personal potential. The following 4 Human Developmental Tasks are necessary Dimensions of Psychological Maturation.

1. **Unique Personal Identity** develops from a functional Observing Ego and realistic Self Worth and Esteem
2. **Emotional Separation** evolves from Ego Boundaries strong enough to resolve Symbiotic Attachment
3. **Interdependence** requires 2 "mature selves" equally committed to needs of both.
4. A functional independently arrived at <u>Philosophy of Life</u> results from moral development, psychological maturation and a broad life focus.

Dysfunctional attitudes and behaviors are traditionally defined as Pathology/Wellness vs Immaturity/Maturity. Theories of Maslow (1954), Kohlberg (1971), Chess (1980), and Pleck (1975) are important exceptions. Although biological or chemical dysfunction may require medication, most psychological distress can be significantly reduced simply by perceiving situations differently.

The Map, based on Developmental, Ego, Psychodynamic and Cognitive theories defines Development in terms of Ego & Cognitive strengths, weaknesses and Maturity level. It leads to growth of an Observing Ego sufficiently mature to face Reality and Accept the Truth.

Most clients seeks treatment only after all else fails. Successful intervention must provide a model for anxiety reduction and functional living skills. Clients respond quickly, more positively and with less anxiety with emphasis placed on Immaturity instead of Pathology. A clear, logical Model of psychological maturation helps clients identify and increase levels of Ego and Cognitive development.

CHAPTER 4

Task #1—Unique Independent Thinking

"Who AM I?"

. . . a Unique "Self" or a reflection of someone else?

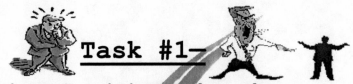

Task #1—

Unique Cognitive Independence

"Do I feel competent? . . ." able to think. for myself?"

Development of COGNITIVE INDEPENDENCE

Human Beings are born with a seed of "Uniqueness". No one else, in the history of the world, has ever been born exactly like us. As Human Beings we can choose to explore and develop our "Gift" of Potential…. or not. Psychologically mature adults can clearly define the principles underlying their personal values. They are able to compromise, problem solve and respect personal differences. Although certain values may be nonnegotiable, personal integrity seldom demands attempts to convince others of either the correctness of our own principles or the error of theirs.

At the core of **Psychological Immaturity** lies the disabling inability to feel safe and behave separately. The **"Faces"** we grew up with contribute to our perception of the world. **Self-image** is a result of our perceptions of how we believed others saw us. Respect for a child's ability to explore innate competence gives a child permission to develop unique personal potential.

Internalization of realistic positive **Self Esteem** and personal **Worth** results from having learned to believe we were Worthwhile, Strong and Competent enough to learn to make our own decisions and solve our own problems. Personal decisions can then be made from a thoughtful focus that while taking emotions into consideration does not allow feelings to assume the most relevant position within the decision making process.

Psychological Maturation is the result of an Observing Ego sufficiently developed (the ability to stand far enough away from our emotions and personal biases) to face reality and accept the truth.

The "Map"

Where is the "real" Me?

Examine Your path Closely *For Clues*

TASK 1
DEFINITIONS OF CHARACTERISTICS
NECESSARY
FOR UNIQUE PSYCHOLOGICAL DEVELOPMENT

♦ **OBSERVING EGO—ABILITY TO Think for myself**
An Observing Ego is the part of us able to 'see" the truth about our situations and ourselves. It allows us to think about our feelings, choose to respond to them or not, face reality, accept the truth, delay gratification, tolerate frustration and assume personal responsibility.

♦ **INTERNALIZING OUR SELF CONCEPT—"REFLECTING"**
Others Opinions of ourselves
Self Image results from "mirroring" our perceptions of others opinions of our worth and abilities. These perceptions are formed in childhood usually in relations with parents, grandparents, siblings, etc.

♦ **SELF ESTEEM—"Mirrors" of Personal Worth**
Positive **Self-Esteem** leads to a sense of self worth and personal value. It develops in childhood from feeling competnet, loved, and valued by important others. Positive Self Esteem is the internal knowledge that we are competent, valuable and able to solve our own problems appropriately.

Definitions And Characteristics Of Ego Functions

OBSERVING EGO

ABILITY TO Think for myself

- What are the characteristics of a strong, stable self?
- Where does it's strength & self confidence come from?
- How does it develop?

An **Observing Ego** is a part of ourselves that is able to 'see" the Objective Reality about our situations and ourselves. It allows us to think about our feelings, choose to respond to them or not, face reality, accept the truth, delay gratification, tolerate frustration and assume personal responsibility.

Our **Observing Ego** is that Adult part of our self that has learned to think about our feelings and choose whether to respond to them or not, based on what is best for us and others, in the Long Term. The Ego is not the Person. The Ego is the part of the Psyche that mediates between the Person we are and Reality. The Ego's function is to perceive (think about) Reality as it "really" is (not as we think it should be, or wish it were, or expect it to be) and adapt to it.

The Human Ego has an organization. We can learn to 1) think about the self's physical and mental functioning, and our behaviors,2) adapt to reality, 3) know the difference between our feelings and thinking and 4) choose to respond to emotions or not based on what is best for us & others in the long run (self preservation & safety). In addition we can learn to 5) balance the external demands of reality vs internal needs & wants of our Id (our unconscious), 6) reconcile conflicting ideas and 7) perceive the realistic truth of a broad external reality vs a narrow personal focus.

The functions of a Human Beings Observing Ego develop gradually. Development depends on physical maturation, genetically determined growth of the central nervous system, and experiences of the developing person. Ego strength is the degree to which the functions of the Ego are able to be maintained even in the face of overwhelming feelings from the Id. Most importantly, the Ego (becomes strong) & learns to deal with Reality as a result of unsatisfied needs.

At birth an infant cannot tell the difference between the self (where they stop) and external reality (where others begin). The child perceives the mother to be part of him/herself, not as a separate person. This is the result of being fed when hungry, changed when wet, etc. and associating satisfied needs with wishes, desires, etc. This Egocentricity (self as center of the universe) of a child (or an adult who has not developed and matured) is called <u>Primary Narcissism</u>. Primary Ego satisfaction (being nurtured and getting needs met) for the infant is normal and necessary. As a result, the infant/child learns to perceive others as existing for the child's satisfaction. When parts of Reality do not bring pleasantness, Reality is seen as <u>not</u> to be tolerated.

An infant at birth can be understood as an emotionally **"empty cup"**. This child "drinks" down & internalizes the parental "Reflections" of himself. If the parents see him as wonderful and meets his needs promptly and lovingly, the child learns to view himself as worthwhile. He learns to trust that his needs will be met and that he is safe and secure in the world. If the child "interjects" or internalizes a parent who perceives her child as a bother, a nuisance or as a person unworthy, unloved or not respected, the child learns to see himself as not valuable, and develops low self esteem. And in the case of a child who has developed low self esteem, **because the child is egocentric** (perceives himself as the center of the Universe) he may even perceive himself to be the **most unworthy person in the world**.

As a child matures, the longing for **Primary Narcissism** (to continue to feel as though he is the center of the universe) is **perceived as Reality** by the child. Only as time goes by and development occurs does the child learn to see both the needs of himself and others as equally important.

<u>Self Esteem</u> is the result of feeling strong, worthwhile, & competent. To become truly independent and mentally healthy it is necessary to feel lovable, loved and with a sense of belonging. True **Self Esteem** is the result of being able to live up to one's realistic standards and solve our own problems. In order to feel & behave autonomously, independently, and with high self esteem it is necessary to develop **frustration tolerance** and <u>learn</u> to **delay gratification**. Development of frustration tolerance is essential for the growth of a strong healthy Ego. A child who feels **egocentric** (center of the Universe) and **omnipotent** (able to be in charge of the rest of the world) eventually encounters the Reality that others are equally important and that all efforts to the contrary will not change Reality.

This lesson is learned as a **result** of needing to tolerate the frustration that anxiety brings. The **ability** to **tolerate frustration** results in **learning** to **delay gratification** which in turn leads to feelings of strength, independence, worthiness, competence, etc. If **Frustration Tolerance** is **never** developed, a person continues trying to control others, often meeting personal needs at the expense of the realistic needs of others.

Summary of Ego Functions

The **Ego** cannot develop without the tempering influence of learning to **tolerate frustration** & **delay gratification.** Ego development is the result of resolving the anxiety generated by **conflicts** between the Underdeveloped Ego and Reality and mastering them. The Ego becomes strong (learns to deal with Reality) as a result of **Unsatisfied** needs. It is impossible to develop Ego Strength, Self Esteem, Independence, without mastering the developmental tasks of Learning to Delay Gratification, Face Reality and tolerate Frustration. The Observing Ego's ability to think about Emotions and choose whether to respond or not is the **hallmark** of **Psychological Maturation**

Why was I born?   What is my Mission in the World?"

WHO AM I?

MIRROR

Am I my "real" Self?"
....or a Reflection of
someone else?"

OBJECTIVE Mirrors of PERSONAL Reality

THINKING FOR MYSELF (OBSERVING EGO) — about
myself, my feelings and the direction of my Path through the Universe.

What do I want to do with my life?

"How can I **finally** be sure this
is
the "Real" Me?"

What is my duty to
Myself?....To
Others?" What do I
"really" think?
Why? "Are my
beliefs true?" "How
do I know?"

"What is the "truth" about my existence?"

" Are my lifestyle conflicts attempts to "Fit"
in?"….." Or could I be trying on identities of Others
in an effort to "decide which of many human
characteristics are truly "Mine?"

"Is there a reason for my life?" "How can I
make sure I don't waste it?" "How do I
want to be remembered when I am gone?"

The **Observing Ego** resolves conflicts between
wants, needs and objective reality. The ability to stand
far enough away from our emotions and personal biases
to see and accept reality grows as a result of ability to
delay gratification and tolerate frustration. A
Psychologically Mature "Self" is able to face reality
and accept the truth.

What are my strengths?
weaknesses?
What is my Potential?

"I am "Unique"."
"No one is exactly like me".

Where is the "Real" Me.
Examine Your path **Closely** *For Clues*

Internalization of self image
Mirrors of Self Esteem

INTERNALIZING SELF CONCEPT—"REFLECTING" Others Opinions of ourselves. Self Image results from **"mirroring"** our perceptions of others opinions of our worth and abilities. These perceptions are formed in childhood usually in relations with parents, grandparents, siblings, etc. **Internalization** is the process of incorporating something outside ourselves and learning to think of it as becoming an intricate part of ourselves. **Self Esteem** is a good example of something that has been internalized.

A mother who loves her child and see him as the most wondrous gift she has ever received will look into the eyes of that baby with such adoration that it can only be internalized by the child as the seed of future positive self esteem. Picture the child as an "empty cup" and the mother as a full to overflowing cup of love and caring. The child . . . looking into his mothers adoring face, drinks into himself . . . the love from the mothers eyes and soul . . . and becomes the manifestation of the mothers love. This is the **birth** of positive **Self Esteem.**

On the other hand, a mother who views her child as a chore and a burden, who resents attending to his needs, who allows the child to cry for food, attention or a change of dry clothes, who handles him roughly and without love and caring will learn to perceive himself in a negative way. A child who sees a mother full of frustration, anger, rage, or resentment will drink into his **"empty cup"** a mixture of "self perception" that defines himself in negative terms. Similarly a child who is treated with love and caring on one occasion and with frustration and anger the next will not internalize a consistent sense of self esteem.

Some writers of Psychological theory speak of **incorporation** and **Introjection** as the mechanism whereby internalization takes place[6]. Incorporation and Introjection are psychiatric terms that describe a

---

[6]   Psychiatric Dictionary, Robert Campbell, 1981

process where by something outside the self is incorporated in some way into the self.

SELF ESTEEM—"Mirrors" of PERCEPTION OF EXTERNAL OPINIONS Positive **Self-Esteem** leads to a sense of self worth and personal value. It develops in childhoodfrom feeling competent, loved, and valued by important others. **Self Esteem** is the internal knowledge that we are competent, valuable and ablee to solve our own problems appropriately.

Self Esteem is the most important element of Mental Health, but also the most difficult to clearly define. This is because, in order to have a high self concept and high self esteem, you must first be able to think of your self and your accomplishment in positive terms and be proud of yourself. However, in order for this to come about, it is necessary to develop a **Set Of Standards** against which to compare your values, accomplishments and self worth. The question then becomes **"How is this to be done? Against what authority do you compare your self, your worth, your achievements?"** And when a standard has been put into place, **what authority** decides if it is it a realistic standard, in terms of mental health, principles, duty, human growth, expectations of parents, authority, etc. Who or what is to be set up as the Final Authority? A tall order, Yes, but one that can be accomplished with some thought and a great deal of growth.

As a Psychologist, my work has been to help people work toward becoming more mentally healthy, assume more responsibility for themselves, and face reality and accept the truth about themselves and their worlds. However, in the years I have been doing this work, I cannot remember a single person who came into therapy specifically for help in raising their level of self esteem. As a result, a rise in the level of personal self esteem has usually been a by-product of some other goal of therapy. This does not mean that **Self Esteem** should only be considered as one of the wonderful by-products of Successful Psychotherapy or Self Exploration and Growth. It is possible to start your journey toward growth and mental health by attempting to raise your level of Self Esteem at the outset.

"FAMILY FACES" FROM THE TREE

The Happy, Angry, Sad, Loving or Judgmental Faces we all grew up with contribute to our level of Self Esteem and how we view the world. Self Image and feelings of Personal Worth result from internalizing "reflections of our worth" seen in the eyes and faces of those entrusted with our care. .....Most of us accepted those "Mirrors" truth.

INTERNALIZATION OF SELF CONCEPT

How do you think your parents, grandparents, siblings and friends felt about you? How did they show it? How did it effect you? How did you contribute to it? How did these experiences contribute to the way you feel about yourself today?

<u>What </u>is Self Esteem?

There are many <u>definitions</u>. Nathan Brandon [7] (1992) says that Self Esteem is the experience that we are appropriate to life and to the requirements of life. It is 1) Confidence in our ability to think and cope with the basic challenges of life and 2) Confidence in our right to be happy, the feeling of being worthy, deserving, entitled to assert our needs and wants and to enjoy the fruits of our efforts.

Others have expressed their <u>definitions </u>of **Self Esteem** as 1) the comparison we place on ourselves to others in areas that are important to us (James, 1890[8]), and 2) personal judgment of worthiness in attitudes held toward the self (Coopersmith, 1981[9]).

Most people start life with feelings of smallness, inferiority, and a need to look to authority for answers. This is a **possible** result of being taught such things as "Adults know best", "Children should be seen and not heard", "Don't ask too many questions", "Don't disagree with Authority", "Always be polite", "If you can't say something nice don't say anything at all", "Being told by this authority or that one that if you knew the whole story you would probably agree with their point of view", etc. It is no wonder that most of us grow up not quite trusting our own perceptions or having expectations for ourselves, others and situations that are not truly in line with reality.

<u>Who</u>, then, is to set the standards against which we define ourselves, our worthiness and our expectations for ourselves? The questions become "Shall I think for myself or not?" "If I do think, how do I know I am thinking rationally? How do I know that I haven't made any mistakes? What value judgments shall I base my decisions on?

---

[7]   The Power of Self Esteem, 1992 Nathan Brandon

[8]   The Principles of Psychology, 1890 William James

[9]   The Antecedents of Self Esteem, 1981 Stanley Coopersmith

The roots of **Self Esteem** lie within ourselves. If we place them outside ourselves we will never be free from self doubt. **Self Esteem** is the result of facing as much of the reality as we are able to perceive and accepting the truth about ourselves, others and our situations. It is taking appropriate responsibility for ourselves, defining our own values and morals and developing integrity. And finally, **Self Esteem** is doing the very best we can and living up to our own values.

"MIRRORS" OF SELF Image

Self Esteem looks you straight in the eye and allows the Dignity of the Human Spirit to reveal itself. It resides in us at Birth, but is often lost as we try to fit into the expectations of others. When we look into the eyes of another who possesses it, it looks back at us as its equal. Its only request is to be shown the caring, respect and love due the majesty of "Gods Handiwork", the Human Spirit.

"I'll Never Amount to anything!!"

"No one cares about me. Nothing ever works out for me.

"I'm a looser"

I can solve my own problems. I can take care of myself

"I am A "Winner". I can rely on myself."

"I don't care if anyone likes me or no".

"I am worthwhile and have many friends."

Self Image "Mirrors" (accepts as truth) <u>our</u> perception of what we believed significant others thought about our worth and abilities. Parental respect for human competence allows the child's potential to develop. Positive self esteem rests on knowledge of competence, value, strength and confidence in ability to take care of ourselves.

TASK—1

The following Questions concerning aspects of personal experiences may help arrive at conclusions concerning Unique Independence

- Did you feel loved, worthwhile and respected as a Child? By Whom? How?
- Do you believe others perceived you as strong and competent? By Whom?
- How do you know?
- Did you somehow feel too small, weak, worthless or incompetent to think
- for yourself or make your own decisions? Why? Under what circumstances?

Questions?

CHAPTER 5

TASK 2—EMOTIONAL SEPARATION

"Masks" of Anxiety

We hide our **"*Real*"** selves Behind "Masks" (attitudes and behaviors) unconsciously designed to "shield" the self from anxiety concerning conflict within ourselves or with others.

TASK 2 –
EMOTIONAL SEPARATION

Two Human "Forces" lead toward relationships and becoming a separate, unique person. At birth we can't tell where we stop and the environment begins. Babies perceive themselves as part of others (usually their mother) Symbiotic Attachment. Immature persons of all ages feel uncomfortable being an emotionally independent self. Inability to resolve emotional fusion "feels like being homesick". However, becoming a "whole" person necessitates learning to balance these forces. Too much of either results in anxiety . When balance has not been achieved attempts to control the resultant anxiety (internal and external conflicts) by impossible methods are made. As a result psychological symptoms and syndromes such as dependency, addictions, anxieties and phobias develop.

Many persons of all ages have difficulty understanding and accepting the concept of Ego Boundaries ("Where I stop and others begin"). Problems with external ego boundaries (physical) can be seen in those who touch, hit or otherwise do not respect the personal space of others. Poor internal Ego boundaries are the result of inability to control emotional responses within ourselves. Many people have so much empathy they feel "the pain, pleasure or problems" of others.

Personality can be defined as the "exhibition" of characteristics "MASKS" OF ANXIETY developed to "shield" the self from anxiety about conflict within ourselves or with others. At the heart of immaturity lies excessive dependency fear of rejection and feelings of inadequacy. Fearing emotional independence, "Masks " are donned in attempts to resolve relationship conflicts and avoid the twin realities of human differences and the necessity for healthy emotional separation.

EMOTIONAL SEPARATION

TASK 2—

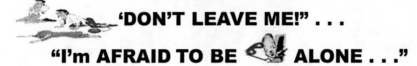 **'DON'T LEAVE ME!"** . . .

"I'm AFRAID TO BE ALONE . . ."

EMOTIONAL Enmeshment-

"It Feels like being Homesick"

Two equally strong forces in Human Life lead toward relationships and becoming a separate, unique person.

At Birth we can't tell where we stop and other begin. Babies perceive themselves as part of their primary caretaker (usually the mother). However, to become a "whole" person each of us must develop the ability to balance these "forces". Too much of <u>either</u> leads to misunderstandings' and an inability to accept reality. When balance has not been achieved we attempt to control the resultant anxiety concerning internal or external conflict with impossible methods. As a result psychological symptoms develop

Inability to resolve emotional "attachment" leads to neurotic behaviors such as dependency, addictions, anxieties and phobias. Resolution of Task 2 demands the ability to feel emotionally separate without undue or unrealistic anxiety. It requires demonstration of loving, caring Emotional Detachment <u>rather than attempts</u> to manage anxiety about feelings of inadequacy to function separately by 1) attempting to control others, 2) Conforming to others expectations, &/or 3) withdrawal from ourself (into repression & denial) or from others (as a manipulation to force their compliance).

There are two innate "forces" in Human Beings, that of being in relationships and that towards becoming a separate, independent person. At birth, we cannot tell where our body stops and that of others or our environment begin. All babies perceive themselves to be part of their Primary Caretakers (usually the mother). However, to become a whole person, each of us must develop the ability to "balance" these two forces. Too much of either leads to distorting and misunderstanding reality.

Typical Pattern of Emotional Fusion in Relationship of Primary Caretaker & Infant. Symbiotic Attachment usually continues into Adult Relationships, causing conflict & emotional pain.

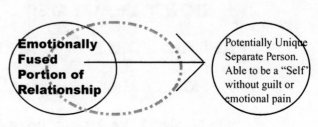

At birth, babies are all emotion (verbal thought processes have not yet developed). No one who has ever been closely involved with an infant doubts this fact. The baby is intensely in touch with his own internal experiences. Whether hungry, contented, Angry, frustrated, or in a rage, the infant feels and expressed them all wholeheartedly and with the whole self. At around age two the superego, or conscience begins to develop and we start to learn what we should or should not do. Although a baby is in touch with his own experiences (independent) he is also emotionally dependent on relationships for survival.

At about two years old, our conscience (the superego), begins to develop. We begin to glimpse what we "should" or "should not" do. Although a baby is in touch with internal experiences (the 'force' toward becoming an independent self) he is also emotionally dependent on others for survival ('force' toward relationships).

The "terrible two's" can be seen as the ***birth pangs*** of a 'Real self'. A baby experiences a forceful "push" to explore his own world and "be" who he is. Mother and other caretakers usually react by quickly applying limits to their child's behaviors and expectations concerning their childs ***appropriate*** feelings. Statements such as "You know you don't really mean that", "You know you don't hate your brother" or "Don't go out in the yard because you'll get hurt", are representative of statements heard by all of us. Unfortunately many of us also hear

such messages as "Don't touch that, you're so clumsy you'll break it", "Stop that or no one will like you", or "Don't say that or Mommy won't love you anymore". However, whether the messages are given in a positive or negative spirit, all of them are messages concerning our personal inadequacy and incompetence. The messages we hear lead to learning to see ourselves as wrong, weak, unable to identify our own feelings, inadequate to protect ourselves from the world, or too clumsy to be inflicted
 upon the world. No wonder most of us grow up with conflicted feelings about our abilities, adequacies, or even our right to function separately.

Fear of emotional separation is the primary problem confronting human beings of all ages. We long to be separate but fear personal inadequacy to become truly independent. We dread abandonment from others believing we could not survive their loss. Intense emotional pain and anxiety are the result of these usually unconscious conflicts. When someone we love disagrees with us, we tend to perceive it in terms of rejection and loss of love. This fear of emotional separation is the primary problem which confronts human beings.

Childhood conflicts with others about personal needs and hurt feelings concerning them lead to intense anxiety. The messages heard and felt in childhood from important others (Mommy, etc.) become "I am part of you, you are part of me", "Our needs and feelings *should* be the same" (Symbiotic Attachment), to "I dimly sense I am somehow a separate person", "It's dangerous to be a separate person", and "I shouldn't be different from you or you will disapprove of me and leave me" (Separation Anxiety).

Human Beings attempts to deal with conflict in relationships (and resulting anxiety) in one or more of 3 ways, 1) forcing others to be similar, 2) conforming to others demands and expectations or 3) withdraw from self and others in an effort to avoid, deny or repress knowledge of conflict in the relationship.

A person, who tries to control the other in a conflict, does so by trying to change the others mind about the issues. As a result, the anxiety disappears along with the conflict. Others are so afraid of losing a relationship that they conform. And although the conflict (and anxiety over it) may temporarily disappear, the buried resentment lingers, causing other problems in the relationship. Withdrawing into sleep, divorce, pouting, emotional distance, drinking, drugs, etc. results in temporary repression of anxiety, but also leads to further personal and relationship problems. These methods of dealing with Conflict always lead to other symptoms, neurosis, addictions, etc. It is much better in the long run to deal with the problem so that the needs of each person in the relationship are fairly addressed and solved so that resentment and frustration are not the result.

Various emotional problems and patterns of behavior result from fear of being an emotionally separate person. The need to resolve conflict by attempting to control others can be seen in those who angrily demand conformity from others, try teaching others how to do things **right**, refuse to take "No" for an answer or attempt to prove others are **wrong**.

Many of us grow up with Separation Anxiety Problems similar to a young woman who felt there was no one in a room when she was there alone. The behavior of
conforming to solve relationship conflict are the results of fear of abandonment, need for approval to receive love, feelings of inadequacy, inability to function alone, or need to avoid conflict at all cost.

As a result of conforming to please others, many of us become emotionally cut off even from ourselves. In an effort to keep our cut off feelings buried, we become depressed or try to hide our repressed anxiety by taking drugs, drinking, sleeping, eating, etc.

Many people develop 'patterns of withdrawing' from others to protect themselves from pain in relationships. A male client looked so angry he away people with his looks. Sitting in my waiting room with eyes down cast you could almost see a cloud of anger rising from him. Clients often told me he looked so angry they hesitated to sit by him. What I couldn't tell them was that if they had been able to look deeply into his eyes they would have seen a terrified little boy, so afraid of relationships he needed to keep everyone at arms length.

Successful resolution of Symbiotic Attachment is most easily achieved in our families of Origin when there are continued love, commitment and respect for each others abilities to learn to care for ourselves. According to Psychological Theory[1] "The struggle against seeing oneself as an individual is the core of every neurosis" and the "universal defense against individuality (**emotional fusion**) is a delusion". The true conflict is between recognizing the fact of one's aloneness and our need to avoid and deny it".

---

[1] Hellmuth Kaiser (Effective Psychotherapy, 1965

EMOTIONAL ENMESHMENT

Roadblocks and Detours on our "Path"
to psychological Maturation.

Although Emotional Enmeshment (inability to know where we end and others begin) is the norm for babies and Mothers most of us faced stumbling blocks in our family of origin as we attempted to resolve this basic developmental task. As a result of not learning to be comfortable with emotional independence we continue the struggle in our relationships with others both inside and outside our family of origin (friends, spouses, siblings, parents, etc). Successful resolution of this developmental task leads to being a loving, caring a separate self in our relationships with others. Inability to achieve emotional separation results in attempts to manage internal anxiety by controlling others or withdrawing from ourselves (into repression, denial, alcohol or drugs) or from others (as a manipulation to force their compliance).

Statements designed to resolve the conflict and preserve the emotionally enmeshed Relationship

- You came from my body. You are part of me.
- Stop, you'll get hurt. It's too dangerous out there
- You're too stupid to make it on your own.
- You know I'm right. Do it my way.
- Women (or men) aren't supposed to do that.
- You never do anything right, here let me show you how?

Persons in
the emotionally Fused
Relationship

Persons in
the
emotionally
Fused
Relationship

Emotional
Independence
is never
reached

Emotional Fusion

MORE
Statements designed to resolve the conflict and preserve the emotionally enmeshed relationship

- I'll do it your way, just don't leave me.
- You're right, I can't survive alone.
- If you don't let me do my own thing, I'll run away
- If you really loved me you'd do what I want

PERSONAL AND RELATIONSHIP
CONFLICT AND ANXIETY are dealt with through
controlling, confirming and/or withdrawal behaviors.

Attempts to covertly
Control the other and
preserve the relationship

Conforms to the other
in attempt to preserve
the relationship

Withdraw from the self or
other in attempt to avoid the
conflict and preserve the
relationship

"See you later!". "I'll be fine."
"I can take care of myself". "I love you". Differentiation

SUCCESSFUL RESOLUTION OF
SYMBIOTIC ATTACHMENT
IN OUR FAMILIES OF ORIGIN

Healthy Emotional Detachment is being achieved. There will be continued love, commitment and respect for each others abilities to care for themselves. A citation from psychological literature states "The struggle against seeing oneself as an individual is the core of every neurosis" and "the universal defense against individuality (emotional fusion) is a Delusion". "The true conflict is between recognizing the fact of one's aloneness and our need to avoid and deny it*".

THE AREA OF EMOTIONAL FUSION IDEALLY GETS SMALLER AS WE MATURE

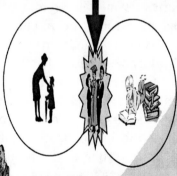

PATH to Differentiation

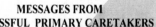

MESSAGES FROM
SUCCESSFUL PRIMARY CARETAKERS

- You are competent and can care for yourself
- It's Ok to make mistakes. The only people who don't make
- mistakes are those who never do anything
- We love you. We will be here if you really need us.
- We are sure you can make successful personal choices and
- decisions.
- You will be a success.
- You have unique potential to offer.
- We are dedicated to your own growth and development.
- Our job as a parent is to teach you to care for yourself.

RESPONSES FROM
SELF CONFIDENT "OFFSPRING"

- I'm confident of my abilities to care for myself
- If I make a mistake, I can learn from it
- If I want advice I can ask my parents, my friends or some other source of objective information
- My parents still love me.
- My parents want me to learn to care for myself

*Hellmuth Kaiser (Effective Psychotherapy, 1965)

EGO BOUNDARIES

It's difficult to discuss the concept of <u>EMOTIONAL SEPARATION</u> because its components, 1) Ego Boundaries, 2) Anxiety and 3) Symbiotic Attachment (feelings of fusing or melting with another) are so closely intertwined. Levels of ability to feel both physical and emotional separation result from development of higher levels of psychological maturation. Some people have no idea they are either physically or emotionally separate. Others may realize they are physically separate but feel emotional "stuck" in relationships with others. They have no idea how to help themselves. Strong Ego Boundaries can help identify what is real in these "stuck" relationships and what is not.

There are two categories of **Ego Boundaries**, **External** and **Internal**. Strong **External** boundaries define where your personal "space" stops and that of another begins. Strong **Internal** boundaries have two functions, to protect you from being bombarded by repressed unconscious material and provide healthy separation of your feelings from those of another. Anxiety about feeling and behaving separately is the basis for most emotional problems. Developing the ability to both feel and behave emotionally separate is the basis of true psychological maturation. The ability to feel emotionally separate is the result of Ego Boundaries sufficiently strong to define personal "space" as belonging to you, and knowing how to keep your emotions from becoming inappropriately "hooked" by someone or something "out there"

<u>Example</u> **of Internal Ego Boundary Fusion**
A new born infant cannot tell where his body stops and that of another begins. He perceives himself as his mother's loving arms, sweet voice and nurturing breast. Everything and everyone in the environment is "me" and therefore "mine". He is the center of the world. Only slowly with time does a child learn others or things outside of himself are not him.

<u>Examples</u> **of External Ego Boundary Fusion**
Effective External Ego Boundaries represent the amount of Personal Space necessary to keep from being physically "too close" to others. People who are physically violent toward others, those who force

others into sexual activity, insist others behave in ways they don't want to behave, etc all exhibit enmeshed External Ego boundaries. Anxiety contributes to a person with Ego Boundary deficiencies feeling unreal or as though they are somehow floating outside their bodies (derealization). A sense of too little physical separation results in distorted perceptions of what control we have over events and persons outside ourselves. Most of us have experienced someone who talks to us so physically close we feel the need to back away. That's External Ego Boundary Deficiency. Deficiency is also seen in those who constantly touch others with out permission, hit, slap or otherwise treat another as a *physical property*. Immature people of all ages, "stuck" in their relationships, see and treat others as a possessions. Enmeshment is seen not only in those who attempt to control others physically but by those who believe others have the right to physically control them.

CONTINUUM OF EXTERNAL EGO BOUNDARY DEVELOPMENT

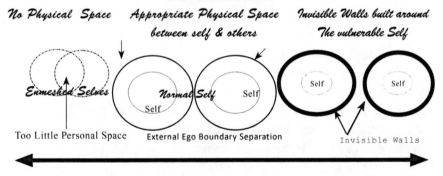

External Ego boundaries can be more easily understood as occurring on a continuum of behavior with severe characteristics of dysfunction at each end and normal in the middle. Sometimes characteristics of behavior falling between one end of dysfunction and the middle of the continuum may be seen as "Normal".

EXMAPLES:

A good example of this (enmeshed end) is a parent who perceives their child as a "part of themselves" or of their family identity. They may spank a child to teach, punish, etc. Statements such as "No kid of mine is going to act that way", or "There's no way my son isn't going to play Baseball. All men in our family are into sports" are common.

However, although the perception of a child as a possession falls within the category of enmeshed External Ego Boundaries, our society accepts this Enmeshment as normal.

A parent who routinely applies abusive physical punishment or perceives a child as having no existence outside of family identity is clearly abnormal. Those who physically control the behavior of a child by spanking, slapping and hitting, often believe a child is not only their property but that the child has no identity of his own. This is partially a result of our culture's message that a parent is not only responsible for a child's attitudes and behaviors but that unacceptable behavior of the child is the *fault* of the parent. The belief and feeling that others are our *possessions* is the result of enmeshed ego boundaries and cultural messages that contribute to immature attitudes and behaviors.

INTERNAL EGO BOUNDARIES

Internal Ego Boundaries are invisible partitions inside and between yourself and others. When strong these boundaries keep Unconscious (Id) material repressed and help keep our Emotions and Feelings from being inappropriately controlled by someone (anothers painful remarks) or something (events) outside of ourselves. All of us, during times of falling asleep or waking up have experienced unconscious material floating in our minds. Waking quickly from dreams, dream fragments seems to float slowly back into the deeply buried, hidden place in your mind from where they came. Unconscious images that just moments before had been so vivid, are instantly forgotten.

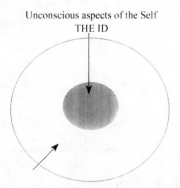

Unconscious aspects of the Self
THE ID

Consciously known aspects of the self

CONTINUUM OF <u>INTERNAL</u> EGO BOUNDARIES

ENMESHMENT
Feelings are vulnerable
to the feelings of others
& outside influences

NORMAL
Feelings are Separate from those
of Others

INVISIBLE WALLS
Built around feelings. May cut off
feelings from Self and/or Others

Painful remarks of another may lead to emotional pain over which you mistakenly believe you have no control. You may see another remarks as somehow "causing" your own emotional or impulsive responses. All of us (especially during times of intense stress) may respond impulsively to others. Those with strong more healthy **Internal Ego Boundaries** have learned to think about feelings and choose to respond to them or not.

EXAMPLES OF WEAK INTERNAL EGO BOUNDARIES:

How do you react to the hurtful remark made by another? Is it true? If it is, can you accept and admit it. People with Psychological Problems routinely overreact, feeling unable to control their responses to people or situations outside themselves. They tend to over personalize and respond to others' behaviors unrealistically, almost entirely from a *subjective* position (a personal or emotional point of view rather than one of objective reality).

A woman was told by a friend that her new dress was a *disaster.* An emotionally strong person could take this blunt (if unkind) comment in stride. She might laugh about it or ask herself if there was any truth to the comment. She could then either disregard it or plan a shopping trip to rectify it. An emotionally vulnerable person however would be devastated, either believing she was worthless for choosing the wrong dress or becoming angry at her friend for having different tastes in clothes. Enmeshed people have almost zero tolerance for differences. Many people have trouble defining where they stop and another begins.

<u>EXAMPLES OF PERSONAL INTUITIVENESS</u>: While feelings of "stuck togetherness" are characteristic of immaturity, inability to feel separate may also be the result of a strange type

135

of 'we-ness". This type of intuitive closeness is often reported by identical Twins, intensely emotionally close spouses, long time loving friends, or those who somehow intuitively *know something* about another.

Ego Enmeshment (with its emotional inability to separate the self from others) is the basis of both immaturity and psychosis. But if enmeshed ego boundaries were the only explanation for intuitive knowledge of another's feelings and thoughts, psychics and clairvoyants would need to be diagnosed immature or psychotic. And psychics and others with the inborn or developed ability to intuitively "know" something about someone else are as mature, immature or normal as any other group of people. They just possess a mysterious ability to "tune in" to another's emotional or cognitive *wave lengths*.

Trying to separate intuitive knowledge, emotional closeness and ego boundary dysfunction can sometimes be challenging. Unfortunately, the destination of Nirvana remains only a longed for illusion. The closest any of us ever come to this paradise is the orgasmic "bliss" felt when our soul touches that of a beloved. It may also be felt in the romantic breathlessness of a new love affair. The lover is perfect, everything is wonderful, we both love the same kinds of food., nothing the other does irritates us. Anticipating each others needs we sometimes find ourselves saying words in the mind of the other before they can be said. Unfortunately or fortunately, before long, usually within a few months, our enmeshed ego boundaries *snap back* and sanity returns. But for some unusual few a type of intuitive knowing, or spiritual clairvoyance is a normal state of affairs.

EXAMPLESOFEMOTIONALEMPTINESS(PSYCHOLOGICAL IMMATURITY) At times most of us have found ourselves searching for a way to fill that *empty spot* in our 'self'. That emptiness may be the result of trying to recreate a dimly recalled, wonderful symbiosis (remnant of the time we could tell where we stopped and another began) between mother and newborn. It may even be a result of some dimly sensed remembrance of life in the womb.

Drug addicts, dependent personalities, borderline personality disorder also display Enmeshment problems. People with weak internal ego boundaries feel a kind of naked transparency as though they are helplessly vulnerable and at the mercy of threat from outside *ourselves*. Feelings of someone or something outside ourselves causing impulsive behaviors or emotional responses is common.

Although all of us (during times of stress) may sometimes respond impulsively to others, those of us with healthier Internal Ego Boundaries are usually able to think about our feelings and choose whether to respond to them or not. Emotionally immature people (and those with Psychological Problems) however, are often unable to control their responses to others or situations. They over-personalize and respond to others from their own subjective positions. Many people with weak ego boundaries develop psychologically induced ailments such as ulcers, gastric problems, extreme oversensitivity to stress, panic attacks, etc. They feel they must "walk on the path" of others.

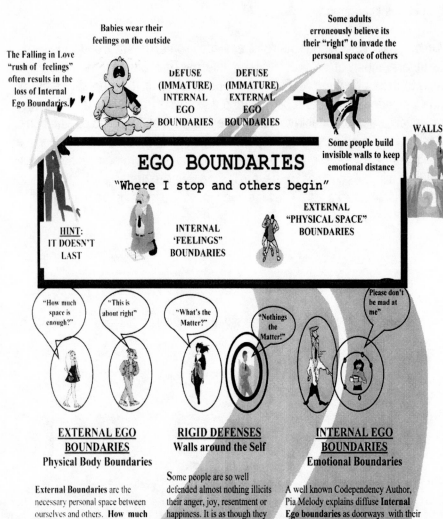

EXTERNAL EGO BOUNDARIES
Physical Body Boundaries

External Boundaries are the necessary personal space between ourselves and others. **How much personal space do you need?** Problematic external boundaries are displayed by those who hit, kiss, touch, etc others without permission. "What do you think about people who eat off the plates of others without permission.? Children are spanked and wives beaten by those who lack adequate external ego boundaries.

RIGID DEFENSES
Walls around the Self

Some people are so well defended almost nothing illicits their anger, joy, resentment or happiness. It is as though they have built **Walls around their feelings** so no one can get into them. Most people with such rigid defenses do not realize they have built these walls until under extreme stress some "break" down into inexplicable depression or Psychological disorganization.

INTERNAL EGO BOUNDARIES
Emotional Boundaries

A well known Codependency Author, Pia Melody explains diffuse **Internal Ego boundaries** as doorways with their "handles" on the outside into their feelings. As a result anyone can open them...even without permission. Adequate Ego Boundaries are explained as doorways with handles on the inside so only their owner is able to open them or not as they see fit. "**Are your Handles on the Inside where you are in charge of your responses to Others and External events?**"

"MASKS OF ANXIETY"

Personality can be understood as the "exhibition" of characteristics developed to "shield" us from anxiety about conflict within ourselves or with others. At the heart of Psychological Immaturity lies excessive dependency, fear of rejection and feelings of inadequacy.

Anxiety is composed of both physical and psychological characteristics. The physical signs of anxiety often consist of increased heart rate, trembling, sweating, b®reathing difficulties, etc. Those who experience anxiety attacks know many of these symptoms intimately, often mistaking them for heart attack, breathing obstruction, or some other serious physical illness.

Psychological anxiety may be associated with painful awareness of being powerless in a personal matter, a feeling of impending and inevitable danger, or an exhausting alertness as if facing an emergency. Anxious persons may feel such great self absorption that it interferes with effective solutions to real problems, or as an irresolvable doubt about the nature of the threat. Anxiety must be separated from realistic fear. Freud believed Anxiety arose automatically whenever the psyche is overwhelmed by something too threatening to be mastered or faced.

It is helpful to think about their personalities as existing within three psychic layers. The Outer/Behavioral Layer contains all consciously known facets of a person, all actions and behaviors and all cognitive functioning. The Middle Layer is that unique combination of characteristics (known as Personality) that reveal the "self." It includes a persons psychological defenses, personal resources, and individual character structure. It manifests personal ability or inability to cope with anxiety and achieve personal goals without undue conflict. The Core Layer (Id) contains all unconscious needs, emotions, drives, fears, conflicts, anxieties and inborn temperament of the self.

"Personality" is a demonstration of our **coping style** within our life space. I call these coping styles **Masks of Anxiety**. These **Masks** can then seen to be a "showcase" that exhibits our ability to see reality (vs fantasy), focus our thoughts (vs feeling confused, fragmented, vague, forgetful, etc.) and set and achieve our goals (vs floundering in rationalization, denial, drugs, alcohol, anxiety, illness, etc.).

Our **Masks of Anxiety** (the defenses we use to "ward off" anxiety) are seen by others (and often ourselves) as our personality characteristics and temperament. If our behaviors show patterns of anger, passivity, suspiciousness, etc. we need to ask ourselves "Why?". We can often understand ourselves and others more easily when we look for answers to such questions as "What am I doing?", "Why am I doing it?", "Is it working?", "How do I feel when I do it?". The methods we finally chose to keep Anxiety out of our consciousness can tell us a great deal about the meaning of our personality and the state of our mental health.

A person with a strong functional personality successfully achieves realistic goals, solves problems, and meets personal needs without undue guilt and anxiety. Conversely, a dysfunctional personality gets needs met at the expense of others, often without realizing it or sometimes even assuming other's needs are less important than their own.

Anxiety is the result of conflict, uncertainty, feelings of being unloved, unwanted or worthless. It is the result of fear, depression, or alienation. Its characteristics form a **cloak** that is often mistaken for our "Real Self". Cowing beneath its "contours" as a defense against pain we eventually become a fundamental part of its "falseness". Tragically some of us completely loose sight of our "self ", frantically exhibiting our **Masks of Anxiety** as though they were authentic.

"Masks" of Anxiety

We hide our "*Real*" selves Behind "Masks" (attitudes and behaviors) unconsciously designed to avoid anxiety, fear of abandonment & emotional independence. "Masks" of Anxiety are donned in attempts to settle both internal and external conflict without resolving issues that interfere with attaining emotional independence.

"Masks of Anxiety"
may include

- Attempts to control the beliefs, attitudes and behaviors of others
- Conforming to the demands of others to keep peace in the relationship
- "Hiding" from the rself in sleep, drugs, or denial to avoid facing conflicts
- Withdrawing from others to avoid solving the conflict
- The need to prove your "right" to
- Independence implies personal doubt

Where is the "real" Me?

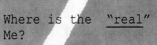

Examine Your path **Closely** For Clues

141

SELF ESTEEM

A NECESSARY CHARACTERISTICS FOR EMOTIONAL SEPARATION

At birth we can't tell where we stop and others begin. Problems with External Ego Boundaries (Physical) can be seen in those who touch, hit or otherwise do not respect the personal space of others. Problematic Internal Ego boundaries are the result of inability to control emotions. A Person with problematic internal ego boundaries feels as if there is no control over their own emotional responses to other people or external situations. Self Esteem is the most important element of Mental Health, but also the most difficult to clearly define. This is because, in order to have a high self concept and high self esteem, you must first be able to think of your self and your accomplishment in positive terms and be proud of yourself. However, in order for this to come about, it is necessary to develop a set of standards against which to compare your values, accomplishments and self worth. The question then becomes "**How is this to be done?** Against what authority do you compare your self, your worth, your achievements?" And when a standard has been put into place, what authority decides if it is it a realistic standard, in terms of mental health, principles, duty, human growth, expectations of parents, authority, etc. Who or what is to be set up as the Final Authority? A tall order, Yes, but one that can be accomplished with some thought and a great deal of growth.

As a Psychologist, my work has been to help people work toward becoming more mentally healthy, assume more responsibility for themselves, and face reality and accept the truth about the themselves and their worlds. However, in the years I have been doing this work, I cannot remember a single person who came into therapy specifically for help in raising their level of **Self Esteem.** As a result, a rise in the level of personal self esteem has usually been a by-product of some other goal of therapy. This does not mean that **Self Esteem** should only be considered as one of the wonderful by-products of Successful Psychotherapy or Self Exploration and Growth. It is possible to start your journey toward growth and mental health by attempting to raise your level of Self Esteem at the outset.

What is **Self Esteem?** There are many definitions. Nathan Brandon [2] (1992)says that Self Esteem is the experience that we are appropriate to life and to the requirements of life. It is 1) Confidence in our ability to think and cope with the basic challenges of life and 2) Confidence in our right to be happy, the feeling of being worthy, deserving, entitled to assert our needs and wants and to enjoy the fruits of our efforts. Others have expressed their definitions of Self Esteem as 1) the comparison we place on ourselves to others in areas that are important to us (James, 1890[3]), and 2) personal judgment of worthiness in attitudes held toward the self (Coopersmith, 1981[4]).

Most people start life with feelings of smallness, inferiority, and a need to look to authority for answers. This is a possible result of being taught such things as Adults know best, Children should be seen and not heard, Don't ask too many questions, Don't disagree with Authority, always be polite, If you can't say something nice don't say anything at all, being told by this authority or that one that if you knew the whole story you would probably agree with their point of view, etc. It is no wonder that most of us grow up not quite trusting our own perceptions or having expectations for ourselves, others and situations that are not truly in line with reality. Who, then, is to set the standards against which we define ourselves, our worthiness and our expectations for ourselves. The questions become "Shall I think for myself or not ?" "If I do think, how do I know I am thinking rationally? How do I know that I haven't made any mistakes? What value judgments shall I base my decisions on?

The roots of **Self Esteem** lie within ourselves. If we place them outside ourselves we will never be free from self doubt. Self Esteem is the result of facing as much of the reality as we are able to perceive and accepting the truth about ourselves, others and our situations. It is taking appropriate responsibility for ourselves, defining our own values and morals, developing integrity. And finally, Self Esteem is doing the very best we can and living up to our own values.

---

[2]   The Power of Self Esteem, 1992 Nathan Brandon

[3]   The Principles of Psychology, 1890 William James

[4]   The Antecedents of Self Esteem, 1981 Stanley Coopersmith

"I am discovering the "Real" Me
and learning to Walk on my own path"

Removing THE "MASK"
A CHECK LIST FOR "BEING" A "REAL" ME

___Assume a Non-judgmental attitude. ___Define the Problem. ___Decide what you must do or will settle for. ___Do not belittle the thoughts or ideas of the other. ___Listen politely to the other's position. ___State your decision calmly and politely. ___Do not argue. ___Ask for possible understanding from the other concerning your decision. ___If you don't agree decide if it's possible to agree to disagree.

AN EXAMPLE

A "MASK" OF WITHDRAWAL
"I told you I don't want you to go back to school. If you do, I'll be angry. You know when you do things I don't like I don't talk to you. So do what you want."

TAKING OFF THE "MASK"
"I'm sorry your angry at me". However, I do not agree with any of your reasons why I should not return to school. I love you and value our relationship. I know that in the past I usually backed down because I hate confrontation and having you mad at me leads to pain. However, this is very important to me. I will be starting school on Monday. I hope you understand my decision and value my right to make it. I hope you will not continue to be angry." "I love you".

TASK 2

WHICH OF THE FOLLOWING ATTITUDES AND BEHAVIORS DO YOU USE TO KEEP FROM FACING FEARS OF ABANDONMENT AND INADEQUACY?

TRY TO CONTROL OTHERS. If I can force you to see things from my point of view, my anxiety will dissolve and resolve the conflict. I need to be correct.

CONFORM TO OTHERS THE RELATIONSHIP. I will do things your way so you will not leave me.

WITHDRAW FROM MYSELF. I may need relationships for the independence. I withdraw into sleep drugs, denial to avoid facing the idea that pleasing others is more important to me than my own integrity.

WITHDRAW FROM OTHERS into anger, indifference, etc. To avoid anxiety in the relationship about conflict. I force you to change or find someone else who will agree with me.

FEEL THE NEED TO PROVE TO OTHERS THAT I HAVE THE RIGHT TO BE A SEPARATE INDEPENDENT PERSON. The need to prove independence reveals unresolved symbiotic attachment.

 **Questions?**

CHAPTER 6

TASK 3—Interdependence

BEING "SEPARATE" IN RELATIONSHIPS

Where is the "real" Me?

Examine Your path Closely... For Clues

TASK 3-INTERDEPENDENCE

**Relationships need two "Winners"...........not ....
a Winner & a Loser.**

We Can learn to be a separate "Self" in a Relationship.... being true to our Separate & Individual Needs, while showing respect for the integrity and needs of others. This means getting our needs met but not at the other's expense. Many of us have been taught that people who love each other "should" agree, especially spouses, with whom we "should" be one. However, since we all have many differences, it is unlikely we will find another person exactly like we are. The problem then often becomes, one person in the relationship must "disown" part of the "self" for the sake of the relationship. Another scenario involves two participants in the relationship fighting to "control" the other, trying to prove the other is "wrong". The Answer? Learn to develop relationships with room for both "whole" selves.

Egocentricity—SEVERAL VIEW FROM THE CENTER OF THE UNIVERSE—All children see them selves at the center of the Universe. The psychological concept of egocentricity can be understood on a continuum with Egocentricity (My needs are more important than yours) at one end, over socialization (Your needs are more important than mine) at the other end and our needs are equally important in the center. The legitimate needs of human beings are equal in importance. It is necessary to learn "how" to meet the legitimate needs of both persons in a relationship.

Adult Ego State— The "Computer" that "lives" in my mind— This Developmental aspect of the Human Psyche is called the Observing Ego. E. Berne* discussed it as the thinking process of a person able to perceive the world without feelings (wants, needs, etc) or duty or morality (shoulds, oughts, etc). He described it as similar to a computer because it objectively considers wants and duties of a given situation and make a decision based on Reality and what is best in the long run. It is a normal part of maturation and development. Those who are not able to achieve this stage at all are often seen as immature, overly duty oriented, etc.

Interdependence is the Psychological Term for the type of behavior between two equal people within Relationships who are able to be independent and depend on each other. Each is free to meet their own needs (if not at the expense of the other), agree or disagree, share their feelings honestly and be comfortable with their differences.

*The "Map"
To
MATURATION*

From Maturation: The Adult Paradigm

E. Berne— Transactional Analysis

TASK 3—Interdependence being "separate" in relationships

Two "whole" selves reside in successful **INTERDEPENDENT RELATIONSHIPS**. Each self is comfortable with personal differences while maintaining loving emotional detachment and deep commitment to the relationship and to the other. Both have developed necessary techniques to resolve relationship problems in ways that compromise neither personal or family integrity nor respect for themselves and each other.

We can learn to be a separate self in a relationship, being true to our individual needs, while showing respect for the integrity and needs of others. It is important to understand our own and others behaviors and attitudes in terms of the following Definitions:

- **Egocentricity—the feeling or belief that personal needs are more important than the needs of others?**
- **Oversocialization—Having leaned to believe that others needs are more important than yours or that**
- **The fear of having no right to be a "Real Self"—having learned your personal beliefs and needs are irrelevant.**

Ego DEVELOPMENT in context of

INTERDEPENDENCE

Egocentricity—several views FROM the center of the universe

The continuum of Egocentricity places those who are too Decentered at one end (others Needs are more important than mine are) and those who are egocentric (My needs are more important than yours are) at the other.

Egocentricity is a Psychological term that describes the state of mind we hold about our personal importance. All babies are born feeling as though they are the center of the universe. And although this is natural for an infant, it is not conducive to good personal relationships for an adults.

During the socialization process that takes place in the life of each child, we all settle on a perception of our importance in relationship to the importance of others. This perception can be seen as a continuum running from:

- "I am the **MOST** important person (Grandiose) in the world
- "I am the **least** important (Negative Egocentrism) person in the world

CONTINUUM OF EGOCENTRICITY

←――――――――――――――――――――――――――→

GRANDIOSE CENTER

1. I am the center of the Universe.
2. My needs come before everyone else's.
3. I am the most wonderful person in the world. Everyone must be instructed to understand this truth.

NEGATIVE CENTER

1. I am the center of the world.
2. Everyone in the world is constantly scrutinizing my behavior and attitudes and judging me in negative ways.
3. Everyone agree that I am the most worthless, stupid and undeserving person in the world

Narcissism has traditional been defined as a perception of one's self and needs in terms of important IN comparison to others, grandiosity, omnipotence and selfishness. However, others perceive **Narcissism in the—Negative** terms of I am the most worthless person in the world, I deserve nothing. The Psychiatric Dictionary—Fifth Edition (Robert Campbell) defines Negative Narcissism as an "exaggerated under-estimation of oneself. It is particularly expressed in states of melancholia, characterized by ideas of inadequacy, unreality and self accusation". (Feels like nothing and may or may not present self as Grandiose as a defense against feelings of worthlessness>

There is much disagreement about what is normal and what is abnormal **Narcissism.** Too much or too little are equally maladaptive. At the center of the continuum is a personal position that perceives the self and others as equally important. This I'm OK-You're OK position (Eric Berne-Transactional Analysis) is the most conducive for good relationships with others.

Traditional Psychology equates (understands) **Egocentricy as Narcissism.** [1] and Patients seen as presenting with the Traditional symptoms of Narcissism—**feelings of omnipotence, grandiosity and entitlement.** This type of Egocentricity usually bring them into conflict with the reality of the world and the rights of others.

The other side of the coin (and one that describes many of the patients I have treated in therapy) describes a person who feels so useless, empty and worthless that functioning in ways necessary to get their own needs met, if indeed they believe they deserve to have any needs at all, is difficult.

Kohut, Heinz 1971 and Kernberg, Otto (1975) are the major contributors to the theory of **Narcissism.**
Both agree that the genetic level of the difficulty is the stage of Separation-Individuation (before age 3).
Both agree that it is the result of their interpretations of their interactions with the primary caretaker (usually the Mother).

- Kohut's view is that these patients are extremely **sensitive to failures, disappoints and slights** and their self esteem is extremely labile.
- Kernberg believed the trauma is a result of development of an **abnormal grandiose self.**

---

[1] Kohut, Heinz 1971 and Kernberg, Otto (1975) are the major contributors to the theory of Narcissism. Both agree that the genetic level of the difficulty is the stage of Separation-Individuation (before age 3). Kohut's view is that these patients are extremely sensitive to failures, disappoints and slights and their self esteem is extremely labile. Kernberg believed the trauma is a result of development of an abnormal grandiose self. Both agree that it is the result of their interpretations of their interactions with the primary caretaker (usually the Mother).

It appears that **Egocentricity** is a natural function of Human Development and it's level is a measure of the persons self focus and self concern. Although over concern with the self is usually seen by others as too much self esteem, this is not the case. An excess does not equate with a positive self image. A low level of **Egocentricity (I am not the center of the universe)** appears to signal negative self esteem and placing a low value on personal worth **because everything and everyone else is more important and valuable than I am**. It is important to realize that a person with high esteem understands everyone's needs are of equal importance and in the absence of serious special circumstances, one's assuming no more importance than another's.

EGOCENTRICITY

"DO YOU LIVE AT THE CENTER OF THE UNVERSE?"
.............................."WHERE IS IT?"

WHAT BELIEFS do you hold ABOUT relationships

My needs are more important than Yours

Your needs are more important than mine

our needs and beliefs are equally important

Interdependency

Two "Whole" selves in a relationship

A Mature and healthy relationship has room for two whole persons, each with equally important needs. In a mature relationship it is necessary to "Be ourselves" and solve our problems fairly and equitably. Problem solving in relationships may be approached from many avenues. Some times we may do it my way, another time your way. Another time we may need to find a "third" solution to the problem. Conflicts in relationships can often be traced to unrealistic expectations for other behaviors, concepts of sex role behavior or gender as a determinant of personality characteristics. In healthy adult relationships an attitude of learning, empathy and understanding is assumed. In this way both partners can try to empathize with each others point of view and solve the problem. The ability to do so often rests on perception of sex role, feelings that both persons are equal, ability to see shades of gray and androgyny.

We must learn to be a self in healthy relationship, being true to our own values and allowing the other person in the relationship to do the same. Many of us have been taught that those who love each other "should" agree, especially spouses, with whom we should "be one". Psychologically this advice is not sound. Since we all have many differences, it is unlikely we will find another person who is exactly like us.

Interdependence involves the ability to problem solve and work through any conflict we may have with others in appropriate ways which do not compromise either our self respect or that of the other. It is the principle that the needs of each person in a relationship is equally important. This belief enables the ability to develop successful solutions to relationship conflicts. In the event that resolution of conflicts cannot be attained, interdependent persons will not continue indefinitely in relationship at the expense of realistic personal autonomy. Feels like a separate person in a relationship.

1. Being a Self

We must all learn to be a "self" in relationships, being true to both our own Values & needs and those of the "Other" within the relationship. This means getting our needs met in Relationships, but not at the Others' expense. Many of us have been taught that people who love each other "should" agree, especially spouses, with whom we "should" be "one". Psychologically, this advice is not sound. Since we all have many differences, it is unlikely we will find another person who is exactly like us. The problem then often becomes that one of us disowns part of the "self" for the sake of the other, or each may fight for control of the relationship. The answer? Learn a method for development of relationships with room for both "whole" selves.

2. Problem solving and Conflict resolution overview

Resolving Conflicts works best when it is "problem" oriented, looks for the truth and accepts reality. It must be objective vs subjective and maintain an attitude of respect for the others point of view. There must be as little blame placing as possible. Searching for "who is right or wrong" usually doesn't work very well either. People are Unique and different and usually have reasons which make good sense to them in support of their behavior. To solve Problems effectively giving up the goal of blaming someone is almost always the first objective.

SEX ROLE DEVELOPMENT

The behaviors, attitudes and appearances exhibited by a person in terms of what the culture considers to be masculine and/or feminine. The learning and performing of socially accepted behaviors and characteristics for a given Gender.

GENDER/ SOCIAL EXPECTATIONS AS DETERMINANTS OF SEX ROLE

Development.—Much research has been undertaken in the area of behavioral gender differences. By the time children reach the age of two, many behaviors can be clearly differentiated as to gender. Boys are more aggressive in both play and fantasy (Hattwick, 1937). Girls tend to be more verbally aggressive than boys (Sears, 1970): Jersild & Markley, 1935;Bandura, 1962, 1963). In support of social attitudes and role modeling as determinants of sex roles, child consciously realize what games and activities are "normal" for boys and girls (Schell & silber, 1968).

As children develop, sex role typing increases. Males show independence (Singer & Stefflre, 1954) practicality (Walter & Marzolf, 1951):achievement and power orientation (mcClelland, Atkinson, et al, 1951) aggression(Anastasi, 1958: and dominance (Brim, et al 1962). Females become social (Sinter & Stefflre, 1954), nurturant and affiliation oriented (Fitzgerald and Pasewark, 1971, McClelland et al., 1953), aesthetic and conforming (Nakamura, 1958; Allen & Crutchfield, 1963).

Several studies have examined children's' gender preference that found that as early as age three there is a preference (i.e. girls prefer to be females and boys prefer to be males (Brown, Hrtup and Hetherton, 1956,60, and 67.) In a longitudinal study on sex role development from childhood through adulthood, Kagan & Moss (1962) demonstrated that societal and cultural standards are the main determinant of whether a particular behavior remains stable or not from childhood through adulthood.

The preference becomes stronger in boys as they grow older, seeming to prefer their own gender. These studies report that girls tend to have a similar or even slightly stronger degree of feminine preference in the preschool period. In Western culture it seems that more girls prefer to be male than boys prefer to be female. This conclusion is supported by reports from adults that indicate that between a third and two thirds of women wanted to be male at some point in their lives. A reason for this may be that the male is more highly regarded in most societies (Rutter, 1970). Men have more job opportunities; most religions point to male superiority, and even the heroes in children's stories are more likely to be male.

It is at the point of development of adolescence and adulthood that questions regarding the appropriateness of benefits of developing firm sex roles begin to be raised. Mussen (1961;1962) noted that although high masculinity in boys in adolescence is correlated with positive psychological adjustment, it has been correlated in adult males with high anxiety, neuroticism and low self esteem. In females, a high incidence of femininity has been correlated with high anxiety, low self esteem and low social acceptance (Sears, 1970) further general intelligence and creativity has been found in men and women who are to some extent cross sex typed.

Gender differences in attitudes, choice of games, et are almost certainly socially determined. What is regarded as masculine in one society may not be seen as such in another.

CHURCH AS A DETERMINENT OF SEX ROLES

Religious Dogma has Traditionally viewed the Role of the Husband and Father as one of Leadership for the family. Even today many Marriage Vows still include that of the new couple becoming "one flesh", with the husband cleaving to his wife and she obeying her husband. His role can be better understood when one can view men as possessing innate, inborn qualities of independence, leadership, assertiveness and courage, while the qualities of nurturance, passivity and functioning best with the confines of a protected relationship can be applied to the innate qualities of women.

<u>GENDER</u> as a Determinant of Personality Characteristics

The Personality characteristics identified by Chance et al. (1978) as emerging in the child appear to describe a unique "human being", and refute the stereotypic profile of either a "traditional male" or a "traditional female". Until recently, stereotypic views of females (passive, dependent, nurturing, etc.,) and males (independent, aggressive, rational, etc.) have largely been accepted by society as being innate characteristics, biologically determined.

It is the belief of a number of writers that most gender differences are not innately determined (Larwood, Wood and Inderlied, 1978). It is their belief that most traditionally viewed gender differences result from preprocesses of socialization, stereotypical mythology and role modeling among others.

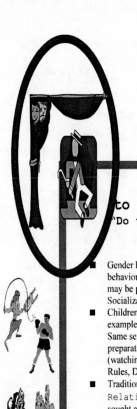

Where is the
"Real" Me?
Examine Your path Closely *For*
Clues

"Roles" we may have learned to "play" in relationships
"Do they work?" "What is their effect on your relationship?"

- Gender has traditionally been a determinant of social expectations for behavior. **Gender roles** are taught by modeling and reinforcement. Models may be parents, peers, sibling or cultural hero's (rock stars, actresses, etcs). Socialization does not come from within the brain or biology.

- Children are taught **Traditional Roles** from biblical, church or family examples. These Roles are learned through rules, discipline and examples. Same sex identification is accomplished through activities (team sports, food preparation, etc), apprenticeships (alter boys, scouting, etc), modeling (watching Mommy, Daddy, Priest, Policeman, etc) and instruction (learning Rules, Directions, Duty, Morals, Responsibility, etc).

- Traditional marriages can often be characterized as **Complementary** * Relationships in which a state of balance and relationship harmony is sought as a result of mutually supplying each other's lack. For example behavior of one sort (dominance) by one spouse is met by behavior of the opposite sort (submission) by the other spouse.

- **Transcendence of sex roles** is the Psychological theory that Traditional Sex Roles (socially expected behavior for males and females) are a stage of development between the role confusion of childhood and psychological androgyny* in accordance with inner needs and temperaments of persons (regardless of their gender) who have attained self actualization*.

- **Scientific research* into gender differences** indicate that stereotypic view of male (independent, aggressive, rational, etc) & females (passive, dependent, nurturing, etc) although   accepted by society as innate are the result of socialization, role modeling and stereotypes and not biologically determined.

*Complementary Relationships—V. Satir   *Transcending Sex Roles—Pleck, J
*Self Actualization—Maslow, A   * Research—Larwood, Wood & Inderlied (1978) Kagan
& Moss (1962) , Mussen (1969)

SCIENTIFIC RESEARCH INTO SEX DIFFERENCES—

Differerences & Similarities between males and female

Gender differences not seen as innately determine

Until recently, stereotypic views of females (passive, dependent, nurturing, etc. And males (independent, aggressive, rational, etc) have largely been accepted by society as being innate characteristics, biologically determined. However, research indicates that most gender differences are not determined and that most tradionally viewed gender differences are the results of socialization, stereotypical mythology and/or role modeling to name a few (Larwood, Wood & Inderlied, 1978).

One study ((Kagen and Moss 1962) demonstrated that societal and cultural standards are the main determinant of whether a particular behavior remains stable or not from childhood through adulthood. Parents must promote their child's positive sex development by reward and punishment of appropriate and inappropriate behavior as well as provide suitable sex role models (Mussen, 1969). For most of our societies history we have viewed sex roles as being innate to our gender. However there is much research that contradicts this concept.

Garai & Scheinfeld (1968) declared the following differences to be the most certain. Females are more sensitive to sound, touch and pain than males. Males are more visual. Males excel in spatial perception and arithmetic reasoning, females in verbal fluency and rote memory. Girls speak early and use language skills for theory development and problem solving. Boys have greater mechanical ability, girls superior manual dexterity. Girls remember general information and things.

Macoby and Jacklin's research (19740 found only four fairly well established differences between males and females 1) males are more aggressive 2) girls have greater verbal ability 3) boys excel in visual spatial ability and 4) boys excel in mathematical abilities.

The conflicting evidence concerning males and female differences seem to highlight a point that has not been routinely taken into consideration. Because humans are so unique and diverse, applying labels to them has been found to be extremely difficult, if not impossible. Although many males may excel in visual spatial ability, many females are also able to excel in those same abilities. When examining research findings we must therefore keep in mind that biologically determined behavior must occur across cultures, show species continuity, be reactive to biochemical manipulation and appear early in life.

It is important to remember that one cannot absolutely know how the environment affects a person because we are all unique combinations of personality characteristics. Pogrebin (1980) writes that although there is a great variability between behaviors of male and females, there is also great variability among members of the same gender.

It may be therefore, that we are human beings first and members of our gender second with a potential capacity to exhibit a full range of human behaviors when our temperaments and characteristics allow them to be manifested.

TRANSCENDING SEX ROLES STAGE

A stage of transcending sex roles has been documented by such theorists as Bem, 1974, Johnson, 1973, Pleck, 1975 and Rebecca, Hefner and Oleshonsky, 1975. These theories describe a subsequent state of sex typed behavioral level, where both masculine and feminine aspects are integrated into a more androgynous definition of optimal human behavior.

Pleck (1975) reported that role dichotomies are dysfunctional and that the happiest people are those who outgrow old rigidity. To help us think through a new set of goals for child development, he developed an "alternative paradigm" with three phases 1) the child who is confused over their own gender 2) the child learns the "ruls" of sex roles and conforms to them and 3) Transcends sex roles and norms and develops psychological androgyny in accordance with their inner needs and temperaments. Instead of characterizing sex role behavior as the final stage of child development, Pleck found "femininity" and "Masculinity" to be an intermediate stage to be supplanted by a more responsive, initialized and flexible humanness. Sex role conformity is a phase that children go through which should not set the pattern for life. It's role is limited.

Other Research proposed a final stage of sex role transcendence in which a universal human existence is the solution (Rebecca et al. (1975). Maslow (1970) understood healthy adulthood as a striving towards self realization and optimal development. He referred to Self Actualization as people who do what their potential fits them to do. Rogers (1950) saw self actualizers throughout life becoming increasingly autonomous and standing on their own feet.

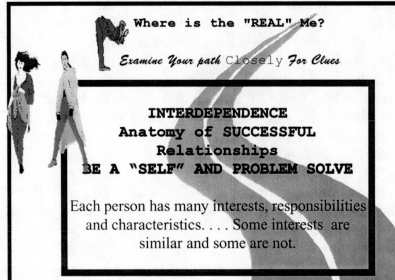

Where is the "REAL" Me?

Examine Your path Closely *For Clues*

INTERDEPENDENCE
Anatomy of SUCCESSFUL
Relationships
BE A "SELF" AND PROBLEM SOLVE

Each person has many interests, responsibilities and characteristics. . . . Some interests are similar and some are not.

ROLES WE HAVE LEARNED TO PLAY IN OUR RELATIONSHIPS—We have all learned to assume certain Roles in our relationships. We often change our Role when we go from one relationship to another. For example we play certain (usually different) roles with a parent, friend, child, sibling, employer, employee, spouse, member of the opposite sex, etc.

HEALTHY ADULT* CHARACTERISTICS—Healthy adult characteristics are similar, whether manifested by a male or female. Everyone has the need to be assertive, independent, competent, dependent, competitive, nurturing and achievement oriented. Problems in relationships are often the result of perceiving these human characteristics as "rightfully" belonging to either males or females. Scientific research shows healthy people have healthy human characteristics.

CONFLICT RESOLUTION—MY WAY, YOUR WAY OR ANOTHER WAY—Learn to be a healthy "self" able to problem solve with other healthy whole selves. Conflict resolution includes "my way" this time, "your way" next time, compromise, a "third" alternatives, taking turns, agreeing to disagree or as a last resort (in a serious values conflict that cannot be solved in these ways and would compromise the personal integrity of one or the other person) leaving the relationship . . .

Pleck, J Alternative Paradigm of Sex Role—Trandensenidng Sex Roles
Broverman,—Healthy adult Characteristics

COMPLEMENTARY RELATIONSHIPS v. Satir

Most marriages between young people in our society fall into the category of complementary relationships. This is probably due to several reasons which may include the sex role we have been taught within our family and society and our temperamental and psychological characteristics.

Since Sex roles are often seen as the Norm in our family and society a passive and timid woman may unconsciously search for and marry an aggressive and forceful man. In this way her need for assertion and relationships can be met. Psychological theory sees this type of situation as meeting the needs of both parties in the relationships since it is likely that the man involved will have problems with his own fears and needs. Another example may be a nurturant, compliant female may marry a withdraw and resistant male. Each partner needs what the others can offer but is unable to provide it for themselves. Marriage to each other provides the two halves they need.

The forces of Human beings include a force toward being a whole separate person as well as being part of a relationship. And as marriage progresses, one or the other of the formerly relationship oriented pair will often naturally grow toward becoming the Individual he/she has the potential to become. When this happens a resistance to the former "role" they had set up for themselves results. When this change comes about the other partner will likely feel a threat and resist the healthy change. The threatened partner will often try to "force" the "growing" mate back into the familiar role they were both comfortable with in the past. This need for the status quo is called maintaining a homeostatic balance.

Psychological Theory maintains that persons in Complementary relationships search each other out in an unconscious manner, resembling a "Hidden radar"
In addition to the natural "force" toward being a whole separate individual, all human beings have had patterns

163

of relationships with their parents and roles they have fallen into within them. Most relationships from childhood required us to assume certain "positions" within them. Most of us were not comfortable with these roles, but because they were in relationship to some type of authority we didn't know how to comfortably or appropriately change them. This nonresolution of our childhood relationships propels us to look for and enter similar types of relationships when we leave home in an unconscious quest for resolution. As a result of this need for completion that we find others to play out the unfinished relationships from our past in a quest for resolution. Only as a result of coming to some conclusion can we comfortably put the old "problems" away" and get on with our live in a new direction.

People who continually marry persons with addictive behaviors can be seen as never having resolved the problem within the relationship interaction. Other examples are those who hate being told what to do but become involved with a mate who feels the other can't take care of themselves, those who live a chaotic lifestyle and marry another who is very structured, etc.

Androgyny—Sandra Bem Research

Androgyny is defined as the possession or manifestation of a near equal degree of femininity or masculinity within a person.

Androgyny is a set of human characteristics seen to fall on a continuum from the most to the least. For example, passivity at the end of one continuum and aggression at the other. The Continuum is not divided in the center with females at one end and males at the other. Society has encouraged this complementary perception of human traits. Research indicates that all humans have a set of characteristics that can be developed. The most healthy type of person has developed all the characteristics within him/herself and may be called androgynous, self actualized, or possessing human characteristics rather than a restricted few that have been proscribed by "something" out there as being appropriate for males or females.

Sandra Bem did not see Masculinity and Femininity as polar distinct traits. Each possesses it's own set of positive personality and behavior characteristics. Therefore, masculinity and femininity should be represented on two separate scales and not as unidemensional scales. Gender is physical and sex roles are behavioral and attitudinal. Individuals possessing equal masculinity and femininity are more flexible and adaptable in a wide range of situations.

HEALTHY ADULT FUNCTIONING—

A study by **Broverman**, demonstrated that a possible source of underlying conflict in women may be that the

- Feminine traits of dependence, passivity and nurturance are viewed as <u>healthy</u> for females and <u>unhealthy</u> for males.
- Healthy masculine traits were identified as independence, competitiveness, and aggressiveness.
- These same variables were also seen as being healthy for an adult. This of course, lead to the conclusion that a healthy female cannot be a healthy adult.

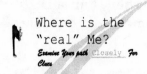

Where is the
"real" Me?
Examine Your path closely For Clues

HEALTHY RELATIONSHIPS

The concept of 2 winners (rather than a winner and a loser) in a relationship is based on the psychological Construct of interdependence. Research underlying equal persons in relationships includes The WIN-WIN* Model of Thomas Gordon and the Problem Solving Model* of Stephen Covey..

■ Research has identified a possible source of underlying conflict in relationships. The traits of dependence, passivity and nurturance were often viewed by randomly selected Research subjects as **healthy adult characteristics*** for females but not for males while independence, competitiveness and aggression were often identified healthy for males but not for females. The traits seen as healthy for males were also identified by the same subjects as healthy adult characteristics. The Conclusion: Healthy females cannot be healthy adults. Marital Happiness Research* indicates the characteristics of both partners in the most happily married were those of independent, equality, no power struggle, age 35 and older, assertive, empathy for each other, children out of the home, both with a sense of identify that includes work.

■ Research identifies Work* as a major source of identity for both males and females

■ Males and females have traditionally been seen as possessing opposite types of personality traits, determined by gender; males as aggressive, independent and competitive and females as nurturing, dependent and noncompetitive. These Traditional Sex Roles have been positively sanctioned by society as appropriate to healthy functioning as males and females. Research* indicates that gender and sex role are independent of each other with gender the physical manifestation of maleness and femaleness and sex role as the attitudes and behavior of a given gender. The concept of androgyny is defined as equal degrees of masculine and feminine characteristics within the same person. Some authors view sex roles as in intermediate step in personal development and point to androgyny as the final transcendent stage of development for both males and females.

■ Logical thinking and acceptance of Reality is seen by cognitive therapists* as the most important aspect of functional life styles and relationships. Cognitive theory is based on rationale that moods, emotions and behavior is determined by our perception of the world and that thoughts are based on attitudes and assumptions developed from our early experiences.

* Healthy Adult Relationships—Broverman   *Problem Solving Model—7 habits of Effective People—Covey, S
* Androgeny—Bem, S   *Marital Research - Paper Presented at aPA Convention (1992)
* Win-Win Model—Parent Effectiveness Training—Gordon, T   * Working—Studs Turkel
* Cognitive Theory—Beck, (1967) * Cognitive Theory—ABC—Rational Emotive Theory—Ellis, A

EQUAL PERSONS IN RELATIONSHIPS

a.   Win-Win Relationships T. Gordon

Within relationships it is best to have two winners and no losers. Even a winner looses because there is always a residue of resentment when we see things in terms of right and wrong, winner and looser.

Thomas Gordon in Parent Effectiveness Training was the first to write of a third method of conflict resolution he called method 111. This was not the I win you lose position of Method 1, or the You lose I win of Method 2. In Method 111, there were two winners because both persons worked on their problems until they came to a position that was acceptable to both.

He advocated a position of agreeing to disagree if such a position could not be found. Recently Steven Covey has written extensively on Win-Win and advocates finding a Third alternative if doing it your way or my way is not acceptable.

b.   I'm OK—You're OK—E. Berne

Eric Berne in Games People Play discusses many interactions between persons as "Games". He refers to the positions they assume in their relationships as generally falling into one of four categories.

These categories are 1) I'm OK, your not Ok, 2) You're Ok, I'm not Ok, 3) I'm not Ok-Your not Ok and I'm Ok your Ok. These positions can be understood on the continuum of Egocentricity (Narcissism) and show relative levels of self esteem and self worth.

The four positions fall along the continuum of Egocentricity (Feelings of being the Center of the Universe

Where is the "REAL" Me?

Examine Your path Closely For

Where is the "real" Me?

WIN-WIN MODEL

WIN-LOSE (Control Other) I get t my way, you don't. When there is a winner there is also a loser. No one likes to lose. Losers don't feel valued. Losers try to get even. Winning is at someone else's expense.

LOSE-WIN (Conform to Other) This is victim or peacemaker stance seeks peace from acceptance by others. It often indicates low self esteem. It covers buried feelings they are afraid to show. Unexpressed feelings cause anxiety, depression, anger, etc.

WIN-WIN (2 winners) Seeks solutions of mutual benefit. All feel good and committed to plan. Sees life as cooperative not competitive. It's not your way or my way it's a better way.

MY WAY? YOUR WAY? Or Another WAY?

Assume an attitude of respect. Mentally define the problem. Is it between equals? Identify what you need and what you want. Do you know the difference?

Is this a philosophical conflict? Can you agree to disagree? Is your integrity at stake?

Are you trying to control something over which you have no control?

Are you taking personal responsibility

Are you attempting to assume responsibility for another?.

Are you facing reality?

Are you making thoughtful vs emotional decisions based what what's best in the long run? (Impulse control)

Is this a moderate, balanced decision? (Crisis oriented)

6 STEPS to PROBLEM SOLVING

Take attitude of understanding and learning (Problem solving attitude, non defensive, non judgmental, objective)

Mentally define the problem— Have a clear understanding of the problem and decide your bottom line.

Address the Problem with the Other. (Is your position Superior (teacher, parent, Employer, etc), equal (spouse, friend, adult child, etc.) or subordinate (Police, employee, student, etc).

Understand the others point of view (Attempt to clarify, understand and empathize with the other. Try to put their view into words and check so they feel heard. It is not necessary to agree or to understand)

Help the other understand You. (Help the other understand your point of view, philosophy of life, values etc.

Arrive at Solutions (May be my way, your way, compromise, taking turns, alternative solution, agree to disagree, etc.

ABILITY TO BE A SEPARATE SELF IN A RELATIONSHIP

Adult Ego State—The computer in my mind
ERIC BERNE—TRANSACTIONAL ANALYSIS

This state can be defined as the ability to think about what is best for us and others in our lives in terms of long-term d decisions. A mature person can chose to respond objectively to life situations and not allow these important decisions to be the result of overly subjective or emotional influences.

The theory of "Ego States" underlies the theory of Transactional Analysis. These "Ego States" organize a Human Being's feelings and behavior into 3 categories: Parent, Adult, Child. The Parent Ego State contains the ideas the child has "internalized" from parents and other Authority Figures such as church, grandparents, teachers, etc as to what we "should/should not, ought/ought not, be thought, said, or done. This Parental state may be either Punishing or Nurturing as a result of the child's internalization's of his Parents & other Authorities attitudes toward him/her and the world.

The Child Ego State begins at birth when the child cannot separate himself from his environment. Everything in the world is experienced as the child's feelings (anger, contentment, frustration, love, hate, pain, etc). Throughout life, the Child Ego State (the Child) influences a persons experiences & relationships. In Maturity, the feelings of the Child hopefully will have become manageable and the person has gradually learned to think about their feelings and "choose" to respond to them or not (a reaction that grows with Maturation). The child Ego State can be recognized by the words of emotion that are associated with it such as "I want, You'd better do it, I can't stand it, etc.

The Adult Ego state begins to develop at around 2 years old and it's "birth" can be recognized by the natural behavior of a child going through the "Terrible Two's". The Task of this Developmental Stage is to help the child learn to "think" for him/herself.

As maturation proceeds, the Adult Ego State must assume the characteristics of a Computer (Objectively evaluating the Data of Reality) and ideally learns to function as a thoughtful Adult like process that is not overly influenced by either the Parent or the Child. However both the Parent and Child must be taken into consideration when decisions are made. The work of the Adult is to critically evaluate the information in the Parent for its' relevancy and the Child for its' appropriateness to the situation at hand. In this way, some of the information in the Parent can be discarded and replaced (when necessary) by concepts that are in line with the thinking of the person as he/she is in the "Here & Now" (vs. continuing to reflect concepts that are not really "ours" and which may be outdated).

Additionally the Child State's feelings may have been irresistible at 2 or 10, but normal development encourages the ability to choose whether the "Child's" feelings are an appropriate way to live our lives. The Child state is divided into "compliance", "rebelliousness" and "The Natural Child", autonomous from parental influences, (the part of us all that is a reflection of our natural feelings and as such is neither right nor wrong). In addition, the Child might contain a component that Dr. Berne's called "the Little Professor. This inhabitant of childhood (and all too often our adult lives as well) is a part of many of us that tries to "trick" or manipulate our world into giving us what we want without our having to face the consequences of our choices. The Little Professor may insist that he/she wants something, but it is only for the good of someone else, or that he/she openly says one thing and secretly does the opposite.

The Adult's function is to monitor Internal Conflicts (guilt about the Parent's "shoulds" and the Child's "wants" or disagreements) and to hopefully shape behavior into functional responses. Transactional Analysis looks for "life scripts" that have been arrived at as a conformity, compromise, or rebellion between the Parental "shoulds" and the Child "wants" & "needs".

Taking this theory into consideration, outline what is contained in your Parent and your Child. Then ask yourself how independently your Adult functions and in what ways have you incorporated or discarded the contents of your Parent. How do you function as a result of inner voice of your child's demands?

ADULT EGO State*
The Computer in my Mind

Where is the "real" Me?

Examine Your path Closely *For Clues*

"I have a well developed Observing Ego able to think about feelings and choose whether to set them aside when necessary." "I am also able to think realistically about the moral and duty oriented aspects of my upbringing and decide whether as an adult I agree with them or not." "If I do I will continue to honor them. "If I don't , I will reexamine the concepts in question and replace them with others in line with my own personal adult conclusions."

The moral responsible, parts of myself. Conscience, duty, morality, religion, values, principles, responsibility.

The Thoughtful Adult Part Of My Self That When Developed Can Realistically Evaluate All Aspects Of A Situation

THE EMOTIONAL PART OF Myself that Wants my own way

Fun Play Anger

Fear Sad

Berne, Eric discusses the Observing Ego in **Transactional Analysis** as the thinking processes of a person that perceives the world without feelings, duty or morality. The Adult Self is a normal part of Maturation. Those who are not able to achieve this stage at all are often seen as immature, overly duty oriented, etc.

OVEREMOTIONAL

Parent
_____
Adult
_____

Child

OVERLYDUTY ORIENTED

Parent

_____
Adult
_____
Child

OBJECTIVE - COLD

Parent
_____

Adult
_____

Child

CHAPTER 7

TASK 4—FIT IN THE UNIVERSE

WHAT IS <u>MY</u> PHILOSPHY OF LIFE?

Essence of the human "spirit?"

"How do I FIT" IN THE UNIVERSE?

Essence of the Human Spirit

Task 4 – PHILOSOPHY OF LIFE

What BELIEFS MAKE UP YOUR PERSONAL PHILOSOPHY OF LIFE ?

GOD

THE BIBLE

A SET OF Universal
Principles underlying the
Universe

SCIENCE

SPIRITUALITY

ORGANIZED
RELIGION

Human
Psychological
Development

Values &
Principles
Moral
Development

Personal PHILOSOPHY OF

"FIT" IN THE Universe

The nature of Human beings requires contemplation of our "fit" in the Universe. We must all learn how we "fit" in life so we will be prepared and comfortable with our unavoidable mortality. Preparing for the end of life is the goal of its' beginning.

The development of an objective personally arrived at Philosophy of Life, given the development of civilization during our life time requires as Broad and realistic View of the Universe as possible into consideration given the development of society and civilization during the time we are in the Universe.

Psychologically maturity requires a broad flexiability able to assimilate and accommodate valid new information as it presents itself whether it formerly was part of our Philosophy or not.

Included in our Philosophy may be science, religion, spirituality, values and principles, God, or Universal Laws of Cause and Effect underlying the Universe rather than a narrow set of beliefs that do not take a broad focus of Objective Reality into consideration.

We must all learn to understand how we "fit" in life so we will be comfortable with our deaths. Preparing for the end of life is the goal of the beginning. It makes little difference, psychologically, if we choose to believe in God, Science, Reincarnation, Principles, Duty, Moral Development, Serendipity, etc. Decisions made from Broad Perspectives (with as much Reality as Science, Spirituality, Values, Religion, etc can provide to us during our life time) allows us to complete our developmental task of understanding our "fit" into the Schema of the Universe, satisfied that we have made our decisions based on as much Reality as our place in evolution and time has provided to us to use. Narrow perceptions on only partial aspects of Reality in the Universe focuses on partial elements of the Universe without providing other necessary elements from which to arrive at realistic conclusions. **Steven Hawkings, in a History of Time (19),** writes that he believes the Universe to be underlain by a set of Principles that relate to all aspects of the Universe, including physical, humans, space, time, etc. He says the conflict between God and Science as an explanation for the Universe does not have to be there.

Most of us have asked questions such as 1) "Why was I born?", "Why am I here?", "Is there a purpose to being alive?" and "If there is a Purpose . . . What is my Mission in the world?" These questions, unique to each of us, can only be answered by asking the additional question "Where is the REAL Me?" Answers to these questions are unique to each of us.

It is uncontroversial that we are each born with a seed of Unique Human Potential. **Development of Human potential** demands **Psychological Maturation**. And only by resolving the problems that deter us from psychological maturation are we free to explore our mission in the Universe.

Personal Choices are presented to each of us on our Path through the Universe in the form of choices, serendipity, synchronicity and problem solving with other people

Psychological Maturation is the doorway leading to a more complete understanding of our unique potential and "fit" **in the Universe.**

Broad Vs Narrow Focus Of Universe And Perspectives Of The World

It is necessary to take as Broad a focus of reality into account as possible when identifying our personal our perceptions concerning of the Universe so our decisions are not arrived at with only partial details about the Big Picture. Trying to live by principles, morals, shoulds, oughts, etc. that are desirable but not psychologically possible are often an important source of conflict within our relationships with others. The development of Personal Principles and Value Systems is necessary for Maturation and successful life styles.

Development of a Personal Philosophy of Life. Demands a Broad View of the Universe that takes as much of Reality into account as possible given the development of society and civilization at the time we inhabit the Earth. Ability to be broad and flexible enough to assimilate and accommodate valid new information as it presents itself is essential for development of an objective perception of the world we live in.

Among the areas representing a valid, Personal Philosophy may include the following. Which may or may not make up your personal philosophy of life? God, Spirituality, Science, Values, Morals Principles, Laws of Cause & Effect? How has this happened" What has happened to result in your perception of life in the ways you do?

I don't believe any of us has the right to chose or overly influence another adults personal philosophy of life. Each of us has the option of setting our own personal philosophy of life and our reasons for doing so.

However, as a psychologist I believe it is important that each of us use as broad a set of reasons for making our decisions concerning our personal choices as possible when making these decisions. It is important that our decisions are supported by individual critical thinking as to what makes sense to us vs an authority we have always relied upon for coming to conclusions concerning important values.

Underlying concepts for developing an objective personal Philosophy might include belief in God, Organized Religion, Spirituality, Values and Principles, Science as well as the belief that everything has a cause and effect. It makes little difference <u>What</u> a person chooses as aspects of a Personal Philosophy of Life. The Big Question concerns the "Why" these aspects of Personal Beliefs have been chosen. It is of paramount importance that our

Belief System lies on the conclusions of our own Critical Thought Processes, not what we believe we should believe or because we think someone else has a better grasp on the situation than we do. The concept of Independent thinking rests on the premise that each of us is responsibile (given our cognitive and ego potential) for learning to make our own choices, decisions and developing methods for investigating complex issues that lead to conclusions we truly believe represents our own inner convictions.

Many areas of Personal Philosophy represent issues that cannot be proven. For example no one can prove that God does or does not exist nor that there is or is not a Spiritual Realm. Such decisions are most wisely left to those looking for answers to their own queries.

However, there is much valid and objective research concerning the objective value of Science, Values, Morals and other Principles of Life . . . including reasons for and against hypotheses why or why not each of thse areas of belief does or does not makes sense.

HUMAN EGO AND COGNITIVE DEVELOPMENT

A. Research on Process & Aspects of Human Adult Development

Taking the Psychological Development (**STRENGTHS & WEAKNESSES**) of a person into consideration is necessary if we are to completely understand ourselves and others.

In the past, emphasis has been placed on the process of childhood and adolescence, development. Recent research has focused on the **Passages** through adulthood. Some Theorists[1] perceived each decade (20's,30', 40, 50, 60, etc) as a Passage with specific characteristics,

More recent Research conclusions about the progression of Human Developmental Stages indicate change as Life Spans become longer

---

[1]   Gail Sheehey—Passages

and Humans are better able to take care of themselves. For instance, the <u>maximum</u> life span for humans (authenticated at 122 years) has probably changed very little in the last several centuries. The <u>average</u> life span, however, has increased greatly[2].

In 1994 the life expectancy lengthened to about 80 . . . a big increase over that of the 1930's when life expectancy was about 40 years. In 1940 a person was willing to retire at 60 or 65. My father, at 88, still worked every day, safely drove his car on the LA freeways and played 18 holes of golf 3 times a week. He took good physical care of himself and had the money to take care of his psychological and safety needs so that his anxiety didn't contribute to somatic complaints. As a result, it appears that Characteristics of the Stages of Life Categories may change due to life expectancy as well as personal differences, goals, situations, etc.

Healthy Old Age is a time for preparing for the end of life. It is experienced by some as a time to withdraw into a smaller, safer space and by others as a limiting of social environment to protect the self from over exertion. Many old people become "more" of what they were when they were young, whether the qualities could be seen as good or bad. Slightly cranky middle aged persons may become severely angry old people and vice versa

Resilience, as previously mentioned, has recently been written about as a characteristic of healthy Human Adult Development. William Glasser, MD[3] in his most recent book "Warning Psychiatry can be hazardous to your mental health" writes "mental health can be taught to millions of people who are unhappy but not mentally Ill". He states that it is possible to learn to "Be Happy" by ignoring what you can't change.

Albert Ellis[4] wrote many books discussing his ABC theory which stated "Its not what happens to us (Antecedent) that causes our problems,

---

[2]   Encarta Encyclopedia—Life span
[3]   William Glasser, MD Author of Choice and Reality
[4]   Albert Ellis, ABC Theory—Cognitive Ideation

it's our Belief about what happens to us that Causes our problems". He discussed the necessity for letting what you can't change roll off your back. His book titled "How to be Happy living with a Neurotic" was a big hit.

The American Psychologist **Carl Rogers** developed the theory of our "Human Drive to achieve full capacity and ability of relating in ways consistent with a "True Self"[5]. **Abraham Maslow**[6] believed all people are motivated to fulfill a hierarchy of needs beginning with physiology (hunger, thirst, etc), through safety and security to belonging and receiving love to the self esteem related needs for status and achievement.

Building on areas of Humanistic, Psychodynamic as well as Reality and Cognitive Choice theory my own theory of **Psychological Maturation** runs on a Continuum of Immaturity/ Maturity vs Mental Illness/Wellness. Psychological Maturation Theory defines most Human Anxiety to be a normal signal from the Unconscious Mind that an underlying ambiguous conflict is present and needs to be taken care of for Psychological Maturation to continue successfully. Psychological Maturation Theory goes a step further positing that the unresolved anxiety in most cases is the result of unresolved emotional attachments (Symbiosis).

Psychological Maturation requires the ability to face reality and accept the truth whether we think reality fair or not or whether we deserve it or not. In addition, in the context of Eternity it appears completely realistic to me, that we come into the world with a Mission, to learn our lessons and grow both Psychologically and Spiritually

---

[5]   Carl Rogers—American Psychologist-Developer of Person Centered Therapy

[6]   Maslow, M (1975)—Theory of Self actualization as the ultimate state of personal fullment.

B. Aspects & Process of of Adult Human Development

1. **MORAL DEVELOPMENT** Following the Work of Jean Piaget Kohlberg [7] Theory of Moral Development published In 1966 posited that moral judgment and logic develop through Stages and Levels. Level 1 (External Locus of Control) is seen principally as similar to a child conforming to obtain rewards). Level 2 (Morality as Conventional Role) is defined as the level where most adults score. This level defines conformity as a method to avoid censure by authority. The final Level 3 (Self accepted Moral Principles) a stage few of us reach is defined as Conforming to avoid self condemnation. As mentioned in a previous section Kohlberg discussed Martin Luther King cognitions and behaviors as representative of Stage 5 (following the Law but actively trying to get it changed) while Stage 6 is the position of those who conform to avoid self condemnation. Examples might include persons who refuses to sit on a death Penalty Jury due to the belief that if Killing someone is wrong it is wrong for the government to kill some one or a person who chooses prison instead of being drafted into the Service due to conformity with his Intrinsic Internal Moral code that killing others is wrong.

2. <u>FUNCTIONAL</u> COPING STRATEGIES & PROBLEM SOLVING—Potential Opportunities for development of personal hardiness, buoyancy, etc (a characteristic of Psychological Maturity) are presented to us each day as we walk down our path of life in the form of situations in which we can choose to face reality and accept the truth . . . or not.

   Successful <u>Coping Strategies</u> within <u>dissonant</u> **Life situations** require increased levels of Unique Emotional Independence as well as Cognitive Maturation in the areas of Frustration Tolerance, ability to Delay of Gratification and objective Cognitive contemplation of emotion (Primary Process Choices) concerning the situation under consideration.

---

[7]   Kohlberg, Lawrence—Theory of Moral Development (1958)

However, Coping Strategies for <u>Life Situations of Tragic Proportions</u> may be more successfully coped with from the Psychological Maturation Dimension of a functional objectively arrived at Spiritual Philosophy of Life. I personally do not perceive a tragedies to fall in the category of God's punishment but rather one requiring exploration of our spiritual Path (Human Mission and Lessons of Life) in the Universe. Increased levels of ability to face reality and accept the truth (Resilience) allows Human Psychological Maturation to develop. Resilience (Psychological buoyancy) is a characteristic of Psychological Maturation

Developing Functional Coping Straggles

The value of Functional (pragmatic) Coping Strategies within our <u>personal</u> **and** <u>relationship</u> situations may be more <u>objectively perceived in the context of cause and effect within our situation</u>. For example: how may my behavior have effected the behavior of the other or what have I been thinking or feeling that keeps me from learning to deal with the reality of my present situation.

It is important we don't misunderstand what we can change and what we can't. or what we believe is fair and what isn't. Drop your expectations, shoulds, oughts, perceptions of fairness, etc. because they do not reflect reality. Realize no one can tell another "how" to face reality and accept the truth" of their own particular tragic situation because learning to cope with reality is an individual psychological developmental process.

To solve the question of "How" to face reality and accept the truth of a situation that seems impossible to deal with, we have to understand what we (or the other) may have been doing or thinking that stands in our way of successfully coping. It is important to understand what types of Defenses we have learned to use in the past and why or why not they have worked well or not at all. Objective reality is truth and must be dealt with. Bitterness and resentment concerning reality is a waste of time. Face reality and accept the truth of your situation because you have no choice. It is important to identify for our self which of our values fall into the categories of negotiable, able to agree to disagree or <u>non</u>-**negotiable.** Only with this knowledge will be able to successfully resolve even the most difficult relationship issues.

<u>COPING WITH ADVERSITY</u>

A list of incomparable tragedies might include but not be limited to the following:

- Being told your illness is terminal
- Being told your illness may be terminal but there is no way to know for sure
- Trying to live with unbearable physical pain
- Be in physical agony of pain one day but not quite as severe the next.
- Being so tired and in such pain many days of your life that getting dressed and attending to essential tasks seems insurmountable.
- Getting your legs blown off in war and having to live in a wheel chair for life
- Trying to live with the devastation of being the victim of rape
- Attempting to face and live life after have all or most of your children die
- Losing your spouse of a life time
- The loss of your home and possessions in an earth quake or tidal wave
- Being blinded for life in an accident
- Loss of freedom—being in jail

Resignation to Life situations of tragic Proportions is not the answer. The alternative is tantamount to saying "Life is too hard to deal with" because my personal life (or what's left of it) is not worth the effort of trying to understand my situation and successfully coping with it. Learning to live with tragedy by not wasting the life you have is the answer.

This is not to say that you should accept the reality of your tragedy with out considering whether or not there is a legal, realistic recourse that can be pursued. Kohlberg's theory of Moral Development cites

Martin Luther Kings response to racism as a level 5 response. He fought injustice by trying to get the laws changed.

- Techniques for **<u>living without loved ones</u>** lost to tragedy may include

    1) taking the hand of the departed and walking thru life with the memories of the loved one that are now part of your present personal essence,
    2) knowledge of growth and lessons learned from the relationship and
    3) giving thanks to the Universe for the Gift of having had the other for the time you had together.

- Techniques for **<u>living without aspects of my former self</u>** (eyesight, hearing, limbs, home, etc) may include

    1) realizing that what is past will never be lost b/c it is part of who we am today.
    2) Realize that you may not know why you are still alive but the fact that you are presents the possibility there must be a reason for it.
    3) Try to plan a new way of life

- Techniques for living with other types of tragedy

    1) Use primary process (cognition) to accept and walk through the Pain (emotional or physical)
    2) Make a list of things that must be done and force yourself to walk through the pain in order to get things accomplished
    3) Visualize cognition rising above the pain and looking at it from a great distance. I will then deal with it for as long as I can. When I can no longer deal with it, I will stop trying for the day and try again tomorrow. In this way, I will help myself live with it for longer and longer periods of time.
    4) Learn to value the life you have been given even though at this time, the emotional or physical pain is so great it is hard to do.

5) Realize that if you are still alive your work on earth is not over. You may still have lessons to learn or your earthy Mission of helping others is not finished yet

PERSONAL PHILOSOPHY OF "FIT" IN THE UNIVERSE.

I really don't believe any of us has the right to chose or overly influence another adults personal philosophy of life. Each of us has the option of setting our own personal philosophy of life and our reasons for doing so. However, as a psychologist I believe it is important that each of us use as broad a set of reasons for making our decisions concerning our personal choices as possible when making these decisions. It is important that our decisions are supported by individual critical thinking as to what makes sense to us vs an authority we have always relied upon for coming to conclusions concerning important values.

Underlying concepts for developing a personal Philosophy might include belief in God, Organized Religion, Spirituality, Values and Principles, Science as well as the belief that everything has a cause and effect. It makes little difference What a person chooses as aspects of a Personal Philosophy of Life. The Big Question concerns the "Why" these aspects of Personal Beliefs have been chosen. It is of paramount importance that our Belief System lies on the conclusions of our own Critical Thought Processes, not what we believe we should believe or because we think someone else has a better grasp on the situation than we do. The concept of Independent thinking rests on the premise that each of us is responsible for our own choices, learning to make our own decisions and developing methods for investigating complex issues that lead to conclusions we truly believe represents our own inner convictions.

Many areas of Personal Philosophy represent issues that cannot be proven. For example no one can prove that God does or does not exist or that there is or is not a Spiritual Realm. Such decisions are most wisely left those looking for answers to their own queries. However, there is much valid and objective research concerning the objective value of Science, Values, Morals and other Principles of Life . . . including reasons for and against hypotheses why or why not each of thse areas of belief does or does not makes sense.

A BROAD UNIVERSAL VIEW MAY INCLUDE THE FOLLOWING BELIEFS

A. Fit with Religion

Fit GOD I believe or do not believe in god, religion or spirituality as it relates to the existence of a God in religion. Does not have to be an organized religion._Belief in the Principles of the **Bible** from different perspectives

B. Fit with Spirituality Lessons and Mission in the Universe

Fit Spirituality I do or do not believe in spirituality, reincarnation, metaphysical Ideas, a spiritual plane, a human soul, higher power, plan of life mission of life, and/or life lessons to be learned. Measures Personal Universal Focus as Broad vs Narrow. To be in line with Reality as broad a focus as possible must be considered so that important aspects of Reality are not ignored.

C. FIT WITH VALUES AND PRINCIPLES

Fit Values & Principles—My philosophy of Life does or does not includes a personally arrived at Set of Values, Principles, Duty, and Responsibility for my self and others. My Values & Principles may include perceptions of DUTY, PRINCIPLES of MORALity, Protestant Work Ethic, Gender Roles, Perception of the world in terms of what I believe "should" or should not be done, Duty to self and others, Moral Pinciples, Religious Ethics and Principles, etc.

D. Fit with SCIENCE

Fit Science I do or do not believe in Science. I may believe that the principles of traditional science do not have the capability of measuring the spiritual realm. I may believe Science has the potential to eventually prove/disprove the existence of God. I may believe that Science as we know it must develop another set of principles that have the capability of investigating the possible existence of a spiritual realm.

E. Fit with UNDERLYING PRINCIPLES of Cause & Effect

Fit Universal Development—I do or do not believe in the possibility there is a set of underlying laws of cause and effect that govern the interactions of the universe. These laws may apply to all aspects of the universe,

PERSONAL SPIRITUAL PHILOSOPHY

Research & Personal Experiences relating to (life after death[5], spirituality[6], God, Science[7], & Human Development)_Although Scientific methods focus on objective reality as that which can be measured and quantified many people report spiritual experiences during their lives or at the death of a loved one that can not be dismissed as psychological dysfunction. About 80% of my clients, after developing trust and being in therapy with me for a while have shared personal spiritual experiences that cannot easily be explained by the Objective Scientific Method. Few of these patients have been significantly mentally or psychologically impaired. Davies, Paul "God and the New Physics" SPIRITUALITY—Metaphysics, Parapsychology Spiritual aspects of life.

LIFE AFTER DEATH RESEARCH

a) **DEATH AND DYING**[8]—Kubler Ross has identified four stages of death and dying to be 1) Denial and

b) Isolation 2) Anger, 3) bargaining and 4) Acceptance. Kubler-Ross & Ron Moody

c) **NEAR DEATH EXPERIENCES**[9]—Ron Moody investigates the core experiences of those who have had brushes with death and returned to describe it. Countless people have had similar experiences which may include some or all of the following: 1) floating out of the body, 2) going through the tunnel, 3) a light at the end of the tunnel, 4) a review of life events, 5) a feeling of overwhelming love, 6) friends and relatives there meeting us, 7) a decision to return or not. Moody, R

d) **SCIENTIFIC PARAPSYCHOLOGY**[10]—K. Ring Views paranormal events such as near death experiences, out of body experiences, telepathy, synchronicity (meaningful patterns of coincidence without apparent causal connections) to be manifestations of holographic reality. Ring, Kenneth—Life at Death A Scientific Investigation of the Near Death Experience.

---

[8]   Kubler-Ross & Ron Moody

[9]   Moody, R

[10]   Ring, Kenneth-Life at Death A Scientific Investigation of the Near Death Experience.

e) **HOLOGRAPHY** is a method of photography without a lens. **Karl Pribram** has proposed in his Holographic theory, that the brain itself functions holographically by analyzing interference patters so that images of objects are seen. Primary reality is said to be composed of frequencies only. plausible by the invention of the hologram. Kenneth Ring believes the world of physics and the spiritual world seem to reflect a single reality.

f) **PARAPSYCHOLOGY RESEARCH OF ROD STEIGER.**[11] A Psychologist, Dr. Charles Taft, University of California. At Davis conducted OBE Research at Univ. Of Virginia Hospital. Research has been extensive in such areas as Mind traveling through time and space, the spiritual body of man, leaving the body during pain, illness, surgery, sleep and at the moment of death. DR Eugene Bernard, Professor of Psychology at No. Carolina University states "It is impossible that so many who are hallucinations. I believe the astral projection theory can be proved and controlled. Once we rid ourselves of the notion that man is separate from his universe. apparently psychologically healthy are having

g) **ASTRAL PROJECTION**—Robert Monroe in his book "Journeys out of the Body" describes his experiences with Astral Projection. Brad Steiger lists 7 types of spontaneous or involuntary out of body e experiences,. Those that occur 1) during sleep, 2) undergoing surgery, childbirth, tooth extraction's 3) at the time of an accident while suffering a violent physical jolt, 4) in intense pain 5) acute illness 6) pseudo-death 7) at physical death when deceased subject appears to someone with whom there has been close emotional link.

---

[11] Pribram, K Langueages of the Brain (1971), Address at APA (1978), What is the fuss all about (1978),
Holographic Memory (1979)
Steiger, Rod Astral Projection (1982) National Psychic Researcher
Monroe, RobertAstral Projection, (1982)

PART III

Dancing to The "Music" of the Universe

THE PATH TO PSYCHOLOGICAL MATURITY
Runs through the fabric of the universe and is paved with realistic laws of cause and effect

DANCING TO THE _"Music"_ OF THE UNIVERSE

Psychological maturation occurs through instructional "processes" of cause and effect underlying attitudes, behavior and communication. Ability to hear and respond to *The Music of the Universe* allows development of personal potential and manifestation of *psychological and spiritual essence.* Initially most psychotherapy clients define "Normal" subjectively. Anxiety and dysfunction commonly result from internalized Rules/Roles many can't or won't live by.

Dysfunction can be classified as manipulation, inappropriate responsibility, distortion and inability to control emotion or "crises". Symptoms of immaturity fall into 3 categories of maladaptive behavior—Controlling, conforming and withdrawing. **Masks of Anxiety** (dysfunctional defenses) are unconsciously donned to avoid rejection, abandonment and emotional independence due to

fears of inadequacy. The goal of immature behavior is anxiety control. Principles of cause and effect teach 5 **Lessons Of Life** necessary for development of personal potential and successful relationshi

**Map of
REALITY**

Laws of
"Cause & Effect"

**Run through the fabric
of the universe**

5 LESSONS OF LIFE

Personal Growth and Mature relationships
(Psychological Maturation) **can occur by adhering
to a set of Universal Principles (Laws of Cause
& effect) underlying objective reality. These
Laws** (Music of the Universe) **are based on** instructional
<u>Processes</u> of cause and effect underlying attitudes, behavior
and communication.

Control

Responsibility

Reality

Decision Making

Crises Control

The "Path"
To Maturity

Lessons of Life

**are based on
Laws of "Cause & Effect**

SCALE 5—CONTROL

Skipi Lundquist Smoot, PhD Finding
the "Real" Me Copyright@1995

191

Maturation: The Adult Paradigm
Follow *The Map* to Unique Personal
Potential and Successful Relationships.

Personal growth and mature relationships (Tasks of Psychological Maturation) can occur by adhering to a set of universal principles (Laws of Cause & Effect) These Laws are based on "Processes" underlying objective reality.

At the core of psychological immaturity lies excessive dependency, feelings of inadequacy and fear of rejection. Fearing abandonment by others "Masks" of Anxiety (Behavioral & Attitudinal Symptoms of Immaturity) are unconsciously donned in an effort to control anxiety and avoid emotional independence.

Follow The Map (Lessons of Life) and learn to dance to the "Music" of the Universe (Cause & Effect).
5 NECESSARY LESSONS OF LIFE
LEADING TO PSYCHOLOGICAL MATURATION

1. **Control**—We can only control ourselves
2. **Responsibility**—Personal Responsibility is necessary for development of Unique Potential
3. **Reality**—Identification of undistorted objective Reality is necessary for development of Human Potential.
4. Successful Decisions must be based on **Cognitive Thought** (Objective Reality) vs Subjective Emotion or Distorted Perceptions or Expectations.
5. A **Balanced and Moderate** LifeStyle limits "Crises"

"WHERE IS THE *Real* ME?"

Examine Your Path CLOSELY for Clues

CHAPTER 8

Lesson 1

CONTROL

Control of others and external situations is an "illusion".

Where is the "real" Me?

Examine Your path
Closely *For Clues*

Do you try to Control people or situations . . . allow others to control you? Why? What are the consequences to yourself and your relationships?

<u>Lesson 1—CONTROL</u>

The only person or situation we can control is ourselves. Attempts to do otherwise lead to anxiety and conflict. Although we may be able to influence another's thoughts or behaviors such demands leads to confusion, anger or resentment. Many of us try to impose compliance by being "right", "manipulating" or "helping" the recipient of our administrations do what we think they "should".

Personal Belief systems are developed from Rules we have adopted concerning how life "should" be lived. These Rules are grouped into categories of regulations which form our Roadmap through Life. Regulations may include mandates about what we believe 1) "shoulds" or "should not" be done, 2) generalities (oversimplifications), 3) statements of what is "always" and "never" true or false (principles to be followed no matter what the circumstances), and/or 4) expectations for ourselves and others (be perfect, be nice, don't hurt people's feelings, never make a mistake, always win, etc). Rules and Beliefs, both functional and dysfunctional are learned from parents, authority figures, tradition, culture or social expectations and are specific to the experiences and environments in which they were learned.

Attempting to live by our Rules we don roles designed to produce the goals previously set for ourselves and our relationships. Goals may be conscious or subconscious, functional or dysfunctional. Similar to Movie Scripts, we organize and play our Roles with others in Life scripts. Scripts can be identified by recurrent themes underlying the Roles we play. Our full range of personal characteristics fit into basic Roles. Core Themes, Red Threads, run through our Basic Roles and reflect the goals our experiences, childhood environment and relationships have proscribed. Less significant or discarded rules may be played out in occasional or peripheral roles in our scripts.

All people need a Philosophy of Life leading to a functional lifestyle. Successful Roadmaps must be based on "Rules" reflecting Objective Reality. Laws of **Cause and Effect** reflect the objective concept that Control of others and external situations is an "illusion" and even seemingly chaotic events have order (cause and effect) even if unknown.

The "Map" of Reality

LESSON 1—Control

The only person or situation We can Control . . . is our self

Controlling Attitudes, Belief Systems, and/or behaviors of others and/or External situations is impossible. To try to do otherwise only leads to anxiety and conflict. In spite of this fact, human beings of all ages attempt to control Others by 1) open demand for compliance, 2) manipulation to hide the appearance of force 3) open defiance of others requests and demands or 4) covert defiance of others requests or demands.

Behavioral "Illusions" of Control (Attempts to Control persons and situations over which we have no control) may be the result of Belief systems, Life Scripts, Rules and/or Roles we attempt to live by. Although at times we may be able to influence others, these attempts will affect our relationships in ways we are unaware of or may not understand. Controlling Types of behaviors may include 1) open attempts to control others, 2) covert manipulation, 3) open defiance and 4) passive aggressive behaviors,.

Many believe controlling behavior is appropriate because the point of view being insisted upon is the "correct behavior". Others attempt to manipulate friends, family or spouses into behaving "correctly" by "helping" others do what they "should".

5 LEVELS OF DEVELOPMENT UNDERLYING PERSONAL BELIEFS

The following discussion of Personal Beliefs may be used as a model to identify which of your beliefs are Functional (contribute to your Realistic understanding of yourself and your world) and/or Dysfunctional (contribute to your anxiety and inability to be successful (personally and in your relationships). They are arranged in Levels of development . . . from primary to complex.

1. **Rules we have learned concerning human behavior**
   RULES (shoulds, ought's, correct behaviors, Generalizations, etc.)_learned as children or adults concerning ways to live, behave or relate to others. These rules have been learned from Parents, Authorities, Church, Teachers, or as a result of our own experiences.

2. **Belief Systems** (Context in which our Rules of Life reside) In addition to the Rules we live by, we hold (consciously or unconsciously) beliefs that are to connected them.

3. **"Roadmaps[1]" of Life** (Model or Paradigm) our beliefs fall into—A "Paradigm" is a Model of the theoretical foundation of our personal Rules of Life.

4. **Life Scripts[2] (Patterns of Beliefs, underlying the Behaviors that make up the Roles we play in Life)** Life Scripts are Methods of Organizing our behavior in an attempt to meet our Goals. Goals may be conscious or subconscious. Life Scripts have underlying Themes. Which can be identified from the Roles we play with others.

5. **Cause and Effect (Universal Laws of Cause & Effect underlying Objective vs Subjective Reality)[3]** Even seemingly chaotic events have order to them and could be explained if the whole situation pertaining to them was known.

---

[1]   Covey, S—Seven Habits of Effective People   Peck, S Road Less Traveled—The Outmoded Map

[2]   Berne, E—Scripts as a means to organize behavior within relationships. These scripts lead to patterns of behavior   that person is used to

[3]   See Scale #4 Fit" in the Universe—Chaos theory, Grand Unification Theory, etc.

DEFINITIONS OF CONTROLLING BEHAVIORS

People who have not resolved the issues of Symbiotic Attachment (and that includes most of us) are uncomfortable with emotional separation. In addition, social and cultural pressure encourages symbiosis and discourage conflict or disagreements with others, etc. As a general rule most groups encourage similarities. For example: Families usually **encourage** it's members to hold many of the same opinions, Church Members usually believe in the same or similar doctrines. Members of various Nations generally exhibit similar cultural expectations for themselves and others within their groups, etc.

Most marital partners feel more comfortable when the spouses are in agreement rather than holding diverse points of view. Scientific Research on Theories of Sex Role[4] identifies expectations for the Male and Female Sex Role and expects the person within the role to exhibit the expected characteristics.

Psychological Theory cites **Anxiety** as a result of conflict within the self or in relationships as the main reason for unhappiness and psychological problems. Few people are mature enough to feel completely comfortable exhibiting their "real" self and allowing others in their life to do the same. **Eric Berne's theory of Differentiation** cites the concept of **"Pseudoself"** as the part of the self that adapts to the expectations of others, authority, society and culture. Characteristics of Pseudoself can be held consciously or unconsciously. Pseudoself is the result of learning. Some people just identify with others ideas and values and never really bother to varify whether or not they themselves are "really" in agreement. Others put up a front and exhibit "Pseudoself" as a fascade, knowing all the time they do not agree but use the facade to serve a purpose.

---

[4] Bem Sex Role Inventory—Gender Role Definition from Wikipedia Encyclopedia

Values Clarification[5] takes this concept furthur and explains the steps to clarification of personal values. The author, Sheldon,) believes that very few values are held that are non negotiable and that few of us deliberately set about to identify values on our own. Apparently (according to Sheldon) most of us assume the values of our family, our culture, or our friends without thinking much about it.

Although many young people during the teenage years or early adulthood go through a stage of rebellion, this stage of life (not explored by everyone) is <u>not</u> **one of "critical thinking"**. Rather it is a stage of "doing the opposite" of what the parents and family want and doing exactly the same as their present group of peers are doing. The adolescent counterculture manifests a general mood of alienation from the larger culture, generally the family. Most adolescents are part of such a group as a means to separate from their family and identify themselves as different from their families. Most adolescents do not take into consideration the fact that they have usually "Joined" another group that takes the place of the family and that they are now following the rules of the Peers rather than those of the Family. More traditional counterculture characteristics may include behaviors and attitudes that are counter to society or the culture.

College is traditionally the time of life set aside for the journey toward clarifying our own values. Classes such as Philosophy, Critical Thinking, Sociology are good examples of situations in which individuals can learn to identify areas of disagreement between the values they have assumed without thinking them through and what they really believe after examination of the issue at hand. Education is an excellent road toward learning to see the broad perspective of the world vs the narrow one that most of us have been trained to assume.

Attempts to control others behavior (so that the anxiety elicited by conflict can be concealed) includes many categories of behavior, such as 1) open control, 2) manipulation of others, 3) withdrawing from the other into anger, silence, distance etc. Sometimes people even 4)

---

[5]   Sheldon, (19) Values Clarifications Valett, Robert Ed.D Self Actualization (1974)

withdraw from themselves in an effort to protect themselves from the knowledge that they are compromising their own integrity. Examples of this may be those who drink or use drugs to avoid facing their problems, becoming depressed, sleeping as avoidance, etc.

Examples of **Open Control ("Do it My Way because I said so")** may be attempts to control others behavior due to expectations for morals, religious beliefs or principles. However, these demands ignore the fact of others independence, psychological development and internal responses. Examples might be The Need to have my own way, insisting "I am right", showing others a "better way", being openly critical of others behavior, etc.

Examples of **Manipulation** (Do it my way without appearing to be controlling) include influencing others to do something they don't want to do to avoid feeling guilty, having to listen to the others whining, etc. Examples of this might be "buttering people up", "hinting" that others might do it differently, crying when others disagree, reminding others of what was done for them in the past or sometimes just stop speaking without explaining why. My own grandmother used the "Stop Talking" technique which she had polished to perfection. When Grandpa inquired out of concern whether something might be wrong, she always replied "No, nothing" and just continued her silent treatment. Finally he would say "Grace I know something is the wrong, what is it?" At which point she would reply "Well, if you don't know, I'm certainly not going to tell you".

Those who **Openly Defy Others attempts to control them** may do so by becoming angry, leaving the relationship, etc. Examples of this might be to refuse a request, openly break rules, disobey laws, etc. Surprisingly to some, this is a position of weakness not strength. Many times those who use it will try to convince the other they have the "right" to do what they want and force the other to agree with them. The need to convince others of their rights shows underling uncertainty concerning personal "right" to live the way they want to.

Covert Defiance of Others is a behavior entered into as a means to keep from being controlled by others without exciting conflict or negative reactions from others. Examples of this include "forgetting" to do what was promised, resisting suggestions, being late, making lots of excuses why it can't be done, etc.

FURTHUR THOUGHTS CONCERING "ILLUSIONS" OF CONTROL

It's interesting thinking about these "Illusions" of Control styles in reference to ourselves . . . and others. Most of us don't really believe our own behavior falls into one of these styles, but the truth is, most of us have "been there done that" with at least one of the styles. Because "Psychological Maturation" is a new way of thinking about Adult Human Development it is important to think about our own behavior in that context. Because most Rules are internalized as children, most of us perceive them as "Correct" and even "Normal". As a result we have never considered our own or others behaviors as Roles played in Scripts with others. However, using personal Rules you believe are correct, consider how you use them in your relationships with others in the context of Roles and Scripts.

- **Describe a recent conflict between you and someone in a relationship with you.**
- **What Control Style did you use? What control Style did they use?**
- **How did you feel as a result of the Control Style they used with you in the conflict?**
- **How do you think they might have felt as a result of the Control Style you used with them in the conflict?**
- **What do you think you might do in the future instead? What does this example reveal to you about the real cause and effect in relationships?**

5 PERCEPTUAL LEVELS
OF PERSONAL BELIEF SYSTEMS

PERCEPTUAL LEVELS	CATAGORIES of Personal Ideologies	
Rules The set of laws we learned as children or adults concerning human behavior.	**MY RULES of Life**	Rule #1 Rules for Correct Human behaviors, Rule #2 Correct Rules for Living Human Life. Rule #3 Lessons learned from Parents. Rule #4 Lessons learned from Authorities Rules # Etc. Etc...from Self & respected Others
Belief SystemS Belief Systems underlie the Rules within our system of Personal Beliefs concerning Human behavior. In addition to the Rules we live by, we hold (consciously or unconsciously) beliefs that are connected to them.	**MY PERSONAL BELIEF SYSTEM**	#1 #2 #3 #6 # ETC. ETC. ETC. ETC. #4 #5
"Roadmap" of Life The Model (Paradigm) our beliefs fall into A "**Paradigm**" is a Model of the theoretical foundation for our personal Rules of Life.	ROADMAP	"Appropriate" Roles / How Relationships Should Work / "My Beliefs" / "My Model of Life" / My "Rules"
Life Scripts[6] Life Scripts (Patterns of Beliefs) lie beneath the Behaviors that make up the Roles we play in Life Scripts organize behavior in attempts to meet Goals. The Goal of Roles & Scripts is to protect perceptions of ourselves and influence relationships (symbiosis). Goals may be conscious or subconscious. Scripts have underlying Themes, which may be identified from Roles played with others.	**Life "Scripts"** organize Roles	Helper Screw-Up Disaster prone "I'm So Nice" Wait to be eaten "always in the soup" Shark CONTROLLER "Do it My Way.. ...Or else" Naïvete "always in crisis" MANIPULATOR "now... ...I got you" Prey VICTIM Waiting for santa "Oh, Foxes" Others "I need"
CAUSE AND EFFECT Universal Laws of Cause & Effect underlie Objective Reality[7] Even seemingly chaotic events have order to them and could be explained if the whole situation pertaining to them is known.	**The Basis of Reality**	Map "Why isn't my life Working out???" Reality Laws of C

---

6   Berne, E—Scripts as a means to organize behavior within relationships. These scripts lead to patterns of behavior   that person is used to

7   See Scale #4 Fit" in the Universe—Chaos theory, Grand Unification Theory, etc.

The <u>RULES</u> we live by and our BELIEFS Concerning them

MY Rules of Life	CATAGORIES of Personal Ideologies
MY Rules of Life The set of laws we learned as children or adults concerning human behavior.	**Category #1 My** Rules concerning Correct Human behaviors, **Category # 2** My Rules concerning Correct Human behavior **Category # 3** My Rules learned from Parents. **Category #4** Rules learned from Authority figures, teachers, etc. **Category <u>#</u> 5 Rules I learned from my own experiences** **Category <u>#</u> Etc . . . Rules learned from respected Others**

We all have **Rules** we at least give "lip service" to trying to live by. These rules, leaned from parents, teachers, authorities, church and our own experiences can be visualized as a Road Map through our life environment Rules may be functional or dysfunctional. We also hold beliefs (some conscious and some unconscious) concerning our Rules. For example, a commonly held rule might be "I must not make mistakes". One person may believe "I will decide when I have made a mistake" while another may decide "Others will decide when I made a mistake"

It is fairly simple to identify the Rules we learned as children or adults. We have all learned many ways to live, behave or relate to others in the world. These rules were learned from Parents, Authority figures, Church, Teachers, or as a result of our own experiences. In addition, it is usually fairly easy to remember from whom or which situations these Rules were adopted

IDENTIFYING OUR BELIEF SYSTEMS

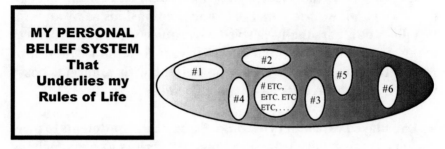

Belief Systems underlie the Rules within our system of Personal Beliefs concerning Human behavior. The following discussion of Personal Beliefs can be used as a model to identify which of beliefs are Functional (contribute to your Realistic understanding of self and our world) and/or Dysfunctional (contribute to anxiety and inability to function successful (personally and in your relationships).

`Belief systems` are inner connected **with our rules for life In addition to the Rules we live by, we (consciously or unco*nsciously*)** *hold beliefs that are connected to them. These beliefs are sometimes harder to identify*, **but with a little effort this too can be done.**

We can often identify them by asking ourselves questions about our Rules. For example, a wife may have a Rule that calls for "letting others know" when they will be late for an appointment. On the surface, the reason for the Rule might be Common Courtesy. However, at a deeper level, this woman realized that her underlying belief about why husbands "should" call was that husbands who did not call, did not love their wives. Therefore, her husbands behavior of not calling her, proved (to her) that he did not love her.

Beliefs concerning possible consequences of our Rules (different for different people) are organized according to `Themes`. For example possible consequences concerning mistakes may include "If I make a mistake it means I am a loser" while another may believe "If I make a mistake I can learn from it".

Rules are used as tools to design our personal Road Map through life. As a result Roles emerge in our relationships as we attempt to follow our personally arrived at requirements for "correct" living. In addition, we often play different Roles in relationships with different people. We may be defiant with a parent, bossy with a friend, or helpless with a boyfriend.

Roles played with others in Life Scripts are attempts to meet our goals (conscious or unconscious). All scripts have underlying themes which may identify the person playing the Role as a victim, looser, winner, complainer, etc.

We, Human Beings, develop our belief systems based on what was taught to us by others (parents, authorities, teachers, etc.), our own perceptions of Reality, and our Emotional Responses to the situations we find ourselves in. Beliefs can be Functional or Dysfunctional. Functional Beliefs usually "fit" Reality. As we develop into Maturity, our thought processes usually make decisions based on balancing our wants & needs with the Reality of what we can realistically and appropriately attain.

It is natural for Human beings to try to avoid anxiety. It's part of our nature to try to defend ourselves against pain. We do not want to be hurt, by others, ourselves, or our situations. Behaving against our value system often results in trying to defend against the reality of what we did by make excuses (Rationalizing) for our behavior. In some cases, we may even defend other people's behavior with Rationalizations.

For instance, a child may excuse a parents neglect with the defense that the parent is too busy to provide the proper attention. This protects the child from confronting the possibility that the parent may not love the child or that the child is not as important to the parent as some other activity of the Parent may be. A more realistic conclusion may be that the parent is unable (due to some maturational or psychological deficiency) to provide the care needed by a child. However, even though this judgment will almost certainly lead to anxiety in the child, in the long run, this conclusion leads to a more realistic understanding of the parent, rather than the erroneous one, that the child is not worth caring for. Similarly, a wife may excuse her husbands neglect of her by concluding his behavior is not really his "fault". In this way she protects herself from facing the possibility that her husband is not able to be a trustworthy husband, that he may find her of little value, or that she may need to make some hard decisions about the state of her marriage.

Children form beliefs about themselves from an interaction between what parents or authority figures tell them and what the child perceives to be true about themselves. A child who reads from the face of a parent, a message that the child is of little value will incorporate that belief into his Belief System concerning Self Esteem. On the other hand, a child who has received a message that he/she is worthwhile, competent, loved and safe will have a much better possibility of going through life believing in him/herself and trusting that the world is usually safe.

Beliefs about the world and how it works can usually be formed without the need for self protection. A Child will usually accept unconditionally what is taught about God, Duty, Morality, Race, Religion, Roles, etc. However, children taught a narrow perspective of any subject, will usually perceive the world narrowly. If, however, a child is taught to perceive the world from a Broad perspective, that child will usually look at the world from a flexible point of view.

1. **Personal problems** are usually the result of a conflict between the way we "see" ourselves and how we "really" are.
2. **Relationship problems** are usually the result of dystonic perceptions (between our view and that of the other) of the way we perceive the world and our place within it.
3. **Communication problems** are often the result of inability to empathize with the other, exhibit flexibility, or truly understand the others point of view.

This does not mean that it is always necessary to agree with the other. It just means that it is often helpful to truly "know" how the other views the situation. And to remember that everyone says and does what they do because they believe there is validity to their point of view. Most of us try to prove to ourselves and the other that we are right and they are wrong. The truth is that there is very seldom a right or wrong way to view a situation. It is more realistic to understand there are many possible perceptions of a given situation.

Many of our beliefs about ourselves (our abilities, worth, etc) others, situations, etc. are dysfunctional. Dysfunctional beliefs are not in line with Reality. As we are able to take a more flexible, broad, and empathetic view of life our views will take more and more of reality into consideration. A Mature Belief Sys tem is able to Face Reality and Accept the Truth. This does not mean that there is a right and wrong. It does mean that as we and our world grow and change, our beliefs must also be flexible enough to grow and change, taking as much of the Truth about Reality as we are able, into consideration. Neither, does this mean we should make "excuses" for others. However, we will experience better relationships with others, if we can find a possible "explanation" of their point of view.

Learning to evaluate our own System of Beliefs in terms of Functionality and Reality is one of the most important aspects of mental health. Much as been written on the "Invisible Bonds" of Dysfunctional Beliefs. Many of us are **Prisoners of our Beliefs (McKay, 19). Albert Ellis** has written many books on changing dysfunctional Beliefs. His message is that it is not what happens to us that causes our misery, but what we think about what happens to us (ABC Model). He states that it is possible to see the world so realistically that it is possible to keep ourselves from being depressed, overly anxious, unhappy, about ANYTHING **"How to keep yourself from being miserable about anything, Yes, Anything" (Ellis, A. 1993).**

Where is the "real" Me?

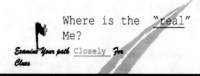

Examine Your path Closely *For Clues*

Follow Biblical Rules

The RULES we live by .....and our beliefs about them

Husbands should never help with housework.

We all have `Rules` we live by. These rules, leaned from parents, teachers, authorities, church and our own experiences can be visualized as a Road Map through our life environment Rules may be functional or dysfunctional.

We also hold `beliefs` (some conscious and some unconscious)concerning our Rules. For example, a commonly held rule might be "I must not make mistakes". One person may believe "I will decide when I have made a mistake" while another will decide "Others will decide when I made a mistake"

Children should be seen and not heard

Beliefs concerning possible consequences of our Rules (different for different people) are organized according to Themes. For example possible consequences about making mistakes may include "If I make a mistake it means I am a loser" and another "If I make a mistake I can learn from it".

Little girls keep house.

Rules are used as tools to design our personal `Road Map` through life. As a result `Roles` emerge in our relationships as we attempt to follow our personally arrived at requirements for "correct" living. In addition, we play different Roles in relationships with different people. We may be defiant with a parent, bossy with a friend, or helpless with a boyfriend.

Roles are played with others in `Life Scripts` in attempts to meet our goals (conscious or unconscious). All scripts have underlying themes which may identify the person playing the Role as a victim, looser, winner, complainer, etc.

Nothing in Life is too dangerous for me

The "Map" of Reality

Families must always be in agreement

"ROADMAPs" (paradigm) OF LIFE

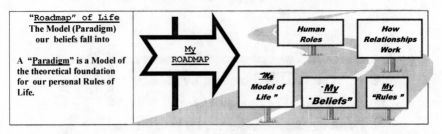

"ROADMAPS" OF LIFE (Paradigms, Categories, Group of Beliefs, Personal Belief Systems) **A** "Paradigm" **is a Model of the theoretical foundation upon which our personal Rules of Life are built.** Our Roadmap[8] contains the categories of beliefs we have placed our Rules for Life within. **Most of us believe our Roadmap hold the "Correct" answers to dealing with life's problems. When our Roadmap falters, a first response is usually to point the finger of blame toward aspects of the situation that do not coincide with our personal Paradigm.**

Our **Paradigm** may define `Rules` we have learned concerning "shoulds" or 'should not" do, perceptions of the world as Black and White or Grey, anticipation of patterns that always or never occur, Principles to be followed, Duty to be done, expectations for self and others concerning mistakes, being perfect, winning and/or losing, etc. Sometimes, the Rules underlying our Roadmap are nebulous or may include unconscious ideology that we have never seriously defined.

An ancient **PARADIGM** defined the World as flat while a later more functional Paradigm currently defines the World as round. Both cannot be true at the same time. Paradigms can be compared to the Model we have assigned our personal and relationship Values into. Some Paradigms are rigidly structured with little or no room for compromise. Other Paradigms may also be highly structured with certain Non-negotiable values but which allow room for compromise on issues perceived as negotiable.

---

[8] Covey, S—Seven Habits of Effective People   Peck, S Road Less Traveled—The Outmoded Map

In marriage counseling I discuss non-negotiable values with spouses as values they believe they cannot deviate from. For instance, consideration of whether to watch a favorite TV program or have dinner out, most of us can agree to do it my way, your way or another way, depending on the circumstances of the situation. However, political ideology, religious convictions, parenting practices and/ or sex role behaviors often fall into the category of non-negotiable values. Such personal issues are more functionally dealt with before marriage than after.

Most of us "Fall In Love" as a result of `chemical attraction` (God's way of perpetuating the Human Race), and because we both "love chocolate ice cream", "Rock and Roll" or "s(he) makes me laugh". Ignorance of the importance of premarital discussion of Non-negotiable Values are of the utmost importance. When the aspect of Marriage or a long term committed relationship comes into view, ignoring or putting off (till a better time) discussion of these topics invariably lead to disappointment, anger, self righteous indignation, confusion, anxiety or depression.

I often share the Theory presented by Virginia Satir[9] that in our early life we often tend to marry those who possess the characteristics we lack in an attempt to feel like a whole person. The problem with doing this is that in mid life when the anxieties connected with Adult Development (Psychological Maturation) becomes difficult to ignore, many of us find ourselves married to those with `Roadmaps of Life` containing Non-Negotiable Values completely opposed to our own.

It is necessary to clearly understand and identify the manner in which our **RULES OF LIFE** do or do not fit into the constraints of Objective Reality. Beliefs are internalized from parents, authority figures, tradition of family and/or culture, social expectations etc. It is important to realize that although all people need a Philosophy

---

[9]   Satir, Virginia—"Conjoint Family Therapy," published in 1964, "Self-Esteem," "Helping Families To Change" and other important research theories.

of Life from which to lead a functional lifestyle our Philosophy of Life and our ability to live up to it must be in line with Objective vs Subjective[10] Reality.

Life Scripts are methods of organizing our behavior in an attempt to meet our goals. Goals may be conscious or unconscious. **SCRIPTS** have underlying themes and can be identified from the Roles we play with others. A person's Life Script may call for them to be a victim, looser, winner, complainer, Pollyanna, etc., in most of their life's situations. In addition, a Life Script often calls for several Roles.

Themes can be identified from the Roles played with others. A person's life script may require presentation of different aspects of our personality in our Roles with different persons who require it. However, our full range of characteristics fit into one or more basic Roles we find ourselves called on to play at different times and in different situations in our relationships with others. For example: a woman may see herself smart, overworked and often overwhelmed. Her new boyfriend may perceive a woman's role as one of Helping. Because the woman wants to be admired for being smart she may assume the role of Helper (which comes with the price tag of being overworked and overwhelmed.

---

[10] Subjective Reality is defined as what we think things "should" be or how we "feel" about the issue.

Where is the "real" Me?

"always in the soup"

Examine Your path Closely For Clues

"Roadmaps" of Life
"Roles" played by many
in Life Scripts

I'm so Nice

Drowning my sorrow

- **Life Scripts** are methods of organizing our behavior in an attempt to meet our goals. Goals may be conscious or unconscious. **Scripts** have underlying themes.
- Themes can be identified from the Roles we play with others. A person's life script may call for a Role of victim, loser, winner, complainer, Pollyanna, etc. in most of our life's situations.
- Our full range of characteristics fit into basic Roles. For instance a **Life Script** may call for several Roles including those of 1) Cinderella waiting for prince charming and fully expecting to try on the glass slipper 2) Loser with men and 3) Successful winner in college and at work.

"always in crisis"

"Do it My way …….. or Else

Overwhelmed

"I need Help!!

Prince Charming

Rewarding the Good Kids

211

"Roles" of control Played IN LIFE scripts

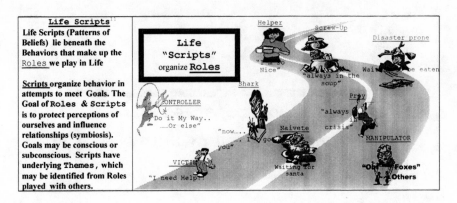

The **Rules** we live by, where they came from and what they mean to us often lie at a subconscious Level. There are appropriate methods to help us decide whether our Rules & Beliefs concerning them are functional or dysfunctional. However, it is imperative that our chosen Methods for deciding must become conscious and objective.

We all have many **ROLES** we have played or continue to play in our relationships with others. These Roles are based on the Goals (conscious or unconscious of our Life Scripts[11] We have learned that certain Roles are necessary or appropriate with certain people we have relationships with. We seldom play the same roles within all of our relationships. For instance, we may play a subordinate or helpless role with a parent, an authoritarian role with a wife or husband, a looser with Men, or a Winner & Achiever at Work or with Peers. It is even possible to take similar roles in most (if not all) of our relationships. Sometimes the roles we take with one person become interchangeable (first one will take the role and then the other will assume that role for a while). For instance, a wife may take the role of a Blamer (the husband doesn't pay enough attention to her). The husband plays the role of the Victim. Then the husband may change roles, blaming his wife for being a nag. The wife then may change her role and become the Victim (seeing her husband as never satisfied).

---

[11]   Life Scripts-Description of Eric Bern's Transactional Analysis Theory. A person is said to develop a Life Script as a method of organizing behavior.

LIFE SCRIPTs [12] **(Patterns of Beliefs) underlie Behaviors that make up the** <u>Roles</u> **we play with others. These Scripts** organize our behavior in attempts to meet our Goals (conscious or subconscious). Scripts have underlying Themes. Themes can be identified from the Roles played with others.

Our **full range** of characteristics fit into the basic Roles within our Life Scripts. These Scripts are played out in relationships with others whose Script fit with ours. A person whose script called for taking care of others might attract another who felt weak. For instance, one of my clients identified her Script as "Cinderella". She waited for Prince Charming and fully expected to try on the Glass slipper and go live in the Castle. However, her Roles included both that of "Looser" (Prince Charming never came) and Winner (she was very successful in College and in Business). Scripts can be flexible enough to take several potential outcomes into account with the Goals call for it.

Red Threads are usually unconscious or feared ideation keeping a person behaving according to the Life Script and Roles that have been adopted. Red Threads consist of a few basic bedrock Personality Characteristics that on which all of our other Personality Characteristics hang. Red Threads can be discerned from the Rules we hold, the Roles we play in life, the Patterns that our Roles seem to follow, and closely considering why we might continue to follow our Life Script (even one that never leads to our conscious goals).

For example, the reason I continued to wait for Santa was because I was afraid that I would be abandoned by those I loved if I did not. The Red Threads underlying the Santa Claus Script that I had adopted were the fears that 1) if I were to make a mistake, 2) could not be perfect or 3) choose to think for myself rather than follow the rules of others, I would almost certainly be abandoned. Sometimes these fears are realistic, sometimes they are not

We might play several Roles within our Scripts with others (winner, looser, fighter, etc.) but Red Threads are Core Characteristics. For example: I was taught that if I was nice to others, they would be nice

---

[12] Berne, E-Scripts as a means to organize behavior within relationships. These scripts lead to patterns of behavior that person is used to

to me and if they weren't it was because I hadn't done it right yet. This Theme can go around and around with a person who believes that if something is wrong it is never their fault because they are perfect. These 2 sets of Immature Red threads can continue indefinitely or until one of the two examines their Red Threads and decides to change them.

It is helpful to examine the Roles we play in our relationships (and reasons for assuming these roles) and decide whether continuing with them is a good idea. A good method of understanding ourselves is to examine the "Red Threads" that run through our personalities. These Red Threads account for most of our personality characteristics and behaviors.

The **"Red Threads"** of Personality can be understood as the Skeleton of **Core Characteristics** (Rules, Roles, Beliefs, etc.) running through our Personality on which all other characteristics hang. Understanding the personality in terms of **Red Threads**[13] was introduced to me in my Doctoral Studies sat California School of Professional Psychology in San Diego, Ca by my Professor of Psychological Assessment, Beverly Kilman, PhD. Dr Kilman's grasp and ability to share methods of understanding the human personality was astounding and invaluable. She explained it by the analogy of Skeleton Bones upon which all nerves and smaller bones hang and fit into. The personality itself can be seen as similar to the Skeletal Pattern of our Beliefs and rules about them.

Over the years, numerous professional theorists and authors including have written extensively on the concept of Core Beliefs. Aaron Beck, & Albert Ellis iwrote extensively about **Cognitive Theory** and **Core Beliefs.** Beck summed up his theory in a 2000 meeting with Albert Ellis said he realized many years ago that the cause of dysfunctional behavior is dysfunctional thinking, and that thinking process are shapped by underlying beliefs. Ellis in his ABC theory is famous for

---

[13]   **Red Threads** analogy of Skeleton Bones (Kilman, B, PhD) upon which all nerves and smaller bones hang and fit into. The personality itself can be seen as similar to the Skeletal Pattern of our Beliefs and rules about them.

his theory that "it's not what happens to us that cause our problems, it's our belief about what happens to us that causes our problems. <u>Kernberg & Kohut</u>— posit Core beliefs to lie at the center of Narcissism. Many other authors and researchers McKay **(19)**. Straight Talk, The Iron Fist and the Velvet Glove. also stress the belief that **Core beliefs** lie at the core of dysfunctional relationships.

<u>THE TYPES & REASONS</u> BEHIND THE USE OF CONTROLLING BEHAVIOR

Over the years, Theorists have written extensively concerning their beliefs concerning "Why" human beings assume the **ROLES** we play in our relationships.[14]. In addition the concepts of `Life Scripts`[15] and **ROLES** assumed by each of us within our relationships (as a means of **organizing behavior within relationships)** has also been extensively discussed, written about, taught and used in Psychological Treatment.

My own thinking les is that Manipulative attempts to control the behaviors of others are made in attempts to resolve relationships conflict, human differences and deny the necessity for emotional separateness. "**Masks**" commonly donned include **overt control** of others, **covert control** of others, **overt defiance** of others and **covert defiance** of others. All these Behaviors have at their core, the need to protect the self from abandonment.

"DON'T LEAVE ME. I'M AFRAID TO BE ALONE" Manipulative attempts to control the behaviors of others are made in attempts to

---

[14]   **Man the Manipulation, The Inner Journey from Manipulation to Actualization (Shostrom, Everett),**
Symbiotic Attachment (Mahler, Margaret Psychoanalyst 1897-1985), and **Differentiation of Self (Bowen, Murray, MD.)**

[15]   **(Berne, E), Maps of Life (Covey, S & Peck, S), Negative Identity (Erickson, E)**_Types of Controlling Behavior—Manipulation, Open Control, Defiance, Covert attem **Egocentricity (Kernberg & Kohut)**, <u>Berne, E</u>—<u>Scripts</u> as a means to organize behavior within relationships. Lead to patterns of behavior.

resolve relationships conflict, resolve human differences and deny the necessity for emotional separateness. **"Masks"** commonly donned include **overt control** of others, **covert control** of others, **overt defiance** of others and **covert defiance** of others. All these Behaviors have at their core, the need to protect the self from abandonment.

OPEN CONTROL—**"Do it My Way"** Attempts to control others is a result of expectations for others to think and behave in ways we expect or want them to. When others believe as we do, the conflict disappears from the relationship

COVERT CONTROL—**"Do it My Way" (without appearing to be demanding).** Manipulative control is accomplished by getting others to "do it my way" through guilt, fear, whining, victimization, being to weak to help ourselves, etc. Examples are "buttering people up", hinting, crying, not speaking until others do "what I want them to do".

Open Defiance—**"I won't do it your way" ("No Way")** Resistance to control by others. Examples may be to refuse a request, openly flaunt rules, disobey laws, etc. Some people may try to convince others they have the "right" to refuse.

Covert Defiance—**" I won't do it your way—(but please don't be mad at me)** This is resistance to control without open conflict. Examples are "forgetting" to do what was asked, resisting suggestions quietly, making excuses, being late, getting lost, oversleeping, etc.

"Hi, there...Big boy..." "

Where is the "real"

Examine Your path Closely For
Please

"My knuckles might be dragging...

"ROLES" OF CONTROL

In Relationships with Others

OPEN CONTROL — "Do it My Way" Attempts to control others is a result of expectations for others to think and behave in ways we expect or want them to. When others believe as we do, the conflict disappears from the relationship

COVERT CONTROL — "Do it My Way" (without appearing to be demanding). Manipulative control is accomplished by getting others to "do it my way" through guilt, fear, whining, victimization, being to weak to help ourselves, etc. Examples are "buttering people up", hinting, crying, not speaking until others do "what I want them to do".

Open Defiance — "I won't do it your way" ("No Way") Resistance to control by others. Examples may be to refuse a request, openly flaunt rules, disobey laws, etc. Some people may try to convince others they have the "right" to refuse.

Covert Defiance—"I won't do it your way - (but please don't be mad at me) This is resistance to control without open conflict. Examples are "forgetting" to do what was asked, resisting suggestions quietly, making excuses, being late, getting lost, oversleeping, etc.

"I'm out of here." "If you don't agree with me I can find someone else who does".!

"ZZZZ...Sorry, I'm so tired....I just can't do it 7777

217

IDENTIFY YOUR LIFE SCRIPT
Where is the "Real" Me?

Examine your Path Closely for Clues

Many authors have set forth the idea that people live according to Life scripts[16]. Some of **Eric Berne's Scripts** included "Now, I've got you, you # @ . . . & **^"" and "I am doomed to be a victim", etc. Some authors discuss navigating life as similar to making a Roadmap of Behavior and following it. In this way it is not necessary to reinvent the wheel in each instance. Some examples of these roadmaps may be 1) doing what we "should" or "should not" do, 2) living by the black and white rules of life that verify what is "always" or "never" to be done, etc. People develop many roadmaps to live by, such as, 1) I must always be perfect, 2) my duty is to help others no matter what it costs me 3) the world is terrifying and therefore I need someone else to take care of me and 4) If I am good I will be rewarded, etc. There are as many scripts of life as there are people to work them out.

Psychiatrist Saul, MD, indicates that Childhood Patterns are worked out by age 5 and that life continues to be lived by them as a result of habit. It is almost as though we work out an explanation of life that makes sense to at in childhood and then continue to live on **"auto pilot"** without critically evaluating whether our ideas make sense in our more adult situations or not. Psychotherapy makes use of the phenomenon as a result of investigating "transferences" within relationships.

Transference[17] is a Psychological concept that can be explained as an emotional reaction to a situation in the here and now that has similar

---

16   Berne, E "Transactional analysis"
17   Transference-Psychoanalytic term for inappropriate emotion felt by the patient toward the therapist that has its roots in a parental relationship from the past. The transference is transferred to the Analyst. Psychological and Psychodynamic therapy uses the term to explain the concept that something in the "here and now" has elicited emotions from the "there

characteristics to something that occurred in the past. For instance, a Mother may become inappropriately and unexplainably angry at her 10 year old daughter who is behaving appropriately in a family therapy session because the daughter reminds the mother of her sister who as a child always tried to show off and got attention from their mother for being a "goody goody".

---

and then". The feelings may have been appropriate to the situation from yesterday, but they are not appropriate in the present situation.

YOUR LIFE PATH TO INNER STRENGTH & PEACE

Where is the "Real Me?

Examine your path **Closely** for Clues

"Directing" others

Instructing Others in the "Correct" way of Life

Fighting for my "Rights"

I wear a suit of Amour

To "Nail" the enemy

Life is Overwhelming

Life is a Time Bomb

Taking the "Edge" off of Life

"Outsmarting" the World

Now I've got you, you *.*#, **.

Getting "Even" with Others

"Eaten Alive" !!!

World is So "Perfect

Always in the soup

Life on a "Limb"

Conforming with the World

Waiting for Prince Charming

Waiting for Santa Claus

Always Needs Broke, help.

IDENTIFY YOUR LIFE SCRIPT

- Identify your **Rules of Life**
- What are your underlying **beliefs** about those **rules?**
- What **Roles** do you play in your life and relationships?
- **Life Scripts** have a sense of repetition to them. They seem to go around and around. <u>**Example**</u>: One client was involved with many people who always tried to control her life style. The Client always fought back. When the Relationship became untenable, she moved on into another Relationship where the same Script repeated itself.
- Put all the above together in your mind and try to summarize it into a short overall description of your **Life Script**
- Life Scripts do not have to be negative. Many Life Scripts are positive.
- Identify the Underlying Fears (RED THREADS) that keep you repeating your Life Script.
- Are your Fears Realistic?
- Do you want to change your Life Script?
- Review the illustrations for possibilities and clues to your own script.

GWSLSRT.PUB

Cause & Effect

The

REALITY UNDERLIE OBJECTIVE Reality

UNIVERSAL Laws of cause & effect

The path to PSYCHOLOGICAL MATURITY **runs through the Fabric Of The Universe and is paved with Universal Laws Of Cause & Effect. Universal Laws of** Cause & Effect **underlie Objective Reality. Even seemingly chaotic events have order and are explainable when the WHOLE situation pertaining to them is known[18]. The principle of** cause and effect **is that everything that happens must have a cause. It concerns the action that causes an effect, or the ability to cause an effect Encarta Dictionary**

A set of **Underlying Laws of Cause and Effect** govern the interactions of the Universe and apply to all aspects of Reality (science, religion, spirituality, psychology, man, animals, physics, space, time, etc). All so called Coincidences are likely to be the result of some type of cause and effect. What appear to be Chaotic happenings may in reality be governed by a set of unseen laws underlying the Universe. Many Scientists believe the task of Science to be discovery of a set of Underlying laws that will explain all cause and effect within the Universe and enable prediction of events.

At any specific time, our situation is a reflection of every decision or choice we have made or allowed to be made on our behalf. Personal choices/behaviors concerning a situation (to act, wait, conform, do nothing, etc.) reflect the antecedents (causes) of what transpired (effects). Choices reflect the rules, roles and beliefs we have assumed concerning attitudes and behaviors in both personal and relationship situations. However, many of these rules and beliefs have little in common with the realities of life.

Choices are presented to each of us in the form of personal decision making, problem solving with others, serendipity, synchronicity, etc. The ability to make choices based on the objective reality of cause

---

[18]   Cause/consequence— is The basis of Reality It is necessary to objectively understand the links of cause and effect within our relationships with others. **Peck, S-**Road Less Traveled-The Outmoded Map

and effect allows the Human Developmental Stage of Maturation to occur.

However, it is important to understand that Cause and Effect as it relates to Psychological Maturation does not refer to a commonly held belief in "reaping what we sow" (alluding to punishment or reward). Nor does it refer to **correlation,** the statistical model used in Scientific Experiments which measures the relationship between dependent and independent variables. An article in the **Encarta Encyclopedia** referring to correlation states "it is natural—but incorrect—to assume that because one variable predicts another, the first must have caused the second. For example, one might assume that frustration triggers aggression, or that friendships foster health. Regardless of how intuitive or accurate these conclusions may be, *correlation does not prove causation.*

The QUICKSAND of Negative Energy

I visualize the concept of Cause and Effect as a force of **Positive Energy** (*Love, Reality, Respect*) floating above the QUICKSAND [19] of Negative Energy (*fear, resentment, unrealistic perceptions and expectations*) that trap our potential mature development within the confines of dysfunction. Only by letting go of unrealistic expectations (Negative Energy) are we able to float free into the Positive Energy (Cause & Effect) of love and respect for ourselves and others.

Human Beings are born with a seed of **Unique Human Potential.** We may choose to explore it or not. Development of Human Potential demands **Psychological Maturation.** I perceive Human Life as a multifaceted arena of Instructional Opportunities within Human Relationships, Life situations and Universal connections (*serendipity, dreams, synchronicity, intuition, meditations*) for development of both human and spiritual potential.

---

[19] **Quicksand-**A deep mass of loose wet sand that sucks down any heavy object falling onto its surface
Quicksand-A hidden trap from which escape is difficult or impossible
(*Encarta Dictionary (English North America)*

I recognize Psychological **Maturation** as the doorway leading to a more complete understanding of our unique potential and fit in the Universe . . . and only by learning to make choices based on the **Laws of Cause and Effect** are we free to explore both our human and spiritual missions as we **Dance to the Music of the Universe.**

PUTTING IT ALL TOGETHER

	Rules	Beliefs about Rules	"Roadmaps" Of Life	Life Scripts static Roles	Red Threads
Person A A woman who believed she had to teach her successful husband the correct ways of life.	• People should follow the rules • People who love their parents follow their parents rules • Anger must be justified • Be Perfect	• When my husband doesn't do what I ask it proves he doesn't love me • Criticism means you think I am not perfect	• Teacher of children • Instructor of the "right" way to live • Observer of others behavior	Teach others the correct way to live	*Admitting others Rules are valid means I have been wrong all my life*
Person B An extremely overweight woman who kept waiting for others to realize she was beautiful inside	• People are mean and unloving • Others cannot be trusted • People always put themselves ahead of me • People value others for how they look instead of what they are like in side.	• People should love me no matter how I look. If they don't it means they are shallow and unfair • I allow Others hold the key to my happiness	• I am a Caterpillar waiting in my cocoon for another to discover me and realize I am a Butterfly and not the Caterpillar I look like.	Waiting in my cocoon to be discovered for the butterfly I am rather than the caterpillar I look like. Eating until I am fat and unappealing.	*I am afraid I am a loser. I eat to get fat and repel others. I can't let others close enough to know me. I am afraid others will learn I am the loser my parents said I was.*
Person C Successful Woman who kept picking Underachieving men	You "should" be able to tell the good guys from the bad guys	If the frog I picked doesn't turn into the prince when I kiss him it proves I am too stupid to pick the right frog.	• High achiever at work and school • Teacher of frogs on how to be a Prince, but the Frogs never learn • Loser with men	Cinderella waiting for Prince charming. I continue to kiss frogs believing each to be the Prince and be disappointed when they are not the Prince.	*I am afraid to stop waiting for Prince Charming b/c I may find out the world is not the way I think it is and want it to be. And I should be able to tell the good guys from the bad.*

Cause & Effect

**Universal Laws of Cause & Effect underlie Objective Reality.
seemingly chaotic events have order and are explainable
when the whole situation pertaining to them is known.**

The

"map"

REALITY

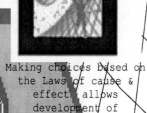

Dancing to the
"Music" of the
Universe

Making choices based on
the Laws of cause &
effect allows
development of
psychological maturation.

searching for REALITY

THE PATH TO PSYCHOLOGICAL MATURITY
RUNS THROUGH THE FABRIC OF THE UNIVERSE
AND IS PAVED WITH REALISTIC LAWS OF CAUSE & EFFECT

Laws of "cause & Effect run
through the fabric of the Universe.

Lessons of Life are based on
the Laws of Cause & Effect.

<u>CHAPTER 9</u>

<u>Lesson 2A</u>
Personal Responsibility

"Directing" your own life

"Directing " your own life

Lesson 2a
Personal Responsibility

SELF LOVE IS NOT SELFISHNESS, but a necessary characteristic of a Mature person. We all have the right to get our needs met unless it is at the *legitimate* expense of another. It is important to understand how the **Rules we live by influence our ability to take appropriate responsibility** for our psychological needs and development. Each of us has the right to get our needs met in order to develop our unique potential but never at the legitimate expenses of others.

TAKING RESPONSIBILITY FOR LEGITIMATE PERSONAL NEEDS IS NOT SELFISH. Many of us are traditionally taught to "turn the other cheek" or take care of others first. Many feel guilty or selfish if the needs of others are not put first. Some of us feel too psychologically weak to care for ourselves at all. Others believe their role doesn't allow it. Still others just don't know how.

APPROPRIATE PERSONAL RESPONSIBILITY includes self-discipline and knowledge of personal competence and potency. Self discipline requires knowing how of set limits, ability to delay gratification and tolerate frustration, organize and plan your life, face reality and accept the truth. Self discipline leads to development of personal potential, successful communication and satisfying relationships.

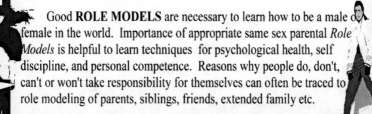

Good **ROLE MODELS** are necessary to learn how to be a male or female in the world. Importance of appropriate same sex parental *Role Models* is helpful to learn techniques for psychological health, self discipline, and personal competence. Reasons why people do, don't, can't or won't take responsibility for themselves can often be traced to role modeling of parents, siblings, friends, extended family etc.

Lesson 2 A—
PERSONAL RESPONSIBILITY

We are responsible for our life, Happiness, Choices, goals, and mistakes.

What is appropriate personal Responsibility?

We are personally responsible for our happiness, choices, life, goals and mistakes. **At any time, our life situation is the direct result of all the past choices we have made. We do not have the right to get our needs met at the expense of another. While a child is at the mercy of others, adults have many choices . . . even if not those we are comfortable with. Personal responsibility demands the clear understanding of the difference between Selfishness and appropriate love and respect for the self. Ignorance of this difference often lies at the core of the inability or unwillingness to assume appropriate personal responsibility.**

Human beings are responsible for taking appropriate responsibility for the self, personal happiness, choices, life goals, achievement and relationships. Appropriate responsibility makes a distinction between Self Love and narcissism (selfishness). Inability to take Appropriate Personal Responsibility may result from 1) feelings of weakness, 2) assumption of a role that precludes personal responsibility, 3) not knowing how to take responsibility for the self, 4) inability to take appropriate care of the self or 5) refusal to take Personal Responsibility.

Development of REALISTIC PERSONAL RESPONSIBILITY is the result of many life experiences including the knowledge of what appropriate personal responsibility includes, the Role Self Discipline plays in our lives, what has been learned from Role Models (siblings, friends, family members, media models, etc) as well as the Role Modeling of our Same Sex parents.

CHARACTERISTICS OFTEN affecting ability to take appropriate personal responsibility

CATAGORIES OF PERSONAL RESPONSIBILITY	
Beliefs about Personal responsibility are often the results of Rules learned as a child. Getting personal needs met is essential for the development of unique potential and maximal psychological development. The following discussion of Personal Responsibility pinpoints specific aspects of Life that influence ability or inability to assume appropriate care of the Self.	
	"Beliefs" about Personal Responsibility "Is getting my own needs met Selfish?" Balancing Self Interest And Self Sacrifice
Where is the "real" Me?  *Examine Your path* Closely *For Clues*	The role of *Self Discipline* In our personal search for self
	ROLE MODELS & MENTORS- The power of influence Personal identity - essence of the self

"Beliefs" about Personal Responsibility
"Is getting my own needs met Selfish?"

Balancing Self Interest And Self Sacrifice

PERSONAL RESPONSIBILITY

Discussion of the problem Overview of the problem

BELIEFS ABOUT PERSONAL RESPONSIBILITY are often the results of Rules learned as a child. Getting personal needs met is essential for the development of unique potential and maximal psychological development. Selfishness can be understood in terms of the Rules we have learned for our life and the Roles we have learned to be comfortable within.

We are personally responsible for our happiness, choices, life, goals and mistakes. Ignorance of the difference between selfishness and appropriate love and respect for the self often lies at the core of inability or unwillingness to assume personal responsibility.

It is important to understand how the Rules we have learned to live by influence our ability to take appropriate responsibility for our psychological development. Self love is not selfishness, but a necessary characteristic of a Mature Adult. Taking care of **legitimate** personal needs is not selfish. Each of us has the right to get our needs met in order to develop our unique potential but not at the expense of others. As mentioned previously, there is a big difference between needs and wants. And while few of us get everything we **want,** we must receive what we **need if we are to develop personal potential.**

Many of us were traditionally taught to "turn the other cheek" or "take care of others first". Many feel guilty or selfish if the needs of others are not put first. Some of us feel too psychologically weak to care for ourselves at all. Others believe their role in life doesn't allow it. Still others just don't know how. Why is this?

Research, Literature and Religious writings contain many distinctive definitions of human characteristics commonly associated with `self interest vs welfare of others`. What is the origin of these mandates for appropriate human behavior and how is it possible to make sense of their contradictions?

Devotion to the **Welfare of others (Altruism)** is clearly revealed in the principle underlying the **Golden Rule**—***Do to others as they would have others do to them.*** Altruism is the English form of the French word *altruisme* created by the 19th-century French philosopher and sociologist Auguste Comte from the Italian word *altrui,* meaning "of or to others[1]." The word has gradually come into more general use. In philosophy **Altruism** describes a theory of conduct that aspires to the good of others as the **ultimate** <u>end</u> **for any moral action.** In theories of ethics **Altruism** is the antithesis (exact opposite) of egoism (self-interest). However, the fact is that p*eople are sometimes **Altruistic.** A a result it is hard to avoid the conclusion that people do sometimes act on non-self-interested, ethical values.*

Self Interest (Egocentricity) is sometimes defined in Literature and Research in terms of two similar sounding words (with different meaning) **Egocentrism** and **Egoism**[2]. A **HighBeam Research** article states although these two words are often used interchangeable in Philosophy they do in fact show a distinction.

- **Egoism** refers to theories in which self-interest is regarded as the primary motivating factor. An *egoist* believes an individual should seek as an end result only his or her own welfare: T*his conduct is characterized by ruthless egoism. APA Dictionary*—***Selfishness and a disregard for the needs of others***
- **Egotism** implies a vain self-absorption as a matter of behavior rather than an ethical principle, and an *egotist* is somebody who behaves in a selfish or self-centered way: *Her egotism*

---

[1]   Encarta Encyclopedia

[2]   *Highbeam—Research site*

makes her ignore other people's concerns. APA Dictionary—An Excessive Conceit Or Preoccupation With One's Own Importance.

- **Egocentricity**—*Piaget. Jean (1896-1980). Swiss Psychologist.* best known for his pioneering work on the development of intelligence in children defined the concept of Egocentricity as perceiving situation from one's own perspective, believing that others also see things from the same point of view and that events will elicit the same thoughts, feelings and behavior in others as in oneself.

My own understanding of these often difficult to separate constructs include

- **Narcissism**—Excessive Self Love and Personal Needs as paramount. Those who perceive themselves to reside at the Center of the Universe and believe their needs and personal perceptions are supreme exhibit an immature personal level of Psychological Maturation that can be defined as Narcissistic.
- **Egocentrism**—Perception of the self as residing at the center of the Universe, inability to identify where personal thoughts and perceptions stop and those of others begin and belief that personal thoughts are the correct and logical ones. Some perceive the self as the most important person in the world while others view the self to be perceived by others as the most disgusting person in the world.
- **Egocentricity** in children is normal and usually grown out of before adulthood. However, Adults who rigidly believe that others (if they knew the truth) would see things from the same point of view and that events will elicit the same thoughts, feelings and behavior in others as in oneself. can usually be identified in the APA DSM Diagnostic Manual as Character Disorders.

In light of the foregoing discussion of egocentricity and altruism, it's obvious that few of us fall into the category of **Sainthood**. And while many if not most of us are taught to turn the other cheek and take care of others first, few of us do so without serious misgivings concerning the mandates we have been taught. As a result many shade the truth concerning their true behaviors, others pretend to misunderstand others requests for help, while others comment they have already "donated to charity" or some other excuse.

My own conclusions concerning these dichotomous situations fall into the categories of both personal Morality and Psychological Maturation. Each of us at times may need to wrestle with a decision concerning whether to put the needs of ourselves or another first. In order to make a Psychology mature decision we must clearly define to ourselves whether the other is able to take responsibility for themselves or not, whether helping the other will clearly result in our own inability to provide for our own need and finally as a result of a clear understanding of the whole situation whether the needs of the other or the self must then take precedence.

Such decisions are often very difficult for parents when an adult child is in need. Such situations are often fraught with pain and anxiety. As a former instructor once told me when I asked for clarification concerning such a situation—"Before pushing our bird out of the family nest, parents must be sure that our bird does not have a broken wing"[3].

Personal decisions must fall into the range of morality as well as the demands of psychological maturation. Decisions are unique to each of us and arrived at through great forethought and a personally arrived at philosophy of life concerning this type of decision.

ABILITY VS INABILITY TO TAKE PERSONAL RESPONSIBILITY

The Test of Ego and Cognitive Development identifies many personal characteristics connected to ability vs **Inability** to assume Personal Responsibility.

- Characteristics correlated with Inability include feelings of weakness, assumption of a role that precludes personal responsibility, not having learned methods for taking personal responsibility, etc. Some people refuse to do so.

---

[3]   Colbert, James, PhD—Lake Forest, Ca—Former Instructor and supervisor

- Conversely, Characteristics correlated with Ability to assume personal responsibility include those reporting achievement of **personal happiness, making good choices, relationship happiness as well as knowledge that Self Love is not the same as selfishness.**

Feelings of Weakness can be seen in those with Low Self Esteem, discomfort with setting appropriate limits for the self, feelings of ineptness, powerlessness and those who can't stand up for themselves. Many reporting feelings of weakness say they feel more comfortable in relationships when others are in charge and helpless when not in a relationship. Reports of being afraid to go to dinner, a movie, or on a trip by themselves are common. Others report the need to be in a relationship to ensure having someone to take care of them. Other comments about feelings of weakness include having always felt too "small" and/or young to make personal decisions. Feelings of powerless to make life changes. Some indicate perplexity concerning reasons whey people often "walk all over me" as well as feeling too weak to "keep people from taking advantage of me". And finally many report allowing others to not only put their needs "ahead of mine but at the expense of mine".

Many with perceived inability to take personal responsibility perceive their expected Role to <u>preclude</u> personal responsible for setting individual goals for their own personal happiness". Assumption of a Role That Precludes Personal Responsibility for Individual Goals are seen in those who believe that many of their own relationships with others do not allow taking responsibility for personal needs, achievement or advancement. These behavioral and philosophical requirements are commonly seen in those reporting **Gender** as the main reason for deferral to marital partners. Others report Religious Philosophy or Cultural Mandates as requirements for their role with others. Some are comfortable with such expectations other are not.

Others find themselves agreeing with others even when perceptions of others belief are incorrect because they don't feel it is their place to disagree. Many of both sexes report believing the man should be the "Head of the Household" and that Men should protect their wives because women are weaker than men. Others don't feel able to "get ahead" at work, because the Role they have been taught to assume in life does not allow them to "stand out". This can be seen in those who often feel like the child they were, rather than the adult they are. Such responses are often made by those who were told in childhood that "Children should be seen and not heard", who obey Rules even when they seem unfair or even unjust and in those who have a difficult time saying "NO". Others say they have a difficult time asserting themselves because of a belief that it is not polite to be in conflict with others.

If some of the above responses from others strike a sore spot in your own life, ask yourself "Where did you learn to think as you do? "Were you taught that getting your own personal needs met is selfish? Did important "Role Models" from your past, accept appropriate personal responsibility for themselves or not? Do you feel free and work hard to identify and develop your individual potential? If not, why not? And finally "Do internal or interpersonal conflicts interfere with acceptance of personal responsibility"?

In Psychology **Locus Of Control** is considered an important aspect of Personality. The concept was developed in the 1950's by Jullian Rotter, PhD (1916-1985) and refers to whether a person believes the main causes of events in life are the result of Internally chosen personal decisions or external facets such as fate, luck or other exterior circumstances.

I help my Clients visualize the concept of **Locus of Control** as a Tree standing in a strong wind. Do the winds of life blow all the leaves off their branches or is their Tree Of Life able to stand firm, bending to Reality when necessary but left to with roots and bark strong enough to rebound. Research indicates that those who rely on an internal Locus of Control for Decision Making are usually more self assured and comfortable with decisions.

It's important to remember, however, that a comfortable level of internal Locus of Control is not the same as that shown by Egocentric Adults who rigidly stick to their own point of view without consideration of all factors that might contribute to an issue at hand.

And finally personally arrived at Moral points of view must be taken into account when important and conflictual decisions are needed. One of my most impressive College Courses presented the quandary of "Who" would you throw overboard if your ship had sunk and you were in charge of deciding which of 6 survivors in the Life Boat must be sacrificed if the other 5 were to make it to safety. Would it be 1) the 5 year old little boy with Down's Syndrome, 2) the 93 year old Rocket Scientist, 3) the young male on his way to his wedding, 4) the President of an important Country, 5) the Pastor of a large religious congregation on his way with a $1,000,000 check to help the poor or 6) himself? Of course such decisions are almost never required by ordinary persons. However, although outrageously unlikely, such an exercise might help each of us arrive at an understanding of what our Personally arrived at Moral Code might entail.

OVEVIEW OF <u>MIND SET FOR PROBLEM SOLVING</u>

Getting appropriate personal needs met is not selfishness. "Beliefs about Personal responsibility are often the results of Rules learned as a child. Getting personal needs met is essential for the development of unique potential and maximal psychological development.

Ask yourself the following Questions (unique to each of us) to help define yourself as a person, understand how your relationships have or have not contributed to your own Psychological Maturation and define your understanding of the Roles played in life and with others and the reasons for them.

- **What is your Mission in Life?**
- **What is your Unique Potential as a person?**
- **What is appropriate responsibility for yourself?**
- **Think of an example of when others needs should come first?**
- **What are your Rules about taking responsibility for yourself. Where did these Rules come from?**
- **Ask yourself if your relationships manifest personal powerlessness, low self esteem and/or LOW self worth?**
- **What are my rights?**

Most of us have asked questions such as 1) "Why was I born?", "Why am I here?", "Is there a purpose to being alive?" and "If there is a Purpose . . . What is my Mission in the world?" These questions, unique to each of us, can only be answered by asking the additional question "Where is the REAL Me?" It is uncontroversial that we are each born with a seed of Unique Human Potential. **Development of Human potential** demands **Psychological Maturation**. And only by resolving the problems that deter us from psychological maturation are we free to explore our mission in the Universe. Personal Choices are presented to each of us on our Path through the Universe in the form of choices, serendipity, synchronicity and problem solving with other people **Psychological Maturation** is the doorway leading to a more complete understanding of our unique potential and "fit" **in the Universe.**

Inability to take Appropriate Personal Responsibility may result from 1) feelings of weakness, 2) assumption of a role that precludes personal responsibility, 3) not knowing how to take responsibility for the self, 4) inability to take appropriate care of the self or 5) refusal to take Personal Responsibility.

Feelings of Weakness and Powerlessness

During my many years of working with clients I have learned that Vignettes[4] and Visualizations[5] are often a very effective method for decreasing levels of personal powerless, increasing levels of self esteem and helping my clients discover successful methods for assuming appropriate personal responsibility for decision making.

During my internship years in an Orange County Hospital while treating adolescents with drug, alcohol and other problems I often used the old adage of having each young person describe themselves in terms of Self Perception to identify unconscious feelings concerning themselves. **"If you were an animal"**, I would ask them, **"What kind**

---

[4] **Vignette—short descriptive pieces of literary writings**
[5] **Visualization—**a vivid mental picture of something either positive or negative in order to promote a desired outcome to a problem.

of an animal would you be?" or **"If you were a Car, what kind of a car would you be?"** Such visualizations of self often lead to important insights concerning personal perceptions and helps arrive at reasons for personal behaviors and ideas. **Feelings of being too weak to take personal responsibility is also seen in many woman who present themselves as** coy, seductive and/or helpless. Over identify with the feminine role and assumption of subtle manipulation is also scored on Psychological Assessment instruments[6].

Grow into your clothes

Many years ago, a client came to therapy with his wife, feeling as though he were the dregs of the world. His father had committed suicide, after telling his son repeatedly that males, (father and son) were worthless. My client was a wonderful, intelligent adult male who had finished graduate school, earned vocational admiration for designing highly successful marketing skills in national companies. It was difficult for this client to ignore the face of the father, who looked back at him every time he looked in a mirror to shave or comb his hair. It took years of SELF reevaluation to give himself the credit he so richly deserved. During treatment, I designed a visualization (**Grow into your clothes**) for him to perceive himself as a little tiny man-child, dressed in the much larger clothes of an adult . . . arms and legs of clothing empty . . . laid out on the floor in front of him. Only by helping this man imagine himself "growing into the clothes of an Adult" was he finally able to perceive himself as the successful Adult is rather than the looser child in the body of a man his father had designed for him.

My own childhood was not much different from many who grew up in the depression era. I can still feel myself shrink in the headlights of my father gaze and stern admonition as his quiet words rang firmly through the formerly happy dinner table atmosphere **"Don't speak unless your spoken to", "Who do you think you are"?, Don't contradict your elders"** and **"Don't show Off"** . . . if I were to offer a personal opinion. But the final painful, confusing edicts was heard over and over again during conversations with family and friends.

---

[6]   FTW (Feel too weak) MMPI Scale 5 Females low T = women

My father's stern abominations were confusing and difficult to understand however, because apparently it was OK to be in dance recitals and singing contests where I was revered for doing well and getting the Superior ratings he wanted me to have. For years although I was encouraged to play the part of the "Big Star" and Winner in Contests I lived in a grey conflicted reality where Personal Decisions were expected to be left to the external discretion of knowledgeable and revered authorities

My professional opinion concerning the consequences of such Parental admonishments as those listed above is that a child hearing them is likely to come to a frightening but logical conclusion **"Don/t challenge authority.** And although the Words were never spoken . . . the message was clear . . . **"Thinking for Yourself"** is a dangerous activity resulting in loss of love and respect of those most dear to our heart. The consequences of a fear driven decision to decline "Thinking For The Self" is a Nail In The Coffin of personal responsibility.

MY ROLE PRECLUDES IT

It is important for all of us to examine **Role Models** we have been exposed to in life and decide whether they have provided rationale for appropriate or inappropriate influence over our current life style. Many women brought up in the eras before woman's lib remembers important females in their lives who made similar strong suggestions to daughters, nieces, etc. as follows:

> **"Remember that men usually think in terms of winning and losing". "Never let your husband think you are trying to tell him what to do". "Always remember 2 things, 1) that men don't like pushy women" and "We must develop methods of getting what we want without appearing to be pushy". "Oh and I almost forgot, HaHa . . . "don't forget the old saying that "That a really smart women can usually think of a way to present the issue at hand so the man thinks it was his idea all the time" . . . "Ha Ha . . . Remember that, sweetie, and I promise . . . They'll never know what hit them". Ha ha ha.**

While it is true that many women are genuinely interested in traditional female roles, I have found that most of my clients are not and come to therapy frantic because they have internalized the belief that God has designed their role as weaker than their mate, unable to care adequately for themselves but needing to take care of their spouse by "walking three steps behind and wiping his butt for him". My own therapeutic response to this is "I'm sure God did not designate ½ of the human race as helpers for the other half" And when I wrote my dissertation on the differences between male and female successful business manager, the Research clearly states that in spite of books such as "Men are from Mars and Women are from Venus" **women and men show few differences.** The major difference of course is gender. However, research also clearly indicates that the differences referred to by many are overwhelmingly the result of social and cultural programming, not biological mandates.

APPROPRIATE REPONIBILIY FOR THE SELF

Much has been written in the literature concerning Negotiable vs Non negotiable values. In my own opinion, conclusions concerning personal definitions of these term is imperative for both personal and relationship comfort.

My clinical definition of **Negotiable Values are** those we can either compromise on or agree to disagree about. In friendships it is often possible to compromise or agree to disagree.

As mentioned in Lesson 1 (Control), we usually "fall in Love" and marry for reasons connected to chemical attraction and love of such mundane things as chocolate ice cream or musical similarities. Unfortunately, however, open, honest discussion of personal **Non Negotiable Values**, are usually disregarded until the chemical attraction wears down, or a child is born and we are forced to identify for our self (and our spouse) issues concerning our true philosophy of life. However, such discussions often require much soul searching and clarification about which of our values are or are not negotiable.

Such Spousal Relationship issues are rarely if ever appropriately left for discussion until after marriage. Why?? Because after the Chemistry wears off, a child is born or an important national election occurs most of us are surprised, upset or even devastated to realize our loved one is "not walking on the same path" as we are. It is unlikely a diehard Republican will ever be happily married to a "dyed in the wool" Democrat. Likewise, it is unlikely a Born again Christian, Jehovah Witness or other devoutly religious person will truly be happy married to an Agnostic. And when a serious Parenting disagreement occurs concerning whether "our child "will be better off in a "Time out" or "Getting a good spanking" the "You Know What" is likely to "Hit the Fan".

For the above reasons, I clearly discuss the importance of having objectively arrived at Personal Negotiable vs Non negotiable values **before marriage or remarriage** (if divorce was the only way for solution of such serious problems in the last relationship). After clients have objectively (clearly thought through) vs subjectively[7] arrived at Personal Negotiable and/or Non negotiable Values, it is very important to be honest with potential Spouses concerning them.

I present the importance of Non Negotiable values and the importance of being our True Selves in relationships with clients in two Visualizations (The Wall Flower at the Dance and Going to the Grocery Store) designed for clear, funny understanding of very unfunny subjects.

I present my visualization of a Wallflower at the Dance as a shy young person sitting quietly on the outskirts of the dance floor waiting for someone to ask for a dance. Maybe 10 out of the 100 at the dance will think she/he is pretty, handsome or interesting enough to consider dancing with. He/she may be interested in 2 or 3 out of the 10 who asked. However, 2-10 out of 100 are not very good odds for picking a life partner.

---

[7] Subjective—Arrived at from an emotional vs cognitive frame of reference

As an alternative to waiting for life to happen, I present the visualization of a person Going to the Grocery Store. Walking to the Produce Department seeking the type of Green Beans needed for a planned casserole this person selects the lighter color beans because they are softer and more in line with the dinner Menu. Strolling through the aisle containing canned fruit the chopper chooses Royal Anne Cherries for the Pie being planning because they are the variety preferred. And finally almost finished, the shopper enters the Meat and Fish department where the softer, more tender Fish instead of Beef briquette is chosen because of a love for Fish instead of Beef.

I discuss **Going to the Grocery Store** in the same vein as presenting yourself to others in social gatherings. Be honest about who you are and don't try to just "fit" in with others to fear others won't like you if you're honest about what you really think. It's true some won't. But it's better to know whether you have a potential fit early in a potential relationship rather than too late.

I remember a Christmas Party in San Juan Capistrano right after receiving my Masters Degree in Psychology. My next door neighbor (apparently being honest after several cocktails) said "Skipi, I hope you don't plan going any further in College. You know most men don't like highly educated women". I realize this is may be true for some men, however, I also know that other men, do like educated women very much. My husband is one that does and my education is one of the things he is most proud of me about.

Happily marital spouses can be visualized as walking on separate but closely connected, paths of life. These relationships contain similar non negotiable values and other Values that can be negotiated, agreed to disagreed about, etc. Their separate Paths, while not overlapping remain close enough to comfortably hold hands as they journey through life.

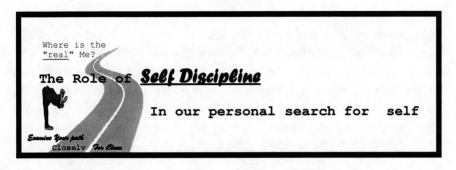

Overview of Problem

THE ROLE OF <u>SELF DISCIPLINE</u> IN OUR SEARCH FOR PERSONAL RESPONSIBILITY

Appropriate Responsibility for the self includes self discipline. Questions to ask the self, concerning why responsibility for myself is or is not taken include 1) knowledge and methods of Limit Setting for the self in relationships, 2) Roles of life played in relationships with others. 3) Feelings of being too weak to take responsibility, 4) Whether my perceived role in life precludes taking appropriate Responsibility for the Self? 5) Do I know how to take responsibility for myself?" and even 6) "Do I externalize Personal Problems as a result denial and rationalization?"

THE SHADOW

 He sat in my office, crying. He had lost his job, again. Over the last 10 years his life had steadily become more desperate. This time, without his job and money for rent he stared into his future . . . homeless, living in his car. This young man could "sell snow to an Eskimo" His silver tongue had opened many doors to good jobs which never lasted In a effort to control the mounting stress he felt, as he tried harder and harder to actually providing an employer what had been promised, he self medicated himself. He bought the "Drugs" from a Dr when he could convince one of the legitimacy of his need or "on the street" when he couldn't Once, under the influence of his medication, his personality changed. Feeling less stress but "On top of the World—his behavior slowly but steadily became strange, angry and insulting. Sooner or Later be would be fired.

243

What happened". I asked gently, knowing the answer would be similar to ones he had told himself & others for over 15 years. "They were jealous of me", he answered angrily "the boss was mad and wanted to get rid of me. He was afraid I would lake his job. He didn't want anyone to know I could do a better job than be could". Tears streaming down his face, the Young Man cried for the poor "victim," he truly perceived himself to be. In agony, he glimpsed **The Shadow**. a "something . . . in the dark recesses of his mind. "What is that", he thought, "could that be what is causing my misfortune?". But as before, he ran from it in tenor. *"Stop"* called **The Shadow.** *"I can save your life",* but the young man was so terrified be continued to run blindly . . . way from **The Voice of Personal Responsibility** . . . as it called vainly . . . for him to stop.

The Masks of Anxiety—Denial, Repression, Rationalization-Externalizing Blame.

DISCUSSION OF REASONS WHY WE CAN'T—WON'T TAKE PERSONAL RESPONSIBILITY

Reasons why many cannot take personal responsibility appears to be a result of many things including inability to control impulses, unconscious causes and conflicts and sometimes even Organicity. Many who are able to take personal responsibility can control impulses, defend against unconscious conflicts, have a good understanding of who they are as a person and often have an above average IQ,

- **Referring to Clients answering Questions on The Test of Ego and Cognitive Development I find** those with high scores on inability to take responsibility answered question identifying reasons as follows: "No matter how hard I try, my life never seems to turn out right and Even though I want to do what I know I should, I am often unable to keep from making the wrong choices. Other indicates disability to being unable to resist doing things I know I shouldn't as well as "I hate the way my life is turning out, but I don't seem able to help myself" and "I often act impulsively and regret my behaviors afterward". Some even chose such flippant responses as "Act in Haste, and Repent at Leisure" is an old saying that accurately reflects my life style" to "I wish most of my past decisions had turned out better" And finally others externalized blame in answering with "Being with Certain friends and family members causes me to do things I shouldn't" to "Society is keeping me from advancing toward success".

- **Others responses included the category of being unwilling to take responsibility for the self due to** defiance, giving up, belief that it's no use as a result of fate, etc. Reasons for those answering in the category of Won't take responsibility for myself included "I refuse to be told what to do", "I often resist following the Rules. " Others responded from a category of legal problems such as "I have often been in trouble because of disruptive behavior" and "I have often been in trouble with the law because I hate to follow rules." Some seem to sent societies rules with answers such as "People should be able to choose whether to adhere to societies expectations or not." and "People should be able to live the way they want to regardless of what the law says". Other reasons for high scores on inability run from "Planning future goals is a waste of time because life is the result of fate", "Nothing I ever tried turned out the way I wanted. I refuse to keep trying.", to I usually just do what appeals to me on the spur of the moment because I hate making plans.".

MIND SET FOR PROBLEM SOLVING
(What caused the Problem)

Self Discipline for children is an area of parenting revered by most parents. However, many attempt to train their children with methods of discipline incompatible for their goals. Many adults have unconsciously internalized the stern eye of a parent whose reproachments "Never question authority", "Don't speak unless your spoken to" and the old favorite "Children should be seen and not heard" continue to reside in their adult subconscious. The Psychodynamic concept of Transference (a feeling about something happening in the present that reminds them of something that originated in the past) is felt by many adults who have no idea what is at the core of their current resentment, feelings of weakness, anger, or other reaction.

Understanding the Problem

Its important that we understand as Adults how the parenting we received in the past effects our present life. Many of us continue to feel "too weak or small" to challenge Authority. As mentioned in a previous section, I find many who still haven't consciously decided on an age when it becomes appropriate to respectfully disagree with authority. I come across this characteristic in many adults who report comfort with stringent structure in the work place, the Armed Services, Police Department, etc. However, it is imperative that those who are comfortable in stringent structure are compliant as a result of their own life philosophy <u>not</u> because they have settled for the Philosophy of a loved one, Work place, Church etc without consciously decided upon personal agreement.

Many who do not understand the reasons for unhappiness, feelings of being put upon by others, watching their life never turn out like they planned do not understand the importance of developing skills related to personal discipline as individuals and in relationships with others. Research cites that a teenager who openly resists parental rules may in fact be more psychologically healthy than one whose conformity bears characteristics of timid submission.

Personal decisions concerning development of assertion skills, methods for setting personal goals, personal decision making and methods of coping with life's disappointments are all closely intertwined within the category of Self Discipline. Many of us do not realize that we have the ability to set personal limits and do not need to continue to live in situations we consider unfair, mean spirited, etc. We have all lived through situations of irritation at others in restaurants (loud voices, drunken conversations), movies (loud whispering, beeping cell phones) or shopping (others cutting in line) when knowledge and use of <u>appropriate</u> **Assertion Skills** could have resulted in more pleasant experiences. Learning Successful Decision Making skills is also an often overlooked behavior that could lead to a more comfortable and successful outcomes.

Functional Coping Strategies within **Dissonant Life Situations** require increased levels of Ego Development (Unique Independence and Emotional Differentiation) as well as Cognitive Maturation in the areas of Frustration Tolerance, Ability to Delay Gratification and factual vs emotional evaluation of the situation under consideration. **Coping Strategies** for **Life Situations of** <u>Tragic Proportions</u> may be more successfully faced from the Psychological Maturation Dimension (Task 1V) of Spiritual Philosophy of Life. I personally do not see tragedy as God's punishment but rather as opportunities to explore our spiritual Path in the Universe and try to understand our Human Mission and Lessons of Life.

The value of Functional (realistic) Coping Strategies within our personal and relationship situations may be more objectively perceived within the context of **Cause And Effect**. For example how may my behavior have affected the behavior of the other or what have I been thinking, feeling or doing that keeps me from learning to deal with the reality of my present situation? Do I consider the aspects of a conflicting situation **negotiable or non-negotiable**? Why or Why Not?

It is important we don't misunderstand what we can change and what we can't or what's fair and what isn't. Literature citing the edict to "Drop your expectations, shoulds, oughts, perceptions of fairness, etc. because they do not reflect reality" is reflected in the ABC theory[8] of Albert Ellis. It is also helpful to understand what types of Defenses[9] we have learned to use and why or why not they have worked well or not at all. Remember, objective reality is truth and must be dealt with. Bitterness and resentment concerning reality is a waste of time. We must learn to Face reality and accept the truth concerning our situations because there is no choice.

Increasing ability to face reality and accept the truth (Resilience) allows Human Psychological Maturation to develop. Resilience (Psychological buoyancy) is a characteristic of Psychological Maturation. And as mentioned in a precious section it is important to take the concept of Locus of Control into consideration for conclusions concerning whether the main causes of events are a result of Internally chosen personal decisions or external facets such as fate, luck or other exterior circumstances.

---

[8]   Albert Ellis, Cognitive Therapy. **A-B-C** theory. It's not the **A**ntecedent (what happens) that causes your problems, it's the **B**elief about what happens that **C**auses your Problems.

[9]   The Psychological defensive mechanisms we have adopted to protect ourselves from Anxiety.

Much has been written about Problem Solving and understanding the concept of who the problem belongs to. Potential Opportunities for development of Psychological Maturity) are presented to us each day as we walk down our path of life in the form of situations in which we can learn to understand others and attempt to find a way to live in harmany. Sometimes it can be done, other times it may not be possible.

RELATIONSHIP CONFLICTS

An increased understanding of the Category of Self Discipline presents the opportunity for learning to deal with the issues of angry resentment and Whose Problem belongs to Who. For Example: Have you ever heard or said something like . . . ?

"Why SHOULD I GO TO THERAPY?? . . . IT'S YOUR FAULT!!!" "I do "everything" for you. Now, it's your turn to do something for me. "You caused the problem. Why do I need help?." "You should go to therapy with me!!! Look at all I've done for you". "You're the one that "screwed" me all up in the first place. Why it now "My Problem?"

Whose Problem is it, anyway? Each of us may believe the other is wrong (has a problem). Although I perceive the other as **"causing"** a me a problem, if they don't agree they are the cause of the conflict, the Problem "belongs to me". We are responsible for solving problems that affect us. A problem becomes "mine" when something outside myself causes me irritation.

Although it would be nice for others to change . . . or even agree to discuss "my" problem (the problem I have with them) they may refuse. Remember, we can only control ourselves. It's true . . . Life isn't fair. We can't force others to change or agree with us. There are many different views of the way life "should" be lived. We each have a right to our opinion. Do I expect others to change and fit into my Map of the "correct" way to live? Do they? Are others willing to change, because I want them to? Am I . . . because they want me to? Do I realize how my attitudes and behaviors effect my relationships?

Even though we believe others would be better off doing things "a better way" (usually my way) they may disagree. I can try to problem solve the conflict with another (if I want to) . . . <u>and the other is free to cooperate . . . or not.</u>

UNDERSTANDING THE "WHY" OF OUR RELATIONSHIPS

Most of us never contemplate why we marry the type of person we choose until problems in our relationships present themselves. However, **It's important to understand whether the type of person we are attracted to is one that will last happily or ends up in problematic situations. I call the following vignette "My Type" because I believe that the type of person we are attracted to is an <u>unconscious </u>response to something we were attracted to in the distant past. It is a type of Transference (Something that happens in the present that reminds us of something that that happened in the past).**

For example a woman who grew up in the 40's attending Movies with her parents staring Betty Grable, Glen Ford or others in movies about Gangsters and the girls who fell in love with them. Although the girls in the movies usually spent a lot of time cryng because the man she loved treated her badly, eventually the Gangster type man she loved realized he was wrong, that she was the one he loved and they walked happily off into the sunset to live happily ever after.

Although as Adults we may consciously realize the possibility of riding off happily into the sunset with our Type, many of us continue to get caught up in some type of past transferences because it feels familiar and we are still so unconsciously attracted to "Blue Eyes", a "Crooked Smile", or some other "Charming" characteristic that we don't stop to evaluate the reality of the situation until it is too late. As a result I always help my clients searching for clarification of why their marriage hasn't worked well to consider whether My Type might be connected with transferences from the past such as a man who reminds me of a favorite uncle who loved me so much (but who was unlucky in love and married and

divorced 3 times) or a handsome man whose voice sounds like that of a long ago family friend (with a self assured attitude and history of a constantly argued with others).

It's sad but true that many of us continue to get involved, marry and even remarry the same type of person that brought us so much pain in the past. I have had this brought to my attention many times recently in the history of 5 or 6 couples (in the 50's or 60's) who have come to therapy not realizing that unsuccessfully trying to adjust to someone who they truly believed was their type has been one of the greatest disasters of their lives.

MIND SET FOR SUCCESSFUL RESOLUTION OF RELATIONSHIP CONFLICTS.
EFFECTS OF RULES AND BELIEFS ON RELATIONSHIPS

It is important to realize the importance of developing and understanding the difference between appropriate skills of **Assertion vs Aggression**. Assertion is the declaration of what is personally acceptable. Aggressive behavior is insisting on others agreement or getting personal needs met at the expense of another. Each of us needs to learn to set personal limits and protect ourselves from aggressive behaviors. However, it is often difficult to understand these two concepts due to the misunderstandings concerning the issue of control

A example of the difference between **Aggression and Assertion** can be seen in an exchange between a Husband and Wife who had agreed to reunite after a 6 month separation. The wife had been residing in an apartment with their 6 year old daughter, while the husband had remained in their personal residence.

During their separation, the husband had taken up shooting and purchased several guns which he stored in their home. Upon learning guns were stored in their home the wife said she could not return home with their child if guns were on the premises. The Husband said they were his guns and would not present a danger, because they were safely locked them in a closet. He insisted she agree to come home under those circumstances. He believed her insistence on living in a home free of guns on the premises was an act of attempted Control. She replied she was not trying to control him and that he could keep the guns on the premises if he wanted to. But, she would not return to a home with the guns on the premises (even under lock and key) due to fear of something happening that could lead to their child being being in danger.

The difference between aggression and assertion can be visualized in an example of a line being drawn in front of the assertive person who is resisting Aggressive (CONTROL) behavior of the other.

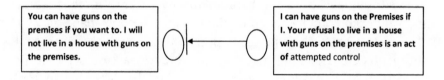

The issue of **Limit Setting** can clearly be seen in this example of conflict in which one asserts the right to live by personal mandates (Assertion) in spite of the others Aggressive (controlling) attempts to control the behavior of the other. Equally important **for appropriate Problem Solving** in relationships are a clear understanding of Mature methods of **Decision Making** and development of effective **Coping Strategies.** Many_ of us believe in Rules that do not allow take appropriate responsibility for yourself? Why might this be? What kinds of Roles do you play with others—Others with you? Where does your Path really Lead?

WHERE DOES MY PATH REALLY LEAD?

Self Discipline10 Assuming appropriate Responsibility for the Self includes not only personal discipline but understanding and living by the realistic principles that lead to others adults being able to live their lives by their own beliefs and rules of life. This does not meana that we will always agree. In fact many times, we will be unable to agree or even problem solve some difficult situation. But

---

[10] Kohlberg-Moral Development Rotter-Locus of Control Theory

the bottom line between adults in significant relationships is that we respect each other, face objective reality and give each other the room needed to live up to their potential and live their lives according to their own personal conclusions about where their path leads.

A tall order, yes, but one that can be attended to with some thought and ability to face objective reality and accept the truth.

I usually end up sharing with clients my visualization of a happily married couple who are able to problem solve, able to agree to disagree and value each other enough to allow each other the space they truly need to live up to their personal potential. I visualize these couples with Paths close enough that they are able to walk on separate Live Paths which are close enough to each other they are able to **Hold Hands While Walking Down Their Own Path**. And while this visualization may seem like a fairy tale or some aspect of life too good to be true it is absolutely attainable for those dedicated to their own and each others personal growth and psychological maturation.

I often discuss Happiness in both Personal and Marital Relationships with my clients in terms of more acceptance and less control of each other. Both need to be comfortable in the relationship, but not at the expense of the other.

A favorite visualization of mine is that of "Throwing Rose Petals". I perceive friends or spouses walking down their Path of friendship or marriage. A suggestion made by ONE to the other can be visualized as a "Rose Petal" thrown softly on the path of friendship. If the OTHER likes the suggestion it may be picked up and curiously inspected. If not . . . it may be left on the path for inspection at a later time or gently thrown off the path. The message of Throwing rose petals is too much pressure or suggestion for the other ruins relationships. A rose petal may one of personal need or need for the other in the relationship. Rose petals are suggestions that can be lived with or without. More specific methods of problem solving can be attained using such techniques as the 6 steps of Problem Solving (that I specifically recommend for my clients).

I have never forgotten a Movie I saw as a child depicting a blind woman who was loved by most everyone in her life. Asked about her "secret" of attracting and holding the love of others she replied. "I perceive my relationships like Birds in my hand". "I open my hand and let the bird lie comfortably on it". "As we talk and get comfortable with each other, I slowly pull my <u>open</u> hand closer to my heart". "I have always found that "Holding Others Close With Open Hands "leads to the best relationships, ones that allow both of us to be who we are".

Helping clients help others feel comfortable in relationships is also the underlying message of a visualization I share with clients of a song popular in the 50's. The Country singer, Glen Campbell sings about **Keeping My Sleeping Bag Rolled up Behind the Couch.** The song concerns a man who wanted love but resisted feelings of being controlled. The man sings of feeling very comfortable in his present loving relationship and that he kept his sleeping bag rolled up behind the couch. But where the woman of his dreams insist on putting the sleeping Bag away in the attic he would become anxious and unhappy. Only as a result of having the option of Leaving if he wanted to, (as a result of the sleeping bag behind the couch) does he feel no need or desire to leave.

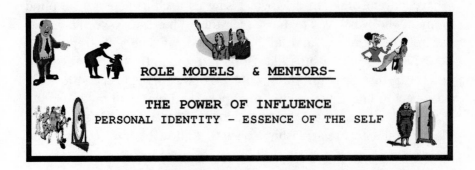

ROLE MODELS & MENTORS-

THE POWER OF INFLUENCE
PERSONAL IDENTITY – ESSENCE OF THE SELF

DEVELOPMENT OF PERSONALITY CHARACTERISTICS

Psychodynamic Theory suggests **Our Path through Life and expectations for personal experiences may be set by the time we are 5.** (find Reference). Other schools of theory might disagree. However, I do agree.

The core structure underlying the above Theory is that before 5 years of age children respond to life from a behavioral often emotional stance. As we grow many of us continue to respond to life from our 5 year old paradigm of expectations, perceptions, etc. This is one of the main reasons why learning to perceive our own experiences from the stance of objective reality is a major factor leading to Psychological Maturation.

Many Psychologists believe that **1ˢᵗ Memories** lie at the basis for many of our unconscious believes about life. I definitely agree that for most of us this is a truth of great importance and can be the basis for negative, positive or other expectations about life. This fact was bought forcibly to my attention one day when I was searching for reasons why my client could never seem to be happy, feel comfortable or expect anything but unhappiness in her life. Attempting to explore her past experiences as a road to some type of enlightenment I asked "What was your 1ˢᵗ memory?". She replied tearfully . . ."My **Grandmother was lying dead, over the steering wheel of our car, with blood running down her face and body.** Until that moment she had no idea that her always negative expectations, waiting for tragedy and believing nothing was ever going to turn out well, were the result of that long ago, experience . . . Lying in agonized pain inside her heart.

Of course all 1ˢᵗ memories are not of tragedy. My own include perceptions of anticipation as I waited for something wonderful to happen. I can still feel the comforting shade of the tall fir trees as dressed in crisp organdy I waited in eager anticipation for the long anticipated arrival of a favorite uncle from his home in Alaska. Many others 1ˢᵗ memories are reported as dimly remembered homes, faint remembrances of long gone parents, dimly recalled family arguments, even recollection of violence. The effect of memories pertaining to parents, family members, places, things or other, long buried, dimly or clearly recalled incidents is, of course, unique to each of us.

INFLUENCES OF ROLE MODELS ON "ESSENCE" OF THE SELF

The Woman Who Walked in Magic

 While I was growing up in a small logging community in Washington state, she sometimes came to visit. I don't remember how she traveled but I think it may have been by train. Her mother, my Grandmother, looked forward to her visits too but not, I'm sure, with the same level of breathless expectation and excitement that filled my small, thin, child's body.

She lived in **CALIFORNIA**, the most "glamorous" and exciting place in the world. As a child, I was sure it was also "the" place that had "somehow" been designated to have perpetually bright blue sky, a sun that always shone, clouds that never rained, and air that was magically filled with anticipation of wonderful things about to happen. I was positive of this because when I had traveled there, several times as a child, the air smelled like no other place that I had ever been (Pure Golden, Glamorous, California).

I can't remember a time when I didn't love this glamorous, kind creature, who resided in the most wonderful place in the world, Hollywood. Her visits provided a "magic carpet" that whisked me out of the every day, rain filled world of tall Douglas Fir trees, that was my life, into the exalted existence that I believed hers to be. In my child's mind, she brought to my ordinary and predictable world, an "aura" that seemed to come from "another" world.

On the first night of each of her visits we would sit up late talking. I was enthralled by the tales of where she lived, her friends, the places she worked. And . . ., I loved her so much. There was not one single thing about her that I didn't admire.

She had pretty blond hair. She was small and petite. We eagerly waited to hear about her life and the magical people she knew. And wonder of wonders, she worked as a Secretary for "movie" people like Jose Iturbi, Walter and Charles Pidgin, and John Wayne. I listened breathlessly. I truly believed she was perfect, that she could do no wrong. I longed to be just like her.

I yearned to somehow "don" her glamour, her wonderful clothes, her pretty blond hair and small perfectly formed body. It seemed to me that she was not just an ordinary every day person. She had in some way assumed the stature of a "special" person. I didn't know how this had happened, but I wanted to have it happen to me too.

Aunt Jane seemed to possess a "magical" quality that set her apart from other mortals. And the most wonderful thing of all was that when she spoke lovingly to me, listened to and valued my opinions, and treated me as though I too, was special . . . I "magically" became beautiful and special. When I was with her, by some mysterious "process" I felt my own small, child's self dissolve . . . and I became beautiful and glamorous, . . . just like she was. In a way that I didn't understand then, and as a result of my special relationship with her, I was able to assume some of her "Magic".

As a result of this, more than anything else in the world, I wanted to feel the same way about myself when I was alone as I did when she was with me. It was not just that her physical self was an expression of glamour and magic, but internally, as well, she was a "separate" entity, a "Real Self". And although as a child I did not understand and could not describe what her Real qualities where, I understood they were there and they were real.

Today, as a Psychologist, I finally understand that it was primarily through my exciting and wonderful relationship with my Father's sister, I have been able to internalized "my" model of how to "be" female in the world. I now understand that some of the most important building blocks that lead to high Self Esteem, value of myself as a woman, and knowledge that I am a "Winner" grew primarily in the fertile soil of my childhood relationship with Jane, my Aunt, a truly magical woman. EXAMAPLE: Psychological Development of a "ROLE MODEL for being Female

EFFECTS OF PARENTAL ROLE MODELING

The Psychological necessity for appropriate Parental Role Modeling is paramount in our human search for personal identity. The importance of **same sex parental role models** for learning how to be a male or a female in the world cannot be overemphasized and can contribute to a child's development either positively or negatively. Modeling of *Suitable* Same Sex Parental *behaviors* lead to development of self discipline, personal competence and psychological health in offspring. Reasons why people do, don't, can't or won't take personal responsibility can often be traced to behaviors modeled by parents, siblings, friends, extended family etc.

Of great importance to my own treatment model for clients has been the discovery that many adults **don't know how** to assume personal responsibility. Clients responses on The Test of Ego and Cognitive Development confirm this finding with responses such as 1) relying on others for happiness, 2) not knowing how to stand up for themselves, 3) feeling life has no direction, 4) difficulty setting personal goals and 5) not knowing what they are or not responsible for. Many adults reside in a life of confusion as a result of childhood environments in which the subject of personal responsibility was never modeled, taught nor discussed. As a result no clear idea of what personal rights are, how to get them met, or methods for living conscientiously. had been addressed. Such findings certainly point to the conclusion that many human beings reach adulthood lacking a reliable compass for safely treading through life's dark waters of fears and uncertainty.

Effects of Opposite/Same Sex Parent Role Modeling

The influence of **Opposite Sex Parent on Sex Roles of offspring** has been investigated by numerous theorists. Many finding point to interesting differences in relationship dynamics between Same Sex parent and offspring (Fathers/Sons And Mothers/Daughters) and Opposite sex parent and offspring (Mothers/Sons and Fathers/Daughters).

My own **Doctoral Dissertation**[11] citing various studies concerning Parent/Offspring relationship dynamics are briefly presented below.

- Children in small family of fewer than 3 siblings, identified strongly with parents, spent more leisure time with parents, used parents as confidants and were more likely to absorb parental points of view. **These offspring** were less concerned with peer evaluations, felt more encouraged becoming autonomous, more internalized and independent and more exploring of risk taking. **These families** shared values that stressed personal responsibility and individual achievement for children and themselves. Douvan and Adelson (1966)
- Daughters of working mothers saw mothers as less negative than daughters of non working mothers. These subjects saw woman as more competent and themselves as more worthwhile. They also saw male and female roles as less polarized. Broverman, et al. (1972)
- Successful women identify with fathers. Daughters in this study are reported to receive attention, approval, reward and confirmation from fathers. Study (Hennig 1973)

---

[11] Relationships among Business Managerial Performance, Gender, Personality Characteristics and the perception of Parental Sex Roles—Skipi Lundquist Smoot—California School of Professional Psychology San Diego—1985

- A significant preference for identification with fathers in successful woman business managers. (Helson 1974),
- The close relationships with fathers of many successful business women may have taken place as a result of being brought up in small families with no male siblings. 20 of 25 subjects in the study of successful business women were the eldest or only child in their family. (Hennig and Jardim (1977)
- Studies to identify Parental Attitudes of children who became successful in their fields were done by Chance et al (1978). Findings indicate most of the achievers' grew up in the 1930 to 1960's, 70% were upward mobile and 60% of achievers were from small families. 60% of the mothers of achievers worked and 70% of mothers had some college education. 67 % of fathers had some college and one out of two of the achievers was a first born or an only child
- The conclusions of (Pincus, et al. (1980) support the original finding of Chance, et al. (1978). Both studies conclude that **Parenting Style** leads to development of certain personality characteristics in offspring which in turn lead toward success and achievement, regardless of gender of the offspring. <u>Parental Characteristics</u> identified as contributing to success in offspring were: **Modeling autonomy, Having interests of their own, and Showing uniqueness without guilt.** <u>Personality Characteristics</u> **in the** <u>Offspring</u> which may emerge as a result of those parental characteristics were See self as an <u>individual </u>without guilt, are <u>Autonomous</u>, Value their own <u>uniqueness</u> and Attempt to <u>live up to their own potential.</u>

Discussion of Research in Context of Personal Experience

Relationships with my own Parents appear to support **many** of these findings. I grew up in the 40's as an only child. My mother worked and had interests of her own. She autonomously modeled "who she was" without guilt. My parents roles were <u>not polarized</u>. Neither tried to control the other.

My father, an autocratic male, valued winning and the rules set by Authority figures. He is also reported to have been quite disappointed I, an only child (until I was 25) had not been born a male. Both my parents education stopped at Grade 10. Apparently those from small western logging communities had no idea concerning the importance of education. Neither was my father a role model for Autonomy. Apparently his philosophy of following the Rule of Authority Figures took precedence over autonomy and uniqueness without guilt.

As an only child my Father said I had been named Skippy after the little Boy in the Funny Papers. No plans for naming a girl had been made during my mother's pregnancy. After my surgical birth (in which my mother almost died), my maternal grandmother told my father <u>she</u> had decided to name me Mildred Grace after my mother's Identical Twin and Paternal Grandmother. Dad however, (although deferring to Parental Authority concerning the name on my Birth Certificate) refused to call me anything but Skippy. I finally (as an adult) had the spelling of my name legally changed to the more feminine, Skipi, because the name of Mildred Grace felt like it belonged to a stranger whom I had never known.

As a 4 year old, petrified to perform in my dance recital, my Dad rushed back stage to tell me that if I didn't "get out there" and dance like I had been instructed to do, he would give me a "good spanking". Needless to say, that solved the problem. Forever afterward I felt like all I had to do in a performance role, was to "Don my Costume" and "get out there".

During my early childhood years my Dad taught me how to dive, swim and shoot a rifle and a bow and arrow. He taught the art of diving first (before I could swim) into the 5 foot deep waters of the Natatorium. He assured me there was "nothing to be afraid of" because he would "catch me and bring me to the surface" before I could say "Boo, to a Jack Rabbit". He never let me down. Eventually, although I learned to Dive off the High Board with grace and precision (Dad loved high diving), I was never much of a swimmer (Dad didn't care about swimming that much).

As a preteen, I eagerly accompanied my Dad to the basement of our house where the Rifle and the Bow and Error he had personally made for me were kept. Although I was extremely near sighted, I found that by trying very hard (and as a result of some miracle) I could shoot an "ant off a hill a mile away". During my Teen Years, I became an expert marksman, able to hit the bull's eye with either a 22 Rifle or a Bow and Arrow. I'm sure these "miracles" were the result of the importance of my need to earn the love and pride of my Dad. It worked, he was.

As a teen ager, my Dad happily drove me to numerous out of State Music Meets where I received A's for outstanding Singing performances. He was always very proud of my winner status (and I believe would have been extremely disappointed in me otherwise). I loved my Dad with all my heart and looking back I believe at that time in my life, I would have tried (until I died) to earn his pride. He was truly my Role Model and if it included winner status, I would try with all my heart to be the someone he could be proud of.

My Dad always longed for personal success, truly believing it would happen as a result of following the rules of authority without question. He waited all his life (with little success) in the everyday world of living from paycheck to paycheck. Eventually, from the age of 65 until his death at 96, he became extremely successful as the Owner Operator of 5 McDonald's Restaurants (a corporation that insists on following their rules or get out).

Although he did not understand the importance of higher education or the concept of autonomy (probably believing both were unnecessary within the confines of deferment to authority) his **Personal Characteristics included** 1) following rules, 2) Striving for Success and 3) being a Winner resulted in his own personal success. This of course doesn't mean that his Personal Philosophy of Life was either correct or incorrect. It does however; prove the point expressed by the concept of Karma (everything has a cause and effect).

<u>EFFECTS OF SIBLING ROLE MODELLING</u>

Many families have no clear idea how important parental as well as **sibling role modeling** is on the development of children in the family. My own personal interest in the relative importance of much older sibling role modeling on significantly younger siblings developed during my Master Degree studies in Marriage and Family Therapy at Pepperdine in Orange County California and has continued to fascinate me probably as a result of my own four sons relationships with each other.

My two older boys, born 1-1/2 years apart were joined 8 years later by a 3rd brother and eight years after that a 4th brother entered our family. The two older, closer in age brothers were often in conflict. But my two older sons, born 8 & 10 years before the arrival of my 3rd son were like uncles or protective care takers to their younger siblings. The same dynamics were evident between my 3rd and 4th sons (also 8 years apart).

Years ago, I seriously thought about designing a research project to investigate the effects of Older Brothers behaviors on behaviors of their significantly younger Brothers. My hypothesis was that "a guitar playing, stay out late older brother" would have a more negative effect on a naïve, younger brother than would a "get his homework done on time, and pick up his own clothes off the floor" 8 year old bother.

Discussion of those who do, don't, can't or won't take responsibility for the self as a result of role modeling of sibling, friends, parents, extended family members, etc. present intriguing questions for research as well as within our own families.

EFFECTS OF PSYIOLOGY ON DEVELOPMENT OF THE SELF
HUMAN FETAL DEVELOPMENT

The Gender Identity Differentiation Model of **Money and Ehrhardt (1972)** concludes that the Process of Gender Identity is continuous, beginning with conception and culminating with emergence of adult gender identity.

- Babies are born male or female. For the first six week a fetus is female. Unless a male hormone changes an embryo's course, it will develop female. All babies have the same sex hormones, only the proportions are different. Pogrebin, 1980)

- **Summary Of Gender Identity** research—**Hampson & Hampson (1961) and Money & Ehrhardt (1968).** 3 points emerge. The initial form of a developing human is female, not male. W/o the addition of appropriate hormones, a developing fetus will develop as a female. For development of a male, two genetically controlled signals must occur. First the appropriate genetic code (XY) is necessary and second, a signal to produce androgens must occur. Without both, a physical male will not develop. The process in females will develop normally with only the signal of the XX genetic pattern. However, the female process can be externally interfered with through drugs which may have been taken during pregnancy that are chemically similar to androgens or if inappropriate hormones were secreted by the fetes during development.

- The developmental message is carried by the sex chromosome of the sperm (X or Y) which joins with the X chromosome of the ovum. The female (XX) or male (XY) then sends instructions to the undifferentiated gonad. Depending on the instructions the gonad will evolve either into a testis (about six weeks into gestation) or into an ovary (about 6 weeks later). The chromosomes, after passing on the genetic message, seem to have no further effect on development. For masculinity the fetal testes takes over as result of two inferred fetal hormones which have not been identified or named. Money and Ehrhardt, 1968 **The Money and Ehrhardt** model show the first inferred fetal hormone, is a Mullerian-inhibiting substance the 2nd is testosterone for development of male ducts into the male reproduce systems.

- Common abnormalities <u>in Biological & Chromosomal Development</u> Examples of common abnormalities include those as a result of improper chromosomal division, causing Down's syndrome or Turners Syndrome when the child looks like a girl, but is short, probably mentally retarded and sterile. There are a number of medical disorders in which internal and external sex organs are incongruent, resulting in mistaken decisions, at birth, as to whether the child is male or female. As a result, biological males may be reared as girls and vice versa. Many of these disorders have bene studied **by money (1961): Money and Ehrhardt (1968): Hampson and Hampson 91961).** All provided support for conclusions concerning the influence of biological factors in **determination of gender identity**

Personal knowledge of Gender Identity

In our Present more scientifically knowledgeable society than in previous times, it has become more and more obvious that Personal Identity may include homosexuality . . . a category seen as unacceptable by some, criticized by others and expeditiously denied by many afraid to accept the truth about the self or a loved one. However, Homosexuality is often a fact of life that must be carefully and critically examined to understand what it is, what it is caused from and how it develops.

Looking at ourselves in the mirror we see a Male, a Female or a someone we may not completely understand in terms of gender identity.

Causes of Sexual Orientation?

There are numerous theories about the origins of a person's sexual orientation. Most scientists today agree that sexual orientation is most likely the result of a complex interaction of environmental, cognitive and biological factors. In most people, sexual orientation is shaped at an early age. There is also considerable recent evidence to suggest that biology, including genetic or inborn hormonal factors, play a significant role in a person's sexuality. It's important to recognize that there are probably many reasons for a person's sexual orientation, and the reasons may be different for different people.

The following information concerning **Homosexuality** is taken from American Psychological Association HELP CENTER **Copyright 2004 American Psychological Association**

- **Is Sexual Orientation a Choice? No,** human beings cannot choose to be either gay or straight. For most people, sexual orientation emerges in early adolescence without any prior sexual experience. Although we can choose whether to act on our feelings, psychologists do not consider sexual orientation to be a conscious choice that can be voluntarily changed.
- **Can Therapy Change Sexual Orientation? No;** even though most homosexuals live successful, happy lives, some homosexual or bisexual people may seek to change their sexual orientation through therapy, often coerced by family members or religious groups to try and do so. The reality is that homosexuality is not an illness. It does not require treatment and is not an illness.
- **Is Homosexuality a Mental Illness or Emotional Problem?** No. Psychologists, psychiatrists, and other mental health professionals agree that homosexuality is not an illness, a mental disorder, or an emotional problem. More than 35 years of objective, well-designed scientific research has shown that homosexuality, in and itself, is not associated with mental disorders or emotional or social problems. Homosexuality was once thought to be a mental illness because mental health professionals and society had biased information. In the past, the studies of gay, lesbian, and bisexual people involved only those in therapy, thus biasing the resulting conclusions. When researchers examined data about such people who were not in therapy, the idea that homosexuality was a mental illness was quickly found to be untrue. In 1973 the American Psychiatric Association confirmed the importance of the new, better-designed research and removed homosexuality from the official manual that lists mental and emotional disorders. Two years later, the American Psychological Association passed a resolution supporting this removal. For more than 25 years,

both associations have urged all mental health professionals to help dispel the stigma of mental illness that some people still associate with homosexual orientation.

- **Can Lesbians, Gay Men, and Bisexuals Be Good Parents?** Yes. Studies comparing groups of children raised by homosexual and by heterosexual parents find no developmental differences between the two groups of children in four critical areas: their intelligence, psychological adjustment, social adjustment, and popularity with friends. It is also important to realize that a parent's sexual orientation does not indicate their children's

MALE AND FEMALE DIFFERENCES

Biological Gender takes 5 forms (chromosomal, gender, gonadal gender, hormonal gender, inner reproductive structures and outer genital structures **(Hampson and Hampson, 1961).**

- This research suggests no correlation between physical gender and internal organs. Even external genital appearance seems to have surprisingly little effect on gender identity. **Nibet (1961) and Ganosib and Ganosib** (1961) found it had been difficult to change a child's knowledge of gender identity after the age of three.
- Studies indicate highly masculine adult males may be very independent but also anxious and with low self esteem Mussen 1962, 1962 Harfor, Willis and Deabler 1967 while highly feminine women, show high passivity, low self esteem and high anxiety (Sears 1970, Webb 1963 and gall 1969.
- Traditionally viewed Gender Differences are not biologically determined but the results of socialization, stereotypical mythology, and or role modeling to name a few. **Larwood, Wood & Inderlied** 1978). Social and cultural standards are the main determinant of whether a particular behavior remains stable or not from childhood through adulthood **Kagen Moss** (1962)
- Macoby & Jacklin (1974) identified only four "fairly well established" differences between males and females. They were 1) males are more aggressive then females, 2) girls have greater verbal ability than boys, 3) boys excel in visual spatial ability, and 4) boys excel in mathematical abilities. However, Hoff (1977) summarized evidence for other differences. And

more recently books such as Women are from Venus and Men are from Mars (John Gray) tend to suggest that males and females are genetically and biologically different (a suggestion I vigorously disagree with).

I was enthralled by a Research project I included in my Doctoral Dissertation concerning influences of Gender on the characteristics of Successful Business Managers. Broverman's subjects identified the characteristics of Normal males as aggressive, independent and competitive while those of normal females were nurturant, dependent and noncompetitive. Asked to identify the characteristics of a Normal Adult the subjects identified them to be aggression, independent and competitive. His conclusions? A normal female is not a normal adult. Broverman, **(1972).**

INFLUENCE OF OTHERS PERCEPTIONS ON THE "SELF"

Much of my understanding of how Personal Identity is developed comes from the concept of Homeostasis. The definition of Homeostasis is maintenance of a stable environment such as seen in a furnace set for 75 degrees—it goes on when the temperature goes below 75 and off when the temperature is above 75. The Psychological ideology behind Homeostasis comes from the work of Murray Bowen, MD[12] in his research and writing concerning Homeostasis in Family Systems.

For over 20 years I have discussed **Homeostasis** with clients as a visualization of a `family swimming pool` in which family members reside. Parental and sibling perceptions, negative and positive, of each other reside in the warm waters of the Pool. Members are comfortable with their own conceptualizations of each other. "I", however, may or may not be comfortable with another's perception of "Me".

Adding to the effectiveness of the Concept of Homeostasis, **Theorist (??19 ?)** presented his visualization of How perceptions of Self and Family Member might be cleverly conceptualized as inscriptions on

---

[12] Murray Bowen, M.D., (13 January 1913, Waverly, Tennessee-9 October 1990) was an American psychiatrist and a professor in Psychiatry at the Georgetown University

the clothes of family members. **T-Shirts** of each family member might sparkle with such short catchy insults or complements as "Weak Dumb Bell", "Trouble Maker", "Winner", "Know it All", or other descriptive phrase.

Voices cry out in shrill discontent when a family member changes behavior (whether for the good or bad) and gets "out of the pool" to stand on the perimeter overlooking the waters of Family Homeostasis. Decreased water levels in the pool (which had previously provided family comfort) has resulted in cries of "Get back in the Pool, our shoulders are cold" to the abandoning person who has gotten out of the pool. It makes little difference whether the abandoning member has assumed different characteristics of either positive or negative attitudes and behaviors.

If the abandoning family member for whatever reason looses the will to behave differently, the family will probably quiet down and allow homeostasis to return on the reentry into the water. If however, the abandoning member refuses assumption of their old role, cries continue for some time, and may eventually reach a new homeostatic point. Whether the abandoning family member's new behavior will ever be welcomed back into the new homeostasis is something individual to each family.

My own experience s with family cold shoulders occurred for 20 to 60 years after I got out of the Pool. After beginning my Graduate Studies in Psychology an Aunt refused contact for 10 years due to her Homeostatic Memory on my T-Shirt that read "weakling in need of vocational direction". In her eyes, I had abandoned the family with my education. The other, a long lost cousin known since teen age couldn't imagine that I had earned a PhD when my T-shirt in her Homeostatic family Memory read "weak dumb bell"

"WHERE IS THE "REAL" ME?

As discussed in Chapter 4, Task 1, infants at birth have no idea Who" they are or even where they stop and others begin. A child perceives their primary caretaker (usually the mother) as part of themselves. This results from associating satisfied needs by others with their own wishes, desires, etc. This perception of residence at the center of the universe (Egocentricity) is normal for a child and is called <u>Primary Narcissism</u>. Although Primary Ego satisfaction (being nurtured and getting needs met) for the infant is normal and necessary for an adult with such needs, it presents a basic conflict with reality.

At birth, an infant can be understood as an emotionally **"empty cup"**. The **"Faces"** we grew up with contribute to our perception of the world. **Self-image** is a result of our perceptions of how we believed others saw us. If a child perceives parental perception of the self as wonderful (meeting his needs promptly and lovingly), the child learns to view himself as worthwhile. If the child internalizes parental perception of the self as a bother, a nuisance or as a person unworthy, unloved or not respected, the child learns to see himself as not valuable, and develops low self esteem. And in such a case, <u>because the child </u>perceives himself as residing at the center of the Universe (<u>egocentric</u>) he may even perceive himself to be the **most unworthy person in the world.**

As a child matures, the longing to continue feeling the self to be the center of the universe) is <u>perceived </u>**as Reality**. Only as time goes by and emotional and ego development occurs does the child learn to see both the needs of himself and others as equally important.

<u>Self Esteem</u> is the result of feeling strong, worthwhile, & competent, the result of being able to live up to one own realistic standards and solve personal problems. Most people start life with feelings of smallness, inferiority, and a need to look to authority for answers. Many of us never learn to completely trust ourselves to make logical decisions without serious "Mistakes". Who, then, is to set standards against which we define ourselves, our worthiness and expectations for ourselves? What type of value judgments (moral, religious, scientific, etc.) shall I base my decisions on?

The roots of **Self Esteem** lie in the Self. **It** is the result of facing and accepting the truth about ourselves, others and our situations. It is taking appropriate responsibility for ourselves, defining our own values and morals and developing integrity. And finally, **Self Esteem** is doing the very best, objectively defining our own values and living up to them. The Road to Psychological Maturity runs through the Valleys of Internalized Opinions of Others. Only by clearly evaluating our Personal Characterisstics and defining the differences between what we really believe and what we believe others expect us to believe are we able to live our lives in harmony with our Essence.

The Following Vignettes describe a woman who lost her Self in a Forest of Pain.

The Memorial Services

Searching for Acceptance in the Eyes of Another

The Memorial Service was held in the common room of the Senior Living Facility to which she had reluctantly returned after the last of two debilitating strokes made a more independent life style impossible. Crying uncontrollably she had extended care of her two beloved cats, Stanley and Mitch to a neighbor who promised to carefully protect them while searching for a secure permanent home.

Chairs for the service were quickly set up as salads, drinks and small sandwiches (favorite foods of the departed) were arranged on a long table. A large beautiful Floral Arrangement, placed at the right of the room provided a circle of beauty for the young man who sat in its shadow playing his guitar. Guitar music, and a slide show showing earlier days in the life of the departed encased the Service.

The Christian Minister's eloquent remark s praising the life and memories of the Departed one floated softly over the 30 to 40 mostly elder attendees. Paying admiring tribute to the woman whose ashes lay upstairs in a cardboard box close to the bed that recently held her dying body he lauded the Departed's unstinting volunteer service at local Medical Treatment Facilities. Special homage was given to her vigorous defense of those she believed had been treated unfairly.

A Friend & former Vocational peer shared memories of the Departed as one with personality characteristics oddly at variance with those recounted by the Minister. The Friend spoke of the Departed's generally high levels of emotional responsiveness, years of medical disability and behaviors reflecting inadequate attention to essential aspects of cause and effect. The Friend's Specific remembrances (presented in a structure of funny comedy) included several accounts of driving practices that lead to the loss of drivers license and auto accidents . . . One of which resulted in running into and over a light pole on a public street in front of the friends home.

Mingling over the delicious food prepared by loved ones of the Departed, many of the attendees shared memories of the departed that were also oddly at variance with each other. Some remembered a Departed who volunteered often at the County Hospitals where she had worked as a Social Worker before her disability forced retirement. Others spoke of incidents in which the Departed "stood up for the underdog" and "fought to end unfairness the Victims may have suffered." Some spoke of the Departed's loving relationship with a female Companion of the past 13 years as common knowledge. Family Members and Other Acquaintances however, knew little or nothing of a Gay Life style so obvious to others.

Some remembered the Departed lack of empathy . . . while others remembered loving concern for others. Some shared memories of the Departed's embarrassing lack of socially acceptable behavior exhibited in poor table manners, loud aggressive conversations and even constant referral to her Volunteer work as a topic of conversation with others.

What life experiences could have lead to such disparity? Why would she behave so differently in one situation from another . . . from one person to another? Photographs of the departed as a young woman show a beautiful, slender and smiling radiance. Middle age photo's reveal weight gains of well over several hundred pounds. The last days of life were spent in a body weighing 130 lbs . . . with flesh on arms, legs and frame hanging empty and loose. What happenings in the life of this poor woman could have lead to such discrepancies in attitudes, philosophies, behaviors

WHISPERS OF PAIN

from an empty apartment

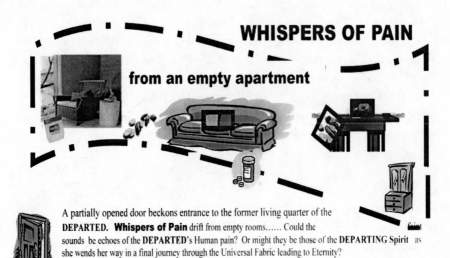

A partially opened door beckons entrance to the former living quarter of the **DEPARTED**. **Whispers of Pain** drift from empty rooms...... Could the sounds be echoes of the **DEPARTED**'s Human pain? Or might they be those of the **DEPARTING** Spirit as she wends her way in a final journey through the Universal Fabric leading to Eternity?

The telephone, recently clutched in the hands of the **DEPARTED** screaming in emotional pain ....now lies silent. **Broken furniture** occupies the apartment. **D**esks with drawers hanging from broken hinges lie abandoned in the empty silence. **F**amily **mementoes**, heirlooms, the likeness of a **young adult daughter, dead from cancer in the prime of her life** peek from a Large Envelope. Pictures of a mother and father as young parents lie covered in dust on top of an aging Photo Album.

Half empty **Pill Bottles** fall from desk and couch to lie in disarray on the floor. Full and empty jars of Vaseline litter the floor and furniture. **Bank books, Insurance policies and financial** records lie open and scattered **around the room.**

In the closet, **Coat-Hangers** no longer cradle the ripped and worn outfits that covered the formerly large body of the **DEPARTED**. An **Arrow through a Heart** drawn on a **Paper Towel** – lies cradled on the desk beside the phone. The words **"I will love you for ever" "You are my Life"** .....are reminders of a Lost Love that was neither openly acknowledged nor abandoned.

The **BED** from which the **DEPARTED** entered Eternity rests against corner walls in the silence of the present. Sheets that cradled her dying body lie partly covered by blankets in disarray as they fall to the floor. In the midst of the Chaos ......beneath a table with a broken leg lies an **Empty Cup** – on its side- without contents of any sort. A **Cardboard** *box* holding the Ashes of the **DEPARTED** rests on a Couch a few feet from the bed where she died.

Are the **Whispers** drifting through the Present, echo's of the DEPARTED's past pain?....Or are they **Whispers** of the DEPARTED's Spirit now at peace and understanding the Past? Is the DEPARTED here in this empty apartment? Or are the Whispered sounds merely wisps of air escaping from damaged heating vents built into apartment walls ?

A JOURNEY THROUGH LIFE

The **Life Journey** of the **DEPARTED** began on a path of Negative energy. In Reaction to the birth of a baby brother, she beat her head against the wall in an outrage of abandonment. Brought up in a Strict Baptist environment, an Aunt married to a Baptist Preacher, little room for nonstandard behavior and a Mother, who put her children to bed at 6 PM to "get some time to herself" she tried to understand her place in the world. In the summer, the children were left for hours and days with relatives while mother visited friends. At 17, her father suffering from Bipolar Disorder hung himself in a hallway outside her bedroom door. He was found by her 16 year old brother when he came home from school.

Marriage as young adult and a move to Puerto Rico ended in pregnancy, a swift return home and divorce. She never remarried. Both the **Departed's** Parents were highly educated (MA's). The brother received a BS, taught school, married and fathered a son. **Rejected in Nursing School** for poor social skills and characteristics believed to be inappropriate for a Nursing career she completed a **MA in Social Work** but required social security disability retirement for addiction to medication. The Departed & her daughter continued to live in the Parental Home with a resentful Mother until her Mother's death 20 years ago.

Constant eating and **Weight gain** to over 300 lbs continued for much of adult life. **Moving to the city of her daughter's residence helped "fill her cup" with the "essence" of her daughter.** Living in apartments or Assisted Living quarters' she regularly House-Sat for her educated, successful, well respected and openly **"Gay" Daughter until the Daughter's Death from Pancreatic Cancer at age 35.**

 Apartment living **with a black, significant** Other (a secret kept from many) who could neither read nor write provided some happiness for **13** **years.** Two strokes and loss of well understood speech necessitated leaving her beloved **Cats—Stanley and Mitch** (to a life in the woods outside their old apartment) when she was forced to return to Assisted Living. Citing money and relationship difficulties her Significant Other vacillated over details of a future together and then reluctantly agreed to accompany her into part time Assisted Living.

Requests for her Significant Other to move out resulted in tearful but dignified compliance. After many emotional, demanding and difficult to understand phone calls the Brother arranged a visit. On arrival, proposed outings to ease stress were refused in favor of the purchase of Tennis Shoes, jars of Vaseline and other everyday items. The DEPARTED cried out repeatedly in emotional pain as she tearfully clung to her brother, A final visit to the Old Apartment resulted in the **cats eagerly running from** their temporary home in the Woods as the voice of the **Departed** called their names. Biding them an emotional farewell and promise of a joyful reunion, the **Departed** returned to Assisted Living where she told her Brother goodbye.

Soon after, several weeks of hysterical phone calls from the **Departed** citing **inability to "do this anymore"** began the descent into death. And finally . . . 4 phone calls from Assisted Living personnel and a Doctor stating the discovery of the Departed **lying** in apparent lifelessness in her bed amidst numerous pill bottles and other sleeping medications. Attempts by Emergency Personnel to revive her failed. **Was death suicide or accidental death from Medication??.** She left this world as she began in childhood—an "Empty Cup" in need of fulfillment. Her whole human life had been spent **SEARCHING FOR SELF IN THE FOREST OF PAIN.**

Are the **Whispers** in the Empty Apartment those of the **DEPARTED's** Spirit finally at peace and in possession of knowledge leading to understanding her path through life? . . . Could the **Whispers** be joyful echo's of reunions with Daughter and Parents? . . . Or might the **Whispers** emanate from the Spirit of the Departed, finally at home in the embrace of Eternity as she joyfully understands the meaning of both her Human and Spiritual Essence. Do the **Cats** in the woods still wait patiently for her return? Or is that faint sound **Meow's** of joy that she has finally returned to care for them as they knew she would . . . Only this time from the Other Side, to scoop them up in loving joy, to feed and nourish them, to care for them knowing that **when their time** on earth is through they will once more be reunited with the spirit of the **Departed** in the loving embrace of eternity . . . *In Loving Memory of the Departed*

DIMENSIONS OF PSYCHOLOGICAL MATURATION.

The Path to Eternity (Human and Spiritual Maturation) runs through Fabric of the Universe (Reality) and is paved with realistic Laws of cause and Effect. Most of us begin our journey "dancing" to intense emotional rhythms. Only later, often in great pain do some of us learn to dance to the Music of the Universe.

Respect for human competence allows innate personal potential to develop. Psychological Maturation results from an **Observing Ego** sufficiently developed to face Reality and accept the truth. **Ego Boundaries** must be strong enough to resolve emotional dependency on others and develop unique personal potential. Human Developmental Tasks for Psychological Maturation include A **Unique Personal Identity** (. The Ability to face objective reality, accept the truth and develop personal potential), **Resolution of excessive Emotional Dependency on Others**, *Interdependent perception* of the needs of self and others as equally important and an Independent, thoughtfully arrived at broadly focused **Philosophy of Life.**

We are each born with a seed of Unique Human Potential. **Development of Human potential** demands **Psychological Maturation**. And only by resolving the problems that deter us from psychological maturation are we free to explore our mission in the Universe. Personal Choices are presented to each of us on our Path through the Universe in the form of choices and opportunities for problem solving with situations and other people. **Psychological Maturation** is the doorway leading to a more complete understanding of our <u>unique potential</u> and "fit" **in the Universe.**

The Self and Personal Identity are defined in **MNS—ENCARTA Dictionary** as what is particular about a person, including those qualities that distinguish one person from another and the consciousness of one's own being or identity.

THE **YELLOW** DRESS OF DREAMS

An example of the type of message concerning Emotional Separation and inner balance can be seen in a dream I experienced as an adult while attending a Doctoral Class in Freudian dream interpretation. In my dream . . . I open a box mailed to me from an Aunt containing one of her discarded dresses. I carefully remove the garment and hold it before me. Beautiful red, white and yellow pieces of its silky fabric have been sewn together to form a fitted bodice, long narrow sleeves, high neck with snugly fitted collar. It resembles costumes worn by women from a long past era. I can feel my heart pounding in happiness and appreciation.

Losing myself in reverie, I remember my Aunt's kindness and beauty, her exquisite clothes. I have loved her a lifetime. While I was growing up I was poor. In my dream I am grown . . . able to provide for my own needs. I 'know' this dream dress is not ordinary. It is a symbol of love I have longed for all of my life.

I am somewhat surprised to receive this beautiful gift. Throughout my life my Aunt has almost always given her discarded but still beautiful clothes to my cousin, her only other niece. And always, I had felt left out and hurt. Once, brave enough to ask her to share her discarded dresses with both of us she replied "No, you're too big to fit into my clothes'. I am 2 inches taller than my cousin and all three of us wear size 6 or 8 dresses. My Aunt is 2 inches shorter than my cousin. Hiding emotional pain of rejection behind a facade of understanding, I smile my acceptance of her explanation. But now, at last, my dream self felt accepted and truly loved. This time, I had been chosen to receive her dress.

Happily, lovingly I raised the dream dress high over my head and slid its silky fabric over my hair. Its silky folds cascaded down my body and swung around my legs. Reaching to zip it up the back I saw it wouldn't close. Disappointment overwhelmed me. In frustration I stared at the too tight bodice, the too short skirt. Sadly I realized the designated loops on the sleeves were too short to reach their assigned buttons. I burst into tears as the the too tight collar cut into my throat, leaving red scratches on my neck.

Alarmed at my tears, my 9 year old son, Ted, put his arms around me. "Throw it away, Mom', he said 'it doesn't fit . . . it's too small. Besides its old and out of style". Choking back tears, I replied "No, maybe I can "fix" it. I might be able to alter it. I could cut the neckline lower or let out the sleeves'. 'The skirt doesn't have to be so long", said my dream self. "I can wear it knee length'.

Entering my dream in a flash of brightness I heard Reality whisper 'Look closely'. Thoughtfully I observed my dream. There in the shadows I glimpsed the anguished face of Desperation crouched in unrealistic longing to "fit" into the clothes of another.

Slowly, as I realized an individual must learn to stand alone, I felt a lifetime of sadness and resentment fade into the past. I see clearly my own truth may never fit into the distinctive shape of another. I finally know the truth. Personal integrity can never be the price of another's acceptance . . .

DEVELOPING A FUNCTIONAL SELF

It is important to those searching for solutions to reasons why we behave as we do and why our relationships are the way they are to examine the role modeling of others as we grew up. An opportunity for such study can be seen in an examination of our Family Genograms.

An understanding of the relationship between our parents, their expectations for each others and their children provide insight into our own unconscious beliefs and Roles in Life. The relationships between our self and siblings also are deterministic in development of Personal Identity. Questions such as "Did I identify with mother, father, a brother or sister? Why or Why not? How do I think the characteristics of these family member might have influenced my perceptions of my own personal identity?.

Other methods of identifying aspects of our life leading to how Psychological Maturation has or has not been developed can be seen in a Psychological Technique called **Celebrate your Life.** Initially this technique was designed as a Person thinking about their own funeral. Questions such as how old do you think you will be when you die, how many marriages and/or divorces will you have had, how many children and grandchildren will there be at these services.

However, during Seminars I presented, I decided that Birthday Parties for Family and Friends can provide equally important information about the self without the aspect of tragedy that a Memorial Service would be likely to include. As a result, I designed and called this Technique **Celebrate Your Life.**

The Birthday recipient is instructed to Picture themselves at a Celebration designed to acknowledge characteristics you would like others to remember about you. List what you would like each of your parents, children, sibs, other professions in your field, other important persons in your life to remember about you, your accomplishments, etc. List your philosophy of life, what direction you want your life to take, what is their hierarchy of importance,. Include your goals for self, relationships, vocation, education, etc. Ask yourself whether or not these conclusions fit with the research presented in this book on successful development of Adult Characteristics as well as those of Psychological Maturation.

During my early career, I used this technique in Hospital Treatment while working with Acting Out Teen agers. It was very helpful for identifying the thought processes, life expectations, perceptions and expectations of the Teen who had been hospitalized for Depression, Anger Management, Anxiety, etc.

As mentioned in Chapter 1—Stages and Ages of Human Development, comparatively little research has focused on Adult Development as that on Childhood and Adolescent Development. The exceptions—Self actualization, Social Processes of Adulthood, Androgyny, Transcending Sex Roles and Becoming Adults are presented below:

⬥ Abraham Maslow 1908-1970[13] spent his professional life researching and writing about SELF-ACTUALIZATION—the fulfillment of one's greatest human potential. His work was greatly influenced by evolutionary theory and the social nature of experience and behavior,

⬥ George Herbert Mead (1863-1931[14]), American pragmatist, philosopher and social psychologist emphasized the natural emergence of the self and mind within the social order. He argued that the self emerges out of a social process in which the organism becomes self-conscious. This self-consciousness arises as a result of the organism's interaction with its environment, including communication with other organisms. I can't help observe that he must have had siblings as well as peers and parents in mind when he made his observations.

⬥ **Peter Ustinov 1921-2004** presented his observation that Parents are the bones on which children sharpen their teeth—As a parent and Psychologist I couldn't agree more.

⬥ **ANDROGENY** is defined as the equal degrees of masculine and feminine characteristics within the same person. Androgyny is seen by many as healthy and some point to its manifestation as evidence of achievement of the final phase of personality development, an integration of personality traits, both masculine and feminine Functional Adult Development has been researched extensively by another of my favorite theorists, **Sanda Bem** who studies the specific area of Androgyny.

⬥ Some authors view **sex roles as an intermediate step in personal development** and point to androgyny as the final transcendent stage of development for both males and females. **Rebecca, Hefner & Oleshonsky 1974, Bem 1974**

⬥ Research Studies point to the final transcending phase of human development as a level, which when reached, allows both sets of traits (Masculine and Feminine) in the same

---

[13] Evolutionary Theory & Social Nature Of Experience And behavior Abraham Maslow 1908-1970

[14] George Herbert Mead (1863-1931born in South Hadley, Massachusetts. Educated at Oberlin College, Harvard University, and in Europe, he taught at the University of Chicago from 1894 until his death.

person to become one whole . . . **A completely functioning human being is the result. Pleck**—1975.

🔸 **Relationships Among Business Managerial Performance, Gender, Personality Characteristics, And The Perception Of Parental Sex Roles**—Skipi Lundquist Smoot—Cal School of Professional Psychology—San Diego Doctoral Dissertation—1985

🔸 **Maturation: The Adult Paradigm**—Skipi Lundquist Smoot, PhD—1994

🔸 **The Test Of Ego & Cognitive Development**—Skipi Lundquist Smoot, PhD—1996

Overview of Research on Sexual Identity

❖ <u>**Macoby & Jacklin**</u> (1974) 4 differences b/t males and females

❖ <u>**Broverman**</u>—Normal males (aggressive, independent and competitive and normal females (nurturant, dependent and noncompetitive). Asked what a normal male is, a normal female is and a normal adult—Normal females can't be normal adults.

❖ <u>**Bem, Sandra**</u>—ANDROGENY—the equal degrees of masc and femin char within the same person. Seen by many as healthy and some point to its manifestation as evidence of achievement of the final phase of personality development, an integration of personality traits, both masculine and feminine <u>**(Rebecca, Hefner & Oleshonsky 1974, Bem 1974**</u>. Some authors view sex roles as an intermediate step in personal development and point ot androgyny as the final transcendent stage of dev for both males and females.

❖ <u>**Mussen 1962, 1962 Harfor, Willis and Deabler 1967**</u> Highly masc adult males maya be very indep but also anxious and low self esteem Highly feminine women, show high passivity, low self esteem and high anxiety (Sears 1970, Webb 1963 and gall 1969

❖ <u>**Pleck**</u>—1975 defined the final transcending phase of human development as a level, which when reached, allows both sets of traits to become one whole. A completely functioning human being is the result.

❖ **Larwood, Wood & Inderlied** 1978) Most gender differences are not determined and that most traditionally viewed gender differences are results of socialization, stereotypical mytholody, and or role modeling to name a few.

❖ **Kagen Moss** (1962) social and cultural standards are the main determinant of whether a particular behavior remains stable or not from childhood through adulthood

❖ **Nibet (1961) abd Ganosib abd Ganosib** (1961) found it had been difficult to change a child's knowledge of gender identity after the age of three

❖ Pogrebin, 1980) babies are born male or female. For the first six week it is female unless a male hormone changes an embroy's course, it will develop female. All babies have thed same sex hormes, only the propotions are different.

❖ Money and Ehrhardt (1972) Gender Identity DifferentiationModel—Process continuous, beginning with conceptuion and culminating with emergence of adult gender identity.

❖ Money and Ehrhardt, 1968 The develop message carried by sex chromosome of the sperm (X or Y0 which joins with the X chromosome of the ovum. The female (XX) or male (XY) then sends instructions to the undifferentiated gonad. Depending on the instructions the gonad will evolve eith into a testis (about six week of gestation) or into an ovary (about 6 weeks later. The chromosomes, after passing on the genetic message, seem to have no further effect on development. For masc, the fetal testes takes over. This happens as result of two inferred fetal hormones which have not been identified or named. **Money and Ehrhardt** model show the first is an inferred fetal hormes Mullerian-inhibiting substance the 2nd is testosterone for dev of male ducts intomale reproduce systems. Examples of common abnormalities are those as a result of improper chromosomal division, causing Down's syndrome or Turners Syndrome (incurrent div of sex chromosomes). Turners' syndrome child looks like a girl, but is short, prob mentally retarded and sterile.

❖ Biological gender takes 5 forms (chromosomal, gender, gonadal gender, hormonal gender, inner reproductive structures and outer genital structures **(Hampson and Hampson, 1961).**

There are a numbe of medical disorders in which internal and external sex organs are incongruent, resulting in mistaken dicsions, at birth, sas to wheter the child is male or female. As a result, biological males may be rearded as girls and vice versa. Many of these disorders have bene studied **by money (1961): Money and Ehrhardt (1968): Hampson and Hampson 91961).** All provided support for conclusions concerning the influence of biological factors in **determination of gender identitidy**

❖ Hampson and Hampson (1961) suggests no correlation b/t psych gender and internal organs. Even external genital appearance seems to have surpisingly little effect on gender identity.

❖ SUMMARY OF GENDER IDENTITY research—**Hampson & Hampson (1961) and Money & Ehrhardt (1968).** 3 points emerge. The initial form of a developing human is female, not male. W/o the addition of appropriate hormones, a developing fetus will develop as a female. For dev of a male, two genetically controlled signsals must occur. First the appropr genetic code (XY) is nec and second, theing the maturation process a signal to produce androgens must occur. Without both, a physical male will not develop. The process in females will dev normally withonly the signal of the XX genetic pattern. However, the female process can be externally interfered with ttthrough drugs which may have been taken during pregnancy that are chemically similar to androgens or if tinappropr hormes were secreted by the fetusus during development.

❖ **Research in knowledge of Gender Identity, Hampson & hampson 1961) Money and Ehrhardt 91968 and Money 1961)** summarized with the statement that although boil factors do inf gender identity, evidence from studies indicat that the most important factor to the knowledge of gender identiy is the gender the child has been assigned by parents and the gender in which he/she was raised.

❖ APA HELP CENTER **(c) Copyright 2004 American Psychological Association**

❖ **What Causes a Person To Have a Particular Sexual Orientation?** There are numerous theories about the origins of a person's sexual orientation. Most scientists today agree that sexual orientation is most likely the result of a complex interaction of environmental, cognitive and biological factors. In most people, sexual orientation is shaped at an early age. There is also considerable recent evidence to suggest that biology, including genetic or inborn hormonal factors, play a significant role in a person's sexuality. It's important to recognize that there are probably many reasons for a person's sexual orientation, and the reasons may be different for different people.

❖ **Is Sexual Orientation a Choice?No,** human beings cannot choose to be either gay or straight. For most people, sexual orientation emerges in early adolescence without any prior sexual experience. Although we can choose whether to act on our feelings, psychologists do not consider sexual orientation to be a conscious choice that can be voluntarily changed.

❖ **Can Therapy Change Sexual Orientation?No;** even though most homosexuals live successful, happy lives, some homosexual or bisexual people may seek to change their sexual orientation through therapy, often coerced by family members or religious groupsto try and do so. The reality is that homosexuality is not an illness. It does not require treatment and is not

❖ **Is Homosexuality a Mental Illness or Emotional Problem?**No. Psychologists, psychiatrists, and other mental health professionals agree that homosexuality is not an illness, a mental disorder, or an emotional problem. More than 35 years of objective, well-designed scientific research has shown that homosexuality, in and itself, is not associated with mental disorders or emotional or social problems. Homosexuality was once thought to be a mental illness because mental health professionals and society had biased information. In the past, the studies of gay, lesbian, and bisexual people involved only those in therapy, thus biasing theresulting conclusions. When researchers examined data about such people who were not in therapy, the idea that homosexuality was a mental illness was quickly found to be untrue. In 1973 the American Psychiatric Association confirmed the importance of the new, better-designed research and removed homosexuality from the official manual that lists mental and emotional disorders. Two years later, the American Psychological Association passed a resolution supporting this removal.

❖ For more than 25 years, both associations have urged all mental health professionals to help dispel the stigma of mental illness that some people still associate with homosexual orientation.

❖ **Can Lesbians, Gay Men, and Bisexuals Be Good Parents?** Yes. Studies comparing groups of children raised by homosexual and by heterosexual parents find no developmental differences between the two groups of children in four critical areas: their intelligence, psychological adjustment, social adjustment, and popularity with friends. It is also important to realize that a parent's sexual orientation does not indicate their children's

Many areas of conflict can be solved by problem solving, agreeing to disagree or considering alternatives. However, many others areas of divergent philosophical expectations such as parenting styles, religious convictions, political ideation, sex role expectations, divergent educational background as well as social and cultural differences cannot.

It is unfortunate but true that most couples never have the slightest idea how important these areas of differences are and often don't even know they exist until after four or five years or until these areas of possible conflict come into view.

CHAPTER 10

LESSON 2B
Responsibility for Others

How Much responsibility for others is 'Too Much"??

LESSON #2B –
RESPONSIBILITY FOR OTHERS
What is 'too much" responsibility for others?

- **We are _not_ _responsible_ for the lessons of others.** To try only leads to our becoming crutches and their becoming crippled. We are, however, responsible for teaching our child to care for themselves. Children are not our possessions. They are loaned to us in trust, until hopefully we have helped them learn to assume appropriate personal responsibility for their lives, choices, and lessons.

- **Personal behavior in relationships in heavily influences by Social expectations.** Society puts great sanctions (often punishment) on those who do not follow or live up to their expected roles. Many women are taught they should be nurturing and "fix" others problems, always act in helpful ways and take responsibility for family members who are weak or not well.

- **THE CODEPENDENCY MOVEMENT STATES THAT PEOPLE BEHAVING IN CODEPENDENT WAYS** (inappropriate assumption of responsibility for others) **ARE NOT HELPFUL AND ARE AT LEAST PARTLY RESPONSIBLE FOR THE BEHAVIOR OF ONE WHO IS ILL OR IRRESPONSIBLE.** Although it is inappropriate to assume inappropriate responsibility for others, it is often extremely difficult to know the exact position of the line between appropriate help and letting people "sink" or swim. Sometimes, people are not able to save themselves. Sometimes, it is hard to tell (without the help of a trained professional) whether another is able to care for themselves or not and even then it may be impossible to know for sure.

CATEGORIES OF RESPONSIBILITY FOR OTHERS

Directing others

Are you frustrated because other people won't take your "direction", allow you to "help" them, or instrust them in the "correct" ways to live? Directing "Others" doesn't work. They often...

.............run away

.... Fight back ...

Or become Psychologically crippled
& .... unable to care for themselves."

EMOTIONAL DETACHMENT

Respect For The
Personal Competence
Of Others

We are responsible for teaching our children to learn to appropriately care for themselves

The "Map"

LESSON 2B
RESPONSIBILITY FOR OTHERS

*WE ARE **NOT** RESPONSIBLE FOR THE LESSONS OF OTHERS*

To try often leads to our becoming a crutch and the crippling of the other. Parents are responsible for teaching a child to learn appropriate methods of how to care for themselves. However, the proper balance between assuming appropriate responsibility for others and trying to "fix" problems of others that are rightfully theirs is a potentially blurry line . . . often fraught with pain, uncertainty and devastating choices.

Personal Beliefs concerning Responsibility for Others as well as the Self are closely connected and heavily influenced by Family Belief Systems, Role Modeling of Parents and important others as well as Religious beliefs and perceptions of parental and family responsibility.

CODEPENDENT VS INTERDEPENDENT RELATIONSHIPS

Although we are each personally responsible for ourselves, and as parents responsible for helping our children learn appropriate methods of self care, this obligation does not, except in certain exceptional circumstances include automatic assumption of responsibility for other adults. It is often extremely confusing to ascertain where these obligations begin or end as a result of unscrambling the categories of **Codependency** and **Emotional Detachment**.

This perplexity is frequently the result of ambiguous definitions of both categories as well as their causes. In addition, many confusing issues result from personal Belief Systems (what we should or should not do), the idea of helping vs ignoring the problems of others, the belief in an obligation to Fix the Problems of others who are uncertain about their choices, in need of advice, etc. And some people just feel the obligation to "set others straight" on "proper" behavior or methods of problem solving.

Research and literature on the subjects of **Codependency** (the state of mutual dependence) and **Emotional Detachment (Mental Assertiveness**) is extensive.

What is Codependency?.

The concept of **Codependency** originated in the 1970's by alcohol counselors. **Codependency**[1] is defined as 1) the state of being mutually dependent, for example, a relationship between two individuals who are emotionally dependent on one another or 2) a dysfunctional relationship pattern in which an individual is psychologically depend on (or controlled by) a person, who has a pathological addition (eg alcohol, gambling, etc.)

My own observation of the causes, symptoms and behaviors observed in of Codependency falls into the category of unresolved issues of **Symbiotic Attachment** (inability to perceive the self as a separate person able to make their own decisions and solve their own problems. **(Task 2)**. According to Psychological Theory (**Effective Psychotherapy Hellmuth Kaiser 1965) "The struggle against seeing oneself as an individual is the core of every neurosis" and "the universal defense against individuality (emotional fusion) is a Delusion". "The true conflict is between recognizing the fact of one's aloneness and our need to avoid and deny it*".**

Understanding Codependency in Relationships

It is often confusing to differentiate the many aspects of Codependency and Healthy Detachment in the relationships we have with others. Healthy Detachment is usually easier to understand in Spousal Relationships, Friendships and in those of our Adult children and our own Parents. However, it often becomes extremely difficult to identify and work through the many issues connected with these categories in relationships with our Teenagers, **Mentally Ill family members**, friends **and family with Alcoholism and Drug problems,** those showing clear Psychological Symptoms or our children or other family members suffering from **Learning Disabilities.**

---

[1]   APA Dictionary of Psychology

What is Healthy Detachment?

The Psychological theory underlying **Emotional Detachment** differentiates between an <u>inability to connect emotionally</u> with others (as a result of psychiatric symptoms[2]) and the concept of **Mental Assertiveness**. **Mental Assertiveness (Emotional detachment)** is a positive and deliberate mental attitude which avoids engaging the emotions of others. It is often applied to those who are in some way emotionally overly demanding. It is not to be confused with being willfully cold or unpleasant, because it is a positive mental attitude[3]".

EMOTIONAL DETACHMENT is defined here as both Respect for the Self and Personal Competence of others. It is the Ability to say No when appropriate, to differentiate between Helping, becoming a crutch and having developed the ability to set appropriate limits for the self and knowledge of when to do so.

EMOTIONAL DETACHMENT is an aspect of the Psychological **Maturation characteristic of Interdependence described in Chapter 6 Task 3. As previously discussed** Interdependence is the Psychological Term for the type of behavior between two equal people within Relationships who are able to be independent and depend on each other without loosing emotional connection. Each is free to meet their own needs (if not at the expense of the other), agree or disagree, share their feelings honestly and be comfortable with their differences.

Reason for taking "too Much or Too Little Responsibility

Many clients come to therapy without a clear understanding of what Should or Should Not be done for the self, in relations, when to help others and even what an appropriate method of helping self or others consists of. However many others report strong beliefs in **Shoulds/Oughts, Black/White**

---

[2]   Narcissism, severe stress, anxiety, disassociation, disinterest or anger at others, etc.

[3]   The Wikipedia Encyclopedia—Mental assertiveness.

perception of world and/or Generalizations such as always, never, etc. Many feel an obligation to instruct others in the way the "Other" "should" behave, what their responsibilities are, etc. For example, many clients report feeling an obligation to 1) let people know when they have done something wrong and 2) to assist others (close friends or relatives) with their problems even if they don't ask for my help. Others report a Belief in a mandatory right and wrong way of do things and often try to help others do things "Right". Some report they would not hesitate to point it out an insignificant mistake a friend had made to help them do better next time.

Many feel a duty to help others **fix their problems.** Some believe their own behavior "causes" the responses of others. Parents may believe it is a duty to continually get their child back to "Square One" of responsible behavior. Some Parents believe their child's dysfunctional behavior is the direct result of mistakes made in parenting vs the concept that mistakes are the result of many variables (temperament, heredity, peers, environment, social class, personal characteristics, etc.) contributing to both functional and dysfunctional behavior. Answers to questions on the Test of Ego and Cognitive Development have included such items as 1) "I believe I am responsible for how others feel about me".2) "People who love each other should always try to shield loved ones from experiencing unpleasantness". 3) "I sometimes find myself helping to fix the problems of another who I believe is too weak to help themselves even when I don't really want to", 4) "It is Ok to write an Excuse for a child who has "played hooky" from school rather than allow the child to take responsibility for their own behavior", 5) "It is usually the parents' fault if their teenager acts irresponsibly and therefore, the parents duty to fix the problem".

Many report "The personal function, behaviors, attitudes, morals, legal problems, etc of other family members are my own moral (& sometimes legal) obligation and duty to fix". This may be the result of believing that parenting skills are the only cause of dysfunctional behavior. Others report believing 1) "Family members behavior is a direct statement about the worth of their family." 2)" I feel torn between my feelings of pity, duty and /or obligation to help a family member who repeatedly gets into trouble vs my belief that people learn best from taking the consequences of their own behavior." 3)" If an adult child behaves irresponsibly, it is the parents duty to somehow find a method to change the dysfunctional behavior." 4) "Parents should take the blame (and the credit) for the way their child turns out because an offspring's behavior is the usually the direct result of parenting techniques." 5) "If a an older Teen or adult child becomes involved in Drugs or Alcohol it is usually the result of inadequate parenting." FMR—

Others responses on the TECD indicate 1) "the need to correct others when the other doesn't do things right", 2) Things should always be done perfectly, that 3) making a mistake is always wrong, 4) Mistakes are a cause for embarrassment because they show a person does not know how to behave correctly, 5) Geel a need to be perfect, 6) Others (my family, friends, etc) often need my help to get things done correctly and 7) There is a right and a wrong way to do most things.

"HOW MUCH "HELP" IS "TOO MUCH"?"

The Concept of **Codependency** includes the ideology and behaviors that result in "Helping or receiving too much help in personal relationships" As previously mentioned the concept of Codependency was begun in the 1970's by Alcoholic Counselors.

Characteristics of those described in Alcoholics or Adult Children of Alcoholics (1987[4]—Recovery Publications) were feelings of isolation, fear of authority, need for approval, lose of identity, fear of anger and criticism. Others characteristics identified included becoming or marrying alcoholics, living life from a viewpoint of helping victims, an overdeveloped sense of responsibility, avoidance of looking closely at themselves, feelings of guilt when standing up for themselves, addiction to excitement, confusing love with pity, stuffing feelings and/or lose of ability to feel or express feelings. Also identified was Low self esteem (often compensated for by trying to appear superior) and dependent personalities that fear abandonment.

---

[4]   Copyright 1987 Recovery Publications, San Diego, Ca—Authors Notes
       as presented The 12 Steps for Adult Children of Alcoholic and Other
       Dysfunctional Families

Psychological FACTORS underlying difficulty resolving Symbiotic Attachment (the Human Development Stage discussed in Chapter 5—Task 2) include trouble developing ability to define the self as an emotionally and physically separate self (strong Ego Boundaries[5]). **Margaret Mahler,** described this Developmental Task as a phase (Separation-Individuation) in the mother child relationship (beginning at about 18 months) during which time the child begins to perceive the self as distinct from the mother and to develop a sense of individual identity. She believed much of the pathology of the Borderline States[6] (unstable impulse control, unstable relationships, moods and self image) to be rooted in failure to have resolved this stage of development.

Jung described Differentiation as the goal of individual personality development. **Murray Bowen** described Differentiation as the ability to be emotionally separate from the "undifferentiated family ego mass" and achieve independence and maturity without losing the capacity for emotional connectedness. He believed that emotional problems are in direct proportion to the "hold" feelings have over the ability to think objectively. The **insecurity and emotional neediness of an Undifferentiated person** is <u>experienced</u> as "forcing" them to hold similar attitudes as loved one **(often resulting in giving up their own individuality).**

<u>Freud, Sigmund </u>described Personality Characteristics as Facades (Pretenses) used to avoid and deny conflict and preserve relationships. He stated that each defensive Facade camouflages its real purpose . . . the avoidance of human differences. As can be seen by the above writings of numerous Theoretical Giants who have contributed to the Science of Psychological, the necessity for healthy emotional separation presents numerous problems to most . . . if not all participants in the relationship.

---

[5]   *Feldern, P (1928) coined   the Phrase Ego Boundaries for the concept of ability to define the self as an emotionally and physically separate self*
Borderline Personality Disorder-The DSMIV

[6]

ATTITUDEs & BEHAVIORS in CODEPENDENT Relationships

Belief systems *and* **personal perceptions of Rules for ourselves and others** *(expectations) all contribute to the Roles we have learned to take in relationships. Rules and Roles are often the result of Cultural and Gender expectations.* ***Belief Systems are a major contributor to*** *Roles played in life and* attitudes concerning what constitutes ***Right and Wrong*** *ways of behaving. These behaviors are often classified as* ***Codependency.***

We have all been exposed or involved with those who can be described as a **"Know it all".** These people feel the need to INSTRUCT OTHERS in the "Correct" way of life. This type of instruction is often seen by those exhibiting it as "being of assistance" to others. Many of these "Helpers" have no idea of the negative effect they illicit in others. This mental set is described in the Psychological Literature, especially in the writings of Ellis, Albert. and Glasser, William as believing and engaging in **GENERALIZATION, SHOULDS, OUGHTS & ALWAYS, and/or BLACK AND WHITE** perceptions of the world.

Many others report a need not only **to Help "Fix" the problems of others** but believe it is their Moral Obligation to do so. Still others believe their own behavior has somehow "caused" the problems they have with others (so they must do everything possible to fix it). Some believe certain others (especially those with different ideas) are unable to assume responsibility for themselves without help. And some believe they need to correct others attitudes and behavior because making mistakes is wrong. Once in a while we find a person who truly believes that most others **NEVER DO ANYTHING RIGHT.**

 The Role of **Instructor** in codependent relationships is fraught with numerous relationship conflicts with fear of abandonment usually at the core of this life role. However, there are some important psychological differences.

Those who assume an Instructor Role may often been seen Withdrawing **from others into anger, indifference, etc. to avoid experiencing** <u>anxiety</u> **in relationships. This type of behavior can be seen in those who** <u>need</u> **others to agree with them can be identified**

in such TECD responses as "I try to force you to change. If you don't change, I look for someone else who might agree with me." Others attempt **to** resolve relationship conflict by Controlling Ideas And Behaviors Of Others And still others feel the need to **"prove to others the right to be "who I am". However, it can be clearly seen, that the need to** prove **my "right "to others reveals unresolved emotional fusion. Why? . . . Because if we really know we have the right to be an individual we don't have to prove it to anyone. If they don't agree, we know they have the right to their opinion, but it doesn't change mine.**

The Instructor role can often be seen in the diagnosis of NARCISSISTIC CHARACTER DISORDER—Symptoms of this diagnostic category may include feelings of Self importance, preoccupation with envy, fantasies of success or ruminations about the uniqueness of their own problems. A Sense of entitlement and/or a lack of empathy may lead to taking advantage of others. Forceful rejection of criticism and need for constant attention and admiration is also common. Characteristics of **BORDERLINE PERSONALLITY DISORDER** is also commonly observed in those who have chosen the Instructor Role. Uncertain about who they are and lacking the ability to maintain stable interpersonal relationships symptoms of BLPD may include impulsive, recurrent suicide threats or attempts, emotional instability, intense, inappropriate anger, feelings of emptiness or boredom and frantic attempts to avoid abandonment.

It is often difficult to understand why certain people appear to abandon their own goals and plans for life in the Role of "Helper". The Role of `Helper` in relationships can be more easily understood when visualized as the behavior  of one suffering from the fear of abandonment. Numerous behaviors can be understood when perceived from the need to conform and do things "your way" so" you won't be angry with me or leave me". However, the underlying anxiety experienced as a result of assumption of the Role of Helper may lead to avoidance of facing the possibility that the need for having a relationship is more important than personal independence. As a result many withdraw into sleep, drugs, eating and denial to repress knowledge that pleasing others takes priority over personal integrity

Needing approval of others so much they have trouble making independent decisions is observed in those diagnosed with DEPENDENT Personality Disorders. These persons may agree with other whom they know to be wrong, fear abandonment, feel helpless when alone and miserable when relationships end. They are easily hurt by criticism and even volunteer for unpleasant tasks to gain favor of others.

However, it is important to clearly understand that numerous reasons exist for **Helper** and **Instructor** types of behaviors besides those symptomatic of mental characteristics commonly described as "Neurotic". Included in the many other Reasons for presentation of behaviors symptomatic of Codependency are the 1) **Rules and Beliefs we have learned during our life time, 2) our perception of appropriate gender roles, 3) things we have learned should and/or ought to be done/or not done** as well as the enormous reservoir of **4) Moral behaviors our families or religions has instilled in our minds and psyches.**

ORIGINS OF "INSTRUCTOR" AND "HELPER" BEHAVIORS

We learn our responses from others in **Family of origin**. Many are taught that if children misbehave it's the parents fault. Others have learned to give, give and . . . give some more while we wait for others to recognize our wonderful behavior. Many learned that those seen as the Good Girl or Boy received the best kind of attention and respect. Many adults have never really learned to think objectively for themselves, believing their role is to follow the rules of authority, the spouse or some respected others because it's the "right" thing to do, because God says so, or because that's the way they got adoration as a child.

Transference [7] as a reason for emotional response and behavior has been discussed in other sections of this book. Transference is one of the most important unconscious reasons why we like someone (or dislike them) on sight. The reason? . . . They remind us of someone we loved, disliked, fear, etc., in the past . . . Usually in our family of origin.

As described in the writings of **Virginia Satir** we are drawn to those who present an unresolved issue or problem we struggled with in our past (usually a parent, sibling, important other, etc.). In our present relationship we respond to others in the same way we did in the past, by conforming, resisting, hiding, helping or behaving in similar ways to those from the past. Some of us continue to behave as we ourselves did previously (conforming, resisting, agreeing, etc). Some of us assume the Role we saw in a respected Parent or other (Instructor, Helper, etc.).

However, many of us, living in extreme pain have assumed the Role Helper due to many other reasons that do not fall into the categories commonly seen as codependency.

WHY DO SO MANY OF US HELP OTHERS "TOO MUCH?
Perception of RESPONSIBILITY for others must depend on examination and objective (vs subjective) answers to many questions within the following groups of relationships. **Codependency**[8] is defined as the dependence of two people, groups, or organisms on each other, especially when this reinforces mutually harmful behavior patterns. Codependency [9] is also defined as a relationship of mutual need in which a person such as the partner of an alcoholic or a parent of a drug-addicted child needs to feel needed by the other person. However these definitions do not identify all of the essential ingredients surrounding such relationships in question.

---

[7] TRANSFERENCE described in Psychodynamic Theory as an emotional response to something that happens in the present that reminds me of an emotional response to something that happened in the past

[8] Encarta Encyclopedia

[9] Encarta Encyclopedia

BELIEF SYSTEMS CONCERNING DUTY

Personal Perceptions of Duty for Others is usually based on Belief Systems, Culture and/or Religious Teachings. People often disagree concerning their conclusions. • Social expectations for behavior in relationships heavily influence personal behavior. Society puts great sanctions (punishment) on those who do not follow or live up to their expected roles. Many women are taught they should be nurturing and "fix" others problems, always act in helpful ways, take responsibility for family members who are not well or weak.

However, it is well to keep in mind that even in difficult situations Psychological Maturation requires learning to live up to personal Potential. For example: A drug Addicted Adult Spouse or Sibling must take responsibility for Sobriety. If they refuse, detachment by the spouse, parent or sibling is usually the answer. However, an Ill or elderly parent may not be able to care for themselves. Is a nursing home or family care the answer?

- **When is it our "duty to help others? Parents, Siblings, Friends? Even if we don't want to?** This is a question to be answered by personal conclusions concerning Morality and Belief Systems.
- **What is my Role with others in terms of helping them Who should we help? Our ill adult parent?? When is it appropriate to detach. Parents are responsible for teaching a child to care for themselves**. The proper balance between helping someone fix their own problem and "fixing" it for them is often a blurry line and fraught with uncertainty and devastating choices. Ill Parents of Adults are another matter and answers to whether to help them or not is usually based on belief Systems. Sometimes, perceptions of duty to help Parents or Siblings may be distorted by Transferences (anger, resentment, fear, abuse, etc.) from the past. It is well to consider all aspects of each situation carefully and from a point of view for Empathy for others before making a final decision.
- **What techniques can I use to make Objective decisions concerning my duty to loved family members and others?** In ordinary family relationship it is important to keep in mind

the importance of communication Skills and Problem Solving techniques for making detachment decisions.

- **Successful** Decision Making is most effective when based on well thought out Cognitive objective points of view vs emotional choices. In most situations, responsibility for sobriety is usually that of the Drug addicted family member. However, there may be exceptions to this mandate in the areas of mental retardation, severe emotional dysfunction, neurological imbalances, etc. Detachment issues with aged or ill parents also fall into the category of difficult decisions based on personal belief system, the personal situation of the person in need, etc.
- TRANSFERENCE (something in the present reminds me of something from the past). Whether unresolved issues from the past, called are able to find resolution in the present relationship is often the result of Objective vs Subjective thinking, Education, Taking a course in Psychology or even treatment in Individual, Family or Marital Psychotherapy.

Transference is sometimes referred to a **"Broken Record"** is because the issues in the relationship go around and around like a broken Record. The writings of **Virginia Satir,** present the new relationships as an opportunity for resolution of problems similar to those from the past. As Adults we have the opportunity to observe similar types of issues in the present and successfully resolve them with different objective types of problem solving methods. If we are able to so this we may resolve our anxiety and solve our problem. If we can't we may continue in our Broken Record Type of relationships.

The "Broken Record"

A serious marital problem can be understood utilizing the concept of Transference in the following situation.

A female client of mine assumed the role of **Instructor** (as did her divorced Mother in parental relationships) in all of her Adult Relationships. The Woman worked at a job that demanded an Authoritarian Role. The Woman assisted her appreciative Mother in continual instruction of her Siblings concerning the Proper way to live their lives. The Woman married a Man who always covertly did what he wanted to (similarly to his behavior in his relationship with his mother whom he was able to deceive). The Woman continued to instruct the Husband in her perception of Proper behavior (expecting appreciation like she had received from her mother). The Husband continued to deceive. The Couple came to Therapy for help resolving these issues. They were offered insight in methods of truthfulness, problem solving and knowledge of individual negotiable vs non negotiable values. The Woman continued to instruct and feel abandoned by a husband who refused to comply. The Husband eventually realized that Psychological Maturation included the ability to state his negotiable vs nonnegotiable values. When attempted problem solving did not result in understanding of each other's point of view he moved on.

As mentioned in a previous chapter Problem Solving in relationships is one of the most important methods of understanding ourselves and others and working out techniques for conflict resolution. It is extremely important that an adult have learned to personally think through and objectively understand which of the many areas of our own Personal Values are comfortably negotiable vs nonnegotiable.

RESPECT FOR PERSONAL COMPETENCE OF OTHERS

In the area of attempting to understand our personal responsibilities in most of our relationships with others including children, teens and older teens it is important to remember that allowing others to take personal responsibility leads to growth. The belief that making a mistake is wrong is a mistake. Allowing a child or teen to take the consequences of their own inappropriate behavior is often a good choice. Covering for a misbehaving teen who plays hooky, is usually a poor choice. Allowing children to take the consequence of their mistakes and work out more appropriate future behaviors are often the most successful parental choice we can make. And although there are certainly exceptions to this directive it is well to remember that Mistakes are nature's way of teaching what works and what doesn't.

Respect for the Competence of self and Others requires the knowledge that it is not always a fact that Family is My Responsibility, that I must Fix Others Problems or that there are many Shoulds and Oughts that must be followed in order for life to be fair or for others to agree with us. Psychological Maturation is the Ability to think for ourselves, face objective reality and accept the truth based on what's best for self and others in the long run.

The area of assuming responsibility for Mentally Ill family members, those with drug problems, learning disabilities, elderly parents, etc. presents another aspect of Responsibility. As a result, it is necessary we understand scientific as well as the Psychological facts underlying each situation. Personal responsibility for family members or others who can't help themselves may include many conflicting aspects of each situation. However, as previously mentioned it is important we understand whether our loved one has a "Broken Wing" and as such cannot easily assume personal responsibility. A loved one may have characteristics of Low IQ, mental illness or learning disorders which result in inability or lowered ability to help themselves. Making well thought out mature decisions in such situations require a broad, objective knowledge of the facts of each. Only then are we able to come to a most appropriate decision for that particular situation.,

EMOTIONAL DETACHMENT

in Successful Interdependent Relationships

Two **"WHOLE"** selves reside in successful **interdependent relationships**. Each self is comfortable with personal differences while maintaining loving emotional detachment and deep commitment to the relationship and to the other. Both have developed necessary techniques to resolve relationship problems in ways that compromise neither personal or family integrity nor respect for themselves and each other. **We can learn to be a separate self in a relationship, being true to our individual needs, while showing respect for the integrity and needs of others.**

The numerous, multifaceted, often conflicting Rules, Roles & Life Scripts learned in our Family of Origin often lie at the core of ability or inability to develop characteristics of healthy emotional detachment (Differentiation). Assumption of both Helper and Instructor Roles are often the result of having learned behaviors of over socialization (others needs are more important than mine) as well as having assumed the duty to "Fix" the Problems of Others. How is this possible?

Childhood impressions (often unconsciously held as an adult) of Self at the center of the Universe are more common than might be expected and lie at the core of much conflict in adult relationships. Many adults report a suspicion of an innate right to be a "separate self" but without much certainty. Such persons often search for permission from important others to justify assumption of independent functioning.

It is relatively easy to understand the Role and belief system of a "know it all" Instructor as occupying a position at the center of the Universe. However, the center of the Universe may also be the position of a Helper who believes them self to be the "worst" person in the universe whose role is to Help deserving others as a means of insurance against abandonment.

Due to lack of knowledge concerning Human Development, it is the atypical parent who teaches techniques for assumption of Responsibility for the self (protecting the self) as well as Respect for Personal Responsibility of Others to their children. Of equal but relatively unrecognized importance is the fact that Internal Ego Boundaries (Emotional) must develop pliability that protects the self from emotional harm without becoming so rigid they close out objective reality. It is equally important to understand that External Ego Boundaries (Physical) be respected from the onslaught of physical damage from others. As a result of educating our children in the techniques of Problem Solving it is possible to easily work out many aspects of personal relationships with others in a manner that respects the integrity of both the self and others.

The reasons for lack of understanding of Human development include the fact that schools rarely, if ever allow the Science of Psychology to be taught in Grade, Intermediate and High School. Only those who take Psychology classes in College become knowledgeable in the many Psychological techniques that may help parents guide their children in developing mature relationships with others. The reasons for this sad state of affairs are varied but often reflect the social, cultural and/or religious Rules & Roles of Life taught in our families of origin. Sometimes these Rules and Roles are appropriate, often they lead to many areas of psychological immaturity and behaviors that conflict in relationships with others.

What Is <u>Healthy</u> Detachment?

Healthy **Emotional Detachment (Interdependence)** has been rigorously studied in the field of Adult Psychological Development. **Eric Berne**[10] **described it as the Adult Ego State, the part of the Psyche—similar to a computer—that is free to objectively consider wants and duties of the self and others and make decisions based on what is best for each in the long run.** He believed it to be a **normal part of a mature Adult and those not able to achieve this stage can be seen as immature.**

Resolution of **Egocentricity**, the Human Developmental Stage of **Separation-Individuation normally** occurring before age 3 can be identified in Adults comfortable with Interdependence. **Kohut, H, Kohut, H. and Kernberg, Otto**[11] the major contributors to the theory of **Narcissism** believed **Egocentricity** (perceptions of the self as the center of the Universe) is normal for children but maturation demands the ability to perceive the needs of self and others as equally important. Kernberg believed Adult Narcissism to be a result of development of an abnormal grandiose self. Both agree that Adult Narcissism is the result of the Narcissistic Adults interpretations of interactions with their primary caretaker (usually the Mother). Kohut's view is that such patients are extremely sensitive to failures, disappoints and slights and their self esteem is extremely labile.

 Although We are not responsible for the lessons of others, we are, responsible for teaching our children to care for themselves. As mentioned in the beginning of this chapter, children are not our possessions, but loaned to us in trust, until hopefully we have helped them learn to assume appropriate personal responsibility for their lives, choices, and lessons.

---

[10] Eric Berne—The adult Ego State

[11] Kohut, H—(1971) Kohut, Heinz 1971 and Kernberg, Otto (1975)

In an effort to teach methods of personal responsibility, we as parents must lean methods of **EMOTIONAL DETACHMENT** from tendencies to take "too much responsibility for those we love. Some of these methods must includes the ability to say No, understanding the differences between helping others vs being a crutch (Detachment) and Setting appropriate limits for the self & others, In the second sense, it is a type of mental assertiveness that allows people to maintain their boundaries and psychic integrity when faced with the emotional demands of another person or group of persons. These definitions are within the framework of psychology and academia, not those of everyone else in the world. This type of emotional detachment does not mean avoiding the feeling of empathy; it is actually more of an awareness of empathetic feelings that allows the person space needed to rationally choose whether or not to engage or be overwhelmed by such feelings.

*The Category of **loving, healthy,*** Emotional detachment must include Respect for the Personal Competence of others as well as a well-informed OBJECTIVE analysis of the characteristics of our loved ones personal competence.

Detachment—TOUGH LOVE—DRUG ADDICTION

The answer to whether Detachment in the form of Tough Love between Parent and Offspring is appropriate "help" depends on specific aspects of the situation in question. For example: Questions such as the following must be examined and faced from the perceptive of complete honesty, Moral Values and well educated critical thinking.

- *How can you detach from one you love?* It is often very difficult to observe a loved one making mistakes and taking the consequences of them. However, it is important to allow a child or other loved one to do so. But here again, you must consider all the aspects of a given situation and help the other take responsibility for living up to their potential.

- *What can I do to help my child or spouse who uses drugs, alcohol, etc?* Appropriate Help for others does not include taking responsibility that is _rightfully_ theirs. However, **objective questions concerning what duties are** rightfully those of another must also include consideration of IQ levels, emotional disorders, cognitive disabilities as well as Drug Abuse, and other facets such as. Psychological development and specific situations including living environment and family relationships.

- *What is Tough Love?* Tough Love is a term for allowing others to take responsibility for their own actions. **The Codependency movement states that people behaving in codependent ways are not helping and are at least partly responsible for the behavior of one who is ill or irresponsible.** However, although it is inappropriate to take complete responsibility for others who can care for themselves, it is often impossible to know where the line between appropriate help and letting people "sink" or swim falls. Sometimes, people are not able to save themselves. Sometimes, it is hard to tell without the help of a trained professional. And even then it may be impossible to know for sure.

- *Does Tough Love work?* It usually is a good idea to carefully consider all aspects of a situation being assessed for Tough Love before deciding whether detachment is the best choice of action. Touch Love with appropriate safeguards is often the best choice. For example, the literature suggests letting a Drug addicted Adult Child take responsibility for their own choices. However, most professionals believe Rehabilitation vs Jail is the best choice for treatment of Drug Addiction. In the case of really hard core Drug Addiction, recovering clients have told me that Jail was for them the last necessary lesson leading to Sobriety. For others, the road from Jail may lead to death.

One of the most logical[12] (and difficult to find fault with) discussions of **Tough Love** was written by an Author who had several sons with severe drug problems. She lived by her own Rules and believed they worked well. She said she would never let a loved one starve. She would always help them get into treatment. However, she would not let them return home to live unless they were sober. If they knocked on the door and requested food she would hand them food to eat, but not allow them to come in. She told them she loved them. But their Drug Addiction was their Responsibility and that she could not contribute to it. She made sure they knew that when they were ready to take Personal Responsibility and go into treatment she would take them there herself and be emotionally supportive. If they could not afford treatment she would help them financially with treatment.

Drug Addiction is a severe and serious problem in many families. Tough Love has been written about and praised by numerous knowledgeable authors. However, there are many well educated as well as moral reasons why family members might decide whether in the long run **Tough Love** will have assumed the countenance of **Savior** or **Villain** in their current conundrum.

The Following Vignettes are examples of 2 Cases in which **Tough Love** was used in attempts to resolve serious cases of **Drug Addiction between Parent and offspring.** Each has aspects that may be seen as supportive and/or non-supportive of **Tough Love.** Read these Vignettes from an Objective point of view and make your own well

---

[12]   TOUGH LOVE BY AUTHOR WHO SAID—GIVE THEM FOOD BUT don't let them live at home unless they agree to become sober.

thought out conclusions concerning which aspects of **Tough Love** you believe might be helpful, under what circumstances and reasons for your decisions

Case One—The Doorbell That Rings At Night

A Mother responds to the concept of tough love concerning a Son's Serious Drug Addiction

I struggle out of sleep at the sound. Is that a sound or just the trace of a bad dream? I feel the familiar knot of anxiety and fear in my stomach. I can feel my heart seems to have assumed an identify of its own as it races madly in panic. Blood pounds in my ears. "What is it this time" my mind cries out in my self? "Is it the police?" . . . "or another plea for help . . . or money".

Arising from my bed I walk into the front bedroom to look out the window. Yes, there it is . . . his car. Nausea, frustration, anger, anxiety all mix in my body as I go to the window overlooking the doorway and call down to the front steps. "Who is it,?" I inquire. "Me . . . it's me" calls my son. "What do you want?" I reply . . . "It's the middle of the nigh". "I need money for gas" my son replies from the step. "I'm hungry".

For over 30 years I lived in a relationship of agony with this son. At 16 we began a journey through horror and pain. As a loving mother, I tried to save my son. My son, in pain, frustration and panic struggled to  find his way. Nothing worked for long. Year after year it worsened . . . some years were better than others. His expectations for himself had always been high. He tried to attain impossible goals. When he failed, he learned to resort to drugs . . . at first just a little . . . to get him over the initial pain. Later, slowly, drugs became an addiction.

Eventually, his addiction becomes a way of life, that threatened not only himself, but the sanity of our family. I found myself in the position of being forced to choose between my son's life and that of my own. Sometimes, **Tough Love** was my welcomed **ALLY,** a weapon to counter insult, offense, abuse and once or twice even violence. Other times, **Tough Love** assumed the face of **ENEMY** to the soul of my starving son who begged on the street and lived in his car.

For many years . . . due to his usually decadent and sometime violent behavior, his two living brothers, refused to speak or allow him in their homes. Only at Christmas, when he knocked on this Parents door would his brothers' stay to welcome him for gifts and dinner.

 Not until the night he arrived home in a Taxi, that brought him from jail did I open the door and let him come home. It was for the last time.

Case One—Continues—Searching for Respect
The Son's Story

He was born 2nd in a family of 5 brothers. After spending 8 and ½ months of his fetal stage in a head first position he unexpectedly "flipped" and drew his first breaths from the breach position. At birth the left back side of his head was flat. A 3rd sibling had died at the age of 5 days from unidentified causes. Hospital records revealed Nurses had held the mothers' legs together until the Dr could arrive at the Hospital. An Oldest brother was a year and a half his senior while a third and fourth brother arrived eight and 16 years later.

 He had great difficulty in school from Learning Disabilities and ADHD. He had a hard time sitting still. He loved telling jokes and laughed heartily while telling them. As a child, without realizing it, he often told the beginning of one joke with the punch line of another. At such times, he seemed surprised that his perplexed audience didn't laugh right away.

In 1960 he was transferred to a school for mentally retarded children His mother, a naïve woman of 23 was surprised by the transfer but believed the school knew best. On a daily basis, the child returned home crying from misery. During the third week the Principal called asking why this little boy with an IQ of 112 had been identified as MR. His mother immediately transferred her child to a private Episcopal Academy where the sisters loved and treated him well although with strictness he resented.

Personal **characteristics** included 1) need for respect 2) need to rely on his own decisions, 3) a perception that deferring to authority of others was result in pain, 4) love of telling silly jokes, 5) need to be seen a "winner", 6) absolutely fabulous wonderful social skills when he chose to exhibit them (he could sell snow to an Eskimo), 7) knowledge of how to work hard, 8) need to be seen as fashionably dressed, 9) need for his possessions to be in perfect shape and order, 10) love of animals and pets, 11) absolute refusal to "give up" in the face of adversity 12) unwillingness to admit defeat 13) and humiliation at the thought of himself as a failure.

 Even as a child, he refused to "give up" <u>trying</u> to do <u>whatever</u> he <u>was intent on</u>. His determined attempts to ride a 2 wheeler bicycle resulted in repeatedly getting on and falling off. He refused all help from others to hold the handle bars or balance the seat. In spite of skinned knees and elbows, he continued his quest to be a "big boy" able to succeed on his own. And . . . at the end of that day, proudly and successfully rode the length of the driveway without falling off.

Family relationships with a Narcissistic, alcoholic husband and father who insisted he didn't need therapy were a nightmare. After many years of emotional abuse from a drunken father who couldn't keep his elbows from slipping off the dinner table the 16 year old son became involved in a physical battle with the father that ended with the son's blood dripping down the wall. The horrified Mother took her 4 sons (17, 16, 8 and 4 months) to a Motel while arranging for a divorce and purchase of a new home for Mother and sons. During his Jr High years, still unwilling to take Direction, his grandfather insisted he be sent to a Military Academy. Several of his High School years were spent in a Boarding School in Arizona. Eventually he returned home to his family.

As a teenager he and his older brother, worked in his Parents Fast Food Restaurant—his brother as Manager and himself an Assistant Manager. He started using drugs as a Teenager, first just a little and then more and more. He was arrested once for being under the influence and released to his Mother.

At 24 he married the beautiful blond Love of his Life in the Chapel on the Campus of the College where his new Wife had eearned a bachelor's degree in Chemistry. Moving to Michigan with his new wife, he worked as a Salesman for several companies. Apparently he still used drugs often and to excess. Eventually realizing their marriage had been a mistake, his wife moved out. He returned to California with a broken heart

 After that, his life began it's **serious**, <u>screaming</u> downhill plummet. He worked at many different jobs . . . in restaurants as assistant manager, in sales and auto supply jobs . . . as salesman . . . In Telemarketing. Sometimes he was able to keep his head afloat and sometimes not. Going from one job to another,. . . relationship to relationship . . . And finally, falling head long into the debilitating drug life style he just stopped trying to live normally. Insisting that Drug usage was not his problem . . . that he could quit any time, if he wanted to . . . **he didn't want to. He was positive he could find a way to use just a** <u>little</u> **. . . and return to the normal life style he came from . . . Any time . . . he** <u>really</u> **wanted to.**

For the next 20 years he went from one disastrous experience to the next . . . in and out of a job . . . living on the street . . . residency in cheap motels . . . involvement with others in such a life style. Once or twice after **pleadings from his mother to enter Sober Living Housing** he reluctantly agreed but left when he wouldn't conform to the rules and regulations. He refused to accept his need for NA Groups.

In 1994 while living on the street in his car his youngest 24 year old brother was murdered,. In emotional devastation, he agreed to seriously try to stay sober. He got a good job as an electrician with Sears traveling from State to State installing new equipment in their House wares department. Eventually he relapsed and lost his job. Again finding himself unwilling to follow the sober living standards of family or group Home, he continued to live in motels, the street or in his car.

In 2001 after his front teeth fell out and being 5150'd, he was let out of jail at 2:00 AM and put into a Taxi without shoes, clothes or a place to live. On that night, he knocked on the door of his Mother and Stepdad's house asking to come home. Saying he wanted to stay sober and try to salvage what was left of his life, his self respect and his dignity he still refused Sober Living, AA or NA. His Parents agreed that if he stayed sober and behaved pleasantly they would give it one last try. He relapsed once for a day.

 2 years later, still afraid to venture out of the house alone for fear of emotional attractions to places he had used drugs in the past, the foundations of his life were again devastatingly shaken by the death of his oldest brother. However, saying he could not relapse for the sake of both his Mother and himself, he remained completely sober. Staying close to home, he gained weight, shopped for family food once a week and planned for the day when he could feel strong enough to work without fear of relapse.

The effects of serious drug addiction, leaves a terrible trail of destruction, to health, brain cells and psychological well being. Being sober, also affects many people with the terrible reality of the effects of their past choices on themselves and others. The result of that reality left him with serious emotional and physical problems as well as the inability to function normally in the work place. But in spite of the many obstacles he faced on a daily basis he REALLY believed that in a short time, he would win his struggle to attain the success he had longed for . . . his entire life.

 On the Night of his 50th Birthday, after eating a Slice of his favorite Ice cream Cake, he arose from his bed with terrible pain in his left arm. After asking his mother to drive him to the Emergency Room he died standing up and fell to the floor behind his mother who was gathering her coat and purse for the drive to the Hospital. He rests in a hillside grave over looking the Ocean a few steps from the Final Resting places of his two brothers who preceded him in death.

CASE TWO—PORTRAIT OF DRUG ADDICTION

A Mother Responds a Son's Serious Drug Addiction

He was lying on the sidewalk in front of the entrance to a closed and abandoned Restaurant where we had agreed to meet. Slowly his large hands pushed his body into a sitting position. Carefully he stood and walked to the passenger side of my car.

Wearing no belt, the waist of his pants slid well below his bony hips. Turning slightly to put one leg inside my car, the half exposed flesh at the top of the crease in his buttocks shown pasty pale over the top of his filthy, too large pants.

As he got into my car his terrible body odor assaulted me. The stench from previously taken drugs, snorted or shot, seeped from the pores of his long unwashed body into his clothing and completely assailed the warm interior of my car. Immediately he began removing his dirty, worn out tennis shoes. He wore no socks. The smell of his feet gagged me. He started to cry.

Late, tired, and resentful over being here, I stared at this filthy young man. Old conflicting emotions again rushed into my consciousness as I felt the twin emotions of love and resentment sweep over me. Once again, I felt trapped and nauseous. I desperately longed for an end to the misery and frustration that this beloved child's tragic and apparently uncontrollable lifestyle had brought to both our lives. It shouldn't be this way, I thought. It wasn't supposed to turn out this way.

"Please let me come home", he begged me "I have no place to go". He poured out his pain. "I was sleeping on my friends porch but they kicked me out. A drug addict acquaintance had taught him to panhandle on the street. Most of the money they collected by begging was used for drugs. "Please, I want to come home". **Again, I told him I would get his truck out of impound and pay for treatment in a recovery home. Only then if he stayed sober and drug free, would I talk with him about the possibility of coming home.** Quickly becoming visibly agitated **the** black points of lens in his eyes, bored into mine. Raising his arm, he shook a finger close to my face, "I'll never do it", he shouted "You let me come home". **Again I quietly explained his need for the help of a long term recovery program.** By now, his screaming ad reached a frenzied pitch. Again, shaking his finger he yelled "If you don't let me come home, Bitch, I'll shoot up on and overdose on heroin and crystal." He lowered his voice to a whisper and ominously continued "How do you like that, Bitch?"

Waves of fear stabbed my chest. My stomach became a knot of panic. Feeling as if I were suffocating, I responded as calmly as I could, "If you don't stop yelling I will leave. Do you want something to eat or not? Do you want me to get your truck out of impound? As quickly as it had appeared "Rage seemed to" retreat and withdraw. His eyes became calculating and unfathomable. Calmly and purposefully he turned, opened the door of the car, and got out. Slowly, he began walking toward the entrance to Shakey's. I swallowed hard. Feeling light headed, I opened the door on my side of the car and followed.

 In the Restaurant my son ordered "All you can eat Pizza and Chicken". He arose twice during his meal to use the rest room. Was he looking for a quiet place to use his drugs or a real need to relieve himself,? I could only speculate. His eyes were glazed. But gone, at least temporarily, was his anger at the "Bitch" he had hated so violently just 1/2 an hour before. Now, he told me he loved me and was sorry for all he had done. He tearfully assured me he was a drug addict and that he would never change. He earnestly told me that he would never go into treatment.

 The next time I heard from him was from the County Jail. He asked me only once to bail l him out. I said "No". He asked me if I could see my way clear to hire an attorney for him. I said "No. They will assign you a Public Defender. You are responsible for yourself. I cannot help you any longer". He quietly accepted my responses. And at that moment, I knew without a doubt that although I was completely unable to help my beautiful son with the problems that he was either unwilling or unable to solve for himself, God had intervened to halt his terrible descent into the hell and misery that he had allowed to become his life. I cried in relief. And in the weeks that followed I slept well, knowing that at least for a while, my son was alive.

CASE TWO—Continues

THE SEARCH FOR BELONGING[13]
The Sons Story Begins . . .

My eyes flew open in the darkness. I quickly arose and walked swiftly towards my 5 year old son's room. To my horror I saw his bed was empty. The blankets on his bed had been thrown aside and he was . . . gone. "Buffy, Buffy", "Where are you", I called running swiftly through the house. Reaching the family room I saw the outside French doors were open. Through the opening I could hear crackling sounds in the woods. Panic stricken, I raced through the door toward the sounds.

In the darkness of the yard, I saw my pajama clad child running through the trees toward the road. Running swiftly I grabbed his small body. Intent on his journey, he tried to pull away from me and run toward the dark road. "What are you doing? Where are you going?" I said loudly. "I'm going to play with Bobby and James," he replied. "Leave me alone, Mommy, they're ridding away from me on their bicycles. If I don't hurry I won't be able to catch up with them" He continued trying to wrench himself from my arms to run toward unseen friends . . . who in some strange way at that moment occupied the "empty" roadway.

---

[13] **References-Social Rejection-Beth Azar—Portland Ore April 2009 Monitor on Psychology**

• Need to Belong, Numb to pain, Rejection Link to aggression

References

• Baumeister, RF, Brewer, LE, Iice DM & Twenge, JM (2007) the Need to belong: understanding the interpersonal and inner effects of social exclusion. Social and Personality Psych Compass 5-6-520

• Williams, KD Ostracism: Effects of being excluded and ignored (2009) Advances in Experimental Social Psych page 279-314

As we came into the lighted rooms of our house, I turned my child toward me and gently told him he could play with his friends tomorrow. He turned, walked into his room and climbed into bed. Within seconds he was asleep. The next morning since he didn't refer to the incident neither did I. It was not until 5 or 6 years later he recalled a "Funny" dream he had as a child in which he had run through the woods, toward the road one dark summer night after his friends, as they rode their bicycles away from him . . . He never caught them.

What did he spend his life searching for? Did he ever find it? I don't know. He spent his whole life searching for something he felt had been lost, feelings of acceptance from others.

THE SEARCH continues . . .

He was born into a loving family that included an Adoring Mother, Grandmother and 3 loving older brothers. His separated Father lived close by. Playing with preschool friends in a San Pedro nursery school he loved giving hugs to his beloved teachers.

Moving to another state, after his parents divorce he lived with his Mother and 13 year old brother. Two older adult brothers (20 and 28) lived close by. At age 5, putting on new clothes to join his mother at the Church he proudly exclaimed "Mommy and Me are getting married today" He insisted on being known by "Jones" the new Last name of his Stepfather.

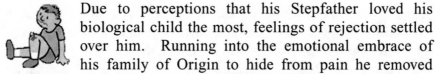 Due to perceptions that his Stepfather loved his biological child the most, feelings of rejection settled over him. Running into the emotional embrace of his family of Origin to hide from pain he removed the Boxer shorts (the type worn by his stepfather), put on Jockey Shorts (like his brother wore) and loudly declared "I'm not a Jones anymore"

In his new neighborhood he searched for, met and made new friends. At the private school where he started school with others kindergartners, he felt himself to be on equal footing and a member of the "In group".

Returning to Ca in the 3rd grade, he searched for acceptance in vain. At the School Bus stop on the first day of school, three 9 years old boys beat up the new kid from Virginia because 3rd graders don't like new kids. He never felt accepted by the other children who had grown up together in their neighborhood.

A family move to a different town, hopefully to feel more accepted revealed the only other child on the street was too shy to come out to play. A 4th grade Public School Teacher encouraged his talent for Art. A potential friend lived too far away to interact on a daily basis. One day Police brought both he and his bicycle home when they found him riding by the side of the Freeway toward his new friend's house.

Searching for Acceptance from new Friends who lived close by, one afternoon under the influence of Marijuana he fell off his bicycle into the thankfully deserted street. Most of the new friends were not bad kids . . . but from a culture where the Role of Males often included doing whatever they wanted. Awakening one night to find his bed empty his mother found he and some friends smoking marijuana in a neighborhood park. Ordering them into the car, she drove to their respective homes, woke up their parents and deposited their wayward children.

A quick enrollment into a Private School did not protect him and came to an abrupt end on the day an older neighborhood boy took him out of School to "hang out". Packing his clothes, he was sent to live with an adult brother in San Pedro while his Mother and Stepfather looked for a new home in a safer neighborhood.

 In a teenage search for Love, he met the love of his life. Unfortunately she was also a troubled Drug Addict. Trying to save her they got an Apartment in San Juan. He got a job in Albertsons Grocery Store. He tried to stay Sober. Realizing he couldn't stay sober and live with her, he drove her to her parents home. The next day she got hit by a Truck.

Every day, he hitchhiked 60 miles to see her in the Hospital. When she recovered, they lived together again. She got pregnant. He desperately tried to save her from Drugs but got hopelessly caught up himself.

An advocate of personal responsibility I did not hire an attorney for my adult son's drug related arrests (under the influence, driving on a suspended license, giving false ID, etc.). I regret it today.

Over the protests of his former probation officer and myself, his own Public Defender and the DA convinced him to plea bargain to a Felony on a wobbler (a charge appropriately pressed as either a misdemeanor or felony). Tried as a misdemeanor, a 1 year county jail sentence might have been the result of driving under the influence of a controlled substance. In exchange for pleading to a Felony, the friendly DA rewarded him with 1) Time served 2) entrance into the prison system (for a 2 weeks turnaround) and 3) the Label of Felon: a category that effectively strips it's recipients of civil rights and allows police to stop, search, stalk like animals and in this case kill him and blame him for his own death.

After his "turn around" into the category of Felon, a relapse (an expected symptom of drug addiction) led to another DUI arrest. But this time, to the prison sentence his "Turn Around" had been designed to engineer. And although I once again pleaded with the judge, parole officer and Public Defender to sentence him to the long term drug treatment he needed, instead of prison, they refused. He served a 1-year punishment at a Fire Fighting Training Program for non-**violent** felons.

He returned home to be met by his family at the train depot. I took him for a week-end celebration trip to Las Vegas for his **24th Birthday. The next week he, his stepdad and I took his 5 year old daughter to Disneyland. He told me he had never realized until "now" that no one but his family ever really cared about him.**

Four months later, on the last morning of his life, he dressed himself neatly in jeans, shirt and new shoes and drove slowly into the cul-de-sac where his friend Chris slept and death waited. At first, drinking a coke, smoking a cigarette and relaxing to his beloved loud music he neither saw the face of death nor felt its cold breath as it crouched on Musial St. preparing to claim him for it's own. Suddenly, amidst angry shouts and violent gun fire, through horrified eyes and rolled up windows, he glimpsed the terrorizing Specter spring forth. In a vain attempt to drive around death, . . . as his clutch slipped and motor died . . . a bullet from the police 45 ripped through the back of his head and upraised left thumb . . . ushering him into the waiting presence of death and outstretched arms of Eternity. As he lay over the steering wheel . . . his truck . . . slowly rolled to a stop. Did his quest come to an end that Thursday afternoon when he died in an unfamiliar neighborhood? Or did he leave the world unfulfilled? It's hard for me to believe he could have looked all his life for answers that were found by accident one hot muggy Thursday afternoon. Did he somehow find the answers to his quest when bullets from the undercover policeman ripped through his brain, silencing it forever? Did the spirit of the man slumped over the steering wheel rise and join Eternity with the knowledge he had searched for since he had been a little boy?

 On October 6, 1994 the tall strong body of my 24 year old son came home for the last time . . . to lie on smooth satin . . . inside a bronze colored box, beneath a green hillside overlooking the Pacific ocean . . . a few blocks from where he was born. His spirit no longer residing in the world had entered Eternity . . . a victim of such intolerable tragedy I can hardly permit its pain to enter my mind . . . Nor can I keep its memory from torturing my existence.

SERIOUS FAMILY RELATIONSHIP CHALLENGES

Under what conditions might DETACHMENT become unachievable?

 Many clients initially report a moral conflict when considering the concept of Emotional detachment in the category of duty for loved ones with serious physical or emotional problems.

The question of whether Emotional Detachment is a valid option in cases of serious family Relationship Challenges is often fraught with extremely difficult choices in many different areas of consideration.

Many presented with the concept **Emotional Differentiation** as a normal part of a mature Human Adult ask such questions as 1) **"How can you detach from someone you love? Doesn't detachment mean you really don't care?" 2) And 3) "Does Detachment really work?"**. Many have serious internal emotional conflict about what they can realistically do to help a child, spouse, parent, brother or sister deal with serious problems. As mentioned in the previous section, questions concerning the characteristics of Tough Love, whether or not it works as well as under what conditions may it fail are common.

Many issues as well as lack of knowledge concerning appropriate responsibility for the self and others underlie **Emotional Detachment**. As previously mentioned **Murray Bowen** described Emotional Detachment in his theory of Differentiation as the ability to be emotionally separate from others, including family. He believed in the importance of becoming personally independent and mature without losing the capacity for emotional connectedness. He wrote that the severity of emotional problems are in direct proportion to the influence of emotion over objective thought. He believed the neediness of an undifferentiated person resulted in feeling it necessary to assume similar thoughts and ideas of loved ones which then lead to loss of personal identity

It is important to realize that Tough Love places Personal Responsibility squarely on the shoulders of the Person with the Problem. However, **Emotional Detachment** is the ability of a Psychological Mature Adult to objectively consider wants, needs and duties of both the self and others and make decisions based on what is best for each in the long run. Under certain situations this task is often an extremely difficult one in which in mature persons recognize the a big difference between **can't and won't** when trying to understand personal responsibility for self and others.

As previously mentioned, few (if any) of us ever receive everything we want. However, it is important to remember that in order to remain emotionally healthy ourselves, we must strive to get our own as well as the **legitimate needs** of our loved ones met. In order to do this, many serious family relationships situations must be faced with the goal of keeping the needs of each <u>in a much balance</u> as possible. Only by keeping this mandate clearly in mind can important decisions be made concerning serious family relationship challenges.

The following situations are examples of Family Relationship Challenges that present serious conundrums for many of us as we travel down our pathway through Life.

Is Tough Love the best or even the only option for a Family member with Serious Drug Addition? (Teen or Adult offspring Drug Addiction, Spouse Drug Addiction

Choices relating to the care of Seriously Drug Addicted Family members, spouses or other loved ones must be based on our best judgment concerning objective facts, research and educated underlying information concerning areas of impairment. Many times, even hindsight does not offer clear explanations for success or failure of our past choices.

To insure as much success as possible in planning treatment goals, decisions must be based on as much objective information (facts vs our emotional reactions to them) as possible. Information for consideration must include Neurological symptoms (brain functioning, LD, IQ Level, Drug usage, ETOH) as well as Emotional Development (levels of self esteem, mood disorders, anxiety issues, rigidity, etc) of the ill one.

For example, Research[14] shows the effects of Methamphetamine on Brain Function and Personality Characteristics are significant.

---

[14]   www.emedicine.com
1. www.kci.org/meth_info/site/meth_psycho.htm
2. Highbeam Research Website
3. www.Psychiatryonline.org
4. Narconon Southern California

High levels of Methamphetamine **usage keep the Firing Neurons releasing Dopamine into the synapse** resulting in severe damage within the **Neurotransmitter environment.** Too <u>Much</u> Dopamine at the synapse is related to symptoms of Psychosis. Too <u>Little</u> Dopamine at the synapse is related to Disorders of Parkinson's.

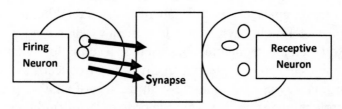

- Meth <u>shuts down</u> and <u>causes damages to the receptive nerve terminals</u> causing <u>shriveling of the brain cells</u>. Brain Damage is result of Chemical N-Acetyle-Asparate in the Cell which indicates loss of mature nerve cells in the brain.
- High levels of Meth at the synapse cause high body temperature, high blood pressure, convulsions, Stroke, Epilepsy, Alzheimer's,
- Smoking Meth causes Tooth enamel to disintegrate and teeth to fall out.
- **Drug craving** last for years due to Toxin retention in Fatty Brain Tissues b/c liver can't eliminate them.
- High Level of **craving** lead to <u>rationalizing reasons for use (I feel good, smart, happy, wonderful, etc)</u>
- **Personality changes** in all Meth Addicts (irrational anger, violence, paranoia) are caused by High Levels of Meth Use.
- Meth short circuits survival system by artificially stimulating the pleasure areas of brain. This leads to increased confidence in meth and less in the normal rewards of life. This happens on a physical level at first, then affects user psychologically. The result is decreased interest in normal aspects of life while reliance in meth increases.
- <u>**Studies of lab animals show they pressed levers for meth rather than eat, mate or satisfy natural drives. They died of starvation while giving themselves meth even though food was available**</u>.

A clear understanding of the numerous Objective Facts (and sometimes our own emotionally terrifying reactions to them) is absolutely necessary when considering if or how we might contribute to the Treatment of a loved one suffering from severe Drug Addiction.

Careful consideration of comments such as "Come Home if you can be sober and pleasant" or "You can come home only after you have gone to treatment and are still sober" is critical. Whether or not a Decision that Tough Love be the Treatment of choice for a severely Drug Addicted loved one must be based on a scrupulous examination of as much Objective Research in the area of concern as possible. Only in this way can our gamble with the life of another provide as much protection as possible from the possibility of finding ourselves staring into the dead eyes of another human being.

Living up to Potential
Adult or child with serious, disabling behavioral, neurological and/or emotional problems

Decisions concerning how or even whether to help a loved one with severe disabling emotional disorders must also be considered in the context of neurological vs emotional symptoms. A Psychologist initially rules out chemical or neurological causes of severe anxiety, mood or other debilitating behaviors and/or emotions. A family background of depression, anxiety, learning disabilities, etc suggests the possibility of neurological, chemical or biological causes. Medication often helps in such cases. However, medications may not be a magic bullet.

Learning Disorders—For many years Learning Disabilities were classified as minimal brain dysfunctions without any clear cut definitions of what they were. Today, according to research[15] a learning disorder involves dysfunction in one or more <u>neuropsychological</u> systems that affect school performance. A child can have poor school performance without having a learning disorder, when the poor school performance is due entirely to emotional, motivational or cultural

---

[15] Bruce F Pennington, PhD—Diagnosing Learning Disorders—A Neuropsychological Framework—Preface Xiii

factors. Five cognitive functions (see below[16]) are separate domains of neuropsychological functioning, Each first emerges early in life, and each is to differing degrees susceptible to developmental perturbation. 15 to 25 percent of the Total Population demonstrate Characteristics of Learning Disorders which includes ADHD, Autism, Dyslexia, Mental retardation and acquired memory disorders. Diagnostic techniques include Psychological and Neurological evaluation with treatment designed for the best possible result.

My own experiences with my son's Learning Disability years ago, included some terribly destructive responses by supposedly knowledgeable school administrators. One, Principal of a Jr High School in Virgina told me he "didn't believe in learning disabilities". Even today, many adults know little about the ideology or treatment of such disorders. Left untreated or responded to with the edict "Your child is just lazy" or "Your child just doesn't pay attention" the situation is ripe for failure.

Many teenagers with LD are terribly embarrassed and perceive themselves as "losers". And although this of course is not the case, many become involved in Drug activities, refusal to go to school, hanging out with poor choice of friends as well as refusal to follow family requests and house rules. As adults, many who suffered LD as a youngster eventually realize they are able to take personal responsibility and learn methods to deal with dyslexia, ADD, ADHD, etc. However, family members of loved ones with such disorders can save themselves and their loved ones years of pain and suffering by learning as much as possible about such disorders as possible now, rather than later.

Learning Disabilities are the result of Strengths and weaknesses in the Brain Hemispheres. By gaining knowledge of where specific characteristics lie in the neurological map of the brain much can be done to build upon the strengths and develop methods for strengthening the weaknesses. Numerous answers to individual quests for successful treatment goals can Techniques. Such assessment be found in the

---

[16] Bruce F Pennington, PhD—phonological processing, spatial cognition, social cognition, executive functions and long term memory—Pg 22

results of IQ Testing, Psycho neurological Screening, and other Psychological Assessment instruments are provided by School and/or Clinical Psychologists who specialize in such areas of diagnosis.

Mood disorders. Many families have the responsibility to face the challenge of a family member with severe emotional disorders. Such Diagnoses may include those in the categories of Bipolar, severe anxiety, Agoraphobia, etc. It is surprising but true that numerous educated persons have little knowledge of the fact that many mental health diagnoses are chemical. Even with the help of medication many of those suffering from Bi-Polar disorder may never reach the level of complete personal responsibility for financial as well as work related obligations. Those in theis category usually qualify for Medicare or Medical.

However, many family members of those diagnosed with severe mood disorders find themselves in the position of needing to contribute to either the living or financial space of the ill one. Such demands place huge pressure on those with limited financial resources or other hesitations. To make matters worse, many otherwise nice people do not understand the difference between those who "can't" and those who "won't". While it is true that some diagnosed with Bi-Polar may fall into the category of those able to recover by working toward resolution of underlying anxiety there are many who cannot. Even, those who fall into the category of Chemical Imbalance may recover partially or completely with medication and treatment others may not.

Research indicates that Bi-Polar Disorder may strike once, twice or numerous times in the life of those afflicted with the chemical and/or neurological predisposition. Some are able to resolve any underlying anxiety and never fall victim to severe depression again. Others many not be able to function minus medication and help from agencies responsible for providing long term disability insurance. However, these persons benefit greatly from the emotional support of family members and loved ones who encourage them to "Try to live up to personal potential". Some are able to hold down part time jobs. Some are not. Some wrestle with the reality that a good job and expectation for ability to care for themselves was followed by another Bi-Polar episode.

An extremely intelligent 50 some years old client suffers from long term neurological and emotional effects of Bipolar Disorder (anxiety, depression, several instances of psychotic ideation, low self esteem and feelings of self loathing) as well as remnants of childhood Learning Disabilities. A lifelong trait of poor interpersonal insight continues. He comes from a family in which he internalized the message that a man only reaches the level of success when he becomes a husband, father and enters a vocational category of Doctor or Lawyer. Earning a BS in his 20's her suffered his first episode of Bipolar Disorder soon after. He recently earned an online MS. He has been able to contain his disorder by constant attention to medication, psychotherapy and contact with others in the environment of advanced educational.

Success in graduate programs leads to feelings of improved self esteem and less tendency to suffer emotional distress or thoughts of personal disgust. However, a Brother in law, married to a younger sister, believes Bipolar Diagnosis will be cured by medication. His messages "Get a job, and get off of Handouts" and "There is nothing wrong with you anymore" have lead to severe stress and discomfort in the family and for the mother who in spite of financial limitations is able to help her son on a monthly basis pay for some of her son's expenses. He lives on $800 a month from receives SSDI. The good grades this man receives in Graduate courses provide perception of himself as working hard to live up to his potential.

Questions such as "Should a man on SSDI be enrolled in Graduate Programs", "Should a mother with limited income pay for any of a mentally ill adult son's expenses?" and "Should a a man whose Mental illness at this time seems contained by medication get a job and stop receiving SSDI" continue to lie unanswered in the vale of uncertainty that surround this family in its search for moral as well as medically successful decisions.

How can a family deal successfully with the Mental Retardation of a Family Member?

Melanie was born the 2nd of 4 daughters. Not until about the age of 8 did the Father relent to others conclusions that something was seriously amiss with his child. She had always been a happy child with somewhat unusual behaviors. For example she didn't understand why her parents were upset when she ran naked in the street one sunny afternoon. In adulthood her mental development never grew past that of an 8 year old.

Her sisters although loving were often uncomfortable when she was around their friends. Their Mother enrolled her during the week in a school in which pupils stayed overnight during the week. On weekends she came home. As she grew older she spent weekends as well at her Live In Group Home. She was happy there and felt comfortable spending time with others more like herself.

Today, at over 50 years of age, she still visits her sister occasionally and is invited to family affairs. At the funeral of her Mother last year Melanie talked happily of her Mother but did not seem to understand the concept of death. She recognized old family members and talked loudly and happily about her remembrances of times past.

Conclusions about family responsibility for loved ones with mental retardation probably fall into the category of the most easily death with compared to other tragedies. This is probably so because the symptoms of the ill one are obvious to all. As a result, most family members agree that the persona with the Mental Retardation must receive the most appropriate Treatment and Living Situation available.

What should be done if a loved one is diagnosed with a serious Mental Illness—

As mentioned in the Preface of this book, I am a Psychologist because of my Mother's mental illness. She was diagnosed with Paranoid Schizophrenia at 44 after the death of her identical Twin Sister. She never completely recovered from the loss and spent the rest of her life searching for the part of herself that had died. One of a set of identical twin girls she had 4 older brothers who doted on their darling little sisters.

After her world came to an end, she listened to voices of Communists over the Loud speakers in airports, heard voices discussing her through solid walls and was the recipient of shock treatment in Napa

Hospital in Cal during the 1940's. She was released when many Mental Institutions were closed and the law was changed to reflect the law of 5150 which states, only those who are a danger to self, others or unable to care for themselves can be institutionalized against their will.

After Neuroleptics were invented, I received a call from a woman at Napa hospital who happily informed me "Good news Mrs Lundquist, your mother is coming to live with you". I was stunned. Over the next few months I researched the requirements for family members of mentally ill persons. I took care of her for over 20 years, in Cal and Va. When she took her medication she lived with me or in apartments I rented for her. She often baby sat or worked at Good Will. When she refused, she lived in Board & Care Homes. She was a loved Grandmother to my 4 sons who grew up understanding the concept of Mental Illness in all its aspects. She died at 76 "waiting for her life to begin".

The following vignettes are true circumstances my own family faced with the Mental Illness of my mother.

THE WOMAN WHO HIDE FROM TORMENTORS

The woman who stepped off the plane looked like a small cold bird. I had not seen her for over 10 years. I could hardly believe she was my mother. She was Excruciatingly thin, the bones of her shoulders stood out clearly beneath her dress. Her face was pale and drawn. Her once beautiful black hair, now white, was carefully combed. Her lipstick, bizarrely bright, stood out starkly on her lips. Her eyes looked haunted.

As I reached out to embrace her, her hands frantically clutched at my arm. Looking up into my face, eyes boring intensely into mine, my mother words, quiet but urgent, brought further concern and confusion into my mind. "Skipi," she whispered, "the Communists are after me. They tried to stop me from coming to Washington State". My mothers mouth, inches from my face, continued to frantically whisper her tortured story. She told me she had hidden from and escaped the Communists in Puerto Rico and Miami. She told me of their effort to catch her by broadcasting her name over the loud speaker while she was in the Miami airport. "Stop that woman", the Loud speakers had blared. "Stop her. Stop Miriam Dobbins, Stop her". My mother, frantic and agitated, begging me for help, was having a hard time making her words understandable. Sometimes she spoke words that seemed to be combinations of several words. I peared at her closely. It was difficult to recognized her as the woman who was my Mother.

I was a small town girl with a husband, 2 little boys and no formal education beyond my High School diploma and a certificate from Grays Harbor Business College. I was confused and astonished by her story. I knew nothing of mental illness.

Since her divorce from my father, my mother had lived with her Identical Twin Sister in California and Puerto Rico. My relationship with her had been strained for much of my life. And, until she had called from Puerto Rico three days before (demanding that I send her a plane ticket home) we had been in touch only occasionally by mail.

To my knowledge my mother had never had political affiliation with Communists or anyone else. And although I could not understand why the Communists would be after her, she had never lied to me. Confused and heart sick, I struggled to believe her story. But at that moment, no other type of explanation for her terrible predicament and strange behavior occurred to me . . . SERENDIPITOUS EVENT in 1952.

My Mother's mental illness was the precipitous event that started my intense interest in mental illness. After her arrival in Washington State I began an investigation of the causes of mental illness and the chances of it's heredity. I learned that although it has a biological basis it is transferred on a recessive gene and those with high levels of ability to deal with stress seldom inherit it. Although she was diagnosed in 1952 with Schizophrenia I believe a more accurate Diagnosis would have been Serious Depression with Psychotic features. For many years my Mother lived in Board and Care homes when unwilling to take her Medication and either with me in Cal Or Va when she complied with medication mandates. The following Vignettes are true interchanges with my mother when she lived in a Board and Care residence in Long Beach, Ca. and often visited me in San Pedro, Ca.

THE "STRANGER" ON OBISPO STREET

My Mother on stood on Obispo St. in front of the Board and Care home she shared with other women who battled mental illness. A breeze rustled her white hair. Her once slight figure, now thick and heavy, was covered by a nondescript dress of the type worn by the other ladies". Belted at the waist. with a V neck, it hung well below her knees. Excitedly getting into my  car, she spoke of her happiness to be "going home". Her voice strange and different had the slow inflexions and rhythms of the South. She sounded nothing like my mother. I asked her if she & Maizie, a fellow resident who had grown up in the deep South had spent the morning together.—Yes", she drawled. "How did you know"" "Just a lucky guess". I replied.—*Loss Of Ego Boundaries*

THE MIRROR—1970's

The large mirror hung on the wall in the front hall. It reflected the images of our two figures. Greeting me happily, my 60 ^{YR} old Mother came out of the guest room announcing her readiness for our shopping trip. She had discarded the clothes she arrived in and carefully combed her white hair into a long popular style of the day. Her once slight, now overweight figure was <u>minimally</u> covered by a short pleated skirt which ended well above her knees and a skimpy capped sleeved blouse. Shiny brown Boots extended well above the calves of her legs. Both knees and a large expanse of stocking were clearly revealed between the top of her new boots and the hem of her skirt.

In the Mirror . . . Imprisoned side by side . . . the figures of my mother and myself revealed themselves. Standing before the Mirror, I starred at my long blond hair, thin legs, short "Hot "Pants" of the 70's and creamy white boots. My outfit looked somehow incongruous beside the garish one worn by my mother. In dismay, I watched as the figure of the older woman smiled at me. "Don't we look nice, Skipi, just like twins." Feeling violated and betrayed, as though my Mother had somehow "stepped into" my identity, I saw my frustration and resentment appear in my glass reflection. Watching in the Mirror as my Mother turned her back to step out, I turned to open the door and follow. As I closed the door behind us the clatter of our footsteps on the sidewalk noisily announced continuation of our journey toward the rest of our lives. From within the hallway, behind the closed door, **THE MIRROR . . .** silently . . . bade us "Goodbye"—*Diffuse External Ego Boundaries of a woman with Psychosis*

THE PATH TO ETERNITY

In 1986 at 76 years of age my mother died in a Long Beach Ca hospital. She had been in and out of hospitals several times but had recovered enough to return to hospice living. On the last day of her life as she drifted in and out of consciousness I noticed water seeping from the pores on her arms. During moments of wakefulness, her speech was often strange, difficult to decipher or in the form of neologism (words she made up). Once upon awaking she earnestly gazed into my eyes and whispered "Skipi, can you imagine a world without me in it?" Later that day, she closed her eyes and drifted off into sleep. During the night I received a call from the Hospital telling me she had never awakened.

My Mother is buried on a hillside, overlooking the Pacific Ocean. Her final resting place lies a few steps from the graves of her three grandsons who also left this earth soon after she closed her eyes for the last time. I often visit the graves of my loved ones . . . usually on a Birthday or other holiday. Sitting on a blanket beside a headstone, I find comfort in letters written during their lifetimes as well as pictures of happy times we spent together. Wandering between Headstones, I hold them close in the loving embrace of memory as I gaze deep into the eyes of their human likenesses etched in their tombstone.

After years of consideration, the answer to the question my Mother posed to me as she lay on her death bed is "Yes". I can picture this world without any of us in it because I truly believe that although our Human body dies our Spiritual Essence returns to the Eternal Universe which lies all around us

I have no doubt that the opportunity to discover our Life Purpose is presented within relationships shared with loved ones as we walk together on our Paths of Life. Life with my mother provided the opportunity that lead to my love for and life work of Psychology. And the path through life with my children lead to motherhood and eternal love for the souls of my three sons.

I believe we are born with a Mission . . . unique to each of us. I perceive Human Life as The training ground for development of both human and spiritual potential. I believe our Paths to E'ernity run through the Fabric of the Universe and are shared with those with whom we have Lessons to learn.

 Standing at the Grave site of my Mother, I feel her spiritual presence drifting down to settle around me. Looking up, a flash of sunlight parts a curtain behind which my loved ones embrace as they walk together on the Path to Eternity. I raise my hand to wave and whisper . . . "Goodbye for a Little While". "I will love you for Eternity and join you there.

Perceptions' concerning Mission & Purpose of Life shared at the grave site of a Loved One.

As a Psychologist with personal experience concerning the need to make decisions pertaining to a loved one with serious mental illness, I tried to make sure my mother's needs as well as those of my family's were met. I believe our Decisions lead to as much success as possible under the circumstances we faced.

I truly believe we come to earth to learn the Lessons needed for both Human and Spiritual Growth. I have no doubt that we can choose whether or not to learn those Lessons. I do not believe all of our Lessons are learned in relationships with Parents, Children and/or Spouses. Sometimes we catch glimpses of them from good friends or acquaintances.

I learned this lesson for myself when throughout my life I kept meeting persons who shared spiritual experiences with me. And although I was always very interested, other things came up and I drifted away from closer scrutiny. It wasn't until after the Murder of my 24 year old son, Blake that I realized I could not go on without exploration of a Personal Philosophy concerning the meaning of Life.

Questions concerning What should be done about conditions of loved ones with serious issues involving Old Age, Alzheimers, etc. must take as much information of the objective facts concerning the as many aspects of the situation as possible.

Circumstances concerning the issues cited above are often dealt with by cultural and social mandates. However, many also present serious confusion, difficultly with choices and in many cases guilt for family and other loved ones.

During middle age, many are faced with an elderly parent in need of care giving. In some cultures an elderly parent is expected to live with the family of a child or children. In others the choices are not so clear due to finances, work schedules or emotional reactions to situations from the past.

Many elderly persons can afford care living at home or needed nursing home expenses. Others would "do anything" to avoid having to give up the autonomy usually expected when living in the home of others. And some, just can't imagine having to behave in ways seen as an imposition of children and family.

In my professional experience I have come face to face with Adult Children and Elderly Parents who expected the elderly parent to live as frugally as possible to save money for a child's inheritance. Other situations include a spouse reluctant to care for a mate with dementia due to scheduling problems, finances etc. The following is a true example of decisions concerning Dementia.

"Living with Sundowner's".

 An elderly couple both previously married realized the wife's memory was becoming more and more unstable. The Husband worried he would not have enough money or time to provide for his elderly spouse who had been diagnosed with Alzheimer's. She often could not remember where she lived or for what reason she had gone shopping. In the evening she often became angry and difficult to be around. He called it the "Sundowner Syndrome".

Although the spouses were similar in age, the wife had taken much more financial responsibility for her spouse due to his often inability to find work, history of alcoholism and a somewhat unwillingness to work steadily. The Wife had spent most of her previously substantial financial resources on her husband's need for help as well as attorney fee's to protect her money from a child who wanted to protect herself from being left out of her mother's will. However, during recent years, the Husband had quit drinking and become something of a celebrity on TV for an Automobile Marketing Program. The Husband really enjoyed his new found fame.

The Husband toyed with the idea (which she hated) of putting her in a Nursing Home. However, she loved her home and strenuously rejected requests to sell it and move into a Care Facility. Finances necessary for providing **In Home Care** did not seem as overwhelming as those of Nursing Homes,

In the end, the Husband's decision was based on what he believed they "owed" each other. After long and careful thought he decided that the Balance in their **Emotional Bank Account** was in her favor. He lovingly remembered all the times she had been there for him financially as well as emotionally when he had no job or imbibed too frequently. He decided that he would hire someone to help her at home for as long as he was financially able to do so. And by doing so, he knew that when the end came and she no longer remembered him, he would be the one to carry loving thoughts of their marriage to his grave with no guilt attached.

CHAPTER 11

LESSON 3

Reality

What Color are your "Glasses" ???

Lesson 3

REALITY IS OBJECTIVE

- What "Color" are my Glasses?

Lesson 3 teaches the ability to Live in the present, perceive objective vs subjective, accept the truth and "see" what is really "out there" now. It demonstrates the ability to separate emotions from thoughts.

Many Distortion (Expectations, Perceptions of the Self, Others and/or Situations) are the result of Emotional Transference's from the past. These distortions may occur as a result of Life Scripts, Belief systems that are not in line with Reality, Social expectations out of line with Reality, Position in the Family of Origin or Family Expectations for Family Members' attitudes and Behaviors.

LESSON 3- REALITY

"MAP OF REALITY"   **LAWS OF CAUSE & EFFECT**

Reality is Objective (what is or did, really happen) However, most of us see life subjectively (our personal points of view).

- **FAMILY CONSTELLATION-** The Family Group we grew up in provides the basic environment in which we develop our belief systems , the Rules we live by, and our Values. This environment provides catalysts for origination of of thought processes and behavior. It can be seen as the birth place of Personality Characteristics.

- **PARADIGMS -** Paradigms are the way we "see" the world. They are often the result of the Rules we have learned to live by. Examples might include Seeing the world as flat rather than round. It is not possible to see the world as three dimensional and flat at the same time. We may believe the human spirit lives after death or when we're dead we cease to exist. We cannot hold both at the same time. Paradigms are conflicting Models of Reality.

- **FAMILY ORDER -** Psychological research indicates that the order we are born into our families influences our personality characteristics. Being oldest children, only child, youngest child, middle child etc., have all been shown to effect our personality characteristics. It is also known that our gender also effects expectations for our attitudes and behaviors. Others may label us as the baby, a crier, a winner, a looser, etc. Labeling also strongly effects the way we see ourselves and our feelings and behaviors.

- **"Red Threads"-** The Psychological skeleton of Personality. All personality characteristics can be summarized into a basic core much like a physical skeleton onto which all other characteristics fit into or fall from. Red Threads of Personality are the result of Conscious and Unconscious Thought processes that lead to **Patterns of Behavior**.

- **ROADMAPS -** We have all learned to live life following whatever Roadmap we have designed for ourselves. These Roadmaps are the result of Rules we have learned about the world, the Roles we play in our relationships with others and our Life Scripts.

DISTORTED REALITY - We all distort reality from time to time. Common ways to distort include 1) distorted expectations for ourselves, others and situations, 2) distorted perceptions of others, ourselves and situations and 3) distortions that result from our emotions. Emotional distortions occur in the present as a result of being similar to situations of the past. A good example is hearing an old favorite song on the radio. It reminds us of people and places from the past. In the present we somehow "magically" return to the **past on** the feelings the song stirs up inside of us.

"Where does your ROADMAP really lead?

Do You Color (Distort) Reality as a result of

❖ Unrealistic Perceptions or Expectations for yourself, others & the World?
❖ Emotional reactions to situations, others behavior or past experiences?

Distorted Unrealistic Expectations

Psychological Maturation requires the ability to face
Objective reality and accept the truth.
Are You Waiting for Santa Claus to reward you for being good?

Or a "Knight in Shining Armor to ....rescue you?."

"How long have you been Waiting?

Distorted Unrealistic Perceptions

What Color are your Glasses? "Do you believe people
"should or ought" to behave in certain ways?",....... "Do
they?" "Are your expectations for yourself and others
realistic?" "Do your perceptions and expectations make
sense?" " Do your Expectations Fit with ....Reality?"

Distorted Emotional Transferences

Do happenings in the Present bring up similar feelings to
something that happened in the past? Do you sometimes feel like
the Child you were, rather than the Adult you are? Are your
perceptions colored by emotional reactions? Do you immediately
respond (hate or love) to a new acquaintance because they remind you of
someone from the past?"

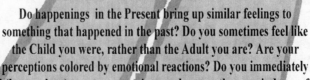

Lesson 3

REALITY IS OBJECTIVE

WHAT "COLOR" ARE MY GLASSES?

HOW PERSONAL PATTERNS OF THOUGHT MAY DISTORT OBJECTIVE REALITY

Distorted Unrealistic <u>Expectations</u> **for self, others and environment.** Such expectations are often based on Distortions concerning religious doctrine, morality of self and others., expectations concerning deference to authority, expectations concerning others responses to our own personal values, etc. Expectations for self and others are usually **based on roles, roles and Scripts we have learned to play in our own Life and in our Relationships with others.**

My own Professional Experiences while gathering Material for writing **Maturation: The Adult Paradigm** and The **Test of Ego and Cognitive Development** supports extensive Research findings underlying Theories of Family and Cognitive Therapy. Responses marked by clients taking the **TECD** reveal numerous types of unrealistic expectations for themselves and others such as the idea that **1) Laws should never be broken. 2) Mistakes should never be made** as well as having great **3) difficulty letting go of expectations for themselves and others.** In addition, many reported 4) **"being seen as inflexible or having difficulty seeing others points of view".** Some report believing in the concept of justice that states **5) "An eye or an eye and a tooth for a tooth".** Some report the expectation that 6) **"People (even adults) should never disrespect their parents or other respected authority by refusing to do what they request".** And of special interest to me as a Psychologist was the expectation that 7) **"People who love each other should know what the other is thinking without being told"** I have never read any research showing Love as the catalyst for mind reading.

Distorted Unrealistic Perceptions for self, others and environment. Such Distortions are often based on Illogical thinking, circumstantial thought, etc. Such conclusions are often the result of distorted perceptions of the big picture (minus necessary details), details too narrow (without perception of the big picture), etc. May be result of mental Illness, psychosis, poor reality testing, hallucinations, neurosis, creativity, etc. Experiences of Déjà vu.

Regression in the Service of the Ego is an explanation for the concept of Creativity. It is seen as arising in the Id and Unconscious mind. When functional persons exhibit creativity they are able to dip into the Id for inspiration and withdraw from it at will. Psychotic persons are seen as those who use Primary Process thought in similar ways but whose reality testing is impaired and therefore cannot tell the difference from the chaotic timeless contents of the Id from the structured framework of reality. The talents of Steven Spielberg Dean Koontz and Other creative writers (whose work is rather bizarre and not understood in the context of reality) can be seen in this way. **Anxiety. Freud**, Psychoanalytic theory,

Many respondents to the TECD answered "YES" to Questions such as 1) "I often make mistakes because I don't pay attention to all the details" and 2) "I often zero in on a few details or small things others don't notice". Others mistakenly place stimuli together that lacks any type of objective connection such as "People often tell me that they cannot see my point of view", "People's behavior causes my emotions and reactions toward them", "Others will never forgive my mistakes" and "My life will never turn out well". Some of these distorted perceptions may well be a result of mental Illness, psychosis, poor reality testing or even hallucinations.

For example the statement that "I sometimes feel people are out to get me" is a cognition stated by some without any real proof or reason for making the statement. However, paranoid thought processes should not be automatically confused with another type of thought process **(sometimes perceived as illogical) that** may occur in mentally stable persons possessed of great creativity, etc. Statements such as "I can intuitively sense what others are thinking", "My creativity often allows me to see connections that others may overlook" are often made by sensitive persons. And who among us has never experienced the unforgettable "Ah, Hah" reaction to experiences of Déjà vu.

DISTORTED PERCEPTIONS—"CHECKING IT OUT"

It is important in relationships to realize that "checking it out" with others (Expectations) is usually a good idea when perceptions of having been treated unfairly or insultingly by another enter our minds. For example: Entering my office, my associate barely takes note of my arrival. However, she immediately turns (in what I consider to be a rude gesture), and quickly leaves the room without a word. I instantly assume she is angry with me for not telling her goodbye last night when I left the office. However, later in the day, after checking it out with my associate, she tells me She hadn't noticed that I had not bade her farewell last night hen I left. She had been buried in work and was trying to finish up to leave for home. And . . . Immediately before my arrival this morning, my associate had been summoned to the office of our boss who has the reputation of "chewing employees up for breakfast" when they do not appear in his office quickly. She assured me she had been so centered on getting to his office as quickly as possible she had not realized her need for speed might be perceived as rudeness by another.

Distortions due to Emotions and Transferences. Such distortions may be result of having assumed a certain type of Life Script, having learned to play certain types of roles in relationships as well as emotional reactions to persons and situations. In some cases even reactions to music, perceptions of how people look, etc remind us of someone or some other time.

Client's replies to TECD Questions include such responses as 1) **When I get to know people, they often remind me of someone from my past,** 2) **I believe in love at first sight.** 3) **I often get involved with the same sort of people that have caused me trouble before,** 4) **My husband/wife often reminds me of my mother, father, sibling, etc**. and 5) **I can't stand people who have similar mannerisms to someone I didn't get along with in the past.** Other responses include 6) **I have Déjà vu experiences when meeting certain people,** 7) **I dislike certain people without knowing why,** 8) **I am sure I can always trust a new acquaintance who has an "honest" face and the**

old favorite 9)and I always fall "slightly in love with" a person who reminds me of famous people, movie stars, etc. A good example of responses to mannerisms of others (Transferences) occurred in my Internship days when Group therapy was a requirement.

COUNTERTRANSFERENCE IN GROUP THERAPY

  During a Supervision session our Instructor requested we consider what types of persons might be problematic for us to work with as therapists. I immediately thought of a male group member whom I "felt" perceived me as unequal to himself. Requested to consider reasons for such a response, I quickly realized the Male Group Member had the same type of look in his eyes when he looked at me that my father used to fix on me when he disapproved of something I was doing. Immediately I realized the situation was a good example of countertransference. Countertransference is  defined in the Encarta Dictionary *"a process that sometimes occurs in psychoanalytic therapy where repressed emotions in the therapist are awakened by identification with the experiences and feelings of the patient"*. I did not however, believe that my Male Group Member experienced me as one whom he disapproved. But I did believe that my own response to him was the result of feelings I had a child when my father looked at me with the same type of expression on his face and in his eyes.

It can easily be seen that all of us, many times in our lives have experienced relationship trouble as a result of having fallen blindly into one or more of the Distortions (perceptions, expectations and feelings from the past) mentioned above. When we understand why these happenings occurred we are in a position to cognitively think about the aspects of each situation and decide what if anything we can do about it. As I have mentioned numerous times during these chapters, we can only control ourselves. For that reason we may have to think long and hard about the circumstances that set these situations into motion.

#1—The Problem of Personal Anxiety

Distortions are the result of subjectivity. Subjective Reality rests upon skewed, biased, slanted and/or one sided decisions that distort the underlying Objective Facts of Reality. These distortions may be a result of the way we remember things, thinking in "shoulds", ought's, right and wrong, etc. (Ellis, [1]Glasser, etc[2].) as well as **Transferences** from our own feelings from the past. In addition, Subjective Reality may be a personal decision based on personal beliefs (**Paradigms—conceptual framework)** we hold about the world.

As mentioned above, some of us distort reality by not noticing certain details, seeing some situations without benefit of detail, not noticing what we don't expect to see, etc. If we are to be in touch with all of the facts in a situation, however, we must learn to clear our senses of these distorted "lenses" and perceive the World in as much of its true complexity as we can possibly learn to do.

Ask yourself the following questions to help bring to light areas of distortions in which personal anxieties lie hidden under Subjective Reality. **"What expectations do we have for ourselves and others?" "What is the result of our expectations?" "Do our thoughts and messages often contain the words should, ought, always, never?", "Am I a perfectionist?", "Do I hate to let others win?", "Do I believe I must be in charge of others because only I can do things correctly?", "Am I still waiting to be rewarded for my good deeds?". And finally, that most dreaded Question of all "Will Santa** Ever **come?".**

Personal ANXIETY, the basis of all distortions arises in our Family of Origin due to human immaturity and inability to feel and behave separately due to feelings of inadequacy, anxiety and fear of rejection and abandonment. According to Hellmuth Kaiser[3] **"The struggle against seeing oneself as an individual is the core**

---

[1]   Ellis, Albert

[2]   Glasser, W

[3]   Kaiser, Hellmuth—**Symbiosis—Family of Origin.??? Reference needed for this statement.**

of every Neurosis and the universal defense (emotional Fusion) against individuality is a delusion". "The true conflict is residing in the fact of one's alones and our need to avoid and deny It".

A complete discussion of the topic of Symbiotic Attachment can be found in Task 2 (Chapter 5). However, in summary, two forces lead toward relations and becoming a separate self. At birth we can't tell where we stop and the environment begins. Babies see self as part of others. Immature persons feel uncomfortable being an emotionally independent self. Inability to resolve fusion feels like being homesick. However becoming a whole person necessitates balancing of forces . . . too much of ether results in anxiety. When balance has not been achieved attempt to control anxiety by impossible methods are made. As a result psychological symptoms and syndromes such as dependency, addictions, anxieties and phobias develop.

Successful resolution of symbiosis in Families Of Origin requires healthy emotional detachment which includes continued love, commitment and respect for each other.

I discuss the topic psychological definition of **ANXIETY** with my clients as a major source of potentially important information concerning what is needed for Psychological growth and Maturation to occur. I emphasize the importance of identifying "**What** I am afraid of, **Why** I am afraid of it, **How** I believe it may have happened, etc".
Personality can be defined as the "exhibition" of characteristics, **"Masks" of Anxiety** developed to shield the self from apprehension about conflict within ourselves or with others. At the heart of Psychological Immaturity lies excessive dependency, fear of rejection and feelings of inadequacy. Fearing emotional independence, masks are donned in attempts to resolve relationship conflicts and avoid the twin realities of human differences and the necessity for healthy emotional separation.

I present the following Visualization as a mental picture to help deal with the stress and anxiety many relationships lead to.

The illustrations in the **Life Boat of Cognition** can easily be used as a tool to instantly focus on Cognition when caught in a web of emotion. The words "When you've fallen into a sea of Emotion

and find yourself going down for the last time, climb into the Life boat of cognition" act as a helpful method of Learning to think about feelings and deciding whether or not to respond to them.

The Basic Ideation underlying **Maturation: The Adult Paradigm** is that **Anxiety arises out of the Unconscious Mind as a signal that something in the unconscious mind needs to be addressed for the process of Psychological Maturation to continue**. I present anxiety as the Developing Ego's signal that an opportunity (underlying unconscious conflict) for attainment of higher levels of Maturation exists. I assure my clients that 80% of those seeking therapy have problems connected to anxiety, not mental illness. The definition of Neurosis remains hazy because the Psychological Coalition doesn't agree on a specific definition. Most do agree however, that Neurosis' may be understood as a term for many types of dysfunctional symptoms and behaviors as as result of defenses used in an otherwise intact base of personality to ward off anxiety.

Within the shadowy confines of **Anxiety** lie most of the common explanations for cognitive and emotional distortions. With the Biological and Genetic exceptions of Learning Disabilities, Neurological deficits, birth injuries, Psychosis, etc., Subjective **Distortions** arise out of our **personally assembled Paradigms, Roadmaps, Family Constellations and the Red Threads** that make up the Psychological Skeleton of our Personality. The Birth Pangs of many personal Categories of **Anxiety** can be remembered either consciously or unconsciously as having arisen in our Family of Origin and account for much of our personal discomfort in adult relationships.

As defined in the **Encarta Encyclopedia,** a cornerstone of modern psychoanalytic theory is the concept that anxiety, institutes DEFENSE MECHANISMS against certain danger situations. As described by Freud, these danger situations are the 1) fear of abandonment by or the loss of the loved one (the object), 2) the risk of losing the object's loves, 3) the danger of retaliation and punishment, and, finally, the 4) hazard of reproach by the superego (conscience). As a result, <u>symptoms</u> form as <u>adaptation</u> (adjustment) to stress that the <u>Ego tries to achieve</u> through more or less successfully <u>reconciling the different conflicting forces in the mind.</u>

Defenses Mechanisms

The **Ego Defenses Mechanisms** help protect the self from emotional distress, especially the suppression of unwanted thought or memories. **Defense mechanisms** operate on habitual and unconscious levels and usually lead to self deception and distortion of reality. Despite this, however, all of us use such defenses. They are essential for dealing with failure, alleviating anxiety and maintaining feelings of adequacy and self worth.

Common Defense mechanisms include but are not limited to Denial ("No, I didn't, you misunderstood), Repression (a child with strong hostility toward his father has so well repressed his feels that he is unaware of it), Escapism (dropping out, not being in the mood, etc), Fantasy (achievement of goals in imagination), Rationalization (justify behavior by inputting logical or admirable reasons for doing it), Projection (Blaming others for our mistakes), Identification (accepting others values as our own as a safety measure), Sublimation (the channeling of impulses or energies regarded as unacceptable, especially sexual desires, toward activities regarded as more socially acceptable, often creative activities, Intellectualization (Grief over senseless death of a child softened by pointing out that "the good die young" or "it was the will of God).

According to the APA Dictionary of Psychology[4] "such Defense Mechanisms range from **Immature** to **Mature** depending on how much they distort reality. Denial is defined as very immature because it negates reality. Sublimation is one of the most mature defenses because it allows indirect satisfaction of a true wish.

4

Defense Mechanisms are seen as normal means of coping but excessive use of any, or the use of immature defenses (Displacement or Repression) is considered Immature

- **Displacement (transfer of emotions or behavior) is** the transfer of emotion from the original focus to another less threatening person or object, or the substitution of one response or behavior for another. For example, an angry child may hurt a sibling instead of attaching a father whom he is afraid of or a wife may criticize her husband instead of her boss whom she fears.
- **Repression**—a mechanism by which people protect themselves from threatening thoughts by blocking them out of the conscious mind. A child with strong hostility toward his father has so well repressed his feelings that he is unaware of them.
- **SUBLIMTION** a high level defense in which an unacceptable sexual or aggressive drive is unconsciously channeled into socially acceptable modes of express. The unacceptable drives are redirected into new, learned behaviors which indirectly provide some satisfaction of the original impulses. Examples might include exhibitionist impulses being channeled into a new outlet in choreography or a voyeuristic urge into scientific research. Or a dangerously aggressive drive expressed no the foot ball field.

I remember how we laughed at an example of **Sublimation** in Graduate school when the instructor presented us with the following possibility for choosing a revered profession: an MD specializing in Surgery may be indirectly as well as subconsciously expressing his aggressive hate toward someone in his past while receiving praise and adulation for the marvelous work being done in surgery. New Clients to therapy rarely have any knowledge of the concept of Defense Mechanisms, either how and why they are developed. However, it is imperative that the theory of Defense Mechanism as well as how they are incorporated into human behavior become familiar to everyone looking for clarification and resolution of relationship conflicts.

#2—FAMILY CONSTELLATION—

Family Faces from the Tree. Basic within **Freudian** theory is that the personality of a child is molded during the early stages of development as a result of the parental behavior toward the child. The child reacts, not only to objective reality, but also to fantasy distortions of reality.

Family Systems Theory defines both the importance of the interrelatedness of family members as well as the difficulty of understanding one member in isolation from the others. **Roles, Rules and Patterns of Behavior in our Family of Origin** becomes evident in **Genograms (d**rawings of Family Systems**). Within our family structure our** Parents Relationships both with us and in their marriage became examples of the Philosophy of Life we came to associate with family roles and marital relationships. In addition, the work of **Toleman, W**[5] indicates that personality characteristics are also a result of growing up within specific constellations (siblings' oldest child, brothers' parents etc.) in our family of origin.

Psychological research indicates that the order we are born into our families influences our personality characteristics. Being oldest children, only child, youngest child, middle child etc., have all been shown to effect our personality characteristics. It is also known that our gender also effects expectations for our attitudes and behaviors. Others may label us as the baby, a crier, a winner, a looser, etc. Labeling

---

[5]   **Toleman, Walter**—Family Constellations, Family Order—FAMILY ORDER—Life Scripts

Bowen, Murray, Satir, Virginia Marriage & Family Theory, Belief Systems, etc. 2007

Redirection of Feelings—In psychology or other psychotherapy, the process in which somebody unconsciously redirects feelings about something onto a new object.

also strongly effects the way we see ourselves and our feelings and behaviors.

Patterns of behavior within **Family of Origin** can be better understood and clearly seen by constructing a Genogram of three to more generations and identifying patterns of behaviors that become apparent. **Genograms**[6] are used by many Mental Health Professionals as a method of identifying Parental Role Modeling, Belief Systems and Transference[7] s associated with Rules and Roles learned in our family of Origin. Many of these transferences signal underlying subconscious conflict and lead to symptoms of anxiety. Genograms are also extensively used in many areas outside Mental Health Services including Career counseling, Child Welfare systems and College Counseling.

GENOGRAMS

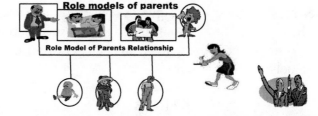

Role Models of parents or siblings can be seen as silent but enormously effective methods of influencing assumption of **similar or dissimilar** philosophical and behavioral identities **in family members**. Angry, unpleasant or warm and loving Parental relationships affect offspring in different ways. Some unconsciously accept the idea that this is the way all parents relate. As a result, depending on our parents' relationship with each other, decisions are made about whether marriage or is not for us or that that's just the way marriage is. On the other hand a child of an Authoritarian father may decide that since everyone jumped to Dads demands that must be a good way to assume management in a relationship.

6

7

The **Role Modeling** presented by a meek unhappy mother may be the nail in the coffin of marriage for a daughter or she may unconsciously assume the role of her father who was the boss. Role Modeling of parents who are happy with each other certainly send a positive message concerning the marital lifestyle, while silently or openly angry parents are characterized by offspring in many different ways.

A **Parents Role with a child** is an important aspect of life that can lead to positive or negative self esteem. Dads who are perceived as constantly critical of one child while praising another also give conflicting messages to offspring about the worthiness of each. It would be difficult if not impossible for a child to ignore statements such as "Stop acting like a Jerk" or "Why can't you be more like your brother"

Introjection of self Image is one of the most important sources of either positive or negative **Self Esteem** and its effects on our life choices. The following Vignette concerning the effects of a dream she had and the conclusions drawn from it was shared in therapy by a large overweight client with an absolutely beautiful face and eyes and extremely low self esteem.

THE BUTTERFLY

The Halloween Party was loud, wild and colorful.

At 11: 45 PM a large woman dressed in a velvety brown Caterpillar Suit arrived. It was soft and full and fitted snugly over the 200 lb. body of the woman who wore it. Standing upright, the Woman dressed as a Caterpillar walked slowly around the dance floor. Her head was encased in a smooth shinny brown satin cap. Two long curved wire antenna's, soft balls of fluff at their ends, extended from high on her forehead and draped gracefully several inches in front of her face. Completely encased in satin and velvet, the only visible part of her body was her absolutely beautiful face. Long graceful lashes swept down from and almost covered the deep, brown softness of her eyes.

In spite of her extreme size and weight, all heads turned to stare at her gorgeous face as the caterpillar continued to make her slow, sensuous way around the dance  floor. At first she kept to the outer edges of the floor, continued to watch her onto the dance floor. she swayed in time toward the Caterpillar admiringly around her. but little by little, as the dancers progress admiringly, she drifted Eventually, standing at it's center, with the music. All eyes turned as the Partygoers gathered First one hand reached out toward the Brown Caterpillar/Woman and then another. Eventually one man touched the top of the zipper under the chin of the woman who wore the Caterpillar Suit. At exactly Midnight, looking into the beautiful eyes of the Woman, the chosen man slowly pulled the zipper down . . . and over the chest and body of the woman . . . who wore the suit. While the music continued to play, all dancing stopped. The transfixed Party Goers' watched in fascinated awe as the tableau at the center of the dance floor continued.

Staring into the beautiful face of the Woman, the arm of the man continued it's gradual descent. As the suit began to slowly drop away from the body of the woman, beautiful long graceful wings of a Butterfly began to appear. Slowly . . . as the brown satiny suit of the caterpillar fell empty to the floor, a beautiful Butterfly emerged. And as it floated gracefully away . . . an amazingly beautifully woman stood among the crumpled folds of soft velvet . . . a Butterfly who had spent her life imprisoned within the body of a Caterpillar.

The effects of **Introjection**[8] (a process in which an individual unconsciously incorporates aspects of reality external to him or herself into the self) on Self Esteem and Self Image are an extremely important Psychological truth for each of us to fully understand.

---

[8] **Introjection**-Psychiatric Dictionary, Robert Campbell, 1981: Some writers of Psychological theory speak of **incorporation** and **Introjection** as the mechanism whereby **internalization** takes place. Incorporation and Introjection are psychiatric terms that describe a process where by something outside the self is incorporated in **some way** into the self.

Working through her thoughts about the dream, the woman realized she had spent her whole life in the role of <u>Caterpillar</u> "waiting in my cocoon for another to discover me and realize I am a Butterfly and not the <u>Caterpillar</u> I look like". She realized she  was eating until she got fat and unappealing because she was afraid she was a loser. Crying softly she whispered "I have always been afraid I am a loser. I ate to get fat and repel others. I couldn't let others close enough to know me. I was afraid others would learn I am the <u>loser</u> my <u>parents said I was</u>."

The effects of siblings on each other are also difficult to ignore. If an older brother skips school or smokes Marijuana behind his parent's backs, younger siblings may grow up thinking that's the way Big Boys are supposed to act.

Using an Educational format, I discuss various Defenses (methods of responding to underlying conscious and subconscious conflict) a client may be using which have been suggested by a close examination of clients Genogram. I explain the concept of both high and low levels of defenses which help protect the self from emotional distress, especially the suppression of unwanted thought or memories.

Clients in Therapy, Graduate students as well Readers of self Help book such as this one, often find clarification of the origin of personal thought processes, rules for life, and belief systems when carefully considering personal family relationships. Drawing a Genogram and studying the characteristics of Family Members and the effects their Roles, Rules and beliefs had on their lives and each others can be extremely helpful in our search for reasons why our life may or may not be working as we hoped it would.

Studying the characteristics of each parents and how these roles effected their relationship, how each parent treated you and your siblings, what their belief systems were and whether these Roles, Rules and Beliefs lead to happiness or unhappiness and/or resentment is a complex but extremely helpful exercise. However, it can be one of the most successful exercises for identifying positive or negative influence of family members on each other. A careful examination of our Family Genogram often results in a more realistic understanding of those we love. And sometimes, although the characteristics and behavior of family members was not what we preferred, we may realize that they did the best they could under the circumstances.

#3 FAMILY ORDER—FAMILY ORDER LEADS TO BEHAVIOR OF FAMILY MEMBERS

Answers to the questions concerning the Characteristics and development of my LIFE SCRIPT can be found and understood within the context of our Family Constellations and Family of Origin Patterns. Each of us, consciously or unconsciously brings into our Spousal and Parenting Relationships Patterns of Behavior and Life Scripts learned in our Families of Origin.

Homeostasis in a family system is a state of equilibrium such as that found in a furnace system. The thermostat is set for 75 degrees. As the temperature drops below the set point of 75 degrees the furnace heats up and comes back to 75. When the temperature rises above the set point of 75 degrees the furnace turns off until the house cools to 75 degrees. In biology, the term is seen as the tendency of biological systems to maintain a state of symmetry.

Homeostasis in a family system can be visualize as a family Swimming Pool. The Family Members can be pictured as living in the warm waters of pool with the water rising to the level of their necks. When a family member gets out of the pool (behaving in unexpected ways) the water level goes down and the other members yell for the wayward member to "get back in the pool" because their shoulders are getting cold. It seldom makes a difference whether the member acts positively or negatively when out of the pool. The main cause of the rumpus is that family members are used to either the negative or positive behavior of the member standing outside of the pool and do not like change. If the abandoning member meekly gets back in the pool, the equilibrium quickly returns to the set point. However, if the abandoning member refuses to "get back in the pool" the other members will eventually respond to the new set point and equilibrium restored.

It is important to remember that a new set point for equilibrium in relationships will not be exactly the same as before a member "got out of the pool". The new equilibrium will be different (negatively or positively) within each of the family relationships. For example: a mother who got along well with an obedient daughter before she got out of the pool may respond angrily or in a withdrawn manner to the daughters new behaviors. A father who constantly criticized a meek fearful son may respond with intense anger to a son who gets out of the pool and refuses to be intimidated. An 8 year old who normally behaved with respect toward parents begins to respond the parental requests with rude refusal after his 14 year old brother who usually "followed the rules" in grade school "got out of the pool" in Jr. High and began smoking Marijuana.

Where do the characteristics of each of us originate? Why do we choose to behave in certain ways?

T-SHIRT LEGENDS IN FAMILY HOMEOSTASIS[9]

An interesting way to think about origins of our personal attitudes and behaviors can be considered more easily by visualizing our Family of Origin as a **Homeostatic** Swimming Pool whose Family Members reside attired in T-Shirts.

T-Shirt Legends can usually be easily identified by asking ourselves what we think others would have written on our T-Shirt. Most of us quickly identify ourselves, our siblings and even our parents with such labels as **"Stupid, Know it all, King, Boss,"** etc.

---

[9]   Homeostasis in Psychologicy—Concept taken from Family Therapy within family and groups. theory of Balance family roles and keeping them stable much as the dynamics of a furnace system.

During our childhood and life in our families of origin parental and sibling perceptions of us result in expectations for our attitudes and behaviors. These perceptions, ascribed in childhood <u>usually</u> continue unchanged unless something of great magnitude occurs. The reason for this? If a younger sibling was perceived as a "Little Princess" it is unlikely (although possible) that those perceptions will change much over the years. A father who is perceived as somewhat scary might be labeled "The Boss" or "The King". A Mother who behaves quietly in an unassuming may still however receive a T-Shirt with the Label of "The Boss". How might this happen? Observed and unobserved Behaviors and expectations may be in conflict For Example: A quiet and unassuming Public Persona of a woman may obscure the "Real Self" of a manipulative Life Script the woman plays in her Roles with others.

In our Family of Origin all of us, <u>even Parents</u> are assigned T-Shirt Labels by other Family Members. What was the legend on the T-Shirt of your Father? Your Mother? Did their Labels clearly define their Roles in Marriage and as Parents? How did their T-Shirts effect their children's perceptions of what a Father, Mother and a Marriage should be? Perceptions of Parental Roles and Behaviors consciously or consciously reflect on our Roles in our own Relationships. Growing up in a family in which Parents never discussed or constantly disagreed about ways to solve a problem cannot help but effect their children's method of problem solving in their own marriage.

Children in a Family Swimming Pool of Sibling Relationships learn methods of relating to each other depending on the characteristics of that **particular** sibling. Learned methods of relating with siblings from our Family of Origin doesn't necessary translate similarly to relationships outside the Family Swimming Pool. However, issues of Transference (something is the present reminds me of something from the past) may at times distort the objective issues between those in a relationship. For example, a look or behavior of a fellow employee may remind of a sibling. As a result we may consciously or unconsciously respond to that peer from a distorted view that may or may not have been realistic in our family of origin.

Research indicates that most of us, do not clearly understand our problems with siblings and often have never learned how to appropriately resolve problems within our Sibling relationships. In addition, few of us learn what type of Parental behavior toward each other or ourselves constitutes Psycholgically Mature behavior. As a result of never having learned Problem Solving Skills that resulted in Positive Outcomes with others of different philosophies we enter adulthood without a clear understand of how to live happily with others, even those with whom we have disagreements.

The Role of a Psychologically Mature Parent is teaching a child to think for themselves, resolve symbiotic attachment and learn to be comfortable being a separate self in relationships with other separate Selves. Along the way, most of us are taught a long litany of "shoulds, Oughts, rights, Wrongs, etc. which many of us never have learned to challenge from our own Realistic Objective point of view.

Ask yourself the following Questions?

- Were your Parents T-Shirt Legends reflective of Traditional, Religious, Shoulds, Oughts, or equalitarian Values?
- Did the Rules and Roles of your Parents including of many "shoulds, Oughts, rights, Wrongs, etc ? Did they agree with each others Rules and beliefs? What were their methods of problem solving?
- Were you labeled positively or negatively (rebel, looser, winner, know it all, etc) as a result of your responses to these Mandates? "Do I agree with these mandates? Why or Why Not?
- Have you removed your childhood T-Shirt, "gotten out of the Pool" and become a "Real" self? Why or why Not?

- Do characteristics of Spouse remind you (positively or negatively) of someone from my Family of Origin? Who? What are the characteristics I am comfortable or uncomfortable with? Why?

"Did I ever get out of the Pool?" Why or Why Not? "Getting Out of the Pool"

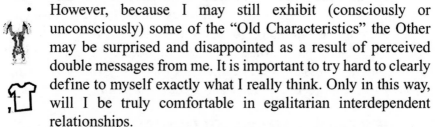

- The role of adult child and parent is respectfully equalitarian (although it may not be similar)
- Roles of Psychologically Mature spouses are equalitarian (belief in equality of the value of each others beliefs).
- Each Relationship is an Opportunity to learn Lessons of Life leading to Psychological maturity
- As we mature, we will more quickly become attuned to identifying "Old Patterns" of characteristics in others we have become uncomfortable with.
- As we mature our "Old Patterns" fade and are replaced with "New Patterns" which might not be interesting to those who were attracted to us in the past.
- However, because I may still exhibit (consciously or unconsciously) some of the "Old Characteristics" the Other may be surprised and disappointed as a result of perceived double messages from me. It is important to try hard to clearly define to myself exactly what I really think. Only in this way, will I be truly comfortable in egalitarian interdependent relationships.

Functional Adult Development

In his Differential of Self Scale Father of Family Therapy MURRAY BOWEN classified levels of human functioning from the lowest to the highest (0—100). The scale attempts to classify human functioning on the single dimension of "Who I am". The Self Scale assess the level of "Self" in a person on the basis of whether decisions are based more on THINKING (High Scores) or Feelings Low Scores)

Murray Bowen's Research in Psychological development indicated that most of us fall at <u>Levels between 40—60</u>. He believed very few Adults reached levels of Logic much above 60. Some Research today (Ellis, Glasser, etc.) indicate symptoms of Neurosis become less as ability to think objectively increases. Ellis concluded it is not what happens that causes the problems, it is our beliefs about what happens that causes the problem (ABC theory). Glasser now describes ability to accept reality as the basis for happiness.

Mild dysfunctional mental disorders (currently defined as Neurosis) are traditionally categorized as Pathology vs Wellness. My own Personal Research, however, suggests such mild dysfunction is not a Mental Illness but a Category of emotional Symptoms indicative of Psychological Immaturity vs Illness. And while serious biological or chemical dysfunction may require medication, most psychological distress can be significantly reduced simply by perceiving situations differently.

I believe Psychological Maturation to be an important "Missing" Link for the functional Resolution of Anxiety and Psychological Growth in which Categories of Mild Dysfunction are Considered on a Continuum of Human Ego Development rather than Pathology/Wellness. Psychological Maturation can be defined a Level of Ego Development necessary for independent Objective, Critical Thinking, ability to Face Objective Reality and Accept the Truth.

STAIRSTEPS OF PSYCHOLOGICAL MATURATION

When relationships become emotionally out of control, it is helpful to think about the situation from a cognitive stance rather than from an emotional one. Since, emotions reside in the most immature Aspects of a self once we have become hit in the "Feelings" it may become difficult to consider the situation from a purely rational basis. In these situations, it is well to climb the <u>Stairs of Cognitions</u> and <u>think</u> about the <u>emotions</u> in the difficult situation <u>from a completely objective rational stance</u>. In especially hurtful situations it is helpful to watch the situation from such a far distance that only the persons involved can be seen as little persons "way, way, down there". In this way, emotions loose their grip because they are too far away to be experienced.

Sometimes formerly close relationships end because one has outgrown the other. Other times, a person in a difficult exchange is at a much lower level of Psychological Maturation than we are. One of the visualizations I use with clients is to ask what they would do if a 2 year old kicked them in the knee or if a Psychotic person insulted them? Of course they would consider the age of the child and mental health of the Insulting adult.

Other considerations may include whether the emotional exchange is between superior and subordinate, equals, teacher and pupil, etc. Always realize that many persons are manipulative while others may be selfish and emotionally immature. Remember, Mature people can choose whether or not to respond to feelings based on the Reality of the situation as well as what is best for everyone in the long run.

#4 RED THREADS—Skeleton of Personality. Red Threads[10] as the Core (Red) characteristics (Threads) that hold the personality together is an interesting way to define the **SCRIPTS** that a person has worked out to live by in relationships with others. Although all personal characteristics fall into the category of Personality, our Core characteristics can be identified as the **Red Threads** underlying the Skeleton of Personality.

The concept of Red Threads[11] was presented to me years ago in a PhD class by my instructor Dr Beverley Killman. As a result of doing Psychological Assessments for many clients over that year, it became obvious to me that our personalities have core characteristics (described by Dr. Killman as Red Threads) that can be summarized

---

[11] **Red Threads** Kilman, Beverly, PhD—Prof of Psychological assessment—Cal School of Prof Psych San Diego 1984

into a basic core much like a physical skeleton onto which all smaller bones, nerves, neurons and skill fit into or fall from.

Ability to perceive and consider personality characteristics and behaviors becomes easier and clear when observed in terms of Core Characteristics (Red Threads) that underlying the more peripheral skeins of characteristics we call personality. Our Personality and behavior is a result of **Conscious and Unconscious Thought processes that lead to patterns of Behavior.**

According to Research in Psychiatric Theory, our basic perception of Life is solidified by the age of 5 years. These Core Perceptions **(Red Threads)** are of course formed unconsciously as a result of our responses to what happens to us in our first years. Most of us have never given a thought to the idea that what happened way back in the hazy or unremembered days childhood is instrumental in our expectations for the here and now. But of course it is.

1ST Memories

It is difficult to overstate the aspect of early memories as unconscious influences of expectations both positive and negative. Asking a client at an impasse in trying to figure out why he or she is so adamant about an issue can often be clarified by asking them to identify and recount a first memory.

Several examples spring to mind: The first as mentioned in another chapter of a client, who found herself always expecting some type of catastrophe was able to understand the influence of such a memory on a 3 or 4 year old child who sat in agony and pain in a wrecked car with her dead grandmother lying bleeding over the steering wheel.

BOWING TO THE "BOSS"

A silently angry and resentful husband who admitted drinking to excess, was baffled by the fact that although his wife spent much of her time arguing with him when he tried to help her understand more "successful ways" of doing things around the house or in the yard, she could quickly put both the issue and her anger aside and seem to forget about it. But he could not.

Asked to think about his first memories he recalled pleasant times playing with his siblings, being held in his mother's lap and going to the ball game with his Dad. Thinking of his wife's family of Origin spent many angrily noisy hours trying vainly to "explain" to each other their individual points of view.

He realized that while his wife was comfortable with disagreement as well as unsuccessful attempts to problem solve issues; his own family memories included almost zero arguments or open discussion of disagreement. He believed his parents may have discussed some differences "behind closed doors" but he wasn't sure.

His father, a retired Military Officer prided himself and others on appropriate behavior. My client recalled his father walking politely away from isagreement with others without making an effort to resolve isunderstandings or understand the others point of view. He remembers when his mother told his Father she would no longer accompany him to Church (one of his revered family values from his own family of Origin) he quietly went by himself once in a while. The matter was politely relegated to the periphery of family life and never openly discussed . . . apparently just buried in the past. His

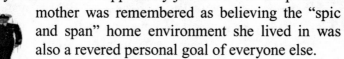

mother was remembered as believing the "spic and span" home environment she lived in was also a revered personal goal of everyone else.

Considering his parents relationships it became clear to the Client that sometimes the "Boss" does not wear the pants and that correct behavior seldom includes arguing with the "Boss". Examination of his own adult perception of life, he believed he had correctly filled his role of "Boss" at work. He really didn't believe the Man should always wear the Pants at home. However, his wife's argumentative behavior confused him because. Only with steady examination of his own Family of Origin in conjunction with his own Personal Philosophy did he bow in surprise to the fact that many do not venerate obsessive cleanliness as the virtue he had internalized as a result of his maternal role model.

It was also obvious to my Client that although he had grown up without parental Role Modeling for successful Problem Solving, neither had his wife's family Role Modeled successful Problem Solving. As a result both husband and wife agreed to try to walk in the Shoes of the Other and politely and without yelling attempt to courteously and respectfully problem solve their disagreements

BEING A SELF IN RELATIONSHIPS

Few of us consider the concept of being a "Real Self" in our Relationships. Because we just assume that the way we are is the way it is. Of course this is not facing Reality. Good Relationships' and happiness in life demand a clear understanding of how our **RED THREADS** of life originated and whether or not, we as adults, really believe in the things we were taught or learned as children.

It is usually only when problems arise in our life and we are afraid that unless things change our situation is unmanageable. At that time, we must remember that the Objective Truth is that we can only change ourselves. With that in mind, the next step is to decide which of our behaviors and philosophies of life are changeable. Follow the steps below to identify your Red Threads and decide whether or not Objective Reality requires changing any of them.

- **STEP 1**—Identify your Rules, Roles and Beliefs systems.
- **STEP 2**—Ask Yourself Where these Rules, Roles and Belief Systems came from. Do you as an adult agree with the Rules and Beliefs your Parents modeled and identified as true? Why or Why Not? Consider the Roles your parents modeled in their marriage. Did they work for them or not? If not, why not? Did your Family of Origin's Rules, Rules and Beliefs encourage family members to think for themselves,

be comfortable with problem solving and critically examining each other's beliefs? "What is your Script for Living? ". "Do you believe people "should or ought" to behave in certain ways?", "Do they?". Do you believe as an Adult that you were brought up in an atmosphere of distorted perceptions and/or expectations? Do you often find yourself upset emotionally by persons or situations outside your control? **Rules, Roles, Beliefs, Red Threads, Roadmaps Where they come from: T1,2,3,4**

- **STEP 3**—Finally, ask yourself what is your Script for Living? How do the Rules, Roles and Beliefs of your family and or yourself fit with the Objective Reality that it is impossible to control anything but yourself, that Personal Responsibility is a mandate of Psychological Maturation, and that only by facing Objective Reality are we able to face the truth. "Are your expectations for yourself and others realistic?" "Do your perceptions and expectations make sense?" "Do your Expectations Fit with Reality?" "Do you expect others to behave in ways the "should?" "Are you able to accept "what is" ? Do you keep trying to convince others of what you think "should" be?" **How they affect our Level of Psych Maturation: Control, Pers Resp, Resp for others, Reality, Cog choices and Bal of Life.**

Once we have been able to understand our own Rules, Roles and Beliefs and identifying whether or not they work successfully with those we share relationships with, we are in a position to identify Why or Why Not our own Roles of Life, Life Scripts and Red Threads interact Successfully with those of others.

#5—ROADMAP OF LIFE

Distortions along our Road of Life are the Result of Conscious and Unconscious Choices (SCRIPTS[12]) we have made or allowed others to make on our behalf. The effects of our Life Scripts on those with whom we have relationships are often complicated and difficult to recognize. In order to clarify why our Life Scripts have been successful or not, it is necessary to identify our **Red Threads** (Core characteristics of Personality). Once we are able to identify the bedrock of our personal identity we are in a position to understand how the personal Red Threads of self and others have affected our Relationships.

Core Beliefs (**Red Threads**) of self and others in <u>contentious</u> Relationships can be visualized as **"Neurotic Circles"** (Behavioral interactions) that go around and around like a **Broken Record.** Research in Family Therapy indicates we unconsciously pick spouses and significant others at our same level of development. Few of us have ever considered our level of Psychological Maturation except to assume that because we are over 18, 35 or 65 we are Adult and able to make successful decisions.

However, the truth is, we pick those at our same level of Psychological Maturation based on issues such as expectations, perceptions, transference and unresolved areas of anxiety acquired in our family of origin. According to [13] author of numerous book and articles on Family Therapy most of us leave our family of origin with many unresolved issues. As a result we are given another chance to resolve our areas of anxiety with others who share similar conflicts.

The problems go round and round like a **Broken Record** Most of us cannot make sense out of the reasons why others don't agree that our ideas and values correct. This is the same type of situation found in the paradigms of Politics. The Republicans believe the Democrats would admit their errors if only they knew the truth. The Democrats

---

[12] Berne, Eric

[13]

of course believe the same concerning the Republicans thought processes. Such prototypes are the same as that found in the World is Flat or the World is round Paradigms from ancient times. Belief Systems as categorized in Chapter 8 Personal may contain many ideologies that have the potential for contentious relationships with others resulting in dancing in Nuerotic circles of Behavior.

Neurotic Circles

 **Neurotic Circles are behavioral** attempts to control others, resist external control, proving our rights, responding to emotion rather than cognition, not having learned successful methods of problem solving, etc. **Neurotic Circles** are usually a consequence  of explicit **Rules** underlying our personal **Belief System**. Such **beliefs** clearly organize our **Rules** into the **Roles** we have learned to play in our **Life Script.**

WHERE DOES YOUR "ROADMAP" REALLY LEAD?

Effects of Culture on Expectations for Roles in Relationships

Belief Systems of Spouses or Significant others from different cultures often have significantly problematic effects on their relationship. Sometimes these conflicts can be worked through but often they cannot. The following examples illustrate such areas of disagreement.

 ## UNEXPRESSED EXPECTATIONS

An **Italian** man and **Caucasian** woman (65-70) with 3 adult children had been married for over 40 years. The wife had successfully managed the family finances during those years and saved close to a million dollars from the income provided by the husbands successful company. Their children were married and self sufficient. There were no debts to be paid off.

The wife came to therapy for closure concerning her anger and resentment that her husband would not sell their company, retire and spend their remaining traveling and visiting interesting sites she had longed to see all of her adult life. The husband was surprised by his wife's expectation that he change his life style at this time in their life. He had no idea she had plans for him to retire. She didn't remember whether she had ever discussed Retirement with him or not. But, she assumed "as any normal person would" that Retirement was an expected part of the last stages of life . . . and her husband should have realized (without her telling him) that she was working so hard to save so much money for a reason.

The wife believed anyone their age (if they could afford it) would jump at the chance of such a wonderful retirement. She was inflexible in her belief she had earned such a "reward" because she had, done without so many things for so many years. She believed her husband owned her a retirement of her choosing in payment for all the things she had gone without over the years. She believed it was now "her turn".

The Wife could not relate to her husband's inflexible stance that a 1) Man s only Role in life is to work, provide for his family and the Role of a wife to assist her husband in his quest for merit.

The husband could not picture himself engaged in any Role except that of Work. Nor could he picture a wife who would value a husband who would abandon his Valued Life Role for a shallow irresponsible life of travel. The wife tried hard but unsuccessfully to help her husband understand her expectations for their final years together but failed in her quest. The marriage ended in divorce. The husband married a much younger woman who he met at her job waiting tables at Wendy's.

Another true instance of undiscussed expectations for Spousal behavior in culturally divergent relationships can be seen in the following Marital Relationships.

ROLES OF FEAR IN A SPOUSAL RELATIONSHIP

 A *"30's Something"* financially successful **Caucasian** businessman Husband married to a **Japanese** Wife came to Therapy for help understanding his wife's anger for not doing exactly as she believed he "should". He was soon joined in couple's sessions by his Spouse.

Of great concern to the Wife was his selfish "unacceptable" behavior one Sunday afternoon when he joined male friends to watch a ballgame. One thing lead to another, several more beers and whiskeys were served as time for dinner came and went. The Husband didn't call his wife to tell her he would be late for their agreed upon time for dinner. He arrived home in midevening with a head spinning from too much whiskey and a nauseous stomach filled with fearful anticipation of expected angry lecturing. He was not disappointed.

Discussion of the incident revealed the Wife believed people who cared about each other called when they would be late. The husband agreed. However, speaking in embarrassed whispers the Husband shared FEAR as the reason for his rude behavior:. Two important areas of trepidation were discussed by the husband. He said he was emotionally afraid to argue with his wife because his stomach always clenched up in a knot. And he was afraid of being labeled by his somewhat Traditional Male friends as a Henpecked "Wimp".

Therapy revealed the Wife believed it was her duty to teach her husband the "Correct ways of life" in spite of the fact he was extremely financially successful in a Business she had no experience with. During discussion of their culturally affected Philosophies of Life, the Husband shared that in his family of Origin, Problem Solving was never discussed. His parents hid disagreements "under the rug" and eventually got over them to the point they were still married, but leading separate lives at age 65 and 67 respectfully.

Consideration of the Cultural expectations for self and others learned in her family of origin the Wife shared the following thoughts and conclusions:

- People should follow the Rules of authority
- People who love their parents should follow their parents rules
- Anger must be justified
- People should strive for and attain Perfection.
- Parents must be the Teacher of Children.
- People who love each other must assume the Role of Instructor of the "right "way to live when a loved one is behaving imperfectly.

After long and thoughtful consideration of the **Rules, Roles** and **Beliefs** originating in her Family of Origin, the Wife realized that although her Script for Living had been that of teaching the correct way to live she had <u>mistakenly</u> assumed that

- If a loved one (husband) didn't do what she asked it proved he doesn't love her.
- If someone criticized her it meant they believed she was not perfect
- Imperfection of any kind was unacceptable
- Admitting others rules and beliefs may be valid even though they were different than those she adhered to was an admission that she had been wrong all her life.

After several long and challenging years in therapy, this couple was able to internalize methods of Problem Solving, examine cultural divergent expectations and come to conclusions comfortable to each. They were able to respect and allow each other's differences, problem solving those that were amenable to cooperation and agree to disagree when possible. Recently I met this couple by accident in a Gardening Shop in California. They were still together in a happy marriage. They invited me to a Christmas Party at their Country estate for friends and family. Of course I could not attend[14].

Problem Solving, Negotiable and Nonnegotiable Values [15]
Where is the "Real" Me?
Examine Your path <u>Closely</u> *For Clues*

Problems can be solved My Way, Your way, Another way, On a scale of 1-10, Negotiable Values or those upon which we can Agree to Disagree. Personal Values must be carefully considered and those identified as Non-Negotiable must be clearly iscussed with the other in the Spousal or Significant Other Relationship. Many of us are able to live comfortably with others whose Non-Negotiable Values can be agreed to disagree about. This philosophy is discussed by Satir, V in her Family Theory Research in the category of Complimentary Relations

Many Negotiable Values are not relationship breakers. Issues in this category are those upon which we can agree to disagree. Non-Negotiable Values often fall into the categories of Spirituality, Religion, Personal Values, Traditional Values, Science, Perceptions of "Shoulds & Oughts, Right & Wrong, Politics, Sex Roles, philosophy of Death Penalty, Parenting Styles, etc.

I clearly discuss the importance of having openly and objectively arrived at Personal Negotiable vs Non negotiable values <u>before</u> marriage or remarriage. Identify whether current Spousal or Significant other characteristics (positive or negative) are similar to those of others in the Past. Identify if any previous choices believed at the time to be

---

[14]   Dual Relationships between client and therapist are ethically unacceptable due to the possible of harming the therapeutic relationship.

[15]   Covey, Steven—**Problem Solving in Relationships**—APA—Convention 1993—**The Happiest Marriages are Egalitarian**-Bowen, Murray **(1913-1990—Family Systems Theory—Differential of self in One's Family of Origin**—Skipi L Smoot—**Walking on Individual Path holding Hands.**

conflict free, contained aspects of unconscious conflicts. If divorce was the only way for solution of such serious problems in the last relationships it absolutely imperative.

After objectively (clearly thought through) vs subjectively (emotionally) arriving at Personal Negotiable and Non-Negotiable Values, it is imperative to be honest with potential spouses concerning them.

Happily married spouses can be visualized as walking on separate but closely connected paths of life. These relationships contain similar Non-Negotiable values and others Values that can be accepted, negotiated, agreed to disagree about, etc. Separate Paths, while not overlapping, remain close enough to comfortably hold hands as they journey through life.

We can learn to be a separate "self" in a Relationship . . . being true to our Separate & Individual Needs, while showing respect for the integrity and needs of others. Relationships need two "Winners" . . . not a Winner and a looser. Two whole selves reside in successful independent relationships. Each is comfortable with personal differences, while maintaining loving emotional detachment and deep commitment to the relationship and to the other. Each has developed the ability to resolve relationship problems in ways that compromise neither their own personal integrity nor respect for the self and each other. Neither believe their needs are more important than the others. Neither believes others needs are more important than their own, fears they may have no right to be who they "really" are and that all personal needs are met.

THE ROAD TO REALITY

A Psychologically Mature Adult is able to face Reality, Accept the Truth and Separate Emotion from Thought.
Perception of Objective Reality is the ability to see world as it is in the "Here and Now" without distortions from past expectations or emotional responses that are not reflective of the present truth.
Lack of capacity to <u>face</u> objective Reality is often a result of Personal Anxiety developed in our Family Constellation. Family, Social and

Cultural expectations can easily be seen as major forces in shaping our perspectives of life and the Roles we play with others. Expectations for self and others are usually based on roles, roles and Scripts we have learned to play in our own Life and in our Relationships with others. However, there is often a big difference between the Reality of the There and Then with the Here and Now. Growing up, it is usually necessary to follow the rules even those we disagree with. However, many of us never realized that disagreement as an adult was an option. Most of us have grown up with distorted emotional transferences as well as unrealistic expectations and perceptions for self, others and life situations.

Distortions of Reality, including expectations for Self, Others and/or situations, are often due to position in the Family of Origin, Family Expectations for Family Members attitudes and Behaviors, Life Scripts, Belief systems and/or Social and Cultural expectations no longer in line with the Objective Reality of the present. As a result, it is necessary to identify Rules, Roles and Beliefs we truly hold as the mature adult we are.

WHERE DOES YOUR "ROADMAP" REALLY LEAD?

Thinking about attitudes and behaviors from the following perspectives may result in a more comprehensive understanding our present life situations. Our **Life Scripts** (what is really happening in the here and now) can be examined to ascertain whether our Paradigm of Life (Rules, Red Threads, Beliefs, Roles) is the result of distortions rather than our true belief systems. "Do you distort reality with unrealistic Expectations, Perceptions or Emotions for people and situations that may have been realistic in the past but are no longer true?"

Distortions—Expectations, Perceptions, emotional Transference of Feelings from the past. Asking the following questions may help clarify the realities of our present life situations. "What expectations do we have for ourselves and others". "What is the result of our expectations?" "Do our thoughts and messages often contain the words should, ought always, never" /an I a perfectionist?" "Do I hate to let others win?" "Do I believe I must be in charge of others because only I can do things correctly?" "Am I still waiting to be rewarded for my good deeds?" Will Santa ever come and reward me for always being good?"

FAMILY CONSTELLATION—Role Modeling of Parents and Others. Family Constellation underlies the Roles, Rules and Belief systems we have been taught. It is necessary to develop an Objective understanding of the possible effects that Family Members perceptions of us (realistic or unrealistic) may have had on our personal Self Esteem and Self Image. Tasks of Maturation include

PARADIGMS—ROADMAP OF LIFE. Recognizing the fact that our Psychologically Mature Methods of organizing our life space and the rules we live by must be in line with Objective Reality, even if the Paradigms we learned as children was not.

FAMILY ORDER—Expected patterns of behavior. Recognition that Birth Order, Family interaction as identified in Genogram and T-Shirts worn in the Homeostasis of our Family Swimming Pool have the potential to result in both unrealistic as well as realistic Roles and Belief Systems. Tasks of Maturation include.

"RED THREADS"—The Psychological skeleton of Personality All personality characteristics can be summarized into a basic core much like a physical skeleton onto which all other characteristics fit into or fall from. Examples might include such distortions as "I'm always right", "People should always do . . .", "I must always try to help others do things the Correct Way", etc.
Tasks of Maturation include.

CHAPTER 12

Lesson 4
The Telescope of Cognitive Observation

**PSYCHOLOGICALLY MATURE PERSONS CAN <u>CHOOSE</u>
TO RESPOND TO EMOTION . . . <u>OR NOT</u>**

Lesson 4

COGNITIVE DECISIONS
VS SHORT TERM EMOTIONAL "FIXES"

"ME"

THINKING ABOUT

MY FEELINGS AND BEHAVIORS.

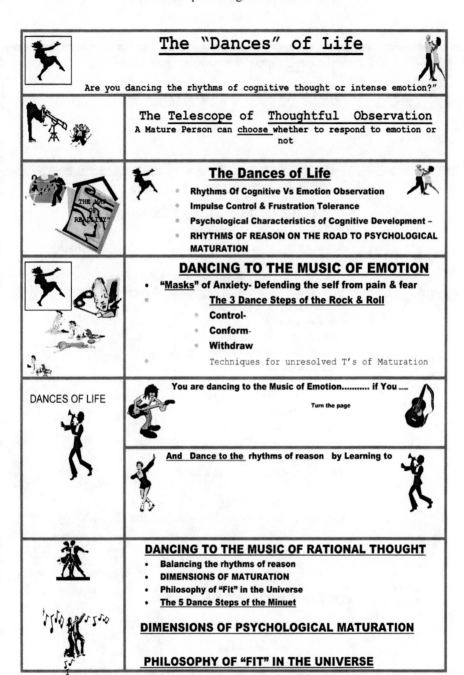

The "Dances" of Life

Are you dancing the rhythms of cognitive thought or intense emotion?"

The Telescope of Thoughtful Observation

A Mature Person can choose whether to respond to emotion or not

The Dances of Life

- Rhythms Of Cognitive Vs Emotion Observation
- Impulse Control & Frustration Tolerance
- Psychological Characteristics of Cognitive Development –
- RHYTHMS OF REASON ON THE ROAD TO PSYCHOLOGICAL MATURATION

DANCING TO THE MUSIC OF EMOTION

- "Masks" of Anxiety- Defending the self from pain & fear
  - The 3 Dance Steps of the Rock & Roll
    - Control-
    - Conform-
    - Withdraw
      Techniques for unresolved T's of Maturation

DANCES OF LIFE

You are dancing to the Music of Emotion........... if You ......

Turn the page

And Dance to the rhythms of reason by Learning to

DANCING TO THE MUSIC OF RATIONAL THOUGHT

- Balancing the rhythms of reason
- DIMENSIONS OF MATURATION
- Philosophy of "Fit" in the Universe
- The 5 Dance Steps of the Minuet

DIMENSIONS OF PSYCHOLOGICAL MATURATION

PHILOSOPHY OF "FIT" IN THE UNIVERSE

THE TELESCOPE OF
THOUGHTFUL OBSERVATION

A mature person can <u>choose</u> whether
to respond to emotion or not.

LONG TERM cognitive decisions
vs emotional "fixes

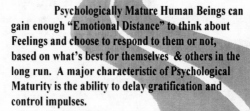

Do you want to get
even but are afraid to
openly solve the
problem with the
person you are angry
at?

Do you often
need a drink
to "Cool" off?

Psychologically Mature Human Beings can
gain enough "Emotional Distance" to think about
Feelings and choose to respond to them or not,
based on what's best for themselves & others in the
long run. A major characteristic of Psychological
Maturity is the ability to delay gratification and
control impulses.

Impulsive behavior is the result of inability
to control impulses, tolerate frustration and delay
gratification. Reasons for such behaviors may be the
result of allow the self to be influenced by others,
excessive need for the love of others or allowing
emotions to dictate the terms of behavior.

Self Discipline, Control, Responsibility,
cognitive Decisions and moderation and balance are
the result of learning to think about feelings and
choosing whether to respond to them or not.

Do you openly
attach others when
they fail to live up to
your expectations

Do emotional
"Tantrums" or Tears
ruin your plans fo
personal success and
relationships with
others?

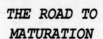

THE ROAD TO
MATURATION

DANCES OF LIFE

ARE YOU DANCING TO THE RHYTHMS OF COGNITIVE THOUGHT ^{OR} INTENSE EMOTION?"

We are born with a mission . . . to explore our own path. Most of us begin our journey "dancing" with abandon to intense emotional rhythms. Only later, often in great pain, do some of us recognize the outstretched hand of Reality . . . and learn to <u>Dance</u> to the Music of the Universe.

IMPULSE CONTROL & FRUSTRATION TOLERANCE

- Do you make impulsive emotional decisions?
- Do you have a low frustration tolerance, feel unable to delay gratification?
- Can you follows rules and make long terms plans?
- Are you unduly Influenced by others?
- Do you feel an excessive need to be liked and respected by others?
- Do you go along with others inappropriate ideas even when you know better?.
- Do you "go along" with others ideas due to fear of anger, abandonment, etc.?
- Are you unable to set limits for the self and others?

Psychologically Mature people can learn to <u>think about their feelings</u> and choose whether to respond to them or not. This ability develops as the result of learning to <u>tolerate frustration</u> and <u>delay gratification</u>. Human Beings can learn to make long term Cognitive decisions based on what is best for ourselves and others in the long run (Characteristics of the Cerebral Cortex) vs. short term emotional "Fixes" (characteristics of the more primitive Limbic System).

Ability to Choose whether to respond to emotions or not is the result of Self Discipline, emotional Control, ability to assume personal

Responsibility, face Reality, make Cognitive Decisions and live a balanced organized life style. Inability to control emotions and tolerate frustration is frequently the result of Psychological Immaturity. Emotionally driven responses are often the result of low impulse control, poor frustration tolerance or never having learned to delay gratification. Underlying <u>causes of these types of behaviors</u> may include allowing the self to be influenced by others, an overwhelming need for the love of others, or impulsive emotional decisions.

<u>Frustration tolerance</u> develops from the experience s of <u>not</u> getting our needs met immediately, learning to wait for what we want (and sometimes not getting it) and making long term plans and goals. A major definition of Psychological Maturation is the ability to tolerate Frustration and delay gratification. This ability seems to be similar to a exercising a muscle (it develops and grows stronger with use). According to Psychological Theory, the Cortex and the Ego develop separately. A main difference between animals and humans is the potential functioning of the Human Cortex. As a result, when a human being has developed a mature level of functioning, that person can choose to think about feelings and decide whether to respond to them or not.

The **Test of Ego and Cognitive Development** identifies many diverse psychological characteristics correlated with personal tendencies toward both Emotional and Cognitive Decision making. Included in these Characteristics are often emotional impulsive decisions, those made out of need for the love of others and as a result of undue influence from others.

Emotional, impulsive decisions are often a result of low frustration tolerance, inability to delay gratification, anxiety or even defiance of others. Many report an emotional tendency towards snap judgments has negatively impacted their personal lives. Other characteristics of emotional decision making include 1) difficulty saving for a "rainy day", 2) wishy-washy tendencies and even 3) discomfort with rigid rules and structure. Some report intuition as a factor in choices while others choose based on thinking about what might be best for the self and others in the long run. And a larger segment than might be expected just "do the opposite of what others want even when we suspect they are right".

On the **continuum of emotion vs thought,** the **need for love and respect from others** plays an enormous role in the process of personal decision making. At the far extreme, are those feeling an excessive, sometimes overwhelming need for love and respect. Fearing anger, abandonment or disapproval, personal thoughts and behaviors are kept to themselves as they silently "go along" with the decisions of others. Some report "almost never trying to change the minds of others due to discomfort with confrontation or anger. A few seldom discuss conflicting topics with others unless knowing the others will not "turn on me". And a segment indicates that few of their values are nonnegotiable, were they to cause a loss of love. At the midpoint of the Continuum are those who sometimes keep plans and opinions to themselves because disapproval is painful. And at the other extreme lie those who even though desiring others approval of their opinions, usually do not change plans to receive good will.

Undue influence by others lies at the core of why many conform or defer to the view point of others without good reason at the expense of personal thinking processes. Many report just "going along with the crowd due to a tendency to think "that if others are doing something, it must be OK". Many rarely tell others what they have originally decided upon and take an opposite point of view because they doubt the validity of their own opinions. Others indicate the belief that Rules have been made for a "good reason" and they seldom bother to question them. Still others believe "others know more about issues then they do. And many report being easily swayed from my initial point of view by another's' persuasive argument as well as almost always being "bested" in an argument.

General Ability In Adulthood

 Normal Biological Development in Adulthood is the result of normal growth and health of Brain and Body. Cognitive Development is the Result of the growth of the mind throughout life. Expected biological and psychological maturation includes development of perception, logic, judgment and reasoning.

Research[1] indicates that of Abstract Reasoning & Vocabulary (left brain functions) as well as Visual Planning (Right Brain function) are resistant to dysfunction once developed. However, <u>many adults</u> remain dependent on external values and philosophies of others due to lack of personal cognitive development, abstract reasoning and problem solving skills (Assimilation & Accommodation).

The Cognitive Ideology (belief system & principles that form basis of philosophy) of admired and respected others are often assumed without adequate thought. Sometimes this acquisition takes place in Adolescence from parents. At other times, it results from interaction with organizations or groups in which we spend time. Often it is the result of Marital relationships in which spouses have not clearly considered the relevance of differences or potential areas of difficulty. During such situations it is often considered the lesser of two evils to "just go along" with the ideology of the loved one. In later adulthood personal Ideology often becomes rigid. According to one Theorist, a cognitive problem of ageing has been well labeled as the "hardening of the categories"!

RIGID THOUGHT PROCESSES—

Unless cognition is or has become impaired by brain or developmental disorders, rigid thinking is usually due to psychological immaturity (inability or reluctance to think for the self, emotional enmeshment, inability to become

---

[1]   General Ability scores (Similarities, Vocabulary and Block Design) on **Wechsler Adult Intelligence Scales (Revised)**

interdependent (our needs are equal in importance) or never having arrived at an Objective personal Philosophy of Life.

The Ideology and Belief systems we have grown up with are often perceived as the "Correct, right way of thinking and doing things etc." Characteristics of Rigidity include all or nothing thinking, numerous shoulds, oughts, generalizations, emotional reasoning, biases, etc.

Cognitive rigidity is often a result of inadequate progression through the Formal Operational Stage of hypothesizing, moral reasoning and problem solving. Such abstracting ability requires incorporating and adapting to new information (Assimilation & Accommodation). Others may refuse to consider the concepts of Assimilation and Accommodation because they believe everything they internalized in the past is the correct way of thinking).

ELDERS

In Elders, Personality often becomes more of what is in subconscious mind. Cognitive change in Elders is complex: some remain unimpaired while others deteriorate. Elder functioning is complicated by physical changes. Speed of motion may slow. Decreased problem solving ability often occurs when new information is required. However, Long Term stored information usually remains relatively unaffected.

Personality Disorders

Personality Disorders [2] are defined as a set of relatively stable, predictable and ego-syntonic[3] habits that characterize the person in his way of managing day to day living: **when those habits are enough beyond the normal range.** Such patterns of relating to the environment are so rigid, fixed and immutable as to severely limit the likelihood of effective functioning or satisfying interpersonal relationships. They are deeply ingrained, chronic and habitual patterns of reaction that are maladaptive in that they are relatively inflexible,

---

[2]   Psychiatric Dictionary—Robert Campbell.
[3]   The acceptability of ideas that are compatible with personal principles.

limit the optimal use of potentialities and often provoke the very counterreactions from others that the person seeks to avoid.

Generic Criteria for Personality Disorder[4]

A lasting pattern of behavior and inner experience that markedly deviates from norms of the patient's culture. The pattern is manifested in at least <u>two </u>of these areas:

- ✓ Affect (appropriateness, intensity, liability and range of emotions)
- ✓ Cognition (how the patient perceives and interprets self, others and events)
- ✓ Impulse control
- ✓ Interpersonal functioning

- The pattern is fixed and affects many personal and social situations
- The pattern causes clinical distress or impairs work, social or personal function
- This stable pattern has lasted a long time, with roots in adolescence or young adulthood
- The pattern isn't better explained by another mental disorder
- Not directly caused by medical condition or use of substances, including medications.

 # THE ROAD TO ADULT HUMAN DEVELOPMENT

No scientifically agreed upon definition of <u>Adult Human Development</u> *exists.* The **Psychodynamic *Theory** (Freud, S & various early authors) of* ego/cognitive development *includes Concepts that 1) The Ego (the thinking part of the Self) arises out of the ID (the immature emotional part of the self) in response to the frustrations and demands (conflict) of reality. According to this theory, the ability of an individual to adapt to life's changing requirements is limited by the degree of psychopathology and the Levels of ego development are the result of techniques used to manage anxiety.*

---

4 DMSIV—Made Easy—Clinicians guide to Diagnosis—James Morrison

The **Humanistic Movement** led by American psychologists **Abraham Maslow** and **Carl Rogers** perceived **Adult Development** as characterized by ability to actualize the true self. According to Carl Rogers, all humans are born with a drive to achieve their full capacity and to behave in ways that are consistent with their true selves. **Rogers,** developed *person-centered therapy,* a nonjudgmental, nondirective approach that helped clients clarify their sense of who they are. The Moral Development research of **Kohlberg,** identified Moral development as the basis of ethical behavior, consisting of 3 levels. The **ABC Mode of Cognitive theory** of **Albert Ellis** states it is not what happens to us that causes our problems; it is the belief we have about it that causes the problems. Similar to Ellis is the belief of **William Glasser,** that Facing Reality leads to the ability to tolerate frustration.

My own conclusions concerning the characteristics of **Adult Human Maturation** are in agreement with the Psychodynamic and Humanistic Theories presented above. However, I add an extra step on the ladder of Psychological Maturation. I perceive Adult Human Maturation to also include an Ego and Behavior component that conceptualizes a majority of Adult Emotional Distress on a continuum of immaturity/maturity rather than pathology and wellness. I believe such a continuum of Ego and Cognitive Development to be a usually disregarded but essential "Missing Link" for attainment of functional (vs dysfunctional) resolution of Anxiety. The Ability to Face Objective Reality and accept the truth is the Missing Link on the Continuum of Emotional Development. Psychological Maturation is a necessary Level of Ego Development for functional comfort with **both** emotional and cognitive independence.

Incorporation of Ego and Cognitive Processes into Human Development[5].

Normal Biological Development in Adulthood is the result of typical growth and health of Brain and Body. Cognitive Development is the

---

[5] **Psychodynamic Theory, Freud & Other**

Result of the mind's state of maturation throughout life. Research cites customary Cognitive growth to include development of insight, logic, judgment and reasoning.

As explained more fully in the Introduction Section[6], **Piaget's theory of Childhood Development** discusses 4 Stages of Human Cognitive Development. During the first *Sensorimotor Stage* **(0-2),** a child perceives the self as the center of the universe. Children at this stage lack ability to conceptualize **ideas** but thinking processes are practical, sensory and action oriented. **During the Second,** *Preoperational Stage* **(2-7)** concept formation begins. The beginning of Language formation enables ability to think about unseen events including their own thoughts and feelings. During this stage there is little awareness of the perspectives of others (Narcissism). **In the 3rd** *Concrete Stage* **(7-11)** the beginning of logical mental processes lead to more careful methodical thinking. And then at about **11 or 12** years of age, **Stage 4** *(Formal Operations)* initiates ability to think about abstract ideas, such as ethics and justice. Piaget did not believe it was possible to hurry through stages.

Characteristics of Adolescent cognitive change during *Formal operational stage*[7] include development of abstract reasoning, deduction, hypothesizing and moral reasoning. The cognitive formulation of hypothesis demands the ability think abstractly, understand the structure of a problem, reason with alternative hypotheses and test conclusions to arrive at an answer to the problem at hand. Passage thru the stage of *Formal Operations* is balanced by Assimilation8 (incorporation of new information into existing cognitive structures) and Accommodation9 (adaptation) which makes room in existing cognitive structures for newly assimilated information.

---

[6]   Introduction section-**Research in Human Development pg 5**

[7]   **Piaget, Jean —(1896-1980), 4 Stages of Cognitive Development**

[8]   **APA Definition—Assimilation-alteration of a new experience to fit existing schemas**

[9]   **APA Definition—Adjustment of mental schemas to match info acquired through experience,**

"AH-HAH"

Many comprehend these concepts as an "Ah, Hah !!! Experience". Some say something like "Oh, I get it now, there's more to this concept than I originally thought". "It's something like a Jig Saw Puzzle." "I'll just move the idea around in what I used to think was the whole design and make room for it.".

I had a client once who said the concepts of **Assimilation** and **Accommodation** reminded her of a situation with a new boyfriend. She learned during their courtship that he had been previously married **(Assimilation).** However it wasn't until speaking with family members did she learn he also had a 6 year son. She said she felt happy to learn her boyfriend was not only kind and sweet to her but that others indicated he was also a excellent father **(Accommodation).**

In addition to biological maturation (physical, sexual, intellectual, etc.) Adolescent Development can be seen as a time for consolidation and integration of **Personal Identity** and **Values.** However, as previously mentioned research cites evidence that <u>many</u> **people never fully incorporate the cognitive building blocks of Assimilation and Accommodation into their personal level of Cognitive development. As a result** many remain dependent upon external values of Parents, Peers, Authority Figures and other respected Icons throughout their lives.

<u>Why</u> are some People, both Adolescents and Adults, able to accomplish the Formal Operations components of **Assimilation** and **Accommodation** while others do not? Putting the concepts of research together in comprehensive order, we understand that biologically, all Human beings follow a similar biological & Cognitive sequence of Patterns[10]. Our Mind, the "Thinking" part of our personality contains the Id, Ego and the superego and has

---

[10]   **Piaget, Jean,** Swiss psychologist, best known for his pioneering work on the development of intelligence in children **(1896-1980)**

the ability to grow. The `Psyche` can be defined as the <u>total</u> **Mind** as distinguished from the Physical and refers to the soul or essence of life.

`Freud` defined the **Id,** as the most primitive component of the personality Located in the deepest level of the unconscious; the ID has no inner organization and operates in obedience to the pleasure principle. The **Id** contains the instinctual, biological drives that supply the psyche with its basic energy. An infant's life is dominated by the desire for immediate gratification of instincts. The **EGO** is the Conscious part of the **Mind. It** grows and learns to deal with emotions and external demands**. Freud** believed the **Ego** arises from **ID** due to the Frustrations of reality. He believed the ability to adapt to life's changing requirements <u>is limited</u> by Level of development and Human Pathology. **The Ego** operates by the rules of the <u>Superego</u> **(conscience).** The American Psychological Association **defines Ego** as the agent of the personality working by the Reality Principle. **According to Classical Freudian Theory the** Level of **human** Ego development is due to Techniques used to manage Anxiety.

Kohlberg's theory of **Moral Development** identified 3 Levels of Moral Development each containing 2 stages of Thinking. <u>Level 1</u> **(External Locus of Control)** appears to be that which most children operate from. Those in **Stage 1** obey to avoid punishment and others in **Stage 2** conform to obtain rewards and return of favors.

Kohlberg believed most Adults operate at **Level 2 (Conventional Conformity)** and continue to function here throughout life. Those falling in **Stage 3** usually conform to avoid disapproval and dislike of others, while those at **stage 4** conform to avoid censure by legitimate authorities. An example would include obeying the speed limit as a method to avoid a speeding ticket.

Level 3 (Internal Locus of Control) contains Stage 5, from which Martin Luther King is widely seen to operate. He obeyed the Laws but due to his moral ideation, actively attempted to get them legally changed And finally <u>Stage 6</u> (**Intrinsic internal morals)** is where **Mohandas Gandhi**, the Indian Nationalist leader, who established his country's freedom though a nonviolent revolution probably operated.

It is at this level a person who truly believes it is immoral to kill another would fall when refusing to be drafted and go to war.

PSYCHOLOGICAL MATURATION: The "Missing Link" On the Ego & Cognitive Ladder of Adult Development

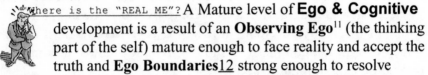Where is the "REAL ME"? A Mature level of **Ego & Cognitive** development is a result of an **Observing Ego**[11] (the thinking part of the self) mature enough to face reality and accept the truth and **Ego Boundaries**[12] strong enough to resolve **Symbiotic Attachment** [13] (emotional enmeshment). A famous Citation from the book **Effective Psychotherapy**[14] by Hellmuth Kaiser states "The struggle against seeing oneself as an individual is the core of every neurosis" and "the universal defense against individuality (emotional fusion) is a Delusion"

A large portion of the Adult population has difficulty understanding reasons for personal discomfort or inability to make well thought out successfully administered personal decisions (Task 1). According to my own Research and interaction with Clients, numerous underlying reasons for this problem reside in the Adult Psychological Maturation Tasks of excessive Emotional Dependency on Others (Symbiotic Attachment Task 2) and resolution of different opinions concerning the circumstances in which the needs of self and others are of equal importance (Interdependence Task 3).

Adolescent Development is a time for identification of both personal identity and moral values. However, as previously mentioned, research cites evidence that **many adults never fully understand the cognitive concepts of Assimilation and Accommodation and**

---

[11] Observing Ego—The ability to think about emotions and personal biases to see and accept reality grows as a result of ability to delay gratification and tolerate frustration.

[12] Ego Boundaries—Knowledge of "where I stop and others begin". Federn (1928).

[13] Inability to feel and behave separately due to feelings of inadequacy, anxiety and fear of rejection.

[14] Hellmuth Kaiser(1965) Effective Psychotherapy

remain dependent on values and ideology of others throughout their lives. Why is this????

Both Ego and Cognitive Development are necessary components of Adult Maturation. Piaget's 4th stage of **Cognitive Development** *(Formal Operations)* identifies **Assimilation** and **Accommodation** as necessary Building Blocks of **Cognitive** Growth. However, without sufficiently developed levels of **Ego maturation** this 4th stage of cognition continues to slip through the fingers of numerous psychologically immature adults.

It appears that Piaget's 4th Stage of Cognitive Development (Formal Operations) ages 11 & beyond has more to do with **Ego Development** than age. Freudian theory states that although the Ego requires frustrations of Reality for Development, the Human Ability to adapt to life's changing circumstances is limited by both developmental levels as well as pathology. **Assimilation requires** successful <u>incorporation of new info into existing cognitive structures</u>. **Accommodation involves** <u>adapting newly assimilated information into existing cognitive structures</u>. **Both** require high levels of Ego Development including Frustration Tolerance, ability to Face Reality and comfort as well as confident thinking for the Self.

Mature Ego development requires a **solid knowledge of Personal Identity. Many of us continue well into middle or old age without a firm knowledge of "Who am I" or even if "I'm a Self or a Reflection of someone or something out there?" As a result of childhood Introjection (drinking down the opinions of others) and absorbing external ideas and philosophies of respected others we often internalize (make them part of ourselves) such external cognitions without adequate thought concerning whether or not such ideas are a true reflection of our own.**

During childhood, **all of us** internalize the admonitions of Parents and respected others in the development of our own Conscience (Superego). And although many of us internalize a positive **SELF IMAGE and resultant high self esteem** as a result of such Introjections, countless others have internalized negative perceptions of our personal worth and abilities. Most of us have heard comments such as "You're just a dumbbell", "There you go again with your stupid ideas" or "Who you think you are anyway? You don't know anything". It's sad but true that overwhelming numbers of intelligent adults continue to be burdened with having adopted such cruel comments concerning personal worth and ability to think for themselves. Of course, many others have heard opposite but equally damaging comments such as "Oh, sweetie, you are the most intelligent person that ever lived", "You're never wrong" or "Your needs are more important than anyone else's needs are". As adults we have all encountered those who believe they are the most wonderful, the worst or the dumbest person that ever lived. Few of us seriously reexamine our internalized Self Image or the T-Shirt worn in our Family Homeostasis in the light of Objective vs Subjective Reality.

In addition, it is sad but true that many of our own personal Adult **Values And Moral Philosophies** are the *result* of having internalized the opinions, values and idea's of others without adequate thought. Such incorporation may be due to fear of personal inadequacy, need for acceptance or fear that unless we agree with a needed or loved other; we will be abandoned and *thrown to the curb*. Most of us have never considered the idea that if such a thing were to happen, the dignity of the human spirit requires getting up, standing tall and growing into our own personal clothes of identity. **Personal integrity can never be the price of another's acceptance.** How do many of us finally come to the realization that it's time as an adult to also become a "Real Self?". Those of us who were not encouraged to do so in their family of origin, may receive such suggestions as a result of talking to others, in Serendipity, in a Dream or in Psychotherapy . . .

 ## WHITE BREAD

She sat huddled in the corner of the couch in my office with tears streaming down her face. "What happened?", I prodded, as gently as possible. "It's such a small thing" she replied "I can't believe I am so upset by it". Tearfully she began telling me the problem she had been having with her husband.

- "I asked him to buy me a loaf of Wheat Bread when he bought the White Bread that he likes, but he said "**No**".
- He said "If I bought a loaf of Wheat Bread for you, I could never eat the large loaf of White Bread during the Week by myself."
- "Well, why can't you get two loaves, one small Wheat for me and one small White for you ?", she asked.
- "Because", he replied, in an angry tone of voice, "one small loaf of White is not enough for my week's lunches."
- "Then, why not buy one small loaf of each". she asked, "one Wheat and one White?".
- "Don't you get it?", he loudly replied in an irritable voice, "I can't eat the large loaf all by myself." "When you eat part of it, it comes out just right at the end of the week. If we each had different loaves of bread, my white loaf would get stale, before I finished eating it"

"He was angry at me for expected him to manage it any other way" she told me. "I don't know what to do". "He only likes one kind of bread and really hates Wheat." "I don't like White Bread either, but I guess it wouldn't hurt me to do it for him." "It's really no big deal." "I don't know why I'm so upset and crying".

It was obvious to me that even at that moment, she didn't see the two children who resided, inside the bodies of she and her husband. The Little Boy, angry and indignant because his needs had not been instantly perceived as paramount by the Little Girl. And the Little Girl, suspicion of her own inferiority laying buried in the dark recesses of her mind, quickly conforming, instantly passive, because she unconsciously feared her own needs were of little consequence within their relationship . . . and maybe . . . even to herself.

Unique Personal Independence (Task 1) results from the ability to face objective vs subjective reality, accept the truth, think for ourselves and develop personal potential. It is likely that many who suffer from symptoms of Anxiety concerning personal decisions have unresolved internal conflict in the areas of **Self Esteem, Self Image** or even sometimes in the appropriateness of developing a **Unique Personal Identity** at all. Many others, although having arrived at a well thought out personal Philosophy of Life, fearing abandonment or loss of important relationships have been unable to devise a method for comfortably sharing their own thoughts with others who disagree (Task 4).

"MASKS" OF ANXIETY

 Maturation: The Adult Paradigm[15] defines Human **PERSONALITY** as **"Masks" of Anxiety"** (exhibition of characteristics) developed to "shield" the self from the pain of conflict within ourselves or with others. It sad but true that many adults have never considered the appropriateness of human differences, the necessity for well thought out vs emotional decisions or arrived at a clear understanding of problem solving skills that recognize negotiable vs non-negotiable personal values.

Searching in vain for the courage to comfortably walk down the Path of Personal Unique Identity as an emotionally independent Adult, many of us continue to the end of life in pain and discomfort. Automatically **reacting to the piercing, deafening percussion of emotion, we don** our preferred **Masks of Anxiety** and head for the Dance Floor where the Trumpets blare. In the darkness of frenzied chaos, brushing up against the shadow of Autonomy we momentarily sense a faint sound. "Wait" . . . **Whispers the imploring silhouette** of **independence "I can help you if you listen". But the blaring voice of emotion, too agonizing to ignore, quickly obscures the murmur of reason. With tears streaming down our face, oblivious to the whispers of personal essence, we turn our back on reason and return to the dance floor where we** kick up our heels in time to the ruckus of emotion as we continue "**dancing to the Music of the Rock & Roll.**

Watching from the depth of the Psyche, the immature neediness of Symbiotic Attachment returns to its post of command and settles down in the recesses of the id, once again safe from the rhythms of reason.

---

[15]   Skipi Lundquist Smoot, PhD   10/4/2009 6:47:00 PM

**Dancing to the "MUSIC" of Emotion
Defending the self from fear**

The 3 Dance Steps of the Rock &Roll

As mentioned in Chapter 2, at the heart of **Psychological Immaturity** lies excessive dependency, fear of rejection and feelings of personal inadequacy. Fearing emotional **in**dependence, "Masks of Anxiety" are donned in attempts to shield themselves from pain, resolve relationship conflicts, avoid the twin realities of human differences and the necessity for healthy emotional separation.

The Dance **Step of Control** is designed to cope with internal Anxiety and control the Cognitive Ideology of others **by** proving the self right and **the other wrong.** If successful, the other admits the error of their ways . . . the conflict in the relationship vanishes and **Symbiosis**[16] lying hidden beneath it's **Mask of Anxiety** breathes a sigh of relief. Variations of symptoms and behaviors within the Dance Step of Control are almost inexhaustible.

The Step of **Conformity** is also designed to resolve anxiety. Some, experts at this step, have become very successful with its results and dance it like the professional they have become. When this happens they can

---

[16] Symbiotic Attachment. Immature persons of all ages feel uncomfortable being an emotionally independent self. Inability to resolve

emotional fusion "feels like being homesick". However, becoming a "whole" person necessitates learning to balance these

forces. Too much of either results in anxiety. When balance has not been achieved attempts to control the resultant anxiety

(internal and external conflicts) by impossible methods are made. As a result psychological symptoms and syndromes

such as dependency, addictions, anxieties and phobias develop.

quickly conform to the needs of others and often successfully hide(even from themselves) the fact they originally had other ideas. Sometimes, however, even these experts need the added persuasion of a few drinks, a sick headache or a trip to the doctor for that mysterious stomach pain, to experience the success they so desperately strive for. However, repressed anger, frustration and psychosomatic symptoms are common symptoms of this **Step of Conformity** even when it is danced with conviction.

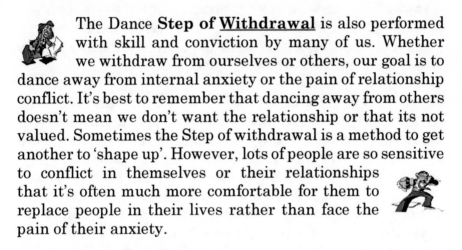

The Dance **Step of <u>Withdrawal</u>** is also performed with skill and conviction by many of us. Whether we withdraw from ourselves or others, our goal is to dance away from internal anxiety or the pain of relationship conflict. It's best to remember that dancing away from others doesn't mean we don't want the relationship or that its not valued. Sometimes the Step of withdrawal is a method to get another to 'shape up'. However, lots of people are so sensitive to conflict in themselves or their relationships that it's often much more comfortable for them to replace people in their lives rather than face the pain of their anxiety.

Many of us have a very hard time dancing away from anxiety within themselves. In an effort to try however, they often drink, sleep, eat, or take drugs as common methods to search for emotional comfort. Apparently this pattern of behavior is attempted by those who need relationships more than they need personal independence. However, such methods, chosen to deal with personal anxiety doesn't appear to work very well.

All three of these **Dance Steps** (with endless variation) lead to psychological and physical symptoms including depression, resentments, anger, ulcers, headaches, asthma, etc. These Symptoms also fall into the psychological categories of neurosis, phobias, addictions, and sometimes even psychosis.

Those of us, who Dance the steps of the the **ROCK AND ROLL** (Control, Conform, Withdraw) distort reality and have unrealistic or illogical expectations and perceptions of themselves and others. **Rock and Roll Dancers** wear **"Masks of Anxiety"** to disguise their "real" selves. These "Masks" are defenses against confronting fears of personal inadequacy and emotional separation from others who are important to us. Some of us hide behind **"Masks"** of chronic anger, self righteous expectations for ourselves and others, violence, or even disregard for the needs and requests of others. Some **"Masks"** hide excessive fears and shyness of the real person beneath. Other **"Masks"** attempt to place blame, be perfect, or instruct others in 'correct ways' to behave. Some *Wait for Santa Clause*[9] to reward them for being good, etc.

We all learn both the Dance Steps of the **Rock and Roll** and our favorite **"Masks of Anxiety"** from our parents, families, authorities, teachers etc. We are taught that certain things are right, wrong, always or never done. We often learn that things are black or white. When we learn that the truth is usually "gray" we put on our preferred style of "Mask" and head for the Dance Hall. Depending upon which Variation of the Dance we have chosen, we kick up our heels, bow to our partner, shove other dancers, grab others to help them perform "correctly", pout, stomp away or angrily shout denunciations when others don't want to dance the steps we have chosen for them. The Emotional Rhythms of the 3 fast slick side steps of the Rock and Roll (with variations) are exhausting. They all lead to pain and some to illness. They are all dances of immaturity learned in a world of fantasy.

The Dances of Life

<u>You</u>   Are Dancing to the Rhythms of emotions

IF YOU.....................

- Make your decisions based on how you feel rather than what you think
- Try to control other People and situations
- Do what others want you to, because you want them to like you
- Get angry, silent, do drugs when you can't face the pain in your relationships
- Believe you are a victim of fate
- *Try to convince others you are right and they are wrong*
- *Think people who love each other should always agree*
- *Have a hard time seeing anothers point of view*
- *Insist on doing things your way*
- *Think your behavior has no effect on the important others in your life*
- *Think drugs, alcohol are OK: or strictly your own business*
- *Usually go along with what your friends are thinking*
- *Think being in love is the most important reason for including sex in your relationship*

Turn the page...........

AND

Dance to the Balanced Rhythms of Reason

BY LEARNING TO:

- Understand yourself and behave as the person you "Really" are
- Live up to your potential as much as you can
- Love and care both for yourself and others in your life without losing yourself in the relationships
- Be a "Real" self in your relationships
- Know how you fit in the overall Schema of the Universe
- Realize you can only control yourself
- Take responsibility for yourself and your own life
- Know the difference between helping others and taking too much responsibility for them
- Face reality and accept the truth
- Make your decisions based on what is best for you and others in the long run
- Never make decisions based exclusively on your feelings
- Live a Moderate, balanced lifestyle
- Live a crisis free life

DANCING TO THE MUSIC OF RATIONAL THOUGHT

BALANCING THE RHYTHMS OF REASON

Mature persons can choose whether or not to respond to emotion. A major characteristic of Psychological Maturity is the ability to delay gratification and control impulses. Human Beings can gain enough "Emotional Distance" to think about Feelings and choose to respond to them or not based on what's best for us & others in the long run.

Scientific Research in Human Development indicates the Ego develop out of the Id allowing Human Beings to learn to think about their feelings and choose whether to respond to them or not. The Id, located in the deepest level of the unconscious mind as defined by Freud is the most primitive component of the Human personality. The Id contains the instincts and biological drives and operates in accordance with the desire for immediate gratification (pleasure principle).

A Child is ruled by the Id until the secondary processes of the Ego begins to form. **Ego** operates by the rules of the Superego **(conscience) and is formed from input of** parents and prohibitions of society, which determine personal standards and aspiration. The Superego Forms at the Unconscious Level thru identification with parents and later admired others. **Ego** [17]1) arises from ID due to Frustrations of reality. 2) The Ability to adapt to life's changing requirements is limited. 3) Limitation is index of pathology and 4) Level of development is due to Techniques used to manage Anxiety[18]. **The American Psychological Association defines the Ego** as the agent of the personality working by Reality Principle

---

[17] **Classical Freudian Theory.**

[18] **Psychodynamic Theory, Freud & Others**

Maturation: **The Adult Paradigm** conceptualizes a majority of Adult Emotional Distress on a continuum of immaturity/maturity. The continuum of Ego and Cognitive Development is a usually disregarded but essential "Missing Link" for attainment of functional (vs dysfunctional) **resolution of** Anxiety.

As mentioned in the Introduction Section of this book, a large proportion of **the Adult Population is unable to Successfully** 1) cope with Stress 2) resolve Personal/Interpersonal Conflict, 3) Make Confident Decisions, 4) understand and set realistic personal goals, or 5) develop a well thought out emotionally satisfying Philosophy for making sense of their lives. Repressed dependency Issues (need for approval, sensitivity, fear of rejection, abandonment, feelings of insignificance, etc) underlie most consciously experienced symptoms of Adult Separation Anxiety19 such as anxiety, indecisiveness, depression, frustration, anger, resentment, guilt/remorse.

Human Psychological Immaturity is a basic reason for personal or interpersonal conflict. Adult Psychological immaturity is a main factor behind high levels of stress, inability to resolve personal and interpersonal conflict, inefficient decision making and inability to derive pleasure from life. Many of us have little understanding of the characteristic attitudes & behaviors of Psychological Maturity nor how lack of those characteristics may effects our ability to successfully cope with life.

As mentioned in the Introduction of this book, the necessity of understanding the concept of Psychological Immaturity in order to resolve the disabling symptoms of Separation Anxiety is almost never considered by the average adult when searching for reasons to explain their own unhappiness and frustrations. However, at the core of Immaturity, is an emotionally disabling inability to feel and behave as a unique, independent and emotionally separate person.

---

[19] Symbiosis—**Differentiation**— M, Bowen, **Differentiation**. M, Mahler

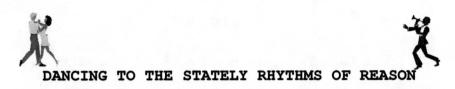

DANCING TO THE STATELY RHYTHMS OF REASON

The **rationality** of the MINUET reflects such mature attitudes and behaviors as Self Discipline, Control, Responsibility, Thoughtful Decisions and a Balanced, Moderate Lifestyle.

Bowing to the stately rhythms of thought rather than emotion is perceived by many as both tedious and difficult. However, its rewards are great. After balancing our needs with others who dance the Minuet, we find our taste for emotional abandon replaced by self discipline, love and respect for each other.

As the loud noisy strains that accompany the excesses of the **Rock & Roll** fade into the distance we objectively realize we have pushed others away with our demands, manipulations and expectations. Our life has been spent dancing alone. Sensing the presence of a Fellow Traveler on the Road Of Life we turn to face a potential partner in the Minuet. Simultaneously bowing to each other we hear the beginning notes of the music of the Universe. Reaching out . . . we take the warm hand of another. Resuming our journeys toward Eternity our shared dance continues . . . down unique but closely positioned individual paths.

Characteristics of optimal Spiritual development include intuition, a sense of spiritual self, altered states of consciousness, knowledge of personal mission in life, an independently arrived at philosophy of purpose of the universe, and a realistic objective workable understanding of its underlying connections.

THE MINUET

DANCING TO THE RHYTHMS OF REASON

The **5 Dance Steps of the Minuet**[20] (thoughtfully balanced Rhythms of Reason) are danced to the positive strains of the Music of the Universe. This music is heard most clearly in the warm, realistic, accepting

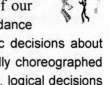

atmosphere of self respect, respect for others, personal responsibility, rational planning and organization of our precious time on earth. The logical, clear, polished dance steps of the Minuet lead to making successful, realistic decisions about life. Any Problem can be evaluated against its realistically choreographed dance steps (a criterion of cause and effect). As a result, logical decisions with a good chance of success can be arrived at because their conclusions are in line with Reality.

Psychological Maturation is the result of facing reality and accepting the truth. Cause and Effect underlies the realism of the 5 **LESSONS OF LIFE:** control, responsibility, reality, thoughtful decisions and moderation and balance. As these 5 **LESSONS OF Life** are accepted and worked into our psychological development, our levels of Psychological Maturity rise. Lessons not understood or incompletely learned are returned to the Fabric of the Universe for further instruction.

The first balanced, measured dance Step of the **Minuet, CONTROL**, presents most of the information we will ever need to learn in order to solve even our most difficult individual and

relationship conflicts. However, executing **Step 1** is exceedingly difficult for most of us. The music leads us to dip and bow to the reality of a fact difficult to accept . . . we have no real control over anyone but ourselves. Attempting to behave otherwise always leads to anxiety and conflict. And although it may be possible to influence another's attitudes and behaviors in various ways, we can never be sure exactly what those "ways" really

---

[20] **Minuet**—a logical, clear, polished dance in measured time was introduced in the 17th century. It possessed rhythmic grace, dignified dance steps, erect posture and respect for others.

are. Actual control of all aspects of specific external situations and others is completely out of our reach. The reason we try to control others is usually a result of certain Belief Systems we have been taught and methods for coping with anxiety we have chosen.

  Assuming the poised, balanced position for the first half of **Step 2**, we find ourselves determinedly gliding in time with the music of the Minuet and stretching to reach the demanding goals of **Personal Responsibility.** We find to our dismay we are responsible not only for our Personal happiness, individual choices, success, goals, achievements and relationships but for our mistakes as well. Bowing to reality, we perceive the impossibility of developing inborn Unique Individual Potential without assumption of personal responsibility. We learn that love for ourselves is not the selfish emotion many of us have been taught it is, but a necessary prerequisite for self respect. Often inability or unwillingness to take personal responsibility is a result of **Rules** we have learned about life or a Role we have been taught to assume in our relationships. Attitudes concerning appropriate personal responsibility are heavily influenced by opportunities to watch an expert same sex Role Model demonstrate the intricacies of **Step 2.** Without such good fortune we find our initial independent efforts to master **Step 2** besieged by criticisms from the side lines of the dance floor by Wall Flowers, shouting misinformed instructions concerning what men and women **"should"** or **"should not"** do.

  Responsibility for Others, the second half of **Step 2**, often presents a challenge to previously internalized personal standards, as we dip very close to the floor in kind, helpful, loving response to another's pain. However, danger may be encountered were we to lose our balance and sidestep our goal of **Personal Responsibility.** However, if we listen very closely to the rhythmic messages of **Step 2**, we hear the music very softly but clearly instructing both ourselves and others to "stand tall" in self respect. As the melody swells in exaltation to human dignity we hear it counsel us in the necessity of personal responsibility as the basis for development of self esteem. Attempts to assume responsibility for lessons rightfully belonging to others /leads to crippling of the other as our inappropriate help becomes their "crutch". 'Appropriate help' is often difficult to see clearly because it lies on such a fine line. As a result, it is probably best to err in the direction of too little help rather than too much. Our decisions about another's' need, often tell us more about our subjective perceptions of another's competence than it does about the realistic ability of the other. When dancing **Step 2** with a partner who frequently asks for help, it is well to ask ourselves the embarrassing question "Does being needed by another build my sense of importance more than it gives actually needed help?" Hearing the Music swell

 into the crescendo of Emotional Detachment we realize we are being beseeched to respect the competence of both ourselves and others.

 The powerful rhythms of **Step 3** loudly attempt to instruct us in the necessity for keeping our eyes wide open as we face **Objective Reality.** We are instructed that Subjective reality is a result of personal distortion. Facing Reality and accepting the truth about ourselves and our world is a necessary prerequisite to developing Psychological Maturity. Our typical **Paradigms** (ROADMAPS) of Life may or may not work well. When they don't, it 's usually the result of **distorted expectations** and **perceptions** for ourselves and others, and/or **emotional distortions from past** **experiences**. Emotional distortion is often the result of Transference, a psychological term used to explain overreaction to something in the present that reminds us of someone or something in our past. Distortions may also be a result of some consequence of Family Birth Order or expectations held for us by someone else in our family.

The legato rhythms of the Minuet's stately **Step 4—Cognitive vs Emotional Decisions** smoothly point out the advisability of well thought out decisions concerning what's best for us and others in the long run rather than those based on **Short Term Emotional** **"Fixes "**. Those addicted to emotion **may** see this Step as tiresome or uninteresting. However, the consequences of emotional impulsivity usually lead to problems while those of thought are more likely to insure success and achievement.

The choreographic nodding of **Step 5** to **MODERATION AND BALANCE** encourages a life reflecting a healthy balance of personal, relationship, and life style characteristics. Living such a life demands planning ability, good judgment, and organizational skills. Precluding a life of obsessions and addictions, a well thought through life with "built in" crisis control is dedicated to a full range of human endeavors including love, work, family, struggle, pain, pleasure, fun and happiness.

Immature personal characteristics such as those of impaired **Impulse Control**, lack of **Frustration Tolerance**, and inability to **Delay Gratification** encourage Dancing to the ROCK & Roll's emotional rhythms. The **rationality** of the **MINUET** reflects such mature attitudes and behaviors as **Self Discipline, Control, Responsibility, Thoughtful Decisions** and a **Balanced, Moderate Lifestyle**. Bowing to the stately rhythms of **thought** vs **emotion** is often perceived by many as both tedious and difficult. However, it's rewards are great. After balancing our needs with others who have learned the dance steps of the Minuet we find our taste for emotional abandon replaced by **self discipline, love and respect for each other**.

As the loud noisy strains that accompany the excesses of the **Rock & Roll** fade into the distance we objectively come to realize that we have pushed others away with our demands, manipulations and expectations. Our life has been spent . . . dancing alone. Sensing the presence of a fellow traveler on the road of life we turn to face a potential partner in the Minuet. Simultaneously bowing to each other we hear the beginning notes o f the music of the Universe. Reaching out we take the warm hand of another. Resuming our journeys toward Eternity our shared dance continues down unique but closely positioned individual paths.

Maturation: **The** <u>Adult</u> **Paradigm**

Follow the "Map" and discover The Path to Psychological Maturity runs through the Fabric of the Universe and is Paved with Realistic laws of cause and effect

Respect for human competence allows innate personal potential to develop. Psychological maturation results from an Observing Ego sufficiently developed to face Reality and accept truth. Ego Boundaries must be strong enough to resolve excessive emotional dependency on others and develop unique personal identity & potential.

The **4 Tasks Of Human Psychological Maturation include 1)** Development of Unique Personal Identity, 2) Resolution of excessive Emotional Dependency on Others, 3) Perception of the needs of self and others as equally important and 4) Personally arrived at broadly focused Objective Philosophy of Life.

The Road to Psychological Maturation is paved with **5 Realistic Laws of Cause and effect** based on **"Processes"** underlying objective reality.

1. The only Person or situation we can <u>Control </u>is our self.
2. We are<u> Personally Responsible </u>for our life, happiness, choices, goals and mistakes. We are not responsible for the lessons of others.
3. <u>Reality </u>is objective. Most of us see life from our own Subjective "points of view". Ability to perceive Reality results in Objective decisions.
4. <u>Cognitive Decisions</u> vs emotional "fixes —This ability develops as the result of learning to <u>Tolerate Frustration</u> and <u>Delay Gratification</u>.
5. <u>Balance & Moderation in Personal Decisions and Life Style</u> Results in resolution of Crisis Control

The Philosophy of "Fit in the Universe"

Most of us have asked questions such as 1) "Why was I born?", "Why am I here?", "Is there a purpose to being alive?" and "If there is a Purpose . . . What is my Mission in the world?" Answers to these questions are unique to each of us. It is uncontroversial that we are each born with a seed of Unique Human Potential. **Development of Human potential** demands **Psychological Maturation**. And only by resolving the problems that deter us from Psychological Maturation are we free to explore our mission in the Universe. **Psychological Maturation** is the doorway leading to a more complete understanding of our <u>unique potential </u>and "fit" **in the Universe.**

Human Life CAN BE PERCEIVED AS A Multifaceted arena of Instructional opportunities for development of both Human and Spiritual Potential. The following points of view are a culmination of my Personal and Professional experiences combined with Educational and Professional knowledge. I am convinced that

1. **Psychological Maturation** is a Human **Developmental Stage** resulting from the ability to **Face** (objective) **Reality, Accept the Truth** of Cause & Effect.
2. I perceive Human **Life** to be a multifaceted arena of **Instructional Opportunities** within **Human Relationships**, **Life Situations**, and **Universal Connections** (serendipity, dreams, synchronicity, intuition, meditation, dreams) for development of both human and spiritual potential.
3. I believe the **Path to Eternity (Spiritual Maturation)** runs thru the **Fabric of the Universe** (Map of Human Reality) and is paved with Realistic **Laws of C & E.**
4. And I have become **convinced** as a result of my **readings and personal experiences that Scientific Research** (Quantum Mechanics, Hypnosis, Parapsychology, etc.) will eventually discover a method for **validation** of the existence of the Spiritual Realm.

You may ask "Why should any Professional presume to know the answers to the myriad of problems surrounding the lives of other Human Beings?" After all Psychologists are just people too . . . like everyone else". I agree that Answers to Life's meaning is Unique to each of us. But I also know from long personal and professional experience that answers to Human Problems lie in the areas of acceptance of Objective Reality and Critical thought processes.

I hope the words presented here will be of comfort to those searching for answers and resolution of personal pain, uncertainty concerning Meaning of Life and questions concerning Death and Dying . . . Answers to such questions reside in commonalities central to the concepts underlying Human Development and the buoyancy and hardiness of Spiritual Growth.

 We are born at the beginning of our potential path into Eternity. By our attitudes and behaviors we choose to explore it . . . or . . . not.

CHAPTER 13

Lesson 5
Balance & Moderation

AM I ABLE TO BALANCE MY LIFE OR
AM I IN A CONSTANT STATE OF CRISIS?

EXAMINE YOUR PATH <u>CLOSELY</u> FOR CLUES

Moderation and Balance

A Healthy Balance Of
Personal Characteristics

- Unique personal identity
- Personal responsibility
- Self Esteem
- Influence of Belief System on Midlife Crisis
- Healthy Old Age

A Healthy Balance Of
Life Style Characteristics

- Gender Equality
- Emotional Bank Account
- Influence of Ego & Cognitive Development on Relationships
- The Doctor who never came home

Characteristics Often
+Connected With "Crises"

- Judgment
- Planning
- Addiction
- Anxiety: A "Signal" of Unresolved Conflict
- Stairsteps of Psychological Maturation

DEVELOPING FUNCTIONAL
COPING STRATEGIES

- Value of Coping Skills & Techniques for Development
- Opportunities for Development
- Coping with Dissonant Life Situations
- Marriage & family conflicts
- Severe Illness
- Coping with Tragedy
- History of Types of Defenses Used
- Life Situations of Tragic Proportions
- Resilience

Where is the "real" Me?

Examine Your path Closely For Clues

LESSON 5

BALANCE & MODERATION

Am I able to balance my life or am I in a constant state of Crisis?

Do you take Unnecessary & Dangerous chances,
expecting to be rescued?

Do you feel like a "Time Bomb"
about to go off?

Do you often find yourself "In The
Soup? because of failure to anticipate
consequences ?

Is your Life so precarious that you feel constantly in
danger of being "Eaten Alive?"

The "Map"

Are you a shoppaholic? Rememember
Shoppaholic's are not always female?

411

LESSON 5

MODERATION & BALANCE

Living a life of Moderation **pre**cludes a life of Obsession, Addictions, too much to do and too little time to do it. Life with built in Crisis control, is a life dedicated to love, work, family, pleasure, fun and struggle. It is one of the most difficult of the 5 lessons to actually learn to do well.

Lesson 5 teaches skills and reasons why or why not living a moderate balanced Life Style with minimal Crises situations presents problems for many. The ability to see the **Big Picture,** anticipate **Consequences** of our choices, demonstrate good **Judgment** and wise **Planning** is the result of many personal decisions as well as personal potential.

A **Healthy balance of personal characteristics** includes successfully existing within our own life space, including provision of appropriate **nurturance for self and others**. The ability to **think critically** about Reality and **objectively assess** the performances of self and others is an essential component of this Lesson.

Unique Personal Identity must be based on having personally and critically arrived at objective facts and conclusions about ourselves, our abilities and our current and past situations. Many of us have never seriously asked ourselves the question "Where is the **"Real"** me?" or even "**Who** is the **"Real" Me**?" As a result we thoughtlessly and often aimlessly glide through life without paying enough attention to what is necessary for living up to our unique potential or even considering what the characteristic of our personal potential include. Instead, most of us have blithely assumed the characteristics respected others thought appropriate for us. Unless our eyes were opened widely in amazement one day in a College Philosophy Class, few of us have ever really come to the realization that **Unique Objective Thought** processes were an important aspect of arriving at success in life.

Many adults enter therapy when their life isn't working and they don't know why. Others decide to get help when the state of their marriage becomes difficult. Often such difficulties arise when a spouse changes jobs, retires, etc. But in more cases than we can ever imagine, **Midlife Crisis** happens unexpectedly. Casually glancing at our self into a mirror one day we find to our dismay the reflection of an elderly person gazing back at us. At that moment the expression "Time waits for no one" becomes clear. Asking ourselves such questions as: "Whatever happened to my plan of traveling the world, getting a graduate degree, writing my book, etc" we consider our present situation in bewilderment!!! At that time the additional question "Whatever happened to the endless time that I always believed I would have to make and complete my plans" becomes unavoidable.

A HEALTHY BALANCE
OF PERSONAL CHARACTERISTICS

Organization & Planning

Successful Organization and Planning of Personal achievement necessitates the ability to provide appropriate <u>nurturance for both ourselves and others.</u> Such success requires the ability to <u>think Critically</u> about Reality, objectively assess appropriate responsibility for self and others and accurately identify and live up to Personal Potential.

Many of us waste valuable time "Talking about Successfully Organizing our Life" rather than doing anything about it. Numerous intelligent adults have no idea what their level of Personal Potential is, how to assess and live up to it or do what they prefer as a result of anxiety. Why is this? As mentioned numerous times in previous sections, at the heart of Psychological Immaturity lies excessive dependency, fear of rejection and feelings of inadequacy.

Numerous cultural and social expectations combine into requirements for living by external standards. Such requirements may or may not have anything to do with our own personal potential, needs, beliefs or even the attainment of realistic responsibility for ourselves. As a result, it often becomes imperative that Adults who disagree with the mandates and expectations of others learn to identify and live up to personally arrived at objective Philosophies of life. We must **STOP** blindly adhering to what others may consider being normal, appropriate or expected and learn to think for ourselves.

A responsible Adult investigating the mandates of Psychological Maturation must accept the fact that we are all **Personally Responsible** for our happiness, choices, life, goals and mistakes. Ignorance of the difference between selfishness and appropriate love and respect for the self often lies at the core of inability or unwillingness to assume personal responsibility. Do you feel too weak to take responsibility, feel your role precludes it, don't know how, can't take responsibility or won't? Why might this be?

A Healthy balance of Mature Ego and Cognitive development includes effort to live up to Personal potential as well as provide appropriate nurturance for ourselves and others. An important component of **Psychological Maturation is** objective identification of **characteristic of** personal <u>Responsibility</u> in both ourselves and others. Such **evaluation** demands recognition of objective facts within specific personal situations as well as **critical evaluation of both our own and others levels of potential and present performance.**

EMOTIONAL EFFECTS ON PSYCHOLOGICAL MATURATION

Psychologically Mature adults are comfortable asking themselves whether their beliefs are truly their own, reflect the views of someone else, define which of their personal values do or do not fit into the ideology of others and the reasons for possible differences. In addition, Psychologically mature adults are able to compromise, problem solve and respect personal differences. Although certain values may be nonnegotiable, personal integrity does not demand others agree with the correctness of our own principles or admit the error of theirs. Why? Because each of us has been born with and the Gift of Unique Personal Potential. We are like no one else in the history of the world. As Human Beings we may explore and develop our "Gift" of Potential . . . or ignore it.

Many adults have never questioned the validity of their professed Values and Principles or even whether those beliefs were reflective of themselves or another. Cognitive Independence is the result of having developed the ability to think about the Self and our Situations from an <u>objective</u> vs subjective point of view. Such a stance requires internalization of Personal Competence, positive Self Esteem and Self Worth,

Internalization of positive self esteem and worth develops from past perceptions of what we believed others thought of us. If we internalized external perceptions of incompetence or worthlessness we may have grown up believing we were unable to think for ourselves. However, if we perceived respect and competence reflected in the eyes of others we were much more likely to have developed positive self worth and esteem. Ask yourself the following Questions to identify personal levels of Unique Independence and possible reasons for having developed such characteristics.

- Did you somehow feel too small, weak, worthless or incompetent to think for yourself or make your own decisions? Why or Why Not?
- Did you feel <u>loved, worthwhile</u> and <u>respected</u> as a Child? By Whom? How was it shown? c
- Do you believe others perceived you as <u>strong</u> and <u>competent</u>? By Whom? How did you know?

In addition to identification of possible reasons for our own development of personal competence and/or incompetence it is also helpful to fully understand the many characteristics, reasons for and aspects of human emotion.

THE EMOTIONAL BARTOMETER
HIERARCHY OF TYPICAL EMOTIONS

An **Emotional Barometer** and Hierarchy of **Typical Emotions** places **Love** at the highest level, followed by **Happiness** and acceptance. Following at a lower level is **Frustration**, **Anger**, **Depression** and **Despair**.

- **Love** is the knowledge that we are all equally important and unique, that positive energy leads to success.
- **Happiness** is the result of solving our problems and the knowledge of Who I am.
- **Acceptance** is the ability to face reality and accept the truth. It is the knowledge we can only control ourselves, that we are personally responsible for our self and the ability to delay gratification and tolerate frustration.
- **Frustration** requires the knowledge that control of others is impossible and no one is perfect.
- **Anger** is a covering emotion and requires the tasks of identifying the real underlying problems.
- **Depression** is best treated by Cognitive therapy and knowledge of our own Core belief system.
- **Despair** has the four positions of **Rudolph Dreikeur**[1]—I want to please and be valued for positive behavior-I want attention—even negative is better than none—I am nothing-worthless—I have no value

---

[1] **Rudolph Dreikurs**—American Psychiatrist who developed Alfred Adler's system of individual psychology for understanding and

OBJECTIVE CONSIDERATION OF BELIEF SYSTEM

Unless expressed in a narcissistic egocentric framework Self Love is not Selfishness. Love for the Self is necessary for Psychological Maturation. Many of us have been taught (sometimes appropriately) to put the needs of others first. And while it is true that we all have the right to get our own needs met . . ., it is <u>never</u> appropriate to do so, at the realistic objective expense of another. However, such a mandate often presents challenges within our roles and relationships with others. For example, difficult situations concerning potential responsibilities for others might include such questions as:

- What might my obligation be for a <u>severely</u> injured spouse (or other loved one) in need of indefinite 24 hour care? Arrange for care on a daily basis? Hire a care giver? Quit my job and do it myself?
- Should I arrange for care of an elderly parent in an Assisted Living Arrangement? Pay for care in their own home? Try to encourage a sibling to help? Provide care for them in my own horn with my own family?
- In the case of a adult child in danger of bankruptcy. What should I do, if the only way to save that child's home and business is to bail them out with money necessary for my own quickly approaching retirement?
- Such questions cannot be realistically and fairly answered solely from the stance of a Belief system in which we were raised, the advice of respected others, the Minister we see on Sundays or even a Therapist. Such decisions can only be made from a long hard critical assessment of our own <u>objectively</u> arrived at <u>personal</u> Philosophy of life.

Over the years as a Psychologist I have used many Techniques for helping clients arrive at their own conclusions concerning person beliefs and what those beliefs and behaviors must include for personal respect. One of the Techniques I have used both in Sessions and Business Presentations includes "Celebrate Your Life". Look it over and answer the questions based on your own

---

stimulating cooperative behavior without punishment or reward.

beliefs. Identify the things you adamantly believe are necessary to be the competent, moral person you can truly admire.

CELEBRATE YOUR LIFE

You are cordially invited to a testimonial celebration to honor your life and accomplishments on your 90th birthday. Dinner will be served in the Founders Suite Of Life at the Performing Arts Center Of Human Accomplishments. Speakers for this wonderful occasion will include: 1) Your parent(s), 2) your child(ren) 3) Your sibling(s) 4) A professional in your field 5) A community leader of your city 6) Your Spouse 7) Your Best Friend and 8) Yourself. Feel free to include any other person you would like to invite.

List what you would like each of these persons to remember about your life and accomplishments. From the lists, you should be able to compile a general outline of your Philosophy of Life. Include in your Philosophy the following points: 1) What directions do you want your life to take? 2) Hierarchy of Importance? Why? 3)Your goals for:) Self and Relationships 4) List your Real Values (Things that can't change). Ask yourself the following Question: Are you able to be proud of yourself?

FOOTPRINTS IN THE SANDS OF TIME
Laws of Cause & Effect

The "**Map "of Reality** runs through the fabric of the universe and is paved with Realistic laws of cause & effect. Making choices based on the Laws of Cause & Effect allows development of Psychological Maturation. Successful Decision Making requires the ability to face reality and accept the truth.

It is often difficult for people to fully understand the concept of Cause and effect outside of the commonly held assumption that it has something to do with reward for positive behavior or punishment for bad. Such an explanation is the Moral one many of us were taught as children.

Cause and Effect as defined in **Maturation**: **The Adult Paradigm** is the concept that everything we do has a consequence. Consequences may not be immediately seen or even the result of our original intent, but it is there. For example: the decision made by a woman who stays with a abusive husband believing in his vow of regret is the cause of future abuse: not because she deserved abuse but because of her decision to stay. Cause & Effect is an objective truth concerning the fact that everything we do results in consequences whether we realize it at the time of the choice or not. This definition is not the same as the commonly held philosophy of **KARMA**: we reap what we sow (good or bad) either now or in the afterlife. The matter-of-fact definition of **Cause & Effect** is that everything we do (cause) has a consequence (effect). Cause & Effect is just that. The only secret is to learn to make choices based on the "processes" of Cause and Effect underling Reality.

A HEALTHY BALANCE OF
LIFE STYLE CHARACTERISTICS

Many aspects of family life including role modeling of others, cultural and social expectations influence our personal belief systems. Many of us have been taught that specific behaviors and beliefs are correct while the beliefs of those falling outside the parameter of our own ideology are not.

However, Psychological Maturation demands comfort with Unique Independence and ability to rely on ourselves for making personal decisions. It is important that our decisions are supported by individual critical thinking concerning what makes sense to us in the present. Such analysis may not be the same as that previously internalized from even well respected authority figures. Many of us find as we reach adulthood that certain areas of beliefs, accepted without question in the past, do not adequately reflect our adult perceptions. Such divergence of opinion is common in all areas of life and is to be expected and objectively addressed.

Psychological Maturation requires development of our own Personal Philosophy of Life and Belief System. Such conclusions must rest on our own Critical Thought Processes, not what we believe we **should** believe or because we **think** others know more about an issue than we do. If others really do have a better grasp of a situation important to us, it is appropriate to study the matter ourselves, in all its complexity, and then make our decision. The concept of Independent thinking rests on the premise that each of us is responsible for investigating complex issues and learning to <u>make choices based on conclusions</u> which <u>truly represents</u> our <u>own</u> inner <u>factual convictions.</u>

Having arrived at well thought out conclusions of our own, it is important to clearly understand that none of us has the right to impose our beliefs on another. Others may feel just as staunchly as we do concerning their own often opposing points of view. And although attorneys are trained to take the point of view of their client and defend it with conviction, successful, psychologically mature personal relationships demand a much higher level of **interdependence**[2]. As a result every effort must be made to value and respect the standards of the other without compromising those of the self. This is possible because attainment of a high level of **Psychological Maturation** allows mature objective consideration of the others point of view, feelings of empathy for the other or even the possibility of agreeing to disagree. **Why?** Because we have learned to love, respect and value the opinions and rights of another as much as we do our own. Dissonant Life situations of all types require enhanced levels of Emotional Independence as well as Cognitive Maturation in the areas of Frustration Tolerance, ability to Delay of Gratification and objective

---

[2]   <u>INTERDEPENDENCE</u> A type of behavior between two equal dependable persons who respect each other, are free to meet their own needs (if not at the expense of the other), able to agree or disagree, share their feelings honestly and he comfortable with their differences.

Cognitive contemplation of emotion concerning the situation under consideration

Balancing Life style Characteristics in Relationships

A Healthy balance of life style includes personal ability to live life so that a broad focus of suitable possibilities may take place in relationships, work place and other areas of activity. Crises Control, necessitates Good Judgment and Planning abilities as well as ability to see the "Big Picture" and anticipate details of possible Consequences. A healthy, balanced life style includes the Psychologically mature characteristics of ability to Tolerate Frustration and Delay Gratification.

Within this category falls drug or alcohol abuse as well as other addictions. It is necessary to reach full psychological maturation and potential to make room in our lives for a well-balanced life style. Such a broad balance must include time to work, play, successful relationships including those of spousal, family and friends as well as allowing for rest, relaxation and the future. It is difficult at times, but important to understand that one aspect of life must not assume a category of greater importance for any extended period of time.

Influences Of Ego & Cognitive Development On Relationships

Inability to avoid or resolve dysfunction or even crises in both personal and life style balance may be a result of Poor Judgment, Poor Planning or symptoms of Addictive Substance Abuse. In some situations, continued dysfunction or crises may be a manifestation of birth defects, low IQ, minimal brain dysfunctions, symptoms of chemical imbalance, mental illness or other types of Psychologically limited development often identified in current literature as **NEUROSIS.**

Virginia Satire's theory concerning reasons for picking spouses suggests those who appeal to us are at our same level of Psychological development and as a result present opportunities for learning

Lessons Of Life necessary for developing Psych logical Maturation. The Effects of Parental beliefs on development of extreme levels of Immaturity in offspring are often the catalyst for dysfunction in relationships throughout life. Such a situation can be observed in the Family of an extremely Narcissistic male, his wife, Mother and Brother.

The following **Vignette** demonstrates the effects of such a state of affairs. After reading the circumstances confronting the family on a Holiday Afternoon, ask yourself what type of parenting may have contributed to such a dysfunctional situation, what Lessons the wife may have needed to learn from her marital relationship and why learning appropriate parenting skills should never be left to chance.

 ## THE SLEEPING HUSBAND

He lay on his mother's living room couch lips slightly parted in sleep, hands clasped together on his chest just below his chin. Five people sat watching him sleep, waiting for him to awaken, . . . his wife, older brother, sister in law, step father and mother. At 35 he still "sleeps like a baby" thought his mother as she lovingly watched him in a behavior that had somehow become a resented family ritual.

Today, Thanksgiving Afternoon, like any other day after a huge dinner, the young husband had gotten up from the table, and lay down for a nap in spite of the exasperation his behavior produced in the others. Plans had been made by the family to visit old friends a few miles away who even now sat waiting for them to arrive. "Why don't we just wake him up, Mom?", asked the brother who that morning had driven with his wife, 150 miles, to have the Holiday dinner with his family "Everyone is waiting for us". Glancing at her older son, their Mother replied, "Just let him sleep a little longer, you know how he hates not having his nap". The man's wife, sitting in angry silence, drummed her fingers on the arm of her chair and thought . . . "Why is It always like this, his needs so much more important than anyone else's." Abruptly she spoke to the hostile silence within the room, "Why don't we ever do anything to put a stop to this ridiculous behavior", she asked in a loud voice "Why don't we just go?".

"Time Past" stealthily entered the room and settled quietly over the man's Mother as she contemplated her sleeping son. Mysteriously the sleeping man faded into yesterday. No longer did he lay sleeping on the couch. The warm cushions that had supported the man, now tenderly cradled the head and innocently flushed face of a peacefully sleeping child. Without suprise she watched the inhabitant from yesterday replace the man who lived in the present. She often confused the man with the child he had been. As she had on many of those long ago days, the Mother spoke quickly to protect her child. "No,", she answered quietly, "he'll wake up soon and then we can go" Lovingly, she considered her sleeping son, the little boy she had tenderly tucked into bed for his nap so many times, for so many years. "Just let him sleep", she said softly "he really needs his rest"

In reference to the family described above neither the Husband nor his mother ever changed their philosophy of life. The husband refused to attend more than several Marital Counseling sessions because he didn't want to be seen as having problems. As a result, the wife attended Psychotherapy alone for several years. She eventually identified her own reasons for marrying the husband, learned many lessons needed for personal responsibility and eventually got a divorce. Several years after her divorce, the wife married a man with whom she had a similar philosophy of life. The last time I checked she had been happily remarried for 33 years to a wonderful husband whom she describes as a 10 on a scale of 1 to 10.

GENDER EQUALITY

The effects of our personal perception of Gender Roles have the capacity for enormous impact on our family, marriage and relations with others. Many cultural expectations still do not afford women the same footing in society as that of men. Even now (2011) in the United States the situation surrounding equal pay for males and females and the Glass Ceiling remains discriminatory. In 2009 the Senate passed the Lilly Ledbetter Fair Pay act of 2009 allowing workers to sue for long-running pay discrimination. The new law reverses a 2007 Supreme Court decision that put a limit on the time allowed for bringing court proceedings. The office of Sen. Barbara A. Mikulski, D-Md., issued the following press release:

U.S. Senator Barbara A. Mikulski (D-Md.) applauded Senate passage of the Lilly Ledbetter Fair Pay Act of 2009 with 61 Senators voting in favor of the bill today. The Lilly Ledbetter Fair Pay Act, which ensures equal pay for equal work regardless of age, race, gender, religion or national origin, is expected to be the first bill sent to President Barack Obama for his signature. "We say to women today who earn only 77 cents for every dollar her male counterpart makes, it's time for a new day. The Bill was signed by President Obama on January 29, 2009.

GENDER ROLES IN PERSONAL ELATIONSHIPS

Males and Females have traditionally been perceived as possessing opposite types of personality traits, determined by gender: males as aggressive, independent, and competitive and females as nurturing dependent and noncompetitive. These Sex Roles have been positively sanctioned by society as appropriate to healthy functioning. My own Doctoral Dissertation:[3]2 presented research identifying four "fairly well established" differences between males and females to be[34] 1) males were more aggressive, 2) girls have greater verbal ability, 3) boys excel in visual spatial ability and 4) boys excel in mathematical abilities.

The effects of expectations concerning Gender Roles in the family effect such preconceived convictions as who "should" care for the children, the "proper" division of household chores, "who" pays the bills in the family, "proper" assignment of money management chores and numerous other family and spousal responsibilities. The Research of Broverman[5], et al[4] (1972), shown below illustrates

---

[3]   Relationships among business Managerial. Performance, Gender, Personality Characteristics, and the perception of Parental sex Roles-Doctoral Dissertation (Skipi Lundquist Smoot, Phd) California School of Professional Psychology—San Diego 1985

[4]   Maccoby and Jacklin (1974). The Psychology of sex differences. Stanford: University Press.

[5]   Broverman, D, (1972) Sex Role Stereotypes; a current appraisal, Journal of Social Issues

perceptions commonly held by average persons concerning Healthy Human Characteristics.

CHARACTERISTICS OF HEALTHY
HUMAN DEVELOPMENT

Question #1	What are the characteristics of a healthy male?	Response:	Assertive—Goal oriented—Successful—Individualistic—Objective—Thoughtful—Career Oriented
Question #2	—What are the—characteristics of a healthy female?	Response:	Nurturing—Supportive—Non assertive—Emotional—Relationship Oriented—Helpful—Doesn't understand business—Doesn't like numbers—Family Oriented—Good Mothers
Question #3	What are the characteristics of a healthy adult?	Response:	Assertive—Goal oriented—Successful—Individualistic Objective—Thoughtful
Conclusions?	Implication that Healthy Females can't be Healthy Adults		
Taken from Doctoral Dissertation (Skipi Lundquist Smoot, PhD) California School of Professional Psychology—San Diego 1985. Relationships among business Managerial. Performance, Gender, Personality Characteristics, and the perception of Parental sex Roles			

Even in 2009, one popular Radio and Television Marriage & Family Therapist[6] presents her own opinion supporting many aspects of Traditional Sex Role in Marriages. Other fashionable books suggest that Males and Females are from different Galaxies. However, Normal Human Traits can more accurately be understood as occurring on a continuum of Human characteristics such as Strong vs Weak, Emotional vs Thoughtful, Assertive vs Nonassertive, etc.).

---

[6]   Dr Laura Schlesinger

Current Research indicates **Gender** and **Sex Role** to be independent categories: <u>**Gender**</u> the physical manifestation of one's maleness or femaleness and <u>**Sex Role**</u> the attitudes and behaviors of a given gender. **Gender identity**[7] is the result of assuming the gender in which he/she was raised and the psychological identity assigned by parents. However, characteristics identified as masculine or feminine are typical of all human **beings** and different levels of **various** human characteristics such as aggression, passivity, independence, nurturance, etc. <u>are inborn traits of both genders. Every</u> child, as a result of physiology, biology, genetics, etc. may be born with different levels of <u>any human</u> trait, some of which society has **mistakenly** identified as indication of Gender.

Human Characteristics are the result of biology, physiology or other chemical pre-determinates. **Chess & Alexander** (1980) write that it is our inborn biologically based characteristics interacting with every factor of our environment that make prediction of behavior difficult. **Sex Type**[8] is defined as the attitudes and behaviors of masculinity and femininity held or exhibited by a person. These characteristics have traditionally been believed to coincide with gender (male exhibits masculine traits: females exhibit feminine traits). The **Research of Bern**[9]—**The Sex Role Inventory** pointed to the likelihood that acquisition of masculine and/or feminine attitudes and behaviors are separate considerations: **Gender,** the physical manifestation of sexual identity and **Sex Type** the psychological sexual identity of a person manifested by behavior. Current Research views masculinity and femininity as separate characteristics within the same person with each set of characteristics having equal potential for development.

---

[7]   Gender Identity—Gender the person believes themselves to be. The personal conviction of belonging to a particular sex, regardless of whether this corresponds to his or her anatomical sex.

[8]   Sex Type = The Psychological Identity manifested by behaviors. The process of adoption of masculine and/or feminine attitudes and behaviors regarded as appropriate by a particular culture for males and females (APA Dictionary of Psychology-2007)

[9]   Bern—(1974) The Sex Role Inventory

Numerous studies indicate **Sex Role**[10]'development to be the result of social and cultural conditioning rather than inborn characteristics of gender. Three phases of **Sex Role Development (Pleck—1975)** [11]identifies 1) **Amorphous** (child has unorganized sex role concepts including confusion over their own gender:2) **Conformist** (child learns the "rules" of sex roles and motivates self and others to form to them: and 3) **Transcendent** (individuals transcend these sex roles and norms and develop **Psychological Androgyny** in accordance with their inner needs and temperaments.

Freud believed Sex Role Development to be the result of Oedipal conflict. The child identifies with the parent **of the** same sex and adopts the qualities of that parent including sex role and attitudes. Social Learning theory indicates children imitate the adult who has the most power over resources such as rewards (whether Mother or father). Cognitive Development Theory (Kohlberg (1966)—states a Child discovers that gender is permanent. The Research of Bern (1976)—indicates that Gender is physical and Sex Role behavior—attitudinal. Additional studies of Bern (1972, 74, 75, 76) show individuals who possess both masculine and feminine attributes are more flexible and adaptable in a wide range of situation. Jung—in his Theory of Anima and Animus believed the need for equilibrium (within the same person) between the unconscious masculine and feminine archetypes was necessary for healthy development of the human psyche. Some authors view **Sex Roles** as an intermediate step in personal development and point to **Androgyny**[12] as the final transcendent stage of development for both males and females. Research of Sandra Bern (1974) indicated 30% of her subjects to be androgynous. Other Research indicates similar findings.

---

[10]   'Sex Role = The Role the person has learned to play

[11]   Pleck, 1975 Masculinity-Femininity: current and alternative paradigms. SEX roles. 1,(2) 161-178.

[12]   9 Androgyny is the possession or manifestation of near equal degrees of femininity or masculinity within a person.

- **QUESTION: If Androgyny (equal levels of Masculine & Feminine characteristics in one person) is the final transcendent phase of development, why don't we see it manifested more often?**
- **ANSWER**: It may be that its development has not been noticed or that it has been discouraged by traditional expectations of society.

My *own* Philosophy and conclusions concerning Gender as a determinant of Sex Roles acquisition are in agreement with Scientific Research identifying Sex Roles to he more a manifestation of social and cultural conditioning than biological determination of Gender. I believe the inborn Gender of human beings to be Male or Female unless there has been an anomaly. The initial form of human fetus is female. For development as a male 1) a genetic code (XY) is necessary and 2) a signal to produce androgens must occur. Female development will occur with only the signal of the (XX) genetic code.

Acquisition of Sex Roles")[13] can be succulently summarized as follows: Genetics (inborn) and culture (expectations, role models, etc.) form personality and sex role identity. Most male and female Temperamental differences can be explained from a cultural point of view. Sex roles are learned by imitation, praise, encouragement and socialization. Genes and environment set limits on personal potential. Although a pairing of genes from parents establish a blueprint, cultural influences have an impact on how, when and if, the an genetic potential will be realized. A child's early socialization depends on social and cultural structure of the family, childrearing attitudes, customs, practices and experiences. Formation of sex role identity demonstrates the cumulative interplay of genetics and culture in development of the central aspect of our human personality.

We are human beings first and members of our gender second with a potential capacity to exhibit a full range of human traits when our inborn temperaments and personality characteristics allow manifestation. I am convinced that as human beings grow toward higher levels of

---

[13] [10] Human Development—Crace J Craig—University Of Massachusetts At Amherst—Prentice-Hall Inc. Englewood Cliff's, New Jersey 1.976

Psychological Maturation we are able to demonstrate more of the whole individual Personality Structure of our inborn potential.

Gender Roles In The Home

When spouses are in agreement concerning division **of chores**, and **who does what** in the home, things go pretty smoothly. However, as a Psychologist **I** find that many spouses remain in disagreement concerning who is "**supposed**" to do what, who "**should**" bring home the bacon, who "**ought to**" takes out the trash, who "**should**" cooks the meals, etc. My response to such quarries remains the same: Those who are best at it and want to do it would probably be the "best" choice. In the Case of a discrepancy of opinion, **Problem Solving** is likely to be the straightest path to clarification of possible expectations for and disagreement concerning Sex Roles. Sometimes such disagreement is the result of **Traditional** perceptions of **Sex Roles**. However, there are numerous other consciously and unconsciously held expectations for self and others in marriage besides Sex Roles. Among them are family rules we learned as children, role modeling of our own parents and respected relatives as well as what authority figures and other respected persons modeled for us as we grew up.

Investigation without bias of reasons why a spouse expects what they do is a good way to clarify underlying often unconsciously held psychological characteristics. It is also helpful to discuss expectations for self and others in marriage as a path to understand our own an our loved ones negotiable and non-negotiable values.

Many clients coming to therapy for the first time have no idea that others do not hold the same expectations they do as to how to divide the chores, who takes out the trash, who handles the money, who pays the bills, etc. Many clients involved in such disagreements are surprised to learn that other families have not lived by the rules they grew up with. Techniques for Problem solving such issues might reach agreement as a result of deciding if possible about who does each chore best or who really wants to do the specific chore being discussed. When agreement can't be arrived at using this type of conflict resolution, we can take turns, compromise or look for alternative solutions not previously considered.

Many disagreements about dividing family chores are the result of Role Modeling of Parents and what we learned to believe were correct ways of family living. When such disagreements occur it is well to keep in mind that successful problem solving requires getting appropriate needs met but never at the expense of another. Respect for the other's point of view is imperative.

Attempt to solve disagreement by compromise, agree to disagree and identify personal negotiable and/or non negotiable values is important for successful relationships. Most such disagreements can be better understood in terms of Values and Principles, Sex Role expectations and then learning to face reality and accept the truth.

Life Style Balance in Relationships

Marital Partners usually come to the realization that personal Gender Role Expectations for themselves and others are out of sync after they have been married a few years after a child is born or when questions concerning working outside the home come up. Many spouses base these expectations on Traditional points of view while many others do not. I personally don't believe Sex Role expectations are either right or wrong providing the spouses can come to agreement concerning the issue. If agreement is not possible, it is important to realize why such conclusions are impossible.

The **Traditional** roles of spouses has defined a wife's duties to be cooking, cleaning, childrearing, husband as head of the family and financial support of the household. Even though many thoughtful Traditionalists agree with this point of view, problems may arise in the case of a female spouse who has inherited money or earns a significant amount of money herself Answers to such questions are the responsibility of those in the marriage as a result of personal ideation concerning values, principles, religion, culture, etc. However, Psychological Maturation requires the conclusions to reflect the view that each person has the obligation to live up to their own potential and that no one has the right to get needs met at the legitimate expense of another.

Modern Spouses often have nontraditional beliefs concerning whether a wife should or should not work outside the home. Some nontraditional women are comfortable in the role of stay **at** home Mom but not as a housewife who cooks, cleans and lives to wait on her husband, especially when no children are involved.

In the area of **Orange County, Ca**. many women from well to do families apparently enjoy the life of a stay at home spouse, mother who is readily available for family members who need her, country club registrant, bridge player and/or golf enthusiast. Again this life style is a matter of choice. However, it is well to remember that the ability to have a successful career is not written into the Genetic Code of either Males or Females. Nor is the ability to take care of finances, dust the furniture or cook the meals. Such assignment of chores are hopefully the result of respectful decisions made by spouses concerning who wants to do them, who does them best, whether a religious ideology concerning them underlies their expectations and whether both spouses are comfortable with their marital roles.

Many cultures and religious groups have many different beliefs concerning the roles of men and women in marriage and relationships. Cultural as well as family systems often relate to each other as a result of shared beliefs and expectations. Many adult males are uncomfortable unless they are the most successful family breadwinner. In traditional families the Male is still today seen as the Head of the Household as well as the Breadwinner. However, today, more than in years past, many men are comfortable with a working wife who also makes a significant amount of income.

THE $1 DOLLAR BILL

I was surprised one day when a Japanese male client told me that he was very comfortable with a working wife, a wife who made as much income as he did, but not one dollar more a very nice Asian Male who came to Therapy for a short time concerning a search for answers about a business problem. Both he and his wife seemed happy with their life together. She is also Asian, a working wife and mother. Apparently his wife agreed with his monetary position

THE **EMOTIONAL BANK ACCOUNT**
IF YOUR WITHDRAWALS OUT BALANCE DEPOSITS YOUR RELATIONSHIP IS BANKRUPT

DEPOSITS	WITHDRAWALS
◆ Courtesy	◆ Discourtesy
◆ Honesty	◆ Disrespect
◆ Kindness	◆ Taking the other for granted
◆ Keeping commitments	◆ Ignoring
◆ Understanding the other	◆ Being arbitrary
◆ Sharing expectations	◆ Betrayal
◆ Showing respect	◆ Threats
◆ Showing personal integrity	◆ Playing god
◆ Don't gossip	◆ Not keeping commitments
◆ Apologize when you make a withdrawal	◆ Lying
◆ Remember mistakes are human	

BUILDING TRUST in RELATIONSHIPS

Working Full time for over 25 years in the field of Clinical Psychology has given me the opportunity to recognize the social and personal decisions concerning negotiable and nonnegotiable points of view within many cultures. As a result, I have found that helping Spouses, Family members and friends understand the necessity of respect for the rights and needs of each other is of extreme importance. As a way to explain the importance of fairness and equal opportunity in relationships I have put together the Model in the Table above. Because most everyone understands the value and make up of Bank accounts, I have used the Paradigm of the Emotional Bank Account as a method for Building justice and Trust in Relationships.

The following Vignette concerns one such marital conflict, the decisions concerning them and the outcome. As you read through the Vignette ask yourself which of the points of view you would consider to be Negotiable, Nonnegotiable and the reasons for your conclusions.

The Doctor Who Never Came Home

During the years they knew each other in High School they loved and respected each other's point of view about life, home, family and Careers. Both wanted to have a family, earn graduate degrees, live with each other and walk through life together until old age and finally death.

After marriage they lived together, worked part time and earned Bachelor Degrees. Placing the future birth of a first child and future family on hold for the present, she felt comfortable going back to work full time so he could enter Medical School and complete requirements of Residency. He finished in the top 7% of his Class, did well in Residency and began writing a book. She continued to work at good jobs, making impressive amounts of money while he searched for a publisher. Finally several years after starting his own medical practice, his book was published to a crescendo of accolades about his Medical Theories. He became an instant success and renounced figure. He was booked for travel all over the country, book signings, and lectures at Medical School and interviews on TV programs.

She was delighted with his success but believed he should now plan to stay home, work in his practice and start their long awaited family, rather than continue traveling, lecturing and teaching in Medical Schools around the country. She believed it was her turn to meet her dreams of Motherhood. He agreed she had put her life on hold for him, given up a lot, waited a long time and was entitled to meet her own dreams but felt he had so much to "give" to others that quitting his job would amount to abandonment of his potential.

She agreed that he had the right to make his own decisions concerning his own future. However, she knew that at 35 years of age her years for motherhood were numbered. But she knew she was still young enough to find a mate who valued family as much as she did. After months of problem solving they decided to go their separate ways. She is currently remarried and the mother of twin girls born just after her 39th birthday.

433

Her second husband work as a bank manager. She is now a stay at home Mom and he is a wonderful husband and father. She looks forward to returning to work when their twins are in grade and middle school. Both he (the doctor) and she (the wife) are happy with their lives, grateful for the lessons and gifts they received from each other. Both are happy with their choices. **Carefully read the research presented below concerning Negotiable vs Non-Negotiable Values.**

Negotiable vs Non-Negotiable Values

Problems can be solved My Way, Your way, Another way, On a scale of 1-10, Negotiable Values or those upon which we can Agree to Disagree. Personal Values must be carefully considered and those identified as Non-Negotiable must be clearly discussed with the other in the Spousal or Significant Other Relationship.

Many of us are able to live comfortably with others whose Non-Negotiable Values can be agreed to disagree about. This philosophy is discussed by Satir, Virginia in her Family Theory Research in the category of Complimentary Relations Many Negotiable Values are not relationship breakers. Issues in this category are those upon which we can agree to disagree.

Non-Negotiable Values often fall into the categories of Spirituality, Religion, Personal Values, Traditional Values, Science, Perceptions of "Shoulds & Oughts, Right & Wrong, Politics, Sex Roles, philosophy of Death Penalty, Parenting Styles, etc.

The importance of clearly discussed and objectively arrived at Personal Negotiable vs Non negotiable values before marriage or remarriage is imperative. Identification of whether current Spousal or Significant other characteristics (positive or negative) are similar to those of others in the Past is an extremely import area to consider well before marriage. Also Identify if any previous issues believed at the time to be conflict free, contained aspects of unconscious conflicts. If divorce was the only way for solution of such serious problems in the last relationships it absolutely imperative to make sure such problems do not occur again. After objectively (clearly thought through) vs subjectively (emotionally) arriving at Personal Negotiable and Non—Negotiable Values, it is imperative to be completely honest with potential spouses concerning them.

Happily married spouses can be visualized as walking on **separate** but **closely connected paths** of life. These relationships may contain similar Non-Negotiable values and others Values that can be accepted, negotiated, agreed to disagree about, etc. Separate Paths, while not overlapping, remain close enough to comfortably hold hands as their journey through life continues[14].

We can learn to be a separate "self" in a Relationship . . . being true to our Separate & Individual Needs, while showing respect for the integrity and needs of others. Relationships need two "Winners" . . . not a Winner and a looser. Two whole selves reside in successful independent relationships. Each is comfortable with personal differences, while maintaining loving emotional detachment and deep commitment to the relationship and to the other. Each has developed the ability to resolve relationship problems in ways that compromise neither their own personal integrity nor respect for the self and each other. Neither believe their needs are more important than the others. Neither believes others needs are more important than their own, fear they may have no right to be who they "really" or worry that important personal needs will not be met.

Relationship Balance In Vocational Situations

Position of Responsibility in Work Situations

The <u>GOAL</u> of Personal Responsibility in Vocational Situations is to Clearly understand and function appropriately in your role. Your <u>ATTTUDE</u> toward another in work related problem situations must reflect your position in the relationship. Decide whether your position in the relationship is one of equality, subordination, or authority. In all cases your attitude must be polite and nonjudgmental. Your goals must be clear. Be able to discuss the facts of the problem and your feelings about it in an appropriate manner.

---

[14] Skipi L Smoot—**Walking on Individual Path holding Hands.**

REMEMBER that in **Win-Win** situations **between** <u>Equals</u> (Spouse, Adults and parents, Partner, etc.) both get what is needed and <u>a</u> fair amount of what is wanted. In Situations in which You arc the **Superior** (**Employer, Parent, etc**) you need to <u>understand the other's needs and wants</u> and get what you need while helping them get what they feel is important to them. However, **the** <u>final</u> decisions are yours. In situations where you arc the **Subordinate** (such as your employer, authority, teacher, police) you must get what you need and at least part of what you want. However, you may need to defer to the other or be prepared to leave the situation. You can use the Sandwich technique[15], "I" messages, "You" messages, make clear comments and learn to <u>think about your emotions</u> and <u>decide whether to respond to</u> them or riot.

Giving and Taking Criticism Appropriately

THOUGHTS ABOUT TAKING CRITICISM

No one is perfect. Sooner or later you will make a mistake. Some of the time it will be noticed and commented upon. The way you react to criticism limits you more than perhaps any other reaction in business & personal life. 1. The most difficult job for many mangers is to criticism their employees job performance. Many times they don't have all the facts. Their position is shaky. Almost all people offer some resistance to admitting they were wrong. When people make excuses to rationalize their behavior and performance, they may think they are making a strong case for themselves. Others see them as unwilling or unable to change. Resisting criticism causes stress and wastes energy and time. People who take criticism badly, even those who do an otherwise good job, are often the most difficult people for management to deal with. You are more trouble than your worth if you offer resistance to valid criticism.

---

[15] **SANDWICH TECHNIQUE** = the meat of the complaint sandwiched in between two positive statements. For example "1) 1 know you try hard to do the right thing, 2) however, I felt sad when 1 heard you had criticized me. 3) 1 know that in the future you will not criticirx me without talking to the about it first in private.

The secret of criticism is turning the situation into one where you are asking for advice. Your value is determined by the way you deal with your mistakes. It is your capacity for growth. The person who constantly makes the same small mistakes, is the loser: while the one who profits from a big mistake, learns his lesson and moves on is the success. If you try to avoid mistakes at all costs you are making a bigger mistake than the one you are trying to avoid. Over caution, losses your spontaneity and ability to adapt. People who are going to amount to anything make mistakes all the time. They just admit them and learn from them.

The source of criticism is important. If you don't trust the criticizer, you will not be open to his comments. Negative people are the worst criticizers. They stalk their prey to express vengeance. Dealing with negative people with a legitimate complaint is especially difficult. They feel because they have caught you they now have an excuse to dump on you. Its easy to be dragged into conflicts at times like this. Most unreasonable arguments are about combating negativity while struggling to hide your flaws. Negative people try to provoke others to fight when they have a defensible case against them. Don't!

TECHNICS TO DEAL WITH CRITICISM from NEGATIVE PEOPLE
Think of yourself as a matador sidestepping an attacking bull. Offer no resistance. Keep your distance. Be nimble. Observe and stay detached. Remember that whatever you have done has tapped into their reservoir of unexpressed anger. They are likely to blow it out of proportion. Don't take it personally. Don't retaliate by criticizing their outburst. Like all people who hold in anger, negative people have low self esteem, bear grudges, and externalize it by blaming anyone they catch making a mistake. If you resist, you will be the target of their outburst and trapped in the wrong issues. Remember they have a case. If you react with emotion or defensive you will be drained and angry and have sunk to their level.

ACTIONS FOR DEALING WITH NEGATIVE AND UNREASONABLE CRITICISM

Minimize conflict by being open. Let their comments pass through you. Interview and question them. Let them feel free to criticize and express their feelings. Help them be clear. Ask their advice. Think of yourself as healthier than they are (they are using you as an emotional whipping boy). Realize that by not reacting to their unreasonable attack you are acting in your own best interests. With negative and unreasonable people, their hostility is their problem even when directed at you even if they have authority over you, your responsibility is still to keep them from polluting your consciousness. Don't fight with them. You will never win. TURN CRITICISM INTO OPPORTUNITY. ASK FOR ADVICE. BE OPEN, ACCEPTING AND EXPECT TO GROW.

OFFERING CONSTRUCTIVE CRITICISM

It is more difficult to give criticism than receive it. People are inhibited about telling others what is wrong with their work. Most people do not want to hurt the feelings of others due to fear of rejection when pointing out a truth others are unwilling to face.

Offering criticism as INSTRUCTION or EXPLANATION, however, usually presents less difficulty because business criticism is prompted by necessity, it is often neglected until severe problems develop. It may then be given abruptly and under stressful circumstances. Supervisors should try to keep an objective distance, so they can be effective and stay in contact. If errors are pointed out as soon as they are noticed, employees will not be allowed to fall into serious trouble. As difficulties grow, workers feel more self conscious about mistakes and are likely to become defensive about hearing criticism. When criticism is withheld too long, irritation and discomfort increase. Feelings build and the supervisor may then OVERREACT. If you keep communication open by taking opportunity to praise, you won't have trouble pointing out shortcomings as they arise.

Criticism and Praise go hand in hand. The old Idea that if you don't say anything, everything must be fine, is maladaptive. If you only criticize, people will equate you with suffering and a blow to their self esteem. They will hide or be defensive no matter how good your criticism.

Make your criticism an extension of some praise by remembering to use the Sandwich Technique. Even though it is truth that Negative behavior is more likely to get your attention praise of good behavior is important. A basic reason for criticism is oiling the squeaky wheel. We focus on weaknesses, because pain is our greatest teacher. When things go well, everyone wants to take the credit. When a problem occurs, people attempt to hide their deficiencies and deny their role in them. Although people know they have room for improvement, they publically deny their weaknesses while secretly dwelling on their shortcomings as they question their competence and fear discovery. In the absence of openness, people blame others and search for a scapegoat. Oil the squeaky wheel but examine and adjust the others as well.

The **Goal Of Correction** is creating an open work atmosphere in which criticism and praise flow as part of the work, where people do not dread being singled out, but expect and are pleased to receive attention and instruction when they need it.

GUIDLINES FOR CONSTRUCTIVE CRITICISM

Clear objectives are important. Know what you want to accomplish with the criticism. Establish open communication between you and the one receiving the instruction. You probably won't be able to make all the corrections you want, but opening the relationship to instruction will be your greatest asset for improving communication. Keep in mind that having a lot of criticism to make reflects a **closed** relationship, in which negative feelings have built up inside both parties. Be diplomatic and deliberate. You are opening the relationship up to a greater depth of honesty. Be slow and gentle. Pick the time and place. Because you want to be heard avoid quitting time when everyone wants to leave. Pick a place that is private and friendly. Put yourself in the others place. Harsh public criticism alienates others and created mistrusting atmospheres. Be positive. View the problem as an entity, not the person as the problem. Talk about the problem with distance. Encourage the other to discuss the problem with distance. The object is to acknowledge the problem and find ways of talking about it that produces results not conflict. If the Other Person doesn't admit there is a problem present your evidence simply and without emotion.

The older your complaints, the less immediate and believable your criticism will sound. Explain you want to review the problem from the beginning and that you didn't comment earlier because you believed the problem would clear up. Admit your judgment was wrong because the problem has persisted. Accept some of the blame for the problem. Perhaps you misunderstood and didn't express yourself clearly or failed to make sure the other really understood. Maybe the other didn't feel comfortable approaching you. Perhaps you seemed critical.

VIEW THIS AS OPPORTUNITY TO DEVELOP CLOSER COOPERATION AND OPENNES.

Once you agree about the problem allow the other to share their perceptions. Interrupt as little as possible. Use short questions such as How did that happen, what was your reasoning, What did you think was happening. Invite the other to critique their own behavior. Ask how the work could be improved and similar mistakes prevented.

The strong worker is aware of shortcomings and is working on them before you point them out. They welcome communication and guidance. The weak worker avoids examining the problem and denies their input into it. Your job is to help people make corrections and take responsibility for their improvement. Provide support and praise when they improve. Offer your point simply and directly. Make sure you are both talking about the same thing. If you find the same situation over and over consider if the other is correctable. Ask the other if they see it as correctable. Do they want to change, are they willing to change? If the situation cannot be corrected decide if it is in your best interest to have that person working for you.

Working in Situations that insults moral responsibility

Sometimes, a responsible, highly motivated person will find themselves in a Vocational environment that uses actions and expectations for your working skills that are not acceptable under your Moral Code. Many companies do such things as skirt the truth, lie to get their bottom line as high as possible, expect employees to lie to customers, etc. If this is truly the situation, get out as soon as possible.

THE *STAIRSTEPS* OF COGNITION
Cognitive perception of Problematic Relationships

When relationships become emotionally out of control, it is Helpful to think about the situation from a cognitive stance rather than from an emotional one. Since, emotions reside in the most immature aspects of a self once we have become hit in the "Feelings" it may become difficult to consider the situation from a purely rational basis. In these situations, it is well to climb the Stairs of Cognitions and think about the emotions in the difficult situation from a completely objective rational stance.

In especially hurtful situations it is helpful to watch the situation from such a far distance that the persons involved can only be seen as little persons "way, way, down there". In this way, emotions lose their grip because they are too far away to be experienced. Sometimes formerly close relationships end because one has outgrown the other or because one has begun to grow in an opposite direction from that formerly traveled. Other times, one of the persons in a difficult exchange may be at a much lower level of Psychological Maturation than the other.

One of the visualizations I use with clients is to ask what they would do if a 2 year old kicked them in the knee or if a Psychotic person insulted them? Of course they would consider the age of the child and mental health of the Insulting adult. Other considerations may include whether the emotional exchange is between superior and subordinate, equals, teacher and pupil, etc. Always remember that many persons are manipulative while others may be selfish and/or emotionally immature. Remember, Mature people can choose whether or not to respond to feelings based on the Reality of the situation as well as what is best for everyone in the long run. Consideration of an emotionally difficult situation with a close friend, spouse or family member is often more clearly perceived when both of the combatants are considered from a psychological maturity point of view. Remember that a psychologically mature adult can think about feelings and choose whether to respond to emotions or not based on what is best for the self and others in the long run vs than the short run.

Personal & Life Style Characteristics *often connected* with "Crises"

A life of Moderation will more often than not preclude s a life of "Crisis", Addictions, too much to do and too little time to do it. Life with built in Crisis Control is a life dedicated to love, work, family, pleasure, fun and struggle. It is one of the most difficult of the 5 lessons to learn.

Inability to avoid or resolve Situations of DISAGREEMENT in both personal and life style balance may be a result of Poor Judgment, Poor Planning or symptoms of Addictive Substances. In some situations, continued connection with Crises may be a manifestation of birth defects, low IQ, minimal brain dysfunctions, symptoms of chemical imbalance, mental illness or other types of psychologically time development often identified as neurosis.

JUDGEMENT

Judgment as defined in the Psychiatric Dictionary[16] is the ability to recognize the objective relationships of ideas. This ability is called critical judgment. Inefficiency in management of Personal And Relationship Life Style may result from numerous issues including Poor Judgment, Poor Planning, Addictions, Anxiety, Attention Deficits, opposional defiance, Depression and/or Cognitive Deficiencies such as Low IQ, Learning Disabilities, Attention Deficit disorders to name a few.

Poor judgment may be a result of chemical imbalance, Organicity, anxiety, low frustration tolerance, low IQ, being overly influenced by emotions or the ideas of others. It can also result from preconceived unrealistic ideas, subjective vs objective reality and poor self discipline. Some people have a hard time with understanding how cause and effect of their own behaviors influences the consequences

---

[16]   Psychiatric Dictionary fifth edition by Robert J. Campbell

of those choices. Many clients enter therapy with symptoms of Poor Judgment. Citing situations over which they have difficulty many make such statements as: "My impulsive behavior has hurt me in achieving my goals", "I often find myself in trouble without really understanding how it happened", "I often find myself in situations from which I need to be rescued" and "I am seldom able to anticipate negative consequences"

As mentioned many times in the previous pages, Psychotherapy with me is often Educational and comparable to taking a course in Psychology. Along with helping clients understand how their family role models, self esteem and self image may have contributed to personal and relationship behaviors I help clients identify areas of needed change.

Many report a life filled with crisis, inability to deal with impulsive behavior, feelings of guilt when doing something they believe others might disapprove of. Many others report feeling the obligation to put others needs first and never knowing how to arrive at the "right" answer to problems. Numerous others say they are always getting into trouble without understanding how it happened. Some report a history of picking the wrong friends and inability to anticipate negative consequences.

When Biological Reasons for Poor Judgment are the focus of Treatment, Autism may lie at the core of the problem. When Autism is PRIMARY, it seriously effects Social Contact and Understanding of social situations. Autistic thinking can be narcissistic, egocentric, fantasizing, daydreaming with little or no connection to reality. It is thinking with emphasis on self absorption rather than disconnection from reality. **Autism** is a disorder of neural development characterized by impaired social interaction and communication, and by restricted and repetitive behavior. These signs all begin before a child is three years old.[2] Autism affects information processing in the brain by altering how nerve cells and their synapses connect and organize; how this occurs is not well understood.[3] It is one of three recognized disorders in the autism spectrum (ASDs), the other two being Asperger syndrome, which lacks delays in cognitive development and language, and Pervasive Developmental Disorder-Not Otherwise Specified (commonly abbreviated as PDD-NOS), which is diagnosed when the full set of criteria for autism or Asperger syndrome are not met.

Many adults have little understanding of Cause and Effect or how their own behaviors influences their relationships either positively or negatively. **The** Definition of cause and effect **(Encarta Dictionary). states the principle that everything that happens must have a cause. It concerns the action that causes an effect, or the ability to cause an effect. Other reasons for poor Judgment may include b**eing overly influenced by ideas of others, having internalized unrealistic ideas or being overly influenced by emotion or subjective perceptions rather than **objective reality**.

<u>TREATMENT</u> techniques include development of more **reliable Coping Skills,** techniques for better Decision Making and more reliable Planning Techniques as well as Techniques for improving Frustration Tolerance and ability to Delay Gratification. **Coping Skills may include learning to make more successful decisions, learning to** think for the self, learning different types of Planning Techniques and becoming more comfortable thinking about feelings,

PLANNING ABILITY

Poor Planning Abilities may be a result of inadequate problem solving skills, never learning to consider Long term solutions as well as too little overall understanding of human development, Good planning abilities is often the result of having established mature levels of Ego and Cognitive development—<u>Self Discipline</u> and—<u>delay gratification</u>.

Clients cite cognitive and behavioral characteristics such as "My motto is "live every day like it's your last", "I am unable to balance my budget until next payday" and "I can never schedule my time so I am able to get all my daily goals accomplished". Other clients with Ego and Cognitive Immaturity issues make such statements as "I am late everywhere I go, "I don't try to work first and play later", "My life is often in crises" and "I have never been able to adopt a plan (technique) for successfully solving my problems".

Many others indicate inability to make sure family and work receive adequate attention, ability to budget time so they get all daily goals accomplished. And most problematic for many is the inability to balance work, family, recreation and ability to feel proud of themselves.

Poor planning may be the result of too little FLEXIBILITY. Such problems may be rigidity in thought processes, responding to an erroneous beliefs concerning how things should be done or continue to do things in spite of the fact that their system isn't working.

Other reasons for the dysfunction of Poor Planning may be a result of a disorder called **SELECTIVE ATTENTION**. Selective attention is a cognitive process in a similar category as Assimilation and Accommodation. Both are supposed to develop as a child reaches Adult hood or during the Teen years. In Overinclusive (sees the trees but not the forest), may focus on one thing in the observation (1 details) and exclude the rest. However, in Underinclusive (sees the forest (many aspects) but not the trees), attends to a great many things. This happens to all children but for those who the phase lasts longer can be labeled as **DISTRACTIBLE**.

At about 12, a child enters the selective attention stage which requires ability to focus on relevant and suppress irrelevant and unnecessary aspects of the situation. Requires the ability to pay attention to the important issues and make room to get them done.

Other reasons for poor Planning include DISTRACTIBILITY, poor attention Span, ability to focus or Inability to tune out irrelevant stimuli. Example: Noisy cars on the road outside the window result in inability to focus on what is going on inside the house.

MENTAL HEALTH ISSUES including Anxiety, Depression, Adj Disorder, etc. are also often at the bottom of poor planning. And of course many adults suffer from disorders such as learning disability without realizing it. Many older adults have suffered from LD all their lives but were never diagnosed because until the 80's and 90's many of those in the Educational fields did not realize they existed.

Also of importance in poor planning are ADHD with is primarily a disorder of inattention, impulsivity and hyperactivity. Correlated with ADHD is sleep disturbances and emotional lability. Secondary to ADHD lies low self esteem, poor Social skills, academic problems, substance abuse issues and conduct disorders. ADHD has a strong biological biological basis and is probably inherited, due to association with pregnancy or birth complications.

LEARNED HELPLESSNESS is also sometimes seen in Psychotherapy as a reason for poor planning. Things that lead to feelings of helplessness include lack of motivation and failure to act after exposure to unpleasant events or things over which they have no control (noise, crowds. People learn they can't control environment and this may lead to failure to make use of any control options available. For example: Years ago, animals in research projects were shocked over and over to see what they would do about it. After getting shocked numerous time, they finally just accepted it, sat there and accepted their terrible situation. Abused women may become so traumatized by abuse they fail to leave when they have the option. **Learned helplessness theory** is the view that clinical depression and related mental illnesses may result from a perceived absence of control over the outcome of a situation.

ADDICTIONS

"Crises" can often be more
easily understood to be a result of
Addictions of one type or another.

Many clients come to therapy for help with problematic drinking, use of illegal drugs, tranquilizers or prescription drugs. Many of these clients have found themselves in trouble with the law as a result of alcohol or drugs or been told they would benefit from understanding underlying psychological reasons for their alcohol, prescription or drug abuse.

Many of these clients report finding themselves in Crisis due to "picking the "wrong" mate or friends without realizing it until it is too late". Others report "Getting stuck in the same type of rut over and over". And many cite "Getting into financial trouble due to impulsively over spending, gambling or Credit cards Debt"

I have found over the many years of treating Addictive Disorders in therapy, the Intervention techniques that have been the most helpful are family Genograms, identification of Family Role Models, a Family history for discovery of similar symptoms in other family members and identifying a clear understanding of clients philosophy and principles of life.

Reasons for Addictive behaviors are numerous and often include low self esteem, poor impulse control, anger at others as well as feeling "Life passing me by" and "It's got to be My Turn sometimes". I have often found the Behavioral Technique of Thought Stopping to be a big help for those just about to get into the car for a trip to the Mall or Poker Table. And of course methods for improving impulse control, anger management, planning ability and coping skills are always explored in detail for relevance in the personal situation of each client.

 Addictions are defined in the dictionary as Habit, compulsion, dependence, need, obsession, craving, and or infatuation. **ADDICTION**[17] is defined in the APA Dictionary of Psychology as "A state of Psychological or physical dependence (or both) on use of alcohol or other drugs". It goes on to explain that "the equivalent term Substance Dependence is preferred to describe this state because it refers more explicitly to the criteria by which it is diagnosed" in the DSM-IV[18]. The DSM-IV criteria for substance dependence include tolerance, withdrawal, loss of control and compulsive use of the substance.

As is the case in the definition of Neurosis, there is also a lack of consensus as to a proper definition of **'ADDICTION.'** Some in the medical community maintain that the term addiction is only applicable to escalating drug or alcohol use as a result of repeated exposure.

---

[17]   APA DICTIONARY OF PSYCHOLOGY (PG 18)

[18]   DSM-IV Diagnostic and Statistical Manal of Mental Disorders—Fourth Edition

In other settings addiction is defined as other types of compulsive behaviors such as shopping, gambling, overeating or getting into the same types of negative behaviors over and over. In all cases, the term addiction describes a chronic pattern of behavior, resulting in adverse consequences and inability to disengage. Many addicts long for the ability to end their addictions but find themselves at the mercy of compulsive thoughts, emotions and habits perceived as being out of their control.

It is interesting to note the differences between Definitions of **Physical** and **Psychological** dependence. **Physical Dependence** is defined as a state of an individual who has taken a drug and will experience unpleasant physiological symptoms if he or she stops taking the drug. **Psychological dependence**[19] however, is defined as a "dependence on a psychological aspect of a substance (eating, gambling, shopping, drugs, alcohol, etc.) for the reinforcement it provides" and "is signaled by a high rate of use, craving and the tendency to relapse after cessation of use".

Psychological addictions are a dependency of the **mind**, and lead to psychological withdrawal symptoms. Theoretically addictions can form for any rewarding behavior, or as a habit to avoid undesired activity. Typically, Psychological Addictions only climb to a clinical level in those who have emotional, social, or psychological dysfunctions, taking the place of normal positive stimuli not otherwise attained.

An Addiction is a compulsion to repeat a behavior regardless of its consequences. A person who is addicted is sometimes called an **addict**.

MENTAL HEALTH—OBSESSIVE, Compulsive
PSYCHOLOGICAL ADDICTION
Obsessional neurosis presents a cluster of symptoms which vary over time but as a group are characteristic of the illness and usually start

---

[19]   APA DICTIONARY OF PSYCHOLOGY (Pg 752)

before age 25. Parents of those with such obsessive processes are often identified as being more perfectionist, obstinate, pedantic and parsimonious than normal.

Obsessive/Compulsive Rituals—A traumatic life event (Death, Injury, sexual abuse Etc.) is often associated with onset of symptoms. However, just as often, one cannot be identified. Some fear loss of being in control of personal situations, fear of embarrassment or even fear of loss of mind, **NONE OF WHICH IS A COMMON COMPLICATION OF OCD** Neurosis.

Repetitive acts of counting, touching, fixing are seen in obsessive behaviors. Counting rituals are common in which counting letters or words, feeling the need to do something like laying down their pencil 3 times or stepping on every fifth sidewalk crack can't be resisted. And as ridiculous as it may sound hand washing, emptying ashtrays, counting rituals or picking up pieces of paper in the street, etc. is done because the person feels as though they will explode if they don't do it". A common presenting symptom is fear of loss of control such as hurting another, or the self, fear of germs, knives, etc.

What distinguishes obsessions from delusion is not so much insight (absurdity) but struggle against the experience itself. He strives to free self from the obsession but can't and feels increasingly uncomfortable until the idea 'runs its course" or the obsession act has been completed. Obsession ideas includes thoughts that repetitively intrude into consciousness interfering with normal thought and causing distress to the person. Obsessional images vividly imagined scenes, often of violence or cars colliding, g parents having intercourse, words, phrases, rhymes. Obsessional convictions "thinking ill of son will cause him to die",

Obsessional ruminations: thinking about a subject to the exclusion of other Indecisiveness "What tie shall I wear"?, Did I turn off the gas, lock the door, Ruminations are resisted, tries to turn attention elsewhere but can't. Obsessional fears dust, disease, contamination, of specific situations or doing certain things.

Biological obsessions and compulsiveness can be seen In those who try to hide from fear of loss of control (Keeping everything tidy) to serious (Obsessive Behaviors) of loss of the self. Many years ago I had a recovering Alcoholic client who actually tried to beat the voices from his past out of his mind.

Land of Shadows

Slowly, stealthily, the Shadow figures crept from dark recesses. Approaching closer, they began the dreaded but inescapable Ritual of claiming the mind of the man. Whirling around in his mind, the voices, inhabitants of Land of Shadows became louder and nearer. One by one they emerged from the darkness.

"What a loser", spat a short, dark shadow, called Chuck. "Take that back", responded the man. "Shut your Mouth" the shadow snapped back. "You're too weak and helpless, even to be a man". "Stop saying that", implored the man. "He's right" whispered another shadow figure. As she came closer the man recognized her as the Wife. Materializing from the darkness she approached menacingly. "You don't deserve anything because you never do anything right", hissed the Wife. "Stop, saying that". the man cried out loudly in pain "leave me alone" "Don't say that" . . .

Screaming out in rage, a tall menacing shadow called Mother shouted "Who do you think you are, defending yourself, You sniveling little brat""You're nothing but a loser, just like your father", "You make me sick". "You're so disgusting I can't even speak your Name".

Swiftly, menacingly the **Band of Shadow Figures** approached the man. Grabbing, shoving they pulling him this way and that. Blindly the Man's arms flailed out in a vain attempt to protect himself. The Shadows laughed derisively at the Man as they continued to hurl angry, insulting, humiliating remarks. Clustered around the small man as he lay in a defenseless heap of pain in the center of the shadows, they assaulted his body and head with physical blows. "Stop", screamed the man in agony "Stop". Crying out in humiliation and pain, the man pulled himself from the floor. Rising, he blindly ran from the Land of Shadows as the physical and mental pain of the attack seared into his thoughts and soul. Running, clawing his way out of the Shadows he emerged from his mind. Staring at his fingers the man saw familiar tell tale stains of blood. Standing, he looked at his reflection in the mirror. Once again he saw he had beaten himself in the face and head with his fists until blood dripped from open cuts and down his cheeks to mix with the tears of humiliation flowing from his eyes.

In frustration and rage, the man surveyed the devastation wrought by his own mind and body. Once again he had vainly tried to beat the voices from the past out of his own head with his own bloody and bruised fists . . . "Leave me alone" the man shrieked in anguish at the memory of the Shadow Figures. "Why can't you leave me along". Staring at his reflection, the man asked himself." Why can't I leave the World of shadows? Why can't I let this go?"

Recurrent Obsessive-Compulsive Ritual experienced by a 47 year old recovering Alcoholic Psychotherapy Patient who had been physically, verbally and sexually abused by family members from the age of 3 until he ran away from home at age 17.

SUMMARY& OVERVIEW OF DEFINITIONS

- **Psychological Addiction (Dependencies** of the Mind) can form to a behavior, relationship, obsession, Alcohol or Drugs and leads to Psychological **dependencies and Psychological withdrawal symptoms.**
- **Chemical Addiction (Dependencies** of the body) to drugs, alcohol, etc. Leads to both physiology and Psychological **dependencies** and both physiology and Psychological withdrawal symptoms.

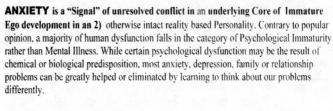

Stair Steps of Psychological Maturation
on the Continuum of Ego/Cognitive

100

Anxiety: The "Signal" of Unresolved Conflict

ANXIETY is a "Signal" of unresolved conflict in an **underlying Core of Immature Ego development in an 2)** otherwise intact reality based Personality. Contrary to popular opinion, a majority of human dysfunction falls in the category of Psychological Immaturity rather than Mental Illness. While certain psychological dysfunction may be the result of chemical or biological predisposition, most anxiety, depression, family or relationship problems can be greatly helped or eliminated by learning to think about our problems differently.

PERSONALITY can be defined as "MASKS" OF ANXIETY. We hide our _"Real"_ selves behind attitudes and behaviors unconsciously designed to avoid anxiety, fear of abandonment & emotional independence Avoiding issues necessary for attainment of emotional independence, **"Masks"** are donned in attempts to ignore internal and external conflict. "The struggle against seeing oneself as an individual is the core of every neurosis" and "the universal defense against individuality (emotional fusion) is a Delusion". "The true conflict is between recognizing the fact of one's aloneness and our need to avoid and deny it"(Reference).

50

Psychological Maturity can be defined as the ability to Face Objective Reality and accept the truth tolerate frustration, delay gratification, think about emotions and choose whether to disregard them based on what is best for the self and others in the long run,. The continuum of Ego/Cognitive Development provides a necessary but frequently _Missing Link_ for conceptualizing normal vs abnormal processes. The intrapsychic characteristics of typical, average, socially conforming individuals are more understandable when categories of mental processes include immaturity in addition to normal and abnormal. Levels of psychological maturation identify a more complete rationale for instances of dysfunctional behaviors often erroneously identified in today's social environment as antisocial, immoral or mental illness. **The Continuum of Ego/Cognitive** Development defines Psychological Maturation as a necessary **"Missing Link"** for a broad comprehensive understanding of human mental processes. Without such in-depth consideration of both **abnormal processes leading to mental disorders and** normal **but** immature **levels of psychological maturation this has often been a confusing task.**

0

0—30 = Lower Levels of Maturation 40-60 = Signals of Anxiety 70-100 Higher Levels Of Maturation

ANXIETY is a **Mood** (unease, depression, phobia, etc) accompanied by **Physical Symptoms** such as racing heart, problems breathing, feelings of faintness, etc. These Dysfunctional symptoms surround **specific underlying conflicts** and occur in an otherwise intact reality based Personality. Questions concerning whether **Anxiety** (a state of distress, unease, dread, fear, uncertainty, helplessness, etc) is a result of **Normal/Abnormal** mental process, **Mental Illness, Neurosis** or **Pathology** have been major sources of disagreement within professional, legal and general populations for decades. Over the years, many ambiguous, conflicting definitions of **"Anxiety"** have evolved. Freud classified Anxiety as **Unconscious Neurotic Conflict** while Rollo May referred to it as an often **Normal** formless state of unease due to realistic causes. However, definitions **of Anxiety appear to** share **the commonality of Troubled** states of mind lacking **unambiguous** causes. According to Donald W Goodwin, MD in his book "Anxiety" all theories share the common element of "**anxiety concerning the presence of a problem that needs to be solved but cannot because the person who has it is unaware of its nature**".

Definitions **of "Neurosis"** have also changed over the years. Most vaguely identifies it as a disorder of nerves. Others classify it more precisely as 1) various functional disorders of mind/emotion (anxiety, phobia etc.), without organic **lesion or change 2)** abnormal **symptoms of behavior or 3)** areas of Dysfunction in an otherwise **intact Reality Base** of Personality. Neither do definitions of **"Pathology"** (any condition that deviates from the normal), **Normal** (average, conforming, typical, the standard or socially acceptable behavior) or **"Abnormal"** (departing from the normal) shed much light on Resolution of Anxiety. With the exception of those suffering from Mental Illness, Psychosis or other disorders falling into the category of being out of touch with reality, Neurosis appears to be another name for the Psychological Immaturity.

Psychological Maturation does not rule out the severe emotional pain and anxiety accompanying the objective reality of **physical danger or Life threatening situations. Nether does attainment of higher levels of ego development rule out the necessity of learning to deal with the challenges of tragedy.** Successful **Coping Strategies**

within dissonant Life situations require increased levels of Ego and Emotional Differentiation (Unique Independence) and as well as Cognitive Maturation in the areas of Objectivity, Frustration Tolerance and ability to Delay of Gratification. However, **Coping Strategies for <u>Life Situations of Tragic Proportions</u>** may be more successfully coped with from the Psychological Maturation Dimension of Spiritual Philosophy of Life. Increasing ability to face reality and accept the truth (Resilience) allows Human Psychological Maturation to develop.

Identification of successful methods for resolution of emotional pain and anxiety is of paramount importance in the psychological profession. Whether Scientific Research will eventually find causes of emotional pain and anxiety to objectively reside in verifiable categories such as neurosis, unconscious conflicts or other areas of dysfunction or pain is at this time unclear. However, successful treatment of Anxiety, whether ultimately found to be normal, abnormal, neurotic or dysfunctional will lead to resolution of emotional pain whether it be found in understanding and working toward psychological maturation, acceptance of reality, human happiness, clarification of philosophical questions or existential enlightenment.

I define **Psychological Maturation** as a Human Developmental Stage (emotional and cognitive) resulting from the ability to face objective reality and accept the truth. **I perceive Human life to be a multifaceted arena of opportunities within human relationships and life situations for development of both human and spiritual potential. I view** Anxiety as a Signal from the Unconscious Mind that an underlying ambiguous conflict is present and needs to be taken care of for Psychological Maturation (Adult Development) to continue successfully. Psychological maturation results from an Observing Ego sufficiently developed to face Reality and accept truth. Ego Boundaries must be strong enough to resolve excessive emotional dependency on others and develop unique personal identity & potential.

Development of Functional Coping Strategies

Maturation: The Adult Paradigm

The Value of Realistic Coping Skills and Techniques for Development

I define **Psychological Maturation** as a Human emotional and cognitive Developmental Stage resulting from the ability to face objective reality and accept the truth. **I perceive Human life to be a multifaceted arena of opportunities within human relationships and life situations for development of both human and spiritual potential.**

I perceive the **Dimensions of Psychological Maturation** to include **4 essential building blocks (Tasks of Ego Development: 1) cognitive independence, 2) emotional differentiation, 3) comfort with personal differences and 4) having arrived at a personally arrived at Philosophy Of Life based on as much objective reality as available during our life time.**

I believe the **Process** of **Cognitive Development**[20] **leading to personal growth and mature relationships can occur by adhering to the Universal Processes of cause and effect underlying reality. 5 Life Lessons teach pragmatic Coping Skills in the areas of 1) internal/external control, 2) responsibility for self and others 3) distortions of reality, 4) cognitive vs emotional decision making and 5) moderation and balance within life and relationships.**

Opportunities for Developing Functional Coping Stragies

Potential Opportunities for development of personal buoyancy, power of endurance, etc (a characteristic of Psychological Maturity) are presented to us each day as we walk down our path of life in the form

---

[20]   Secondary Process—Freud

of situations in which we can choose to face reality and accept the truth . . . or not.

Unwillingness (or less often inability[21]) to accept the truth of **objective reality** lies at the core of much of the stress and anxiety surrounding human situational problems and relationships conflicts. **Objective Reality** can be defined as the Facts concerning a situation. **Subjective Reality** can be defined as distorted emotional responses or those containing slanted or biased perceptions and or expectations for Self/ Others/or Situations.

The value of **Functional (pragmatic) Coping Strategies** within our **personal** and **relationship** situations may be more objectively perceived in the context of considering cause and effect within the Reality of a specific situation. For example: "How may my behavior have affected the behavior of the other?" or "What may I have been thinking or feeling that keeps me from learning to deal with the reality of my present situation?" It is important that we don't misunderstand What We Can Change and What We Can't and/or What Is Fair and What Isn't. Drop your Expectations, Shoulds, Ought's, Perceptions of fairness, etc. because they do not reflect reality and reside in the minds of those who hold them.

COPING WITH DISSONANT LIFE SITUATIONS

Dissonant Life situations may include issues concerning marital conflicts, the possibility of divorce, conflicts in parenting styles, parenting difficult teenagers, problems with extended family members, etc. Such situations may be addressed using techniques of problem solving including, negotiation when possible and identification of non-negotiable values when necessary.

Increasing ability to face reality and accept the truth (Resilience) allows Human Psychological Maturation to develop. Resilience (Psychological buoyancy) is a characteristic of Psychological

---

[21]   Psychosis or other symptoms of serious Mental Illness

Maturation. Few of us are spared the necessity of dealing with dissonant life situations.

Successful **Coping Strategies** **within dissonant Life situations** require increased levels of Ego (Unique Independence and Emotional Differentiation) Development as well as Cognitive Maturation in the areas of Frustration Tolerance. ability to Delay of Gratification and objective Cognitive contemplation of emotion (Primary Process Choices) concerning the situation under consideration.

Psychological Defenses (**Coping Strategies**) range from extremely dysfunctional to highly functional. And although much has been written concerning making choices for successfully **coping** with every day types of problematic situations, few equate this advice with opportunity for development of potential strength to deal with devastating types of life tragedy.

MARRIAGE & FAMILY CONFLICTS

 Ordinary types of Dissonance include Family and Marital Conflict as well as Parenting Issues concerning younger children and teens. Such dissonance can often be solved using Problem Solving Methods in which 2 winners[22] get what they need and at least part of what they want. It is important to also remember to drop the "shoulds, oughts, generalizations, etc[23]"

In all types of dissonant relationships it is important to learn techniques for **"Walking in the Shoes of Others"**. This does not mean that we must agree with the other point of view, only that we have been able to see it through the eyes of others and have developed methods for empathizing with the other. Within marriage, parenting styles for younger children often becomes an area fraught with dissonance. It is sad but true that most of us do not clarify our own ideology of Parenting Style before marriage. Only when children arrive do such

---

[22] Gordon, Thomas—Win-Win Model and Steven Covey—7 habits of Effective People

[23] Albert Ellis & William Glasser—

difficulties become paramount. It is important to calmly and factually attempt to problem solve these areas of important differences. Many differences can be solved using techniques of clear open communication, dropping the idea that everyone thinks the same way we do, etc. However, again here, non-negotiable values must be clearly thought through, identified and clearly discussed

Most of us can remember how it felt to be a Teenager. And although those feelings are no longer the impetus for our adult behavior it is often quite easy for many of us to close our eyes and be instantly transported on our magic carpet of time travel to time past.

With our own teenage child(ren) we will likely get more cooperation if we try to solve our conflict using the empathic techniques of problem Solving. With very difficult, rude or "know it all" teens it may become necessary to discuss the old adage of "The person who pays the bills" holds the defining power. Most teens are able to understand and respect this fact. For those who can't or won't other harsher treatment may be required.

A **Teen's age** is of utmost importance in making decisions concerning rules. The older and psychologically mature the Teen, the more allowance should be given to their own thoughts and requests. It is also important however, to realize that the 18th birthday does not automatically supply wisdom. I am surprised to realize that many adults give their 18 year old complete control of their lives if when the offspring still resides in the family home and pays little or nothing toward expenses. I personally believe that the persons who owns the house, puts food on the table and pays the bills has the right to insist that all residents follow important rules of the house. When an 18 year old (or older) moves out, has a job pays their own bills, etc. they can then set their own house rules.

AGING—RETIREMENT

Many clients new to the concepts of therapeutic intervention, arrive in their 50's, 60's and 70's, with serious marital problems connected with conflicts presented by retirement. Finding our Place in relationships (siblings, parent/child, friendships, work environments, superior/

subordinate, etc) has always presented many areas of conflict. It is also one of the most contentious areas of conflict in marriage. In changing environments such as retirement, what was previously perceived as a compatible marriage is now the scene of conflicts over territory.

A spouse previously at work for the day or week is now home <u>all</u> day, <u>every</u> day. The Spouse, previously in charge of home duties now faces disagreements about how things that previously went off without a hitch are now seen as dysfunctional.

 A newly retired spouse (the Boss in the previous Work Environment) may pose questions and demands such as "Why do you insist on cooking dinner without the fan turned on?", "Why do you leave the kitchen without putting the dirty dishes in th e dish washer?", "Why don't you run the sprinklers at evening instead of the middle of the day when water evaporates more quickly?" or "I don't like your tone of voice when discussing homework with our grandchild".

Conversely, the spouse confronted with such a retired mate may retort "What do you know about it?", ", I've done it for years without any advice from you." Or "What's wrong with my tone of voice?, I don't like yours much either".

SEVERE ILLNESS

Living with tragedy can be extremely challenging. However, it may be met more productively by facing the Objective Facts of the situation, not turning our backs on the life that is left and considering the possibility that if I am still alive there must be a reason for it. An example of personal tragedy seen as too difficult to deal with can be seen within treatment of a client who became very angry because I could not tell her exactly what steps she must take to deal with her potential fatal illness.

Dancing with the Specter of Death

 A 47 year old, divorced client had returned to therapy after a previous course of treatment concerning vocational choices. This time she had recently been diagnosed with a potentially Fatal physical Diagnosis. However, both her MD's and hospital treatment teams were unable to say for sure whether her illness was fatal or might result in remission.

Some days, the client felt fine, other days terrible. Sometimes she could not get out of bed to take care of her household chores. At that time, she would call her adult daughter to come and care for her. The pain she felt was debilitating, her head ached with migraine, she couldn't eat, sleep or care for herself. On the days she felt better; she got up, dressed, shopped or came for an appointment.

However, the ambiguity surrounding her symptoms, uncertainty concerning potential present, eventual or end of life plans, feelings of horrible pain, terrible anger and resentment concerning the unfairness of life were challenges she felt unable to deal with. She cried and pleaded for a clear, unshakable course of thought concerning successful patterns of thought and methods for dealing with a potentially fatal disorder. She firmly insisted that others could not possibly understand her situation because others had never been through the specific tragedy of her situation. Crying inconsolably she sobbed "I can never accept the reality and objectively truth of my situation because I don't know how". Crying inconsolably she pleaded "Teach me how to face reality and accept the truth of my possible Death".

Coping with Tragedy

Treatment of Clients dealing with incomprehensible Tragedy is an extremely challenging situation. Most are so overcome with Depression as well as the uniqueness of their situation that setting specific flawless treatment goals is extremely difficult if not impossible. However, clients suffering tragedy must realize that comparison of a personal tragedy to that of another is impossible because each is unique. For example how can the trauma concerning the loss of both legs be compared with a loss of all possession in a tornado, to the necessity of begging for food on the street to keep from starving, to watching your loved one die, to the murder of your child, to the deaths of 3 of your 4 children, etc.

Similarly, it's impossible to tell another "HOW" to Face Reality and Accept the Truth within a Personal tragedy because each situation of tragedy contains incomparable specific details as well differences between the personal characterizes of those forced to live through a tragedy.

In spite of such obstacles, Objective **Reality is a FACT.** Bitterness and resentment concerning reality is a waste of time. Face reality and accept the truth of your situation because there is no other choice. However, it is important to realize that resignation to tragedy is not the answer. Resignation is tantamount to saying "Life is too hard to deal with" because my personal life (or what's left of it) is not worth the effort of trying to understand my situation and successfully coping with it.

A list of incomparable tragedies might include but not be limited to the following:

- Being told your illness is terminal
- Being told your illness may be terminal but there is no way to know for sure
- Trying to live with unbearable physical pain
- Be in physical agony of pain one day but not quite as severe the next.
- Being so tired and in such pain many days of your life that getting dressed and attending to essential tasks seems insurmountable.
- Getting your legs blown off in war and having to live in a wheel chair for life
- Trying to live with the devastation of being the victim of rape
- Attempting to face and live life after have all or most of your children die
- Losing your spouse of a life time
- The loss of your home and possessions in an earth quake or tidal wave
- Being blinded for life in an accident
- Loss of freedom—being in jail

Clients who are devastated by such a loss may make comment similar to the following: Why me? What have I done to deserve this?

Why my child instead of me, they had their whole life ahead of them. I'm old. I would gladly change places with them. I don't want to live without them. I can't figure out how to live with it and accept the truth. I need someone to tell me "how".

HISTORY OF **TYPES** OF DEFENSES USED

To solve the question of "How" to face reality and accept the truth of a situation that seems impossible to deal with, we have to understand what we may have been doing or thinking that stands in our way of successfully coping with tragedy. It is important to understand what types of Defenses we have learned to use in the past and why or why not they have worked well or not at all.

In the DSM-IV Psychological Defense mechanisms are explained as an unconscious reaction pattern employed by the Ego to protect itself from the anxiety that arises from conflict. Such Mechanisms range from mature to immature; depending on how much they distort reality. Denial is a very immature because it negates reality.

In the case of tragic loss the conflict may reveal itself in ability (willingness) vs inability (unwillingness) to face the facts of the loss. For example the conflict may be seen in admitting that "Yes it did happen but it's not fair", "Yes, it did happen, but it shouldn't have",. "Yes it did happen, but what did I do to deserve it?". Such cognitions continue to protect the self from finally accepting the Objective Fact of the Loss and learning personal methods of dealing with the truth of the tragedy.

Most of us eventually learn to deal with loss . . . some sooner than others. Some get over tragedy more easily because the Loss did not affect them at a really deep level. Some never really deal with the complete facts of a tragedy which can be seen rising to consciousness under the influence of alcohol or in distressing dreams. Others, however, having learned methods for cognitively facing reality and accepting the truth are able to face and deal with the objective facts of emotional pain rather than denying it. My own conclusions concerning Denial of Reality in the Category of severe tragedy is that emotional responses to the pain of loss must be overcome in a realistic way to foster the continued development of Psychological Maturation.

Life Situations of Tragic Proportions

Realize no one can tell another "how" to Face Reality and Accept The "Truth" of their own particular tragic situation because learning to cope with reality is an individual psychological developmental process which in the case of Life Situations of Tragic Proportions may be more successfully coped with from the Psychological Maturation Dimension of a personally arrived at Spiritual Philosophy of Life.

The following Suggestions for learning to Coping with Tragedy have been used in Therapeutic Treatment with clients as well as in personal situations of my own. Some of them may be more successful than others. Others may be of little interest or help to those suffering pain. However, many of them have lead to emotional relief from the pain of tragedy.

- Possible Techniques for **living without loved ones** lost to tragedy may include 1) taking the hand of the departed and walking thru life with the memories of the loved one that are now part of my personal essence, 2) knowledge of personal growth and invaluable lessons learned from the relationship and 3) giving thanks to the Universe for the Gift of having walked in life with the other for the time we had together.
- Techniques for **living without aspects of my former self** (eyesight, hearing, limbs, home, etc) may include realizing that what is past will never be lost b/c it is part of who I am today. Realize that you may not know why you are still alive but the fact that you are presents the possibility there may be a reason for it.
- Coping with Tragedy presents the opportunity for considering plans for new ways of life.
- Use primary process (cognition) to accept and walk through the Pain (emotional or physical). Make a list of things that must be done and force yourself to walk through the pain in order to get things accomplished. Visualize cognition rising above the pain and looking at it from a great distance. I will then deal with it for as long as I can. When I can no longer deal with it, I will stop trying for the day and try again tomorrow.

In this way, I will help myself live with it for longer and longer periods of time.

- Learn to value the life you have been given even though at this time, the emotional or physical pain is so great it is hard to do.
- Realize that if you are still alive your work on earth is not over. You may still have lessons to learn or your earthy Mission of helping others is not finished yet
- I personally do not see such situations as God's punishment but rather opportunities to explore our spiritual Path in the Universe and try to understand our Human Mission and Lessons of Life.

Choices to be considered for dealing with tragedy

- Reasons why suicide is not a realistic option include need to be there for others, being a good role model for other children and family members, not wanting to give up, trying to be emotionally healthy enough to deal with adversity, not being comfortable with wasting the life we have been given.
- Either resign yourself to being overcome by tragic circumstances or fight for the life that may be the only one you will ever have.
- Go down swinging
- Define your perception of differences between physical vs emotional pain.
- Decide for self which aspects of emotional vs physical pain would be more difficult to deal with and reasons why you believe what you do.

RESILIENCE

The concept of **Resilience is seen by well respected professionals as a long overdue area of need for attention In an APA Article Road to Resilience—Resilience—PTSD—Trauma** Developing resilience is discussed as a personal journey in which people do not all react the same to traumatic and stressful life events. **Resilience is discussed as a p**rocess of adapting well in the face of adversity and "bouncing back" from difficult experiences. Research shows resilience to be ordinary rather than extraordinary. The article goes on to say "This doesn't mean that a person will not experience difficulty or distress". Emotional pain and sadness are common in people who have suffered major adversity or trauma in their lives. **Resilience** is not a trait that people either have or do not have. It involves behaviors, thoughts, and actions that can be learned and developed.

I personally believe that Resilience is an indispensible coping mechanism, necessary for life.—Psych Maturation—Face Reality—Accept truth. My Own Point of View concerning the new focus on Resilience can be stated in three words . . . "It's about time". I have been gathering material, writing this book for over 10 years and teaching my clients the concepts of Resilience for over 20 years. The only difference is that I have been referring to the concept now called Resilience as a Coping Mechanism[24] and an **essential aspect of "Psychological Maturation".**

Living a life of Moderation and Balance precludes a life of obsession, addiction or too much to do and too little time to do it. Life with Crisis control built in, is a life dedicated to work, love, family, pleasure, fun and struggle. It is one of the most difficult of the 5 lessons to acutely learn well. As I mentioned in the Forward and Preface of my Book **Maturation: The Adult Paradigm** "What gives me the strength to face Objective reality and Accept the Truth is the fact that I do not have a choice. Objective Reality is just that: The Truth. I can pretend it's not true, whine about it (making myself and everyone else around me miserable) or learn to walk through the pain of emotion, come out the other side and learn to cope with the reality of truth.

---

[24]   See Appendix 2

PART IV

Chapter 14

Mission & Purpose of Life on Earth

CHAPTER 14

Mission & Purpose of Life on Earth

Finding The "Real" Me—The Path to Human and Spiritual Development

The Human Search for Meaning can be discovered in the many personal choices leading to Human Maturation and Spiritual growth. The **EARTH SCHOOL** has the potential for teaching the Human Lessons necessary for Development of both Human and Spiritual Maturation.

The Human mind has the ability to process information regarding issues concerning Philosophies of life and death. Psychological Maturation (The usually disregarded "Missing Link") to Human Happiness opens the door to both human and spiritual growth. People and Situations (Family, friends, loved ones, spouses, children, environmental and world events) provide opportunities for both human maturation and spiritual growth. Education provides techniques for understanding the self, relationships, world issues, religion and philosophy. The Music of the Universe (Cause & Effect) provides techniques for understanding the Human Self in the world and the Spiritual Self in the Universe. Psychological Maturation can develop as a result of letting go of the

Negative energy (like a field of quicksand) and floating free into the Positive Energy of Cause and Effect.

The **Soul** comes to earth at its Present level of Development for discovery of its Mission in Life on Earth. The soul's plan for Spiritual Growth and Spiritual Evolution of the self can be discovered in the Positive energy Underlying Connections between Human Growth & Spirit. Underlying connections include **Serendipity, synchronicity** (Karma, fate or Accident?), **Altered States of Consciousness** (Alpha, Beta & Out of Body experiences), **Meditation** (Clearing mind for information), **Dreaming** (Tools for understanding the self) and The **spiritual Realm** (Possible Scientific explanation contained in Quantum Mechanics, that something does go faster then the speed of Light}

Human Purpose—**The Purpose of Human Life is to live up to personal potential by growing psychologically and Spiritually. Our Human purpose is presented to each of us daily by Teachers of the 5 Lessons of Life and other instances of Universal connections such as serendipity, synchronicity, etc. I can live up to my purpose in life by facing reality and accepting the truth.**

Human Potential—Individual Human Potential is unique to each of us. Development of Human Maturation leads to growth of self as well as becoming role models for others, allowing others to develop person potential and/or making other contributions to society. Human Adult Maturation leads to Developing Spiritual Growth by recognizing aspects of our human mission in relationships with others as well as situations containing serendipity, synchronicity, fate, coincidences, etc.

Although **Karma** is the belief held by some that a person's behavior in this and previous lives cause certain effects in the current life and/or in future life (both positive and negative), in Buddhist philosophy, especially Zen, the word karma simply means the law of cause and effect. American mystic Edgar Cayce promoted the theory of both reincarnation and karma, but where they acted as instruments of a loving God as well as natural laws—the purpose was to teach us certain spiritual lessons.

<u>Human Personality.</u>—Personality can be understood as the "exhibition" of characteristics **"MASKS" OF ANXIETY"**, developed to "shield" the self from anxiety about conflict within ourselves or with others. At the heart of Psychological Immaturity lies excessive dependency, fear of rejection and feelings of inadequacy.

Human beings are born with a seed of "Uniqueness". No one in the history of the world has ever been born exactly like we are. The human mission is to explore and develop the human "potential" that makes us unique. the ability to develop unique personal identity is the result of feeling competent, strong, loved, worthwhile and able to perceive <u>objective</u> (vs subjective) Reality.

Personality Characteristics developed to shield the self from pain are composed of both physical and psychological characteristics. The physical signs of anxiety often consist of increased heart rate, trembling, sweating, breathing difficulties, etc. Those who experience anxiety attacks know many of these symptoms intimately, often mistaking them for heart attack, breathing obstruction, or some other serious physical illness.

At the core of <u>Adult</u> Immaturity, is an emotionally disabling inability to feel and behave as a unique, independent and/or emotionally separate person. Anxiety is a signal of unresolved subconscious issues in need of solution for the process of Psychological Development to successfully continue Psychological Maturity Can be defined in terms of <u>Secondary Process1</u>, as well as Frustration Tolerance, Ability to Delay Gratification, Face Objective Reality and accept the truth. Most People go to Therapy in Mid Life because their life isn't working and they're willing "try most anything" to feel better. **Psychological Maturation** is a usually disregarded but essential **"<u>Missing Link</u>"** to Human Happiness. Psychological Maturation and Educational Methods for its achievement can be learned to help arrive at more successful life choices.

---

[1]   Freud defined Secondary Process as the Reality Principle vs the Pleasure Principle

Psychological anxiety may be associated with painful awareness of being powerless in a personal matter, a feeling of impending and inevitable danger, or an exhausting alertness as if facing an emergency. Anxious persons may feel such great self absorption that it interferes with effective solutions to real problems, or as an irresolvable doubt about the nature of the threat. Anxiety must be separated from realistic fear. Freud believed Anxiety arose automatically whenever the psyche is overwhelmed by something too threatening to be mastered or faced.

Two innate, conflicting, but equally strong "forces" lead toward Relationships and Unique Independence. Psychological Maturation demands these opposing "forces" be balanced—one assuming no more importance than the other. At the heart of Psychological Immaturity lies excessive dependency, fear of rejection and feelings of personal inadequacy. Fearing emotional independence, Behavioral attempts (**Masks of Anxiety**) to manipulate and control others are made as a way to 1) resolve relationship conflicts, 2) avoid human differences and 3) deny the necessity for emotional separateness. **Masks commonly donned** include attempts to force others to agree with you, Conforming to others points of view to keep peace and avoid abandonment, withdrawing from the self to avoid facing the fact that relationships are more important then integrity and independence, withdrawing from others to pressure others into agreement and feeling a need to prove your "rights" to others.

Psychological Maturation—Respect for human competence allows innate human potential to develop. Psychological Maturation results from an observing ego sufficiently developed to face reality, accept the truth and ego boundaries strong enough to resolve symbiotic attachment. Ego Boundaries must be strong enough to resolve excessive emotional dependency on others and develop unique personal identity & potential.

- **TASK 1—UNIQUE INDEPENDENCE** (Thinking for Ourselves) The ability to "Think for ourselves" develops as the result of having developed Positive Self Esteem and feelings of Self Worth. **Cognitive Independence** requires the ability to think about (our self and our situations and identify Objective (vs Subjective) Reality. It develops from an internalized self perception of competence, strength, being loved and able to solve our own problems. Reality into consideration.

- **TASK 2**—EMOTIONAL SEPARATION. "Don't Leave me . . . I'm afraid to be alone" At the heart of Psychological immaturity lies excessive dependency[2], fear of rejection and feelings of personal inadequacy. Fearing Emotional independence, "M asks" of Anxiety are donned in defensive attempts to resolve relationship conflicts and avoid the twin realties of human differences and healthy emotional separation.

- **TASK**—3 INTERDEPENDENCE the Ability to be a separate self in a relationship. Two whole selves reside in successful interdependent relationships. Each self has developed comfort with personal differences while Maintaining loving emotional detachment and deep commitment to the relationship by resolving conflict in ways that compromise neither personal or family integrity nor respect for themselves or each other.

- **TASK**—4—PHILOSOPHY of Life Independent Personal Philosophy of Human "Fit" in the Universe What beliefs make up your personal philosophy ("Fit in the Universe") of life? Such an understanding needs a broad view of the Universe that takes as much of objective reality into consideration as possible given the present level of development within our society and civilization.

I believe that Cause & Effect is a Natural Law and that All Causes results in some kind of Effects. In relationships the results (Effects) vary according to the Personality of the recipient. Our responsibility is to treat ourselves and others positively. If our relationships are based on the 5 Lessons of Life we cannot continue in relationships that remain negative for either ourselves or others.

The ladder of **Psychological Maturation**—requires recognition of Cause and Effect in relationships.—Personal Responsibility requires development of Maturation in relationships. As we climb the ladder of Maturation we engage in fewer neurotic relationships and very

---

[2]   Symbiotic Attachment

close (spousal, etc.) relationships require the identification of **Non Negotiable** values for myself and others. Living up to Personal Potential requires ability to improve cognitive and ego functioning, identify strengths and weakness and strive to improve what we can while accepting what we can't.

Lessons of Life

- **<u>LESSON 1—CONTROL.</u>** We can only control ourselves. Attempts to do otherwise only leads to anxiety and conflict. Do you believe you are right and others wrong, try to convince others of your rights, use manipulation to control others, use force to control your relationships or use defiance to keep from being controlled by others?
- **<u>LESSON 2A—PERSONAL RESPONSIBILITY.</u>** We are personally responsible for our happiness, choices, life, goals and mistakes. Ignorance of the difference between selfishness and appropriate love and respect for the self often lies at the core of inability or unwillingness to assume personal responsibility. Do you **feel too weak** to take responsibility, feel your **role precludes it**, **don't know how**, **can't** take responsibility or **won't** ?
- **<u>LESSON 2B—RESPONSIBILITY FOR OTHERS.</u>** We are not responsible for other people's life lessons. To try leads to becoming a crutch and others cripples. **Parents are responsible to teaching a child to care for themselves.** The proper balance between helping someone fix their own problem and "fixing" it for them is often a blurry line and fraught with uncertainty and devastating choices. Do you think in **"shoulds", oughts**, need to **"fix" others problems**? Do you think family **is your responsibility** or that **others never do anything right?**
- **<u>LESSON 3—FACE REALITY.</u>** Reality is Objective. What Color are your "Glasses?" Do you distort reality with <u>unrealistic</u> **expectations, perceptions** or **emotional responses** that may have been realistic in the past but are not in the present?

- **LESSON 4—COGNITIVE DECISIONS VS EMOTIONAL "FIXES"**. <u>Mature people</u> can **choose whether to respond to their feelings or not**. We can learn to make long term cognitive decisions based on what is best for ourselves and others in the long run rather than making decisions based on short term emotional "fixes". Are you responding to emotions or realistic thoughts when you make your decisions? Can you think about your feelings and disregard them when necessary?

- **LESSON 5—ABILITY TO LIVE A BALANCED, MODERATE AND ORGANIZED LIFESTYLE.** A life of Moderation precludes a life of Crisis. Life with built in Crisis control is dedicated to love, work, family, pleasure, fun and struggle. It is one of the most difficult lessons to learn. Is your judgment poor, are you able to make successful plans, are you addicted to alcohol, drugs, gambling, eating, etc.

CHAPTER 15

Essence of the Human Spirit

Essence of the Human Spirit

The Mission (Soul's Plan) of the Evolving Dancer, unique to each of us, is growth and development of individual Potential. The Evolving Dancer Comes to Earth at its current state of development to emerge in a continually unfolding process of Human and Spiritual Growth when the necessary conditions for potential growth are recognized. **Human Life can** be understood as a multifaceted arena of **Instructional Opportunities** within **Human Relationships, Life Situations**, and Universal **Connections** (serendipity, dreams, synchronicity, intuition, meditation,) for development of both human and spiritual potential.

The Human Personality can be defined as **Masks Of Anxiety unconsciously** donned in attempts to avoid the Twin Realities of human differences and necessity for healthy emotional separation. **Psychological Maturation, a** Human **Developmental Stage** resulting from the ability to **Face** (objective) **Reality and Accept the Truth** is the Disregarded but Essential "Missing Link" for Functional Resolution of Anxiety. At the core of psychological immaturity lies a disabling inability to feel and behave as a unique, independent, emotionally separate person.

The Music of the Universe (Universal Laws of Cause & Effect) teaches techniques for Development of Psychological Maturation. The Human Ego (Sense of self) and Mind (the thinking part of our Personality) have the ability to grow and deal with emotions and external demands. Human Relationships are the training ground for development of both human and spiritual potential. The Soul's Program teaches lessons of life necessary for development of both physical and spiritual Potential.

Psychological Maturation, the dignity and unique potential of the human spirit, is a bridge leading to the Door of the Spiritual Realm behind which allows understanding of our Human Mission. The **Path to Eternity (Spiritual Maturation)** runs thru the **Fabric of the Universe** (Map of Human Reality) and is paved with Realistic **Laws of C & E. We are born at the beginning of our potential path into Eternity. By our attitudes and behaviors we choose to explore it . . . or . . . not.**

EVOLUTION OF THE HUMAN SPIRIT

The subject of a spiritual meaning of existence is a broad, complex and disturbing one. Many people overwhelmed by the concept blindly accept traditional answers. Some reject the possibility of the soul's existence as unlikely due to the inability of science to prove it. Others just give up thinking about it until at the death of a loved one are forced once again to search for answers.

The death of 3 of my 4 son's has lead to important additions to my books originally planned contents. After my 24 year old son was murdered, I realized a main topic of my book, spiritual evolution, holds a depth of meaning and comprehensives that previously I had not completely recognized. As a result I found it necessary to not only define and discuss spiritual development but to explore as thoroughly and accurately as possible the "role" played by death in the Fabric of the Universe. For over a year I frantically searched for Answers to the question "Where did he go?" "How could he be alive one minute and dead the next?

I searched and found many answers to my frantic questions concerning spirituality and the possibility of Life after death in the research of Quantum Physics[3]. Recent Data of QT has located a "hologragrahic window" capable of investigating the previously invisible realm of frequency. This discovery has lead some writers to speculate on possible scientific explorations of long suspected but statistically non verifiable hypotheses concerning the existence and survival of human essence. As a result Maturation: The Adult Paradigm is now able to weaves strands of psychological theory, spiritual speculation and scientific observation into a richly tapestried blueprint and possible scientific explanation of both Human and Spiritual "fit" in the Universe.

---

[3] Quantum physics is a branch of science that deals with discrete, indivisible units of energy called quanta as described by the Quantum Theory.

CONNECTIONS BETWEEN PHYSICAL & SPIRITUAL REALMS

Of particular importance to development of a clear understanding of opportunities for possible communication between the Physical and Spiritual Realms is the Research concerning **Synchronicity** as the unifying principal behind meaningful coincidence. After many discussions with Albert Einstein and Wolfgang Pauli, Carl Jung, a Swiss psychiatrist came to believe there were parallels between synchronicity (coincidences of time) and aspects of quantum theory **(nature and behavior of matter and energy on the atomic and subatomic level).** Jung was transfixed by the idea that life was not a series of random events but rather an expression of a deeper order, which he and Pauli referred to as *Unus mundus[4]*. Jung also believed that synchronicity served a similar role in a person's life as dreams. As a result of some very powerful synchronistic experiences a new stage in a person's psychological or spiritual development is attained. These revelatory synchronistic experiences are usually associated with major events such as birth, death or crises.

SOULMATE RESEARCH

In 1995 **as** a result of my own experiences after the death of my children, I designed a Research Project for gathering Data on Psychic Experiences which I called the **SOULMATE RESEARCH** project. Types of Spiritual Experiences for research included Premonitions, Dreams, feels presence of deceased, Auditory Experiences, (knocking, phone rings, deceased voice), Lucid dreams. Apparitions, General Theme of Messages (I'm Ok, not Ok, stay in touch, get info to survivor), Unfortunately due to heavy Professional and Personal demands during the ensuing years, I identified 10 Hypotheses for testing that I believed to be significant to the philosophy of underlying spiritual connections. I was never able to complete my plan for the Project which is presented below.

---

[4] Underlying unified reality from which everything emerges and returns to (Wikipedia, the free encyclopedia)

1: Many normal people have psychic experiences
2: The closer the emotional bond the more often psychic experiences
3: Sudden death results in more psychic experiences
4: Mothers have more psychic experiences than : fathers
5: Close siblings have more psychic experiences than less emotionally close sibs
6: There is no difference in rate of psychic occurrences between male and female
7: People are prone to experience one or more type of psychic experience
8: Some People have premonitions of their own deaths
9: Some survivors have premonitions of deceased deaths.
10: Psychic Experiences are more common within 0-1 year after death.

However, today, after working in the field of Psychotherapy for over 20 years I have had the opportunity to learn that a large majority of human beings have experienced psychic phenomena at one time or another in their lives. These experiences appear to happen more frequently after sudden death of loved ones. It has not been my experience that they are more frequent to either males or females but appear to be more common within the first year after a death of a loved one. Dealing with the Reality of Death is a daunting task for most all human beings.

Personal: End of Life Experiences

As a Teen-ager I was faced with the death of my beloved Grandmother who had raised me from birth. I offer the following Vignettes as an example of the Roles of Teacher played by my Soul Mate and Grandmother (Filling my Cup to face life), Grandfather and Death as we walked together as a Family through the Fabric of the Universe.

Saying Goodbye

On the evening of his wife's death my Grandfather entered the Bedroom he shared with his wife of 40 years to find her standing in front of the closet waiting for him. Twilight enfolded him as he entered the room.

Incredulously he stopped, to stare at his wife. He had seen her standing there hundreds of times in their 40 years together, as he lay in bed, readying himself for sleep. It was always the same. She would stand at the closet, remove her clothes, and put on her night gown. "Come to bed, Grace" he said "You know I can't sleep without you here". "Yes, I'm coming, Ted", was her reply. "I'm just going to read a little while before I turn out the light" she would always say softly. Her voice and presence always soothed him. He loved the way she spoke.

Today when the Hospital called to say "You're wife has been brought in . . . Yes, a stroke", he had rushed to her side. She lay in a coma. Even though they tried to be calm, reassuring, their message was that she probably wouldn't live. Late that night, the Dr. urged him to go home for sleep. "Come back in the morning" he said. "There's really nothing you can do here, now". Weary, heart sick he had finally left to get some rest.

But now as he entered the room they had spent so many nights in, to try to sleep, he saw her standing at the closet . . . where she always stood when she told him goodnight. For a moment she stood watching him As he stepped toward her in surprise, she slowly faded away. And he knew, without a doubt that this time she had not stood saying good night. This time she had come to say Goodbye. **Example of Telepathy or Clairvoyance.**

Returning home from the funeral of my Grandmother . . . I entering the room to stand before the bathroom window trying to hide from pain too agonizing to endure.

Rain Drops

Crying softly I watched drops of rain roll quietly down blades of grass and disappear into the earth. Waves of misery and despair washed over me, cut off my breath and filled my body with agony. Trapped between the anguish of reality and the torment of denial I was finally forced to accept the fact that escape from truth was no longer possible . . . My darling grandma . . . my "real" mother . . . was dead.

I remembered her—lying dead in her casket . . . an awful pallor of death covering and distorting her features. Looking like "someone" I didn't know, I reached out to touch her face and felt cold, clammy skin & bones under my fingers. Recoiling in horror and fear of the woman who bore no resemblance to the living person I had known and loved my whole life my mind cried out in aguish "Where have you gone?, "What happened to you, Why don't you look like you always did?".

Turning inward I asked myself "What is this fear in me as I look at you", "Why am I suddenly panicked, afraid the body in the casket might suddenly "open her eyes, get up from death, and come toward me" when all I ever wanted was to keep her from leaving me?". "Was it normal to be afraid of the one person I had loved the most in the world, in the 16 years since my life began?" I asked myself. Quickly switching outward to the God I felt had abandoned me, I screamed in my soul, "Where have you taken her?" "How can I live without her?"

. . . Her lap was safe and warm. a haven. Her stories revealed the life of Cinderella, the Wicked Stepmother, Prince Charming and Billy goat Gruff. Sometimes I laughed. Sometimes I felt sad as the characters in her stories, books and songs became my friends . . .

Her stories and love for the books she read to me, encouraged a door in my mind to open. That door "lead out" into countless places in the world, peopled by fascinating events and situations.

. . . "Look Skipi" she said, "See how pretty the snowflakes are. Do you see the Fairy dancing on the Snow Flakes?" Sitting on Grandma's lap, looking out the window of our house in the Logging Camp, my 4 year old eyes strained to see the beautiful Fairy's dance. "Where was she? Was that her, in the shadows"? And then I saw her, "Yes", I cried "there she is". She was dressed in lavender, with her layered skirt cut in sharply pointed flounces. Her flowing hem cleared the tops of her silver shoes as she danced, first on one snow flake then on another . . .

I was not surprised to see the fairy dressed exactly as my beloved Aunt Jane had been in her Lavender Graduation dress. Even today when I think of that long ago Magic, the graceful Fairy dancing, the softly falling snow, I can hear in memory the voice of my grandmother singing to me, cradling me, loving and protecting me. Enthralled by my Grandmother I snuggled close in her arms.

 Every summer she took me on a trip for 3 weeks. We visited her sister in St Helens and another in Portland. I was allowed to eat Cold Cereal for Breakfast . . . a wonderful treat from the Hot Oatmeal that was served at home. She let me sit on her lap and take sips of her black coffee with my little spoon. She let me sleep beside her, in Grandpa's place, during the week while he was away working at the logging camp. She would carefully wrap a newspaper over the lamp by the bed so the light couldn't shine in my eyes while I slept and she read her books, the Bible, Novels of the Day and Biographies of famous people . . .

 . . . She let me to stay up late. Sitting on her lap while she played Bridge with her family and friends . . . she allowed me to "take the tricks". And when my five year old eyes got heavy with sleep but fearful of the "dark" in the bedroom beyond, she asked the others to wait to finish the game while she lay down with me in the dark so I could find sleep without fear. My family said then and for years afterward, that "Skipi was the most miserably spoiled child that ever lived" . . . But she and I knew better. She was preparing me for life without her, giving me love to last for the rest of my life. She was filling my tiny self with Trust of others, Respect for myself and my needs and giving me the Tools with which to build my self esteem.

In waves of agony the knowledge that she was really DEAD swept over me. I cried and cried, thinking there was no way I could find the courage to walk through life without her . . . the foundation of my life since the day I was born . . . But I did because I had no choice. **Internalization of self Esteem, Compassion, Respect for the Human Spirit, Permission for creativity, Unconditional Love**

As a result of growing up with my Grandmother, I came to perceive the Human Spirit as entering the Human body to touch the lives of loved ones. I believe the living Human body (a receptacle of the Human Spirit) illustrates characteristics of the spirit it contains. After death, the **Spirit evaporates into its essence of Soul (from which it came) and leaves** the Human Body like rain drops on blades of grass as it disappears into an unseen realm. The lifeless Human body retains its elements of physical structure, such as skin and bones but no longer exemplifies the characteristics of the Spirit it once contained. However, although the Spirit has returned to its Essence, the love generated by the **Essence of the Soul** has the power to work miracles and often does in the hearts and minds of loved ones left behind.

I truly believe this to be true because although the life that once resided in the human body of my grandmother has disappeared, her love for me has never left and I know it never will. She is still my strength. She will always be my mother. Her love for me and the teachings she empowered in my heart ignited the flame that became my Self Esteem, respect for the Human Spirit and certainty that we come to earth with a Mission . . . to live up to our Potential . . . by the Lessons we learn from each other.

CLINICAL: End of Life Experiences

A 60 year old client in therapy was finally experiencing Life as a happy adult due to having found the Man of her dream. However, just before their planned marriage, she received word he had died unexpectedly. She was of course devastated. Returning to Therapy when she felt able to discuss her experiences without breaking into tears she reported the following Spiritual Experience

BLUE LIGHT OF LOVE

She stood in the doorway and stared in surprise. Bathed in soft blue rays of light, the night stand and part of the satin covered bed separated from the shadows that held the rest of the darkened room hostage.

She remembered when he had bought the light. At 52 she had been divorced for over 10 years. She perceived the act of love making to be one that belonged within the confines of marriage. And although she had tried hard to wait for the wedding date, she found she could not. He had been 10 years older than she and a man of the world. He laughed lovingly at her sweet naiveness. He said she reminded him more of a young girl than a woman who had lived through a marriage that had produced two sons. He loved her for her morals, principles and perception of love in marriage. In time, their need for each other prevailed over her reluctance.

Always extremely modest, at first she had insisted on the act of love being completed in darkness. Eventually she had given in to his need for not only feeling the physical wonder of their love but for the visualization of it as well. When he bought the tiny blue light she had shyly agreed. For several months the man and the woman made love balthed in the soft blue rays. He called it their Blue Light of Love. She came to love it. When the blue light burned out, she reminded him to replace it. Saying he would do so soon, he nevertheless did not. For months it had been a frequently spoken about task that he did not attend to. The act of love was completed in the warm passion of darkness.

Two weeks before their Wedding Day he died unexpectedly. Heartbroken, she had cried out in pain against the cruel fate that had once again taken away her happiness. Today she had gone to the church & cemetery to tell him goodbye.

Now, as she walked into the room where they had spent so many magical hours, she stopped and stared in surprise. The long ago burned out blue light cast it's soft blue rays into the deepening shadows of dusk. And she knew without a doubt that he was here, loving her, encouraging her to continue with life. She could feel his presence . . . in the shadowy corners . . . in the soft blue of the light rays. For just a split second, she thought she heard his voice whisper, "Goodbye, My Love".

Many years ago, one of my teen age clients, a severely mistreated girl, came to therapy to tell me not only that her verbally abuse stepmother was upset about the death of my Clients Paternal Grandmother. My client had been living with both her father, her grandmother and stepmother. Presented below are the remembrances of my client as she recounted the experiences concerning the death of her Grandmother.

THE grandmother who died in the pool

"I remember lying in bed that afternoon when I was 13 years old". "I had the flu and a temperature of 102 degrees". "My stepmother was in the living room. From the front yard, I heard the sounds of danger. As usual, my Grandmother, old, ill, and mute was in the yard, sitting in her wheel chair. My stepmother always put her out there with a stick through one of her chair's wheels so she couldn't roll down the hill and into the fenced swimming pool area. "Did you hear that?" I called out. "Did you lock the gate into the pool area this morning?" "No" replied my Stepmother angrily "I didn't have time". Calling out in urgency I continued the interchange between my bed and my Stepmother in the next room. "You'd better look at Grandma", I cried out "I'm sure I hear a squeaking sound". "The stick might have come out of her wheel". Frantically, I screamed "It sounds like the chair is going down the hill".

I knew my grandmother could never save herself either from rolling down the hill or going into the pool. Not only was she old and sick, she was helpless and almost paralyzed. If the chair she spent most of her waking hours in began a down hill decent, there was nothing she would be able to do to stop it. She couldn't even call out for help. She hadn't been able to speak for several years. I was furious at the words of my stepmother "I don't care if she does fall in the pool", she called back "Good Riddance".

Jumping from bed I flew into the front yard just as my Grandmother in her Wheelchair toppled into the deep end of the pool. Horrified I rushed to her aid and jumped into the water. Trying to pull her out, I realized that she had, as usual, been tied into her chair. The knots that kept her safe from falling out while on solid ground were holding her steadfastly inside the chair while death waited in the depths of the water.

Horrified at the seriousness of the life and death situation, I frantically continued my attempts to free her. Realizing the knots would not give way to my frenzied clawing, I quickly tried pushing the chair toward the shallow end of the pool. When that failed, I tried to pull the chair containing her limp body and wide staring eyes to the surface of the pool but failed. Over and over I came up for air and back down, trying to remove my grandmother from the water.

When the fire department came, they pulled the still tied, dead body, of my grandmother & her wheelchair out of the water. Quickly they cut the bonds from her body and placed her on the grass. One last attempt to perform the miracle that would save her life was made. Of course it was too late. She just continued to lay dead, on the grass, unresponsive and finally at rest. Hysterically I ran into the house to hide in my room while they took my grandmother away. I knew I had failed to save her life.

After dark, I crept out of my room. I hated my stepmother. I knew she had always hated my grandmother and resented the time required to attend to her needs. She resented caring for me, too, I knew. Her voice from the afternoon, echoed in my memory. ""Who cares if she drowns," I rememberd her calling out to me "Good Riddance". Exhausted from crying, I searched out a corner of the living room and curled up on the floor. Mercifully, sleep overtook me.

Opening my swollen eyes, I looked across the carpet on which I lay into the eyes of my grandmother. For a moment, she too, lay on the carpeted floor ... gazing into my eyes with love and compassion. Before I could respond she faded away. Turning my head toward the kitchen I saw my stepmother ironing. The figure of my grandmother moved toward her daughter-in-law, one arm outstretched. She appeared to be asking for some understanding of the afternoon's events. As I watched, she again faded out of sight. I never saw her again. **Spiritual Experience reported by a Client in Psychotherapy**

THE SOULS PROGRAM FOR EVOLUTION

- **Spiritual Realm—Spiritual Purpose**—Soul enters the Human Realm at its current state of development. —Human experiences provide opportunities for both Human and Spiritual Growth.
- **Underlying Connections b/t Human and Spirit** The spiritual purpose of life is to learn necessary lessons for growth of both human and spiritual essence. Universal connections (serendipity, dreams, synchronicity, intuition, meditation, etc.) provide opportunities for Human and Spiritual development.
- **Human Realm—Path to Human Growth** Human Life is the Training Ground for both Psychological Maturation and Spiritual Evolution— The Map of Reality runs through the Fabric of the Universe and teaches 5 Lessons of Life necessary for Psychological and Spiritual Growth

Growth of both Human and Spiritual Essence are presented to each of us in the form of Personal **choices,** problem solving with other people, serendipity, synchronicity, etc. The ability to face reality and make choices based on the Laws of cause and effect allow the Stage of Adult Maturation to development. I visualize Laws of **cause and effect** as a force of positive energy (love, reality, respect) floating above the quicksand of negative energy (fear, resentment, unrealistic perceptions and expectations) which traps our potential mature development within the confines of dysfunction. To break free from our self imposed bondage, allowing ourselves to bathe in the positive energy of love and respect for ourselves and others, we must face reality and accept the truth concerning ourselves and our environment. Only then are we free as human beings to explore our human and spiritual missions in the universe.

The Fabric of the Universe (physical environment, people, etc) is reflected in the tangible parts of the life (opportunities, choices, people) and **presents opportunities for both Human and Spiritual Growth.** Universal Goals **for Human Development include 1) ability to face reality and accept the truth, 2) increased levels of psychological maturation, 3) development of unique human potential, 4) identification of personal mission in life and 5) ability to respond to Cause and Effect.**

The Music of the Universe (**a "force" of** positive energy **residing in the environment**) is an intangible, invisible process underlying events and relationships that provides opportunities for both psychological & spiritual development. The Music presents opportunities for communication between the spiritual and physical realm through (**serendipity, dreams, synchronicity, intuition**) as well as opportunities for growth within human relationships and/or life situations based on the Cause & Effect underlying reality. Ability to hear and respond positively to the **Music Of The Universe** (Cause & Effect) allows the **Evolving Dancer** to develop higher levels of both physical & spiritual uniqueness of self as a result of ability to resolve personal & interpersonal emotional conflicts. As the ideology of the 5 lessons of realistic cause & effect are internalized, levels of psychological maturity rise.

Psychological Maturation—is a human developmental stage resulting from the ability to face (**objective**) reality and accept the truth of cause & effect. **5 lessons of life (control, responsibility, reality, cognitive decision making, balance and moderation) teach 4 Adult tasks of maturation: Unique Thought, Resolution Of Emotional Enmeshment, Interdependence and development of a** personally arrived **at Objective Philosophy Of Life.**

Psychological Maturation (**being a "real" self**) is the goal of human adult development and leads to higher levels of spiritual maturation. Teachers of the Life Lessons for **human growth** include other people, transference, situations, experiences, empathy for others, etc. Teachers of lessons for **spiritual growth** include serendipity, synchronicity, intuition, 6th sense, etc. The ideology underlying Psychological Maturation teaches life lessons necessary for resolution of emotional dependency on others & achievement of becoming our "real" self. Psychological maturation is the doorway leading to a more complete understanding of our unique potential and "fit" in the universe. The Map of Reality The Map of Reality runs through the Fabric of the Universe and is paved with Objective laws of cause and effect.

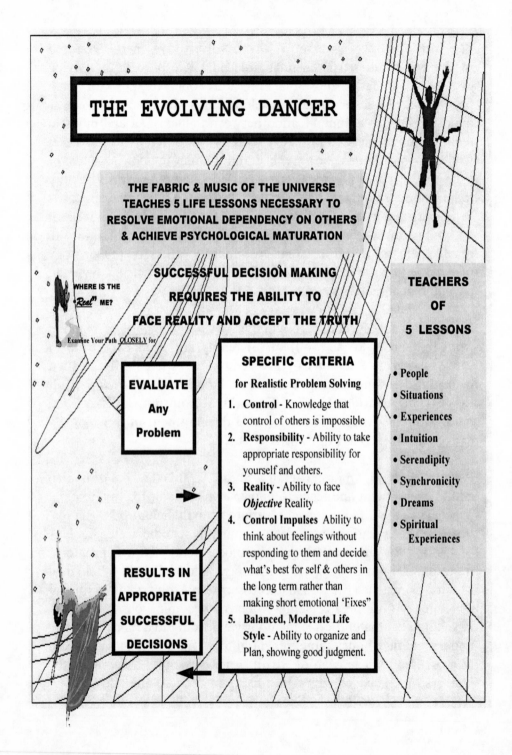

THE EVOLVING DANCER

THE FABRIC & MUSIC OF THE UNIVERSE TEACHES 5 LIFE LESSONS NECESSARY TO RESOLVE EMOTIONAL DEPENDENCY ON OTHERS & ACHIEVE PSYCHOLOGICAL MATURATION

SUCCESSFUL DECISION MAKING REQUIRES THE ABILITY TO FACE REALITY AND ACCEPT THE TRUTH

WHERE IS THE *"Real"* ME?

Examine Your Path _CLOSELY_ for

EVALUATE Any Problem

RESULTS IN APPROPRIATE SUCCESSFUL DECISIONS

SPECIFIC CRITERIA
for Realistic Problem Solving

1. **Control** - Knowledge that control of others is impossible
2. **Responsibility** - Ability to take appropriate responsibility for yourself and others.
3. **Reality** - Ability to face *Objective* Reality
4. **Control Impulses** Ability to think about feelings without responding to them and decide what's best for self & others in the long term rather than making short emotional 'Fixes"
5. **Balanced, Moderate Life Style** - Ability to organize and Plan, showing good judgment.

TEACHERS OF 5 LESSONS

- People
- Situations
- Experiences
- Intuition
- Serendipity
- Synchronicity
- Dreams
- Spiritual Experiences

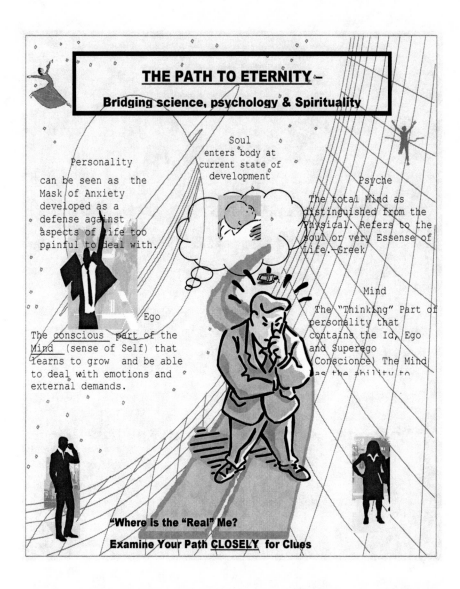

THE PATH TO ETERNITY –

Bridging science, psychology & Spirituality

Soul enters body at current state of development

Personality

can be seen as the Mask of Anxiety developed as a defense against aspects of life too painful to deal with.

Psyche

The total Mind as distinguished from the Physical. Refers to the soul or very Essense of Life. –Greek

Mind

The "Thinking" Part of personality that contains the Id, Ego and Superego (Conscience) The Mind has the ability to

Ego

The conscious part of the Mind (sense of Self) that learns to grow and be able to deal with emotions and external demands.

"Where is the "Real" Me?

Examine Your Path CLOSELY for Clues

Human Life CAN BE PERCEIVED AS A Multifaceted arena of Instructional Opportunities for development of both Human and Spiritual Potential. The fabric of the Universe (Map of Reality) is paved with Realistic Laws of Cause & Effect

CHAPTER 16

Science Knocks on the Door
of the Spiritual Realm

Science, Psychology and Spirituality

FABRIC OF THE UNIVERSE

The Path to Eternity runs through the Fabric Of The Universe and is paved with realistic laws of cause and effect. The Mission & Purpose of Life (unique to each of us) lies in the Souls Plan for human and spiritual growth. **The <u>Fabric Of The Universe</u> presents opportunities for both Human and Spiritual Growth. The Physical Fabric (environment, events, etc.) is reflected in the tangible parts of the Universe (Persons, Opportunities, individual Choices).**

<u>Human Life</u> is a multifaceted arena of Instructional Opportunities within <u>Human Relationships</u>, <u>Life Situations</u>, and <u>Universal Connections</u> (serendipity, dreams, synchronicity, intuition, meditation, dreams) for development of both human and spiritual potential.

The Music Of The Universe is an intangible, invisible **"force" of POSITIVE ENERGY** underlying events and relationships that provides opportunities for both Psychological & Spiritual Development s a result of recognition of <u>Universal Connections</u> (**serendipity, dreams, synchronicity, intuition**) and the Reality of Laws of Cause and Effect. **The Fabric & Music Of The Universe Teach Lessons Necessary for both Human and Spiritual growth.**

Psychological Maturation can be defined as the ability to Face Objective Reality, accept the truth, tolerate frustration, delay gratification and live up to inborn unique potential. The Stage of Adult Ego and Cognitive Maturation requires unique cognitive independence, resolution of emotional enmeshment, respect for the needs of others as equal to our own and development of a personally arrived at objective vs subjective philosophy of Life.

Underlying Connections between the Human and Spiritual Realm dwell within the **Evolving Dancer (essence of the Human Spirit)** and the Spiritual Realm. Interactions may be seen as **Karma, Fate, Serendipity** (Accident), **Synchronicity** (accidents in time) as well as **Altered States of Consciousness** such as **Dreaming** (Alpha, beta) and **Out of Body Experiences.** A possible Validation and Scientific explanation of the **Fabric of the Universe** lies in the Data documented in the scientific research of **Quantum Mechanics** concerning **Multidimensional Reality** (superluminal connectedness results through a higher plane of reality) and **Frequency Domain** (Reality is a frequency domain). **Quantum Theory** defines a **Macro** (real—touchable) Level of reality and a **Micro** (real-Invisible) Level. **David Bohm's** research suggests the **Explicate** (enfolds into the **Implicate** and becomes invisible but does not disappear. It can reappear and become visible again as it again comes in the **Explicate** order. **Bell's Interconnectedness Theorem** proved **Quantum Mechanics** describers correlations that cannot be explained by a Local Mode (less than the speed of light). A paradoxical aspect of quantum theory: two particles once connected are always afterward interconnected even if they become widely separated.

THE FABRIC OF THE UNIVERSE

Multidimensional Reality
Superluminal Connectedness results through a higher plane of reality. **Sarfatti, PhD**

Holographic Universe
Model of reality suggesting the physical universe is similar to a giant hologram. Hologram is a 3 dimensional image, each part of which contains all the information possessed by the whole. Makes sense of phenomena such as telepathy, precognition, etc. **Talbot**

Interconnectedness
Describes connections that cannot be explained by Less than Speed of Light. Two particles once connected always connected. **Bell**

Superluminal
Something does go faster than the Speed Of Light. Superluminal Connectedness results through a higher plane of reality. Possible explanation for telepathy, clairvoyance, etc. **Aspect—**

Fundamental processes of nature lies outside space/time in the Implicate realm of extraneous instantaneous faster than Speed Of light action.

Implicate Explicate
Quantum Theory is incomplete. There is a Macro (real) Level and a Micro (Real-Invisible) Level. Implicate Order is the basic order from which our 3 dimensional world springs. The explicate enfolds into the implicate and becomes invisible but does not disappear. It can reappear and become visible again as it again comes into the Explicate order. **Bohm**

Frequency Domain
is the **Interference patterns** that compose the **Implicate order** Reality is a Frequency Domain. Brain lens that converts frequencies into objective world of appearances. **Pribram & Talbot**

Brain is hardware that plays **the software of the Soul. P Davies—**

Soul enters the body at its current state of development

STRICTLY—SCIENCE
TIMELINE OF SCIENTIFIC RESEARCH

- **1994, Newton, Michael, PhD** Hypnosis Through age-regression technique, he takes clients beyond their past life and uncover a more meaningful soul existence between lives.
- **1991, Talbot, Michael** <u>The Holographic Universe</u> "The most staggering thing about the holographic model was that it suddenly made sense of a wide range of phenomena so elusive they generally have been categorized outside the scientific understanding" including "telepathy, precognition, mystical feelings of oneness with the universe"
- **1983, Davies, Paul,** Brain is hardware that plays the Software of the Soul.
- **1982, Aspect, Alain,** Confirms **Bohm** Research that fundamental process of mature is Implicate (^186)
- **1982, Wolf, Fred,** The **Frequency Realm** is the Interference pattern that compose the Implicate Order.
- **1980, Ring, Kenneth, Near Death Experiences**—Death is shifting consciousness 1 level of Hologram to another
- **1979, Zukov, Gary,** Multidimensional Soul—Material & Nonmaterial Universe is Material & Nonmaterial Personality is Human vehicle (body & Mind)
- **1978, Robert Monroe,** Out of Body Experiences—**devoted to the exploration of human consciousness** <u>Astral projection</u> (or **astral travel**) is a paranormal interpretation of an out-of-body experience achieved either awake or via lucid dreaming or deep meditation.
- **1977, Bentov, Itahak,** Doorway of Time. <u>Altered states of Consciousness</u> allow us to function in realities that are normally not available to us, in our <u>waking</u> state of consciousness. General underlying principle in all psychic phenomena occurs in an *altered state of consciousness*
- **1971, Bohm & Pribram, Hologram** is a 3 dimensional image of object that is photo record of light interference pattern. Each part contains info about the whole. Realm is the Interference patterns that compose the Implicate order (Pribram Talbot p164)

- **1971, Pribram, Karl**—The Holographic Brain—Brain is Lens that converts frequency into macro from Micro. Reality is a frequency Domain. Frequency Realm is interference pattern that compose Implicate Order.
- **1970**, Superluminal is possible <u>explanation</u> for telepathy, clairvoyance, etc.
- **1964, John Bell**, Bell's Theorem—<u>Interconnectedness.</u>— Superluminal. Describes connections that cannot be explained by v186 (Locality). <u>Two particles once connected always connected even if so far apart signals can't reach in v186</u>. QT is Trojan Horse of QT b/c it describes outcomes that contradicts (SOL V186).
- **1951, Bohm, David**—Implicate and explicate Implicate is primary. Explicate rolled into Implicate and can be seen again. QT incomplete. ^ 186.
- **1935, Pandora's Box,** Epr Pandora's Box ^186 Experiment indicated information can be communicated Superluminally (faster than light). **Einstein, Podolsky, Rosen EPR Pater** (Pandora's box of modern Physics
- **1935—Einstein—Quantum Theory Complete. Nothing** can travel faster than SOL v186. Info transmits superluminally (^186). Every Thing is real. We just haven't discovered everything yet. There is a deeper real Macro that may be too small to see.
- **1927, Neils Bohr**, Quantum Theory is Compete._Entity is particle or wave, but not both at the same time. Nothing can go faster than speed of light (186).
- **1890's** Quantum physics dates back to the nineteenth century and is associated with the work of German physicist **Max Planck**. In the 1890's **Planck** postulated that light is emitted in packets of definite size which he called a quanta. Thus light, is being described as a photon in order to solve the riddle of blackbody radiation. The wave/particle duality suggests that either particles can travel beyond the speed of light (a theoretical impossibility), or that everything is connected, and joined together. **Richard Feynmann** "at the subatomic level discrete objects do not exist: our perception of reality may be an illusionary phenomenon.

The Underlying Conflicts in the Present position of Science concerning the Spiritual Realm

♦ A **scientific validation** of the **Spiritual Realm** presents many obstacles for many reasons. Although Philosophy, Religion and human experiences lead to a belief in Spirit and Soul neither Science nor Spirit can "prove" it. The frequency Domain is energy—light, audio, radio beams, etc In spite of the fact that QT proved there are instantaneous (**superluminal**—faster than the speed of light) connections between aspects of the Universe that cannot be explained by Science at its present state of development I believe Science will eventually be able to prove the spiritual realm exists b/c there is already a QT Scientific proof of a type of unexplained connection. QT has shown an instantaneous connection between separate local properties.

♦ In 1964) Bell **proved that** no local model of Reality can do justice to the facts of quantum behavior. A **local model** of reality is one in which all causal connections propagate by **signals that travel at less than the speed of light.** Bell (Interconnectedness Theorem—proved that **Quantum Mechanics** describes correlations that cannot be explained by a Local Model. The theorem considers a variation on that of the **Einstein—Podolsky—Rosen** thought experiment. Experiment: discovered a paradoxical aspect of quantum theory: **two particles that** were once connected **are always afterwards interconnected even if they become widely separated.**

♦ The fact that QM info can be instantaneous forced Scientists to acknowledge a complete understanding of reality lay beyond the capabilities of rational thought. Bohr said QT is complete but beyond the understanding of human. It only explains what happened not how The Copenhagen Interpretation of Quantum **Mechanics said the** Quantum Theory is complete because it works every time. Neils Bohr believed the Quantum Theory **is COMPLETE although it** does not explain the details of what is going on. Einstein (and the Scientific Community) believe nothing can travel faster than the speed of light. However,

Einstein did not accept the idea that QT was complete and believed there must be some other explanation for the Faster than Light.

♦ Einstein and Bohr Einstein says QT is incomplete because info travels superluminally (faster than speed of light. So there must be something else that science has not discovered Einstein and Bohm thought Quantum Theory **is INCOMPLETE** and there was a deeper reality beyond the present understanding of the Quantum Landscape. **Characteristics** that may push the door of Spirituality open a little more.

♦ The faster than light aspect of QT, a characteristic that seems impossible in a Local World suggests an interconnection (Hidden variables) that knocks on the "spooky" door of spirituality. The Incomplete aspect of QT suggests a deeper reality, a Characteristics that may push the door of Spirituality open a little more.

♦ Aspect, Alain (1982) Aspect does. Aspect Experiment—In the early **1980s,** a team of French scientists led by Alain **Aspect,** Jean Dalibard, and Gerard Roger tested **Bohm's thought experiment that t**he fundamental process of Nature lies outside space time but generates events that can be located in space time **and information can be transferred superluminally (Faster than the speed of light).** The results went against Einstein's **belief that nothing travels faster than speed of light. Aspect** and his team found there is a mysterious instantaneous faster-than-light 'action at a distance' between once-linked photons, and presumably between once-linked particles, too.

Reincarnation says we are in the world to learn our lessons, explore and hopefully achieve our mission in life of love and human and spiritual growth. If this is a possibility, how in the world might it fit into the Scientific Research Data of Quantum Physics? Mark Bancroft, MA (**Quantum Physics and Consciousness**) defines **Quantum Physics** as a branch of physics which concerns itself with the study (observation) of the subatomic realm. Physics is defined as, "The science of matter and energy and of interactions between the two." "It is the study of Physical properties, interactions, processes, or laws." It is the study of the natural or material world and phenomenon."

Many PhD's and Physicists accept Superluminal connections as a door to Spirit but are afraid to say so for fear of ridicule by the scientific community. In 1964) Bell **proved that** no local model of Reality can do justice to the facts of quantum behavior. A **local model** of reality is one in which all causal connections propagate by **signals that travel at** less **than the speed of light.**

BRIDGING SCIENCE, PSYCHOLOGY AND SPIRITUALITY

Research data concerning spirituality as phenomena of the frequency realm is presented below.

- **Psyche**—The Total Mind as distinguished from the physical Refers to the Soul or very essence of Life—**Greek**
- **Soul** is non material. stored outside our physical bodies and will not decay. **Zukov**
- Brain is the hardware that plays the software of the Soul. **P Davies**
- Near Death Experiences are a shifting of consciousness 1 level to another level of the Hologram—**Kenneth Ring**
- Hypnosis—Clients go beyond past lives to uncover their soul existence between lives. Newton, M—
- Astral Projection is an Out of Body altered state of consciousness **Monroe, R**
- All Psychic phenomena occurs in altered states of consciousness **Bentov**
- Interconnectedness—Two particles once connected always connected. Describes connections that cannot be explained by less than Speed of Light. **Bell**
  - Multidimensional Reality—Superluminal Connectedness results through a higher plane of reality. **Sarfatti, PhD**
  - Holographic Universe—a model of reality that suggests the physical universe is similar to a giant hologram. A Hologram is a 3 dimensional image,

each part of which contains all the information possessed by the whole. Makes sense of phenomena such as telepathy, precognition, etc. **Talbot**

- Frequency Realm is the Interference patterns that compose the Implicate order (Pribram Talbot p164).—

- Reality is a Frequency Domain. Brain is the lens that converts frequencies into the objective world of appearances. **Pribram**

- Implicate Explicate. Quantum Theory is incomplete. There is a Macro (real) Level and a Micro (Real-Invisible) Level. Implicate Order is the basic order from which our 3 dimensional world springs. The explicate enfolds into the implicate and becomes invisible but does not disappear. It can reappear and become visible again as it again comes into the Explicate order. **Bohm**

- **Quantum Theory** is more general than classical physics, and in principle, could be used to predict the behavior of any physical, chemical, or biological system. Quantum Theory describes outcomes that contradicts Speed of Light Theory.

- **Bohr**—QT is complete. Nothing goes faster than Speed Of Light Einstein—QT is complete. Nothing goes faster than Speed Of Light. T here are hidden variables in the **Macro (Local, real,)** that we haven't discovered.

- **Mind**—The Thinking part of Personality that contains the ID, Ego & Superego (conscience). The Mind has the ability to grow. "Our soul (mind) is information (The software) and runs on the Hardware of the Brain" Paul Davies. **Consciousness**— The awareness of one's own existence. Also defined The process of integrating the local mind (the self) with additional portions of the universal mind (all ideas in the universe)

- **Personality** The "Masks of Anxiety" developed as a defense against difficult or conflictual aspects of life. Personality is the Human vehicle (body & Mind). At death we can play our soul on a different media (heaven, reincarnation, etc.) **Zukov, G**

- **Superluminal**—Something does go faster than the Speed of Light. Superluminal Connectedness results through a higher plane of reality. A possible explanation for telepathy, clairvoyance, etc. fundamental process of natures lies outside space/time in the Implicate realm in a mysterious instantaneous faster than Speed Of light action. **Aspect**

UNDERLYING CONNECTIONS OF THE UNIVERSE

Near Death Experiences are a **shifting of consciousness 1 level to another level of the Hologram. Kenneth Ring**—
Hypnosis—Clients go beyond past lives to uncover their **soul existence between lives**. Newton, Michael
Astral Projection, Out of Body altered states of consciousness **Monroe, Robert**

♦ All Psychic phenomena occur in altered states of consciousness **Bentov. Itahak**

♦ **Superluminal**—Something does go faster than the SOL. Superluminal Connectedness results through a higher plane of reality. possible <u>explanation </u>for telepathy, clairvoyance, etc. fundamental process of natures lies outside space/time in the Implicate realm in a mysterious instantaneous faster than Speed Of light action. **Aspect, Alain**

♦ **Interconnectedness**—<u>Two particles once connected always connected. </u>Describes connections that cannot be explained by Less than Speed of Light. **Bell, John**

♦ **Multidimensional Reality**—Superluminal Connectedness results through a higher plane of reality. **Sarfatti, PhD**

♦ **Holographic Universe**—a model of reality that suggests the physical universe is similar to a giant hologram. Hologram is a 3 dimensional image, each part of which contains all the information possessed by the whole. Makes sense of phenomena such as telepathy, precognition, etc **Talbot.**

♦ **Frequency Realm** is the **Interference patterns** that compose the Implicate order Pribram—Reality is a Frequency Domain. Brain lens that converts frequencies into objective world of appearances. **(Pribram & Talbot p164).**

♦ **Implicate explicate**. Qt is incomplete. There is a macro (real) level and a micro (real-invisible) level. Implicate order is the basic order from which our 3 dimensional world springs. The <u>explicate </u>enfolds into the implicate and becomes invisible but does not disappear. It can reappear and become visible again as it again comes into the explicate order. **Bohm, David**

- **Quantum theory** is more general than classical physics, and in principle, could be used to predict the behavior of any physical, chemical, or biological system. Quantum theory describes outcomes that contradicts speed of light theory. Classical theory—do not explain the behavior of matter and energy on this small scale. Qt is complete. Nothing goes faster than speed of light **Bohr, Neils**

- **Quantum Theory** is complete. Nothing goes faster than speed of light. T here are hidden variables in the **macro (local, real,)** that we haven't discovered. **Einstein, Albert**

- **Mind**—the thinking part of personality that contains the id, ego & superego (conscience). The mind has the ability to grow.

- "our soul (mind) is information (the software) and runs on the hardware of the brain" **Paul Davies. Consciousness**—the awareness of one's own existence. Also defined the process of integrating the local mind (the self) with additional portions of the universal mind (all ideas in the universe) personality the "masks of anxiety" developed as a defense against difficult or conflictual aspects of life. Personality is the human vehicle (body & mind). At death we can play our soul on a different media (heaven, reincarnation, etc.)

- Quantum theory describes unexplained (faster than speed of light) connections **Zukov, Gary**

- Research supports theory of the primacy of an implicate order (real & invisible) and reality as a holographic (multidimensional) universe of superluminal connections **Bohm, David**

SCIENTIFIC BOOKS IN SUPPORT OF SPIRITUAL REALM.

GOD AND THE NEW PHYSICS—PAUL DAVIES

God and the New Physics, written by Paul Davies answers the questions: "Is the mind only the reaction of brain cells?", "Does the Mind disappear when brain dies?" and "Could the Mind survive after death?". His answer is <u>Yes, . . .</u> if a Mind could be played on another medium besides the brain (such as the Universal Mind).

In the chapters of this book Paul Davies[1] discusses modern physics, the new ideas about space and time, order, mind and matter in the search for God. He indicates that much of the new research will confirm the opinions of some that science is implacably opposed to religion and continues to threaten the basis of most religious doctrines. He states it would be foolish to deny that many of the traditional religious ideas about god, man and nature have been swept away by the new physics. But . . . he believes that the new research has turned up many positive signs too. He indicates that the existence of mind, as an abstract, holistic, organized pattern, capable of disembodiment, refutes the reductionism philosophy that we are all nothing but moving mounds of atoms.

Mr. Davies does not try to provide easy answers for religious questions, but only to expand the context in which the traditional religious issues are discussed. He believes **The New Physics** has overturned so many commonsense notions of space, time and matter that no serious religious thinker can ignore it. Mr. Davies cites his deep conviction that only by understanding the world in all its aspects, reductionist and holistic, math and poet, through forces, fields and particles as well as good and evil, that we will come to understand ourselves and the meaning behind the universe, our home.

After long and careful study of this wonderful insightful book concerning the conclusions of Mr. Davies in his book God and The New Physics I believe the following points of view fit well into the

---

[1] Paraphrasing Information written on <u>Pg 229</u> by Paul Davies author of <u>God and the New Physics</u> <u>the following conclusions are cited.</u>

scientific theories of Quantum Theory. The soul is not located in the brain or anywhere in space. The Soul is made of stuff that dreams and thoughts are made of. In answer to the Question: "Where do MEMORIES go when the body dies" the answer is "The same place that music goes, when not being listened to, where software programs go when not being used. Or where Wednesday are on other days of the week. Of course they do not cease to exist. According to the theory of Dualism (Mental Phenomena are in some ways, non-physical), Soul is a thing and separate from the body. Physics operates best at Reductionist level because any complex idea can be understood best when explained at its most basic level.

Software can solve many problems, makes comparisons, and come to conclusions etc based on processing information. The Essential ingredient of the mind is the software (Brain). Cognitive Sciences (computers, psychology, cybernetics, linguists) are systems that process information. Thoughts cause thoughts. Brains and computers are both circuitry and follows physical rules. We are a pattern (plot). Our soul (mind) is information and runs on the hardware of the Brain. At death our soul can be played on a different media (Heaven, reincarnation).

The Seat of the Soul—Gary Zukov
"Treatment of Thought, Evolution and Reincarnation"

Gary Zukov writes in The Seat of the Soul2—that Human & Spiritual Development is on a continuum, from five sensory physical levels to multisensory levels of the spiritual. The whole of human kind is evolving into a multisensory phase vs each soul evolving as it learns its lessons. He writes that Time and space are artifacts of the objective (explicate order) in which we live on earth.

Gary Zukov writes that each Soul is made up of many personalities that contribute to the evolution of the primary soul. The Soul creates each personality (incarnation) to teach lessons necessary for further development of the soul. Personalities are incomplete parts of our soul. He states that the 5 sensory personality is not always conscious

---

2   The above Information has been Paraphrased from the Book the Seat of the Soul written by Gary Zukov.

of other incarnations but a multi-sensory personality may be aware of other incarnations as part of past or future experiences the soul has lived.

The Soul is energy. Authentic empowerment is the alignment of the personality (5 sensory objective solid human) with the soul's (Multisensory, loving, compassionate and wise) journey to evolution. He states that all incarnations exist at once, that personalities are splintered parts of the soul that need to heal and that we are responsible for our intuition. However, he writes that memories of soul's agreement with Universe become dim.

Mr. Zukov believes in guides and teachers and anger causes distance and hostile interaction. Cause and Effect leads to Karma which we may have created it in another life. He writes that Problems are doorways to identification of specific problem areas but also opportunities for growth. The Human and Spiritual GOAL Is Balancing and growth of the soul.

Dancing Wu Li **Master—Gary Zukav** "An overview of the New Physics"

The Dancing Wu Li Master by Gary Zukov[3]. The development of physics has transformed the consciousness of those involved with it. (1935). The **Dancing Wu Li Master** is a book about quantum physics for people who had no scientific background or interest in science, but who wanted to know about this thing called quantum physics. That became The Dancing Wu Li Masters and won the American Book Award for Science.

At a deep and fundamental level, the **separate parts of the universe are connected** in an intimate and immediate way. Like everything else, it is dependent on something which is happening elsewhere. Everything is the result of some kind of cause and effect in either **macro (something you can touch) or micro (too small to see) realms**. **(1964)** Bells' Theorem. A fundamental concept of quantum theory holding that energy sometimes behaves like particles and

---

[3]   The above points are paraphrased from Information on Pg 327 of the Dancing Wu Li Master by
       Gary Zukov

sometimes behaves like waves. So descriptions of energy as one or the other are inadequate. PHYSICS concept that two different models may be necessary to describe an atomic or subatomic system. For example, electrons may be regarded as particles or waves in different circumstances. Bohr's concept explaining wave-particle duality of light Complementarily (Pg 116), The Uncertainty Principle—a quantum mechanics principle holding that it is impossible to determine both the position and momentum of a particle at the same time. Heisenberg133), Quantum Field Theory—a quantum mechanics theory based on the assumption that elementary particles interact through the influence of fields around them and the exchange of energy (Pg 218). Copenhagen Interpretation of Quantum Mechanics. The **Copenhagen Interpretation** was product of **Neils Bohr** and **Werner Heisenberg** and strongly supported by **Max Born, Wolfgang Pauli** and **John von Neumann**. The search for causal laws was declared fruitless because of the claim that the threshold of acausal randomness had been discovered—with the further implication that there is ultimately no objective reality. This is the philosophical essence of the Copenhagen Interpretation of quantum theory. It is an interpretation which does not follow strictly from physics. Among those opposed to the **Copenhagen Interpretation** have been **Albert Einstein, Erwin Schroedinger, Louis de Broglie, Max Planck, David Bohm, Alfred Landé, Karl Popper and Bertrand Russell**. Those supporting the **Copenhagen Interpretation** constitute a "school", those opposed to it have widely divergent views. Those opposing it have been uniformly vilified as too simple-minded or too "old fashioned" to understand such "modern" ideas as **acausality** and **positivism (the scientific method is the best approach to uncovering the processes by which both physical and human events occur)**. Soviet physicists also opposed the **Copenhagen Interpretation**, but on the grounds that it is an "idealism", to be contrasted to a "dialectical materialist" view of reality. (Pg 62)

I have found the reading of the Dancing Wu Li Masters to be extremely interesting and thought provoking. And although I am not a scientist in the same frame of reference as a Physicist, I am a PhD and need well thought out Objective factual information that fits in with what I have previously learned in my studies of Quantum Physics or have experienced myself.

I am very comfortable with the ideology that the Universe consists of 2 organizing systems, Material and non-material. I can also agree that the Universe is a hologram of interacting fields and that DNA contains information to build copies of the body while chromosomes contains blue prints of physical. I am sure that at death we decompose, protein break down into substances of planet they came from, decays and returns to nonmaterial.

As a result of my own thoughts and experiences (the death of my 3 sons) I am sure the Psyche (Non material) —will not decay because it is stored outside our physical bodies. It is non physical and returns to universal mind. I agree that when information concerning phenomena such as telepathy is organized into reasonable order, they are manifestation of consciousness or increasingly higher levels. The concept of the Underlying principle of the universe is consciousness also makes sense to me. As for the scientific concept that It is not possible to measure both motion and postion at the same time because conscious and observation interacts with the experimenter, I will just have to the the Physicists word for that.

Stalking the Wild Pendulum—Itzhak Bentov
On the Mechanics of Consciousness

The following information has been taken from "Stalking the Wild Pendulum by Itzhak Bentov on the Mechanics of Consciousness. During the reading of this book I found I had to study it carefully, take notes concerning the issue of Consciousness and thinking about it very carefully. After long and carefully study I found that I could agree with most of Mr. **Bentov's** observations. The following Information has been Paraphrased from the Book the Stalking the Wild Pendulum by Itzhak Bentov.

The State of consciousness interferes with seeing the "other "side. When I am awake I can't see the "others" until I can alter my state of consciousness thru telepathy, Out of Body Experiences. Etc." This can happen in certain stages of sleep. **Quantum Theory** asserts there is no way to measure some sets of things, together very accurately. Because the **consciousness** of the experimenter interacts with the experiment. When information about ESP, telepathy, psychic healing, spontaneous mystical experiences, etc is organized into reasonable order, we find these phenomena are a manifestation of "**consciousness** on increasingly higher levels.

When we die, we decompose and our proteins, DNA, etc return to the earth. The psyche doesn't decay b/c it is not subject to physical laws but will return to the fund of information of mankind. The window of time when consciousness can leave the body is similar to when the Pendulum on a Clock comes to a full stop and before it starts again. At that time, there is an area in which the causal relationship b/t time and space breaks down and infinite or nearly infinite velocities are encountered. This is because the uncertainty principle [4]is operating on the quantum scale of things. Published by **Werner Heisenberg in** 1927 this principle means that it is impossible to *determine* simultaneously both the position and the momentum of an electron or any other particle with any great degree of accuracy or certainty. Consciousness can leave your body and time stands still. The Window—Between the time the pendulum stops and starts is an area when causal relationship b/t time and space break down in which infinite velocities are encountered. Because of the Uncertainty Principle it is impossible to specify simultaneously the position and momentum of a particle (Space and Time). Speed of light 186,000 miles per second. Day dreaming, mind wandering, OBE's, dreams, meditation are instances when consciousness leaves the body. It travels at above the speed of light.

AUTHORS—Discussing Paranormal & SPIRITUAL PHILOPHY[5].

Sylvia Brown—Writing and philosophy of spirituality is one which I absolutely admire. Her writings and books are interesting and based

---

[4]   **Werner Heisenberg** in 1927, the principle means that it is impossible to determine simultaneously both the position and the momentum of an electron or any other particle with any great degree of accuracy or certainty

[5]   God & the New Physics—Paul Davies—Simon & Schuster 1993, The Holographic Universe—Michael Talbot Harper Collins Publishers 1991, Stalking the Wild Pendulum (The Mechanics of Consciousness) Destiny Books—Iszhak Bentov 1988—Life at Death—Kenneth Ring, PhD (a scientific investigation of near death experiences —Coward, McCann & Georghegan—1980, The Holographic Paradigm (Exploring the leading edge

on her absolute conviction of the truth of the Spiritual Realm. She is said to have begun her work with Research Project Information gathered with Bill Yalroff, PhD. They made a list of 20 former patients (dead and alive) and asked Francine, Sylvia Brown's Spirit Guide to Identify cause of death. 19 of 20 were identified with factual details. Sylvia didn't read Bills mind because he couldn't remember causes of death when he wrote the list.

Sylvia Brown believes that Astral Projection is real. She believes that Ghosts are earthbound spiritis who sees the tunnel and turns or refuses to acknowledge it. They gets caught outside their body between dimensions and probably don't know they are dead. She believes that Imaginary playmates may be earth bound spirits. Other Important and Well Researched book concerning Aspects of the Spiritual Real include the following: **Journey of Souls,** Newton, Michael, PhD, **Destiny of Souls—**Newton, Michael, PhD, **Afterlife Experiments,** Gary E Schwartz, PhD with William Simon. Foreword **Deepak Chopra, Echoes of the Soul—**Echo Bodine, **Never Say Goodbye—**Patrick Mathews, **What happens after death—**Migene Gonzalea-Wipper—**Scientific & Personal Evidence for Survival, Philosophy for Dummies—**Tom Morris, PhD. **Lessons from the Light—**Kenneth Ring, PhD, **Recovering the Soul—Scientific and Spiritual Search—**Larry Dossey, MD, Kuebler Ross,—**On Death and Dying,** Robert Monroe,—**Journeys out of the Body, The Last Laugh—**Robert Moody, etc—**Life After Life**

MY BELIEFS CONCERING THE SPIRITUAL REALM
My Conclusions about Quantum Theory

The Underlying principle of the universe is consciousness. The Universe is a hologram of interacting fields. The concept of Relativity presents the fact that we must compare our frame of reference with another to get meaningful measurement—It is not possible to measure both motion and position at the same time because consciousness and observation interacts with the experimenter's organizing systems: material and non material.

---

of Science) Edited by Ken Wilbur, Shambhala Publications 1985, Contributions by Karl Pribram, Renee Weber, Fritjof Capra, K. Pelletier, Iszhak Bentov, David Bohm, Journeys Out of the Body, Far Journeys, Reunions—Robert Monroe—1987, 1990, 1993

Material from the Macro Levels decays at death and returns to nonmaterial. However, the Psyche (Non-material) will not decay because it is stored outside our physical bodies and is non physical. When information about all phenomena such as telepathy is organized into reasonable order, it is a manifestation of consciousness on increasingly higher levels. The order of life counteracts entropy. DNA contains information with which to build copies of the body (chromosomes contains blue prints of physical). Life organizes random minerals into stable structure and maintains order of life (negative entropy). At death we decompose and protein break down into substances of planet they came from

The Soul comes from the spiritual Realm and can connect instantaneously with Human consciousness. Consciousness is at different levels and accessible through different stages (sleep, hypnosis, dreams, out of body experience's etc.). The soul is composed of consciousness. Purpose of Life and Human Mission is to grow, learn lessons for human and spiritual development.

I believe a frequency realm is composed of atoms, electrons, quarks, etc. within the implicate order. The Frequency Realm is the **Interference patterns** that compose the **Implicate order** (Pribram Talbot p164). Frequency Domain (**Pribram**) Reality of our Macro domain is really a **frequency domain** and our brain is a kind of lens that converts these frequencies into the objective world of appearances. He now uses the term to refer to the interference patterns that compose the implicate order. He believes there are tings in the frequency domain we are not seeing, that our brains have learned to edit out of our visual reality. He thinks that when Mystics have transcendental experiences they are catching glimpses of the frequency domain. I believe science & QT will eventually be able to prove the existence of the spiritual realm thru some type of physics. However, it maybe not QM in its present form.

My Interpretations concerning

The Souls Program

I believe the **spiritual realm** is **Real** (Non Local) but we just can't see it. Nonlocal (Invisible but also real). This is either because its properties are too small to be seen (subtle matter) or are constructed from aspects of energy that have not been identified. The Soul comes from the Implicate Order and resides in human form (Explicate Order). The Soul, composed of consciousness comes from the spiritual Realm and can connect instantaneously with Human consciousness. Consciousness is at different levels and accessible through different stages (sleep, hypnosis, dreams, out of body experiences, etc.)

Soul enters at current state of development. Soul is not located anywhere. It is made of stuff of dreams, Wednesdays. The Soul's agenda is played on the software of the Human Mind in thoughts. The Human Brain is the hardware that plays the software of the Mind (Self). We are a Pattern (Plot). Our soul (mind) is information and runs on the Brain from which we learn our lessons and become self aware. At death our soul is played on a different media.(Heaven, reincarnation)

The Soul is Individual for each of us and leads to individual Missions on Earth. The Soul is not located anywhere in space. It is made of the stuff of dreams and thoughts and is separate from the body.

I believe that the Mind is the thinking part of the self. The Soul's Program is played on the Software of the Human Mind by the Hardware of the Brain. The Soul develops and matures as a result of learning lessons in the earth school with other human beings. The Mind does not disappear. The Mind (software that contains the Program of the Soul) is played on the Hardware of the Brain. Mind doesn't die when body dies. Like a novels theme, it can be put and heard on video and played. QT says nothing ever disappears. It just gets smaller and smaller. The Soul's Program (Like Beethoven's Symphony) can be played on the Software of the Mind while we are alive. The Mind is not just brain cell activity. The Soul's Program can be played on other medium besides the brain (such as the Universal Mind).

Fellow Travelers on the Road of Life
"Good-Bye for A Little While"

The Death of a child (of any age, is an intolerable tragedy). The Murder of a child is a tragedy of almost unbearable dimensions. But the murder of a child by police, an agency designed to protect the public, is an insult of cataclysmic proportions.

On the last morning of his life, my son, Blake dressed himself neatly in jeans, shirt and new shoes and drove slowly into the cul-de-sac where his friend Chris slept and death waited. At first, drinking a coke, smoking a cigarette and relaxing to his beloved loud music he neither saw the face nor felt the cold breath of death as it crouched on Musial St. preparing to claim him for its own.

Suddenly, amidst angry shouts and violent gun fire, through horrified eyes and rolled up windows, he glimpsed the terrorizing Specter spring forth. In a vain attempt to drive around death, . . . as his clutch slipped and motor died . . . a bullet from the police 45 ripped through the back of his head and upraised left thumb . . . ushering him into the waiting presence of death and outstretched arms of Eternity. As he lay over the steering wheel . . . his truck . . . slowly rolled to a stop.

All his life Blake said he would not live to be old. When he was little boy I had a recurring nightmare from which I always awakened in terror . . . Running towards a lake I inevitably found my 4 year old son, dressed in his little green jacket, floating face down in shallow water. His body silent and still, moving slowly back and forth in rhythm with the tide . . . drowned.

Lying in bed at night, gazing at twinkling lights on a far dark hill I long for release from pain. Through my dark window, Desolation enters the room and settles over me. A week before his death, as I lay sleeping, my son entered my DREAM, bent and touched my hand. Sliding to the floor he sat leaning against the bedroom curtain, crying softly. 'I'm all alone,' he sobbed, 'she's gone'. Awakening, I brushed the dream pain from my mind . . . as he disappeared into daylight. Who was my dream son crying for? Was the Dream a premonition of his death? Was he somehow, in my dream, trying to tell me his life would soon be over? That we would no longer be together in life? How could he have known?

A few weeks after his death I dreamed I stood beside the bronze colored box cradling my son's body. Feeling a tap on my shoulder I whirled to find myself staring into the living face of my son. Nervously reassuring me he was "not really dead", he cautioned me to tell no one . . . fearing they would "try to kill me again". A few months later, over the course of several weeks, two women called to share separate but almost identical dreams. Standing at his casket each remembers turning in surprise as Blake approached his own casket, wearing the same shirt and pants he wore in the bronze box. Looking casually at his own dead body he happily assured each of them the lifeless body in the bronze box was not him because he was alive —no longer residing in the body lying on white satin.

About a year after Blake's death, in a strange dream like experience (but not exactly like a dream) I arose from bed and walked down the dark hall to find him waiting for me in my softly lit office next to the room that used to be his. Happily he reached out to hug and assure me he was not dead. I cried with joy to see and touch him. I had waited so long. Sitting beside him on the couch, hugging him I could feel the warmth of his body . . . and smell the uniquely familiar, never to be forgotten scent of his skin.

Later, recalling the extraordinary experience I tried to make sense of it. Contemplating whether I had lost my mind or if the encounter was simply a result of wishful thinking I could find no sensible compelling reason to doubt my own experience, my sanity or the truth of his message to me. About a year later on a trip to Seattle for a Book Convention I asked the Manager of a Publishing House what his impressions of my experiences might be. Looking me straight in the eye he assured me that he had no doubt I had experienced an Out of Body Experience with the Spirit of my Son who had come to reassure me that he was fine and safe in the spiritual realm.

I have since read of similar experiences and personally spoken to other parents[6] of dead children who have seen, touched, smelled and even heard the breathing of a dead child. The place these experiences originate from is difficult for everyone who has experienced them to explain to those who have never had such an encounter. However, I believe there is a rational, scientific explanation for such experiences (common to many) that will eventually be explained by scientific research such as those of quantum mechanics[7].

I will love you forever and Join you there

Eight years after the death of my son Blake, my oldest son, Kurt died of a medication interaction. Having been laid off from his job of seventeen years at Boeing Co in Huntington Beach Ca he was very depressed. In an effort to feel better while searching for work that might temporarily fill the emptiness that had been his Identity he consulted a Psychiatrist who proscribed Medication.

On the hot afternoon of **June 30, 2003**, after trying unsuccessfully to reach my son by phone, I went to his house to verify he would join us for our July 4th celebration. Although his car was parked in the garage he neither answered the knocks on his door nor the rings of his door bell. Using a key he had provided me for emergencies, I entered the house to find him in bed where he had lain dead for 3 days, a victim of an accidental medication interaction that lead to a deep sleep from which he never awoke.

---

6   Meetings of Parents of Murdered Children, Compassionate Friends, Chance acquaintances who related such experiences when they trusted me enough to know I would not automatically diagnose them as Psychotic and recommend they be locked up.

7   God & the New Physics—Paul Davies—Simon & Schuster 1993, The Holographic Universe—Michael Talbot Harper Collins Publishers 1991, Stalking the Wild Pendulum (The Mechanics of Consciousness) Destiny Books—Iszhak Bentov 1988—Life at Death—Kenneth Ring, PhD (a scientific investigation of near death experiences —Coward, McCann & Georghegan—1980, The Holographic Paradigm (Exploring the leading edge of Science) Edited by Ken Wilbur, Shambhala Publications 1985, Contributions by Karl Pribram, Renee Weber, Fritjof Capra, K. Pelletier, Iszhak Bentov, David Bohm, Journeys Out of the Body, Far Journeys, Reunions—Robert Monroe—1987, 1990, 1993

Kurt was a scientist who had worked for years at McDonnell Douglas and Boeing where he negotiated contracts for NASA. As a child he attended Sunday school and was married in the Episcopal Church. During adulthood, he shared with me the doubts he was having about the existence of a Spiritual Realm or even the very existence of a God at all. Over several years we discussed the pros and cons surrounding the concept of the God. However, during the last few years of his life, he confessed that the idea of a Spiritual Realm might actually be the truth.

After Kurt's death, the sale of his house and taking care of his earthly obligations I entered his home for the last time to leave keys for the new owner. In a search for closure, with tears in my eyes and pain in my heart I went upstairs and entered the room where he died. As I stood in the room, I heard the door bell ring. Running down stairs I opened the door to find the front steps empty. Thinking someone had left before I got there, I left the door open. As I turned my back and flipped the light switch that controlled the many colored lights at the top of the stairs to begin my ascent to the second floor the door bell rang again. Turning my head toward the sound I saw an empty doorway. As I walked through the house flipping on one light after another, the sound of the doorbell from the empty doorway continued to echo through the house. "How this could be happening", I asked myself.

A few minutes later, as my son, Ted and his wife Kathy started up the walkway to say one last goodbye, the door bell rang again. Asking my son, Ted (an electrician) to test the Doorbell for an electrical problem, he found none. And as before, as Ted and Kathy went though the house to say one last goodbye to the memory and spirit of their brother, each time they switched on a light, the door bell rang.

As we left the house, after laying the keys on the counter for the new owner we turned to say one last goodbye to the spirit of my son, who I am sure, was telling me he had in fact found the Spiritual Realm to be a Reality . . . a finding that he wanted to share with his loved ones.

<u>DREAM IN THE MALL—"It had to be you"</u>

15 months after the Death of my son, Kurt, my son, Mark, fell dead of a heart attack in the upstairs hallway of our home right behind me on his 50th Birthday. Alive one minute he fell over dead the next into the micro realm where spirituality waits when death of the human body occurs or the heart stops beating. And although I never heard the ringing of the door bell or experienced the smell and touch of a son who had entered the spiritual realm I have no doubt that my son, Mark came from the Frequency Realm to walk with me in a Dream.

It was a very sad dream. I had been having a hard time accepting the fact of his death. On the date of May 24th 2007 three years after his death on December 8, 2004 I dreamed I was in the mall with Kurt, Mark and someone else, I don't know who. We were going shopping for some things for the house. We bought some things but I can't remember what.

Then Mark and I veered off to another part of the mall because I wanted to buy some new bed spreads for Mark. He was very happy to come with me but didn't really think it was necessary to buy any bedspreads or anything else for him. We wandered along together through semi busy corridors of the mall. There were not many people there, but some.

I don't remember if the melody of *"It Had to Be You"* just somehow drifted over us or if we just started singing out loud. Not too loud, but not too soft either. Mark didn't know the words well, but was very happy as we stood there and I continued to sing . . ." *It had to be you, It had to be you, I wandered around and finally found somebody who. . . Could make me feel sad, Could make me feel glad . . . Thinking of You . . . For nobody else gives me a thrill, with all your faults . . . I love you still; it had to be you, wonderful you, no one but you.* Someone in the mall (like a manager or something) called out . . . with a smile and a laugh, "Thank you . . . Skipi Lundquist Smoot". Mark and I both laughed.

Strolling out of the Mall through a set of double glass doors we drifted along an outside corridor. I could feel but not see Mark beside me. Sensing he had somehow disappeared into shallow water that lined the outer corridor, I stood warily expecting his reappearance by my side. Slowly as uncertainty surrounded me, Denial jumped defiantly into command. Mark would reappear, I confidently assured myself. I just had to wait. The conviction, of two living sons resided firmly in my mind. I counted them, one, two . . . yes, one, two. Ted and Mark make two . . . not one. Yes, Ted and Mark were both alive. Mark (although unseen) was still here . . . happy and sweet. I could feel his love around me, enveloping me. So, why did the aura of death refuse to disappear?

Then I woke up . . . jolted into consciousness. by the objective Fact that Mark was physically dead. The shield of Denial had vanished. Mark . . . not just Blake and Kurt . . . but Mark, too . . . had disappeared into an unseen dimension. No longer able to hide from the truth of objective reality, the knowledge of my 3rd sons' exodus from the Macro Level of Human Life into the Micro Level of Spiritual interconnectedness became a Reality.

The Spiritual Realm is sometimes accessible to dreamers searching for loved ones who have passed on to the other side. As I search for words to clearly explain the circumstances surrounding Mark's death, I am convinced that the essence of his spirit (concerned for my mental state of denial) entered my dream in an effort to assure me, he was alive and happy in a micro (real but invisible) frequency realm.

During the year after Blake's murder, in an effort to help myself understand "where he went", "how he could be alive one minute and dead the next" I exhaustively studied Quantum Theory Data and Research concerning underlying explanations for the possibility of the existence of a Spiritual Realm. As a result of that study and my own personal experiences after the deaths of my father and sons I am convinced that Science will eventually identify the Spiritual Realm to be a higher level of Frequency within the interconnectedness of Multidimensional reality. I am sure that when my time comes to personally explore the underlying connections of the Universe, I will find my loved ones waiting there to welcome me into the joyous embrace of eternal love.

My Beliefs Concerning Spirituality

Many PhD, Physicists accept Superluminal (faster than speed of light) connections as a door to Spirit but are afraid to say so for fear of ridicule by the scientific community. I believe the spiritual realm is **Real** (Non Local) but we just can't see it. It is Invisible but also real. This is either because its properties are too small to be seen (subtle matter) or are constructed from aspects of energy that have not been identified.

I believe the Human Realm resides in the Macro Frequency of Locality (Touch) and that the Spiritual Frequency (Micro—Invisible) is also real but just too small to see. I share my conclusions about the makeup of the Universe with clients who have had spiritual experiences that many things exist in the Universe that we just can't see due to residing in a different frequency realm. For example, before the discovery of electricity we didn't know it existed but it was real and constructed of energy that had not been identified at that time.

Synchronicity was always something I sensed was important in my life. But it wasn't until the last 20 years that I have realized how significantly it has affected my life. It's obvious to me that I choose Psychology as a result of my mother's mental illness, that I moved to Ca and bough a McD's franchise due to my Aunt marrying Ray Kroc and that I was able to pay for 10 years of college due to being able to sell my McD's restaurants.

I have no doubt that the Human Spirit evolves through interactions with other human beings, life experiences and recognition of spiritual information synchronicity, serendipity, fate, etc. I believe there is a spiritual realm because I have had personal experience with dreams, Out of Body Experiences and unexplained frequency realm type phenomena.

My own belief is that the Soul comes from the Implicate Order to reside in human form (Explicate Order) while attempting to learn the necessary lessons for growth of both human and spiritual essence. Some of us are much more in tune with the unseen, intuitively sensing the frequency of the implicate while others need hard facts to convince them. From my own personal experiences, I always knew that there was definitely "something" about Spirituality that I knew I wanted to study but I just never seemed to find the necessary time for it. It wasn't until I found myself surrounded with tragedy of such monumental proportions that I found myself floating in the realm of consciousness.

I am sure that the truth of both the Micro and Macro levels are realistic aspects of Frequency. I am sure as does David Bohm that the Explicate enfolds into the Implicate and becomes invisible but does not disappear. I am positive that Research will eventually prove the reality of a higher plane of reality to be multidimensional. I am positive that such conclusions will eventually be explained by scientific theories such as those of quantum mechanics.

The
"Map"

REALITY

Laws of Cause & Effect

EPILOGUE

Maturation: The Adult Paradigm

WHERE IS the **"Real"** Me?

Examine Your Path <u>CLOSELY</u> for Clues

Epilogue

Laws of Cause & Effect

Maturation: The Adult Paradigm

We are Born With A Mission—to explore our own path. Most of us begin our Journey "dancing" with abandon to intense emotional rhythms. Only later, . . . often in great pain, do some of us recognize the outstretched hand of Objective Reality and learn to Dance to the Music of the Universe.

A majority of Adult Emotional Distress **and** Anxiety **falls on the** continuum of **immaturity/maturity vs** neurosis/wellness. **Although Separation Anxiety is Normal in childhood, symptoms of** Adult Psychological immaturity are a typically underneath but essential "Missing Link" for attainment of functional **(vs dysfunctional) resolution of Anxiety.**

We hide our "Real" selves behind "Masks" of Anxiety in attempts to avoid the Reality of human differences and necessity for healthy emotional separation. **At the core of Adult Psychological Immaturity lies disabling inability to feel and behave as an Independent, emotionally separate person.** Anxiety is a Normal signal of underlying ambiguous conflict in need of resolution for the processes of Ego and Cognitive Development to successfully continue. Levels of Self Worth, developed over a life span, significantly effect Adult ability to live up to unique inborn potential and resolve conflict concerning personal competence and interpersonal differences.

Loving, well meaning Parents, Authority Figures and many admired others often teach confusing, contradictory **Rules** & **Roles** of life such as "**Never make mistakes,**" "**Authority knows best**", "**Think for yourself**", "**People who really love each other should always agree**", Don't talk back", etc. Most children and Adolescents are instructed that **Normal** Behavior requires **Deference to Authority.** Sadly, **Walking on the Path of others** does not automatically lead to **Normal** Development but often to Anxiety and other symptoms of ego & cognitive **Immaturity. Psychological Immaturity** in Adulthood often results from inadequate self esteem, reluctance or inability to think for the self and fear of abandonment for disagreement with loved ones or respected authority figures. Levels of Self Worth and Esteem developed over a life span, significantly affect Adult ability to live up to inborn unique potential and resolve conflict concerning interpersonal differences.

 A clear Boundary between adolescent and adult development has not been identified. No Agreed upon definition of **"Normal"** adult ego & cognitive development currently exists. Most perceptions of Normal behavior includes typical, socially conforming, responsible or functional conduct. However, those identified by others as responsible, high functioning people do not always exhibit typical, common or even socially approved attitudes and behaviors. In addition, responsible behavior sometimes **requires** socially nonconforming, atypical or currently socially disapproved behavior.

 Successful progression through the Adolescent Stage of Emotional Seperation **(Separation-Individuation) into Adulthood** may rest on realistic knowledge of how an unconscious redirections of feelings from the past **(Psychological Transference)** into the present may continue to entrap our Adult relationships in the emotional bondage of childhood enmeshment.

Psychological Maturity can be defined as the ability to Face Objective Reality, accept the truth, tolerate frustration, delay gratification and live up to inborn unique potential. The Stage of Ego and Cognitive Maturation requires unique cognitive  independence, resolution of emotional enmeshment, respect for the needs of others as equal to our own and development of a personally arrived at objective vs subjective philosophy of life

The <u>Map of Reality</u> Runs through the **Fabric of the Universe** and is paved with **Universal Laws Of Cause And Effect**. <u>Human Life</u> can be perceived as a multifaceted arena of Instructional Opportunities within <u>Human Relationships</u>, <u>Life Situations</u>, and <u>Universal Connections</u> (serendipity, dreams, synchronicity, intuition), meditation, dreams) for development of both human and spiritual potential. **Personal growth, mature relationships** and development of **Unique Potential (Psychological Maturation)** can occur by Learning to recognize the underlying **"Processes" of Reality. The** Music <u>Of The Universe</u> is an intangible, invisible process underlying events and relationships providing opportunities for both Psychological & Spiritual Development.

The Evolving Dancer (Essence of the Human Spirit) comes to earth to emerge **in a continual Unfolding Process when the necessary conditions for potential growth are recognized.** Psychological Maturation (dignity and unique potential of Human Spirit) is a bridge leading to the Door of the Spiritual Realm behind which allows understanding of our Human Mission.

The Human <u>Mission</u>, Unique to each of Us, is contained in The Soul's Program for Human & Spiritual growth. <u>Human Life</u> is the training ground for development of <u>both</u> human and spiritual potential. Listen closely to the **Music of the Universe** for knowledge **(serendipity, dreams, synchronicity, intuition)** leading to opportunities for spiritual growth within human <u>relationships</u> and/or <u>life</u> **situations.** The <u>Path to Eternity</u> (Spiritual Maturity) runs through the <u>Fabric of the Universe</u> (Map of Reality) and <u>is paved</u> with Universal <u>Laws of Cause & Effect</u>. Dancing to the Music of the Universe allows evolution of the Human Spirit and development of a more complete understanding of Human Mission and Purpose of Life.

 Science Knocks on the Door of the Spiritual Realm.
FOLLOW THE "MAP" & LEARN TO DANCE TO THE "MUSIC" OF THE UNIVERSE

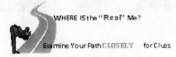

WHERE IS the "Real" Me?

Examine Your Path CLOSELY for Clues

Chapter 16
Science Knocks on the Door of the Spiritual Realm

Blue Arrows = Functional Behavior   **Red** Arrows = Dysfunctional Behavior

THE REAL "ME"
Learning to Walk on Your
Own Path

**A PHILOSOPHICAL DIAGRAM OF THE
FABRIC & MUSIC
OF THE UNIVERSE**

Psychological Maturity

- Unique Objective Thought Process,
- Comfort with Emotional Separation,
- Interdependence
- Personal Objective Philosophy of Life

The Evolving Dancer -
Spiritual Essence
Intuition * Evolution of Human Spirit * Altered States
of Consciousness * Knowledge of Mission *
Philosophy of Purpose * Understanding of Underlying
Connections in Universe

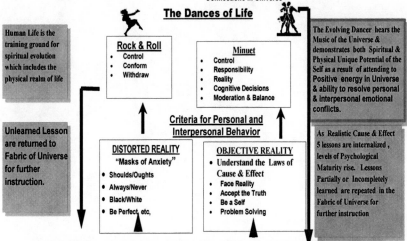

The Dances of Life

Human Life is the training ground for spiritual evolution which includes the physical realm of life

Rock & Roll
- Control
- Conform
- Withdraw

Minuet
- Control
- Responsibility
- Reality
- Cognitive Decisions
- Moderation & Balance

The Evolving Dancer hears the Music of the Universe & demonstrates both Spiritual & Physical Unique Potential of the Self as a result of attending to Positive energy in Universe & ability to resolve personal & interpersonal emotional conflicts.

Criteria for Personal and Interpersonal Behavior

Unlearned Lesson are returned to Fabric of Universe for further instruction.

DISTORTED REALITY
"Masks of Anxiety"
- Shoulds/Oughts
- Always/Never
- Black/White
- Be Perfect, etc,

OBJECTIVE REALITY
- Understand the Laws of Cause & Effect
- Face Reality
- Accept the Truth
- Be a Self
- Problem Solving

As Realistic Cause & Effect 5 lessons are internalized , levels of Psychological Maturity rise. Lessons Partially or Incompletely learned are repeated in the Fabric of Universe for further instruction

THE MUSIC (Laws of Cause & Effect) OF THE UNIVERSE teaches **5 LIFE LESSONS** which allow

resolution of **Emotional Dependency, Psychological Development** and **Evolution Of The Human Spirit**

TEACHERS OF LIFE LESSONS include **People-Situations-Experiences–Serendipity-Synchronicity**

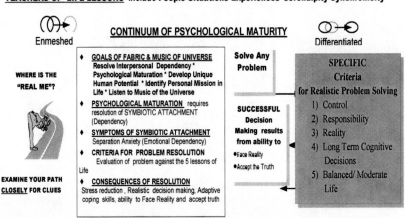

CONTINUUM OF PSYCHOLOGICAL MATURITY

Enmeshed

Differentiated

**WHERE IS THE
"REAL ME"?**

♦ **GOALS OF FABRIC & MUSIC OF UNIVERSE**
Resolve Interpersonal Dependency *
Psychological Maturation * Develop Unique
Human Potential * Identify Personal Mission in
Life * Listen to Music of the Universe

♦ **PSYCHOLOGICAL MATURATION** requires
resolution of SYMBIOTIC ATTACHMENT
(Dependency)

♦ **SYMPTOMS OF SYMBIOTIC ATTACHMENT**
Separation Anxiety (Emotional Dependency)

♦ **CRITERIA FOR PROBLEM RESOLUTION**
Evaluation of problem against the 5 lessons of
Life

♦ **CONSEQUENCES OF RESOLUTION**
Stress reduction , Realistic decision making, Adaptive
coping skills, ability to Face Reality and accept truth

**Solve Any
Problem**

**SUCCESSFUL
Decision
Making results
from ability to**

● Face Reality
● Accept the Truth

**SPECIFIC
Criteria
for Realistic Problem Solving**

1) Control

2) Responsibility

3) Reality

4) Long Term Cognitive Decisions

5) Balanced/ Moderate Life

**EXAMINE YOUR PATH
CLOSELY FOR CLUES**

REFERENCES

Maturation: The Adult Paradigm—

CHAPTER 1—

The Search for Normal—Mental Processes

- ❖ **DSM-IV MADE EASY, JAMES MORRISON** (PAGE 8-9)—Def of Mental disorder paraphrased, is "Mental disorder is a clinically important collection of syumptoms (behavioral or psychological) that causes an individual distress, disability or increased risk of suffering pain, disability, death, or the loss of freedom" He adds that Mental disorder describe disease not people, there is no sharp boundary between disorders or any disorder and normality.
- ❖ **Ideology** A cohesive set of beliefs, ideas, and symbols through which persons interpret the world and their place within it. The term was coined in late eighteenth-century France in reference to a projected science of ideas, but soon came to refer to a view of the world based on irrational beliefs as opposed to objective knowledge.
- ❖ Unable to function normally as result of disease or impairment

Stages & ages of Human Biological Development

- ❖ **Piaget, Jean**, **Swiss Psychologist (1896-1980)** best known for his pioneering work on the development of intelligence in children **Encarta Encyclopedia Child Development**
- ❖ **Human Cognitive Development**
- ❖ Kohlberg's Theories of Childhood Reasoning and Moral Development follows closely the work of Jean Piaget's Theory of Cognitive Development and perhaps even extends his predecessor's work. **Kohlberg, Lawrence (1927-1987**

Aspects of Adult Functioning

- ❖ Murray Bowen, MD—Family Therapy in Clinical Practice—Copyright 1978 Jason Aronson
- ❖ Reprinted from Website of **Bowen Center for the Study of the Family** on Murray Bowen's research on Differentiation.
- ❖ (1970) Father of Ego Psychology—Hartman, H
- ❖ **Hellmuth Kaiser (Effective Psychotherapy, 1965)**
- ❖ Psychoanalytic Concept of Primary Process thinking—basic tendency toward immediate gratification
- ❖ Mature Observing Ego—Psychoanalytic Theory—Secondary process thinking—Freud Reality Principle
- ❖ (1970) Father of Ego Psychology—Hartman, H
- ❖ Immature **Observing Ego**—Campbill, R Psychiatric Dictionary (1981) Psychoanalytic Concept of primary Process thinking—Basic tendency for immediate gratification. Mature **Observing Ego**—Psychoanalytic Theory—Secondary process thinking—Freud Reality Principle

PERSONALITY "Masks" of Anxiety

- ❖ **Maturation: Adult Paradigm** (The Map) adapted from Psychological Theory underlying **FINDING THE "REAL" ME**—Learning to Walk on Your Own Path (Unpublished Book).
- ❖ **Skipi Lundquist Smoot, PhD** Copyright@ 1995—Psychological Theory underlying **FINDING THE "REAL ME"**—Scientific Theory, Data and Research.

Maturation: The Adult Paradigm

- ❖ Goodwin, Donald W, MD Anxiety
- ❖ (Encarta Dictionary)
- ❖ (American Heritage Dictionary)[20] "The Struggle against seeing oneself as an individual is the core of every neurosis" wrote Hellmuth Kaiser. He spoke of the "universal defense" against individuality, fusion, as a delusion. He saw the conflict to be between recognizing one's aloneness and need to deny it. Contribution of Hellmuth Kaiser from Effective Psychotherapy (1965) by Fierman, Louis.
- ❖ <u>Symbiotic Attachment</u>. Symbiotic Attachment defined in Psychodynamic literature as a phase in mother-child relationship when child dimly recognizes mother as a need satisfying object and functions as through they formed a single omnipotent system (Mahler, 1975). Much of the Borderline States is believed to be rooted in failure to progress satisfactory through the separation-individuation stage (Campbell, 1981). See Reference Section.
- ❖ <u>NEUROSIS</u>=just <u>another name for</u> Anxiety. Dysfunctional symptoms (anxiety, depression, phobia, etc) in otherwise intact Reality Base of Personality. surrounding Specific underlying conflict. Various functional disorders without organic lesion or change. Dysfunctional Emotional Behavior. **Norm**

CHAPTER 2

- ❖ Albert Ellis—RET—Irrational, Illogical thinking processes—1950's Glasser—Reality Therapy— What behaviors caused the problem.-1960
- ❖ <u>Hartmann, H</u>—Father of Ego Psychology—Concept that thought develops independently from the Ego
- ❖ <u>Berne, E</u>—Adult Ego State—Transactional Analysis—Think about feelings and choose to disregard them
- ❖ Hartsman, H—Father of Ego Psychology. The Cognitive (thinking) processes develop separately from the Ego Ego Psychology—Emotional structure) <u>Impulse Control—Delay of Gratification</u>—Ego Boundaries—Codependency Beattym M

CHAPTER 3

- ❖ Peck, s Road Less Traveled Serendipity Pgs 305, 308 Synchronicity Pg 308
- ❖ The Road Less Traveled" by Scott Peck, MD Chapter 1V, the Miracle of Serendipity (pg 253).
- ❖ Karma (Hinduism & Buddhism) is the sum and consequences of a person's actions during the successive phase of his existence, regarded as determining his destiny. "New College Edition of the American Heritage Dictionary"
- ❖ ???? Jacque Costeau, 19 pg

PART II—THE MISSING LINK

ENDNOTES

[i] **Ego Boundaries**—Hypothesis that Ego Boundaries operate as peripheral sense organ of Ego was introduced by **Federn,** (1928).   Defined in Psychodynamic Literature as two main Ego Boundaries (inner=Feeling and outer=Physical) sensing and discriminating real from unreal.

[ii] <u>Individuation</u> Described in Psychoanalytic Literature as the Process of forming individual personality that leads to source of psychic existence-the inner core Self. (Jacobi, 1942 and Bowen, 1978).

[iii] **Interdependence**-Defined in Psychodynamic Literature as state of feeling and behaving as equal persons in relationships. Underlying theory contributing to concept includes positions on scale of Narcissism: 1) Egocentric = Center of Universe (**Kernberg, 1975 and Kohut, 1971**): 2) Decentered = Others needs more important than mine (**Exner, 1986)** Rorschach Ink Blots research: 3) = I'm OK, You're OK Our needs are equally important **Berne, 1961 and Harris**, 1969)-. See Reference section

[iv] **Ego Boundaries**-Hypothesis that Ego Boundaries operate as peripheral sense organ of Ego was introduced by **Federn,** (1928). Defined in Psychodynamic Literature as two main Ego Boundaries (inner=Feeling and outer=Physical) sensing and discriminating real from unreal.

[v] <u>**Individuation**</u> Described in Psychoanalytic Literature as the Process of forming individual personality that leads   to

source of psychic existence-the inner core Self. (Jacobi, 1942 and Bowen, 1978).

vi **Interdependence**-Defined in Psychodynamic Literature as state of feeling and behaving as equal persons in relationships. Underlying theory contributing to concept includes positions on scale of Narcissism: 1) Egocentric = Center of Universe (**Kernberg, 1975 and Kohut, 1971**): 2) Decentered = Others needs more important than mine (**Exner, 1986**) Rorshach Ink Blots research: 3) = I'm OK, You're OK Our needs are equally important **Berne, 1961 and Harris**, 1969)—. See Reference section

vii Theories of Psychology contributing to Maturation: Adult Paradigm (*The* Map).

- **Developmental Psychology** Study of processes of maturation of the intellectual, emotional, attitudinal and social aspects of organism. Child cognition (**Piaget**, 1937):, Temperment (**Chess and Alexander 1980**) Stages (**Erickson**, 1959) Self Esteem (Brandon, 1992), Pleck, (1975) and Adult Development (**Colarusso and Nemiroff** 1983).
- **Ego Psychology** Hypothesis that Ego development (autonomous functioning) follows a developmental path independent of conflict resolution and arises out of a conflict free sphere of ego. These functions evolve according to an innate biological timetable. This environment (**Winnicott, 1965**) is free of major trauma yet not without frustration or the need for adaptation. Concept that Ego & Cognition develop from the same common matrix but form two separate parts of the Ego (**Hartsman, Kris, Lowenstein, 1946**).
- **Psychodynamic Theory** Concept that ego arises in response to the frustrations and demands of reality (conflict) on the organism: The ability of an individual to adapt to life's changing requirements is limited and the degree of limitation is the index of psychopathology. Levels of Ego development is result of techniques of anxiety management (**Freud,** S. & various early authors) Resolution of Symbiotic Attachment and Separation Anxiety (**Mahler**, 1975), Resolution of Egocentricity narcissistic position : self as the center of the Universe.(**Kernberg, 1975 and Kohut, 1971**)

PART II—Tasks of Human Psychological Maturation

Chapter 4

Task 1—Unique Independence

❖ Bernstein-Warner (1981) Introduction to Contemporary Psychology—Introspection—Unconscious Assimilation of "something out there" into the self—Psychoanalytic concept of Introspection —Ego develops the ability to observe the Self.

❖ Brandon, Nathan The Power of Self Esteem 1992

❖ Coopersmith, Stanley 1981 The Antecedents of Self Esteem

❖ Hartmann, Heinz—Father of Ego Psychology—(1976) Concept that Thought develops independently from the Ego

❖ Hartmann, Heinz, Kris & Lowenstein (1946) Parents of Ego Psychology. The Psychoanalytic Study of the Child Comments on the formation of psychic structure. Concept that ego does not develop from the id but that id and ego develop from a common matrix.

❖ James, William 1890 Principles of Psychology

❖ Principles of Psychology (1890), INTERNALIZATION Psychoanalytic Concept that describes a process of assimilation (Introjection, Incorporation, & secondary Identification).

Chapter 5

Task 2—Emotional Separation

❖ Hellmuth Kaiser (Effective Psychotherapy, 1965

❖ The Power of Self Esteem, 1992 Nathan Brandon

❖ The Principles of Psychology, 1890 William James

❖ The Antecedents of Self Esteem, 1981 Stanley Coopersmith Berne, Eric—Scripts as a means to organize behavior within relationship. Lead to patterns of Behavior.

❖ Berne, Eric—Scripts as a means to organize behavior within relationship. Lead to patterns of Behavior.

❖ Berne, Eric **Emotional Differentiation**

- ❖ Bowen, Murray—Differentiation—
- ❖ Exner, John—The Rorschach: A Comprehensive System—Egocentricity Scale
- ❖ Failberg (1969) Object Constancy
- ❖ Failberg—Object Constancy
- ❖ Federn, Paul (1928) Ego feeling. Viewed as maintaining equilibrium. In it's absence depersonalization would occur (a loss of the sense of wholeness and cohesion of the sense of self. A feeling of unreality.
- ❖ Fierman, Louis (1965) Effective psychotherapy: the contribution of Hellmuth Kaiser.
- ❖ Freud, Sigmund—Concept that Anxiety is the manifestation of an Unconscious Conflict —
- ❖ Kernberg, Otto—(1975) Borderline Conditions and Pathological Narcissism
- ❖ Kerr, MD—Family Evaluation,
- ❖ Kohut, H (1971) Analysis of the self. Kohug, H & Wolf, E (1978) the disorders of the self and their treatment
- ❖ Mahler, M—Symbiosis Mahler, Margaret Differentiation
- ❖ Psychological Theory (Hellmuth Kaiser—1965)
- ❖ Winnocott—Transitional Objects

Chapter 6

Task 3—Interdependence

- ❖ **Berne, Eric** discusses the **Observing Ego** in **Transactional Analysis** as the thinking processes of a person that perceives the world without feelings, duty or morality. The Adult Self is a normal part of Maturation. Those who are not able to achieve this stage at all are often seen as immature, overly duty oriented, etc.
- ❖ Beels, C *Whatever happened to father.* New York Times, Aug. 25, 1974.
- ❖ Bem, S (1972, 1974, 1975, 1976) **Androgyny**
- ❖ Berne E—**Transactional Analysis** Three Ego States (Parent, Adult, Child)
- ❖ Berne, E—Transactional Analysis—Adult Ego State
- ❖ Bowen, M—**Differentiation**

- Broverman—**Characteristics of Normal males and females**
- Chance et all (1978) Gender as determinant of Sex roles Traditional Male-Traditional Female
- Covey, S "Seven Habits of Effective People"
- Elder, RA Traditional and Developmental concepts of Fatherhood *Marriage and Family living* 1949.
- Exner, J The Rorschach: A Comprehensive System— **Egocentricity** Scale Page 392-396.
- Gordon, T "Parent Effectiveness Training
- Hattwidk (1937) Bandura (1962) Kagan & Moss (1962) **Gender-Sex Roles**
- Kernberg, O (1975) Borderline Conditions and Pathological **Narcissism**
- Kohlberg and Ullian, *Stages in the **Development of Psychosexual concepts** and attitudes* (1974).
- **Kohlberg, L** "*A cognitive developmental analysis of **children's sex roll concepts** and attitudes.*
- Kohut, H—Narcissism (1971)
- Kohut, H & Wolf, E (1978) the **disorders of the self** and their treatment
- Kohut, H (1971) **Analysis of the self**.
- Macoby, the **Development of Sex Differences** (1966).
- Parsons, T & Bales, RF *Family, socialization and interaction Process*.
- **Zelditch,—R**ole **Differentiation in the Nuclear Family** (1955).
- Parsons, T & Bales, RF *Family, socialization* **and interaction Process**
- Pleck, J alternative Paradigm of **Sex Role**
- Zelditch, **Role Differentiation** *in the Nuclear Family* (1955

Chapter 7

TASK 4—FIT IN THE UNIVERSE—WHAT IS MY PHILOSPHY OF LIFE?

A BROAD UNIVERSAL VIEW MAY INCLUDE THE FOLLOWING BELIEFS.

A. **Fit GOD** Fit with Religion—I believe or do not believe in god, religion or spirituality as it relates to the existence of a God in religion.
B. **Fit Spirituality** I do or do not believe in spirituality.
C. **Fit Values & Principles**—My philosophy of Life does or does not include a personally arrived at Set of Values, Principles, Duty,and Responsibility for my self and others.
D. **Fit with Science** I do or do not believe in Science.
E. **Fit Universal Development**—I do or do not believe in a set of underlying laws of cause and effect that govern the interactions of the universe. These laws may apply to all aspects of the universe,

PART III—

Lessons for Development of Psychological Maturation

Chapter 8

Lesson 1—CONTROL

❖ Beck, & Ellis, A—Cognitive theory and Core Beliefs—behavior that person is used to
❖ Berne, E—Scripts as a means to organize behavior within relationships. Lead to patterns of behavior.
❖ Bowen, M—Theories of Differentiation
❖ Bowen, Murray & Mahler, M Differentiation and Symbiosis—Behavior as a method to control anxiety in Relationships

- ❖ Covey, S—Seven Habits of Effective People—Problem Solving
- ❖ Kernberg & Kohut Psychoanalytic theory of— Narcissism.
- ❖ **McKay (19).** Straight Talk (The Iron Fist and the Velvet Glove)
- ❖ Peck, S—Road Less Traveled—The Outmoded Map

Chapter 9

Lesson 2A—PERSONAL RESPONSIBILITY

- ❖ Bem, Sandra,—Androgyny—**Sex Roles**
- ❖ Bowen, Murray—Differentiation, Emotional Fusion
- ❖ Broverman,—Normal Male & Female Behavior—**Sex Roles**
- ❖ Chess, S 19) Tempermeantal Fit with others
- ❖ Hartsman, H Ego Psychology
- ❖ Kohlberg—Moral Development
- ❖ Kohut & Kernberg—Theories of Narcissism
- ❖ Hartsman, H Ego Psychology
- ❖ ROTTER—Locus of Control
- ❖ Psychological Theory of Human Development
  - ❖ Chess, S (19) temperamental fit
  - ❖ Rotter—Theory of Locus of Control
  - ❖ Sex Roles and Gender Expectations for taking care of family members, children, etc.
  - ❖ Social Learning Theory,
  - ❖ Marriage & Family Theory,
  - ❖ Parental Belief Systems—Roles played in life.
  - ❖ Family Order —
  - ❖ Smoot Skipi—Doctoral Dissertation —Differences b/t males and females

Chapter 10

Lesson 2B—RESPONSIBILITY FOR OTHERS

- ❖ Codependency **Resp for Others**
- ❖ Emotional Detachment
- ❖ Social Learning theory,

- ❖ Marriage & Family Theory,
- ❖ Ellis, Belief Systems,
- ❖ Glasser, W, Cultural and social expectations
- ❖ Beatty, M—Codependent No More and other writings.
- ❖ Sex Roles and Gender expectations for taking care of family members, children, elderly family members and those who are seen as unable to take proper responsibility.
- ❖ Ellis, Albert—Should, Always & Generalize—Rational Emotive Therapy. ABC theory. Problem Solving, Reason & Emotion, Growth through Reason,

Chapter 11

Lesson 3—REALITY

- ❖ Beck, Ellis,), Cognitive Theory
- ❖ Michenbaum Cognitive Theory
- ❖ Berne, E), Life Scripts
- ❖ Exner), Psychological assessment of Perceptual distortions
- ❖ Kilman, B), Prof. Of Psychological Assessment—California School of Prof Psychology 1984—Red Threads (Strong Patterns) that run through Life
- ❖ Toleman), Family Order
- ❖ Deja vous, Anxiety (Freud) as an explanation for confusion and distortions,
- ❖ **Emotions** and other Psychological factors as disruptors of reality,
- ❖ Freud, Sigmund Psychoanalytic and Psychodynamic theories of **Transference**
- ❖ Homeostasis (Family Therapy) within family and groups. theory of Balance family roles and keeping them stable much as the dynamics of a furnace system.
- ❖ Kris, E—Creativity—Unconsciously reaches for the more primitive layer of thinking to facilitate creativity or promote empathy
- ❖ Paradigms (Belief System)

Chapter 12

Lesson 4—TELESCOPE OF COGNTIVE OBSERVATION

- ❖ <u>Ellis, A,</u> **Cognitive theory** and **Core Beliefs** 1950s American psychologist Albert Ellis developed one of the first cognitive approaches to therapy, *rational-emotive therapy,* now commonly called *rational-emotive behavior therapy.*
- ❖ <u>Beck, Aaron,</u> Cognitive Theory Causes of Depression Irrational Thinking n Beck's view, depressed people tend to have negative views of themselves, interpret their experiences negatively, and feel hopeless about their future. He sees these tendencies as a problem of faulty thinking.
- ❖ **Michenbaum, Donald** You Can change your emotions by changing your ways of thinking . . . & vice versa **Cognitive—Behavioral Theory**
- ❖ **Glasser, William Glasser, William 1960's.—Developed Reality Therapy, after working with severely disturbed schizophrenic patients. Believed that it was important to help individuals take personal responsibility and blame othrs less.**
- ❖ Hartsman, H—Father of Ego Psychology. The Cognitive (thinking) processes develop separately from the Ego Ego Psychology—Emotional structure) <u>Impulse Control—Delay of Gratification—</u>
- ❖ Smoot, S—Pschological Immaturity vs Maturity A set of attitudes and Behaviors seen as Dancing to the Music of the Universe (Cause & Effect) Objective Reality.
- ❖ Smoot, S —Adult Seperation Anxiety
- ❖ Smoot, S—Dancing to Emotion—Dancing to Cognitive Thought Frustration Tolerance _ Delay of Gratification
- ❖ Colarus;so & Nemeroff (1983) Adult Development: A New Dimension—Adult Separation Anxiety
- ❖ Adult Seperation Anxiety—Fears of rejection, inadequacy
- ❖ Winnicott (1965) Ego develops according to Biological time table including need to adapt to frustration.

Chapter 13

Lesson 5—BALANCE & MODERATION

- ❖ Covey, Steven—**Problem Solving in Relationships**—
- ❖ APA—Convention 1993—**The Happiest Marriages are Egalitarian**
- ❖ Bowen, Murray **(1913-1990—Family Systems Theory—**
- ❖ **Differential of self in One's Family of Origin**
- ❖ **Covey, Steven** Seven Habits of Effective People
- ❖ Coopersmith, S—Self Esteem DepressionAddictgions
- ❖ **Ellis, A, Ellis, A, Cognitive theory** and **Core Beliefs** 1950s American psychologist Albert Ellis developed one of the first cognitive approaches to therapy, *rational-emotive therapy,* now commonly called *rational-emotive behavior therapy.*
- ❖ **Beck, Aaron. T. Cognitive theory** and **Core Beliefs. Theories of Depression.** Ways of thinking learned in childhood may not be consistent with reality.
- ❖ **Bandura, Albert Social Learning Theory**—Educational Psychology, Child Development theory
- ❖ **Michenbaum**—Cognitive Theory—You can **change your emotions by changing your thinking**
- ❖ (Berne, E) Berne, E—Transactional Analysis—Adult—Child—Parent Ego State
- ❖ **Scripts** as a means to organize behavior within relationships. Lead to patterns of behavior. **Berne, E—Covey, S**
- ❖ **(Dusay, John**

Miscellaneous References used in The Map

- ❖ APA Convention—1993—The Happiest Marriages are Equalitarian
- ❖ Beatty, M—Codependent no more and others
- ❖ Beck, Ellis, A—Cognitive theory and Core Beliefs
- ❖ Bem, S—Androgency
- ❖ Bentov, I—Staking the Wild Pentulum Davies—God and the New Physics
- ❖ Berne, E—Scripts as a means to organize behavior within relationships. Lead to patterns of behavior.

- ❖ Berne, E—Transactional Analysis—Adult Ego State
- ❖ Bernstein-Warner (1981) Introduction to Contemporary Psychology—Introspection—Unconscious Assimilation of something out there into the self—
- ❖ Bowen, M—Differentiation
- ❖ Bowen, Murray—Differentiation
- ❖ Bowen, Murray & Mahler, M Differentiation and Symbiosis—Behavior as a method to control anxiety in Relationships
- ❖ Brandon,N—PowerofSelfEsteem(1992),James,w—Principles of Psychology (1890), Coopersmith, S antecedents of Self Esteem (1981)
- ❖ Chance et all (1978) Gender as determinent of Sex roles Traditional Male-Traditional Female
- ❖ Cultural and social expectations are major forces in shaping our perspectives of our Roles
- ❖ Ellis, A—Cognitive Therapy—Gordon, T—Win-Win Covey, S Seven Habits of Effective People
- ❖ Ellis, A, Beck, Michenbaum—Cognitive Theory—You can change your emotions by changing your thinking
- ❖ Family Theory—Homeostasis within the family—thoery of Balance family roles and keeping them stable much as the dynamics of a furnace system.
- ❖ Freud—Concept that Anxiety is the manifestation of an Unconscious Conflict—Smoot, s—"Masks of Anxiety" (1995)
- ❖ Friedman—Bridging Science & Spirt Davis, P—God and the New Physics
- ❖ Friedman,—Bridging Science and Spiri Ring, K—Life After Death Moody, R—Near Death Experiences
- ❖ Gender-Sex Roles Hattwidk (1937) Bandura (1962) Kagan & Moss (1962)
- ❖ Hartsman, H—father of Ego Psychology—(1976) Concept that Thought develops independently from the Ego
- ❖ Hawkings, s—Grand Unification theory Bohr, D—Quantum Mechanics
- ❖ Hawkings, S—Scientific Physics theories—Chaos theory, Grand Unification theory
- ❖ Introspection—Ability to Observe the Self

- Kilman, B. Prof. Of Psychological Assessment—California School of Prof Psychology 1984
- Kohlberg (1966) Stages of Moral development
- Kohlberg—Moral Development Rotter—Locus of Control Theory
- Kohut & Kernberg—Theories of Narcissism
- Kohut, H—Narcissism (1971)—Kernbert, Otto (1975)
- Kris, E—Creativity—Unconsciously reaches for the more primitive layers of thinking and feeling to fascilitate creativity or promote empathy.
- Kubler-Ross Moody, R—Near Death Experiences
- Mahler, M—Symbiosis Failberg (1969) Object Constancy Winnicott—Transitional Objects
- Maslow, A—
- Monroe, R—Journeys out of the body
- Monroe, R—Journeys out of the Body, Far Journeys, Reunions
- Ossis & Harroldsson—At the Hour of Death
- Rorshach—Special Scores Dd—W Wais-R = Picture Completion—Details
- Satir, V—Complementary Relationships Pleck (1975) Transcendence of Sex Roles
- SatirSex Roles and Gender expectations for taking care of family members, children, elderly family members and those who are seen as unable to take proper responsibility.
- Sex Roles and Gender expectations for taking care of family members, children, elderly family members and
- Sheehey, G—Passages Adult Psychological Development
- Skipi Lundquist Smoot, PhD—adapted from FINDING THE "REAL" ME—Learning to Walk on Your Own Path Copyright—1994 (Unpublished Book)
- Smoot, S—A set of attitudes and Behaviors that are seen as Dancing to the Music of Cognitions
- Smoot, s—A set of Behaviors that are seen as Dancing to the Music of Emotion
- Social Learning theory, Marriage & Family Theory, Belief Systems, etc. All contribute to Roles played in life.
- Talbot, M—Holographic Universe The Dancing Wu Li Masters

❖ Masters
❖ Toleman, W—Family Constellations, Family Order

Scientific Theories of Psychology contributing to Maturation: Adult Paradigm (The Map).

- Developmental Psychology Study of processes of maturation of the intellectual, emotional, attitudinal and social aspects of organism. Child cognition (**Piaget**, 1937):, Temperment (**Chess and Alexander 1980**) Stages (**Erickson**, 1959) Self Esteem (Brandon, 1992), Pleck, (1975) and Adult Development (**Colarusso and Nemiroff** 1983).

- Ego Psychology Hypothesis that Ego development (autonomous functioning) follows a developmental path independent of conflict resolution and arises out of a conflict free sphere of ego. These functions evolve according to an innate biological timetable. This environment (**Winnicott,** 1965) is free of major trauma yet not without frustration or the need for adaptation. Concept that Ego & Cognition develop from the same common matrix but form two separate parts of the Ego (**Hartsman, Kris, Lowenstein, 1946).**

- Psychodynamic Theory Concept that ego arises in response to the frustrations and demands of reality (conflict) on the organism: The ability of an individual to adapt to life's changing requirements is limited and the degree of limitation is the index of psychopathology. Levels of Ego development is result of techniques of anxiety management (**Freud,** S. & various early authors including Anna Freud, Carl Jung, and Melanie Klein) **Later,** Psychodynamic theories, while retaining concepts of drives and motives to varying degrees, moved toward the contemporary approach, which emphasizes the process of change and incorporates interpersonal and transactional perspectives of personality. Resolution of Symbiotic Attachment and Separation Anxiety (**Mahler**, 1975), Resolution of Egocentricity narcissistic position : self as the center of the Universe.(**Kernberg, 1975 and Kohut, 1971).**

- Separation Anxiety—Separation Anxiety defined in Psychodynamic Literature as fear, anxiety, etc., occasioned by threat or actual separation from mother or home. Implications and concept of Adult Separation Anxiety discussed by Colarusso and Nemiroff (1983) in Adult Development: A New Dimension In Psychodynamic Theory And Practice. Symptms of unresolved symbiotic attachment includes fears of inadequacy and rejection and attempts to control external situations and person. Controlling, conforming and withdrawing from ourselves and others (Bowen, 1978) are attempts to avoid anxiety by preventing conflict and potential rejection. Evidence of these intentions lie hidden behind attitudes and behaviors that when successful, maintain internal homeostasis and/or enmeshment with others. See Reference Section.

- A reference to the **concept that everything in the Universe is somehow connected through processes of cause and effect.** Hawkings (*A Brief History of Time),* perceives the Universe as so exquisitely put together it can only come from a type of Grand Unification theory. Hypothesis of Chaos theory states that everything in the Universe has a cause and effect even if not apparent. See Reference Sectiion.

APPENDIX 1

RESILIENCE—COPING WITH ADVERSITY

A list of incomparable tragedies might include but not be limited to the following:

- Being told your illness is terminal
- Being told your illness may be terminal but there is no way to know for sure
- Trying to live with unbearable physical pain
- Be in physical agony of pain one day but not quite as severe the next.
- Being so tired and in such pain many days of your life that getting dressed and attending to essential tasks seems insurmountable.
- Getting your legs blown off in war and having to live in a wheel chair for life
- Trying to live with the devastation of being the victim of rape
- Attempting to face and live life after have all or most of your children die
- Losing your spouse of a life time
- The loss of your home and possessions in an earth quake or tidal wave
- Being blinded for life in an accident
- Loss of freedom—being in jail

Client who is devastated by such a loss may comment similar to the following::

- Why me? What have I done to deserve this?
- Why my child instead of me, they had their whole life ahead of them. I'm old. I would gladly change places with them. I don't want to live without them.

- I can't figure out how to live with it and accept the truth. I need someone to tell me "how",
- I can't face it because others do not clearly understand my situation, etc.
- I don't understand what you mean by face reality and accept the truth
- I don't understand what you mean by "walk through it"
- I'm not getting the help I need, because the therapist isn't telling me clearly what I must do or think in order to walk through it, accept it, etc.

Possible Therapeutic Situations

- Client is faced with a situation of such difficult that coming to terms with it appears impossible.
- Client believes that therapy is not working, because the Therapist is not clearly sharing a method for coping with the problem (he/she) faces.
- Comparison of situations of such tragic proportion appears to be of little help because each problem is so devastating it presents a experience completely set off from the others.

Choices to be considered for dealing with a tragic situation

- Reasons why suicide is not a realistic option include need to be there for others, being a good role model for other children and family members, not wanting to give up, trying to be emotionally healthy enough to deal with adversity, not being comfortable with wasting the life we have been given.
- Either resign yourself to being overcome by tragic circumstances or fight for the life that may be the only one you will ever have.
- Go down swinging
- Define your perception of differences between physical vs emotional pain.
- Decide for self which aspects of emotional vs physical pain would be more difficult to deal with and reasons why you believe what you do.

The Value of Realistic Coping Skills and Techniques for Development

Definitions

- **I define Psychological Maturation** as a Human emotional and cognitive Developmental Stage resulting from the ability to face objective reality and accept the truth. **I perceive Human life to be a multifaceted arena of opportunities within human relationships and life situations for development of both human and spiritual potential.**

- I perceive the <u>Dimensions of Psychological Maturation</u> **to include 4 essential building blocks (Tasks of Ego Development: 1) cognitive independence, 2) emotional differentiation, 3) comfort with personal differences and 4) having arrived at a personally arrived at Philosophy Of Life based on as much objective reality as available during our life time.**

- I believe the <u>Process</u> of <u>Cognitive Development</u>1 **leading to personal growth and mature relationships can occur by adhering to the Universal Processes of cause and effect underlying reality. <u>5 Life Lessons</u> teach pragmatic Coping Skills in the areas of 1) internal/external control, 2) responsibility for self and others 3) distortions of reality, 4) cognitive vs emotional decision making and 5) moderation.**

Opportunities

- Potential Opportunities for development of personal hardiness, buoyancy, etc (a characteristic of Psychological Maturity) are presented to us each day as we walk down our path of life in the form of situations in which we can choose to face reality and accept the truth . . . or not.

---

1   Secondary Process—Freud

Functional Coping Strategies

- Successful **Coping Strategies within dissonant Life situations** require increased levels of Ego (Unique Independence and Emotional Differentiation) Development as well as Cognitive Maturation in the areas of Frustration Tolerance. ability to Delay of Gratification and objective Cognitive contemplation of emotion (Primary Process Choices) concerning the situation under consideration.
- However, **Coping Strategies for Life Situations of Tragic Proporations** may be more successfully coped with from the Psychological Maturation Dimension of Spiritual Philosophy of Life.
- I personally do not see such situations as God's punishment but rather opportunities to explore our spiritual Path in the Universe and try to understand our Human Mission and Lessons of Life.
- Increasing ability to face reality and accept the truth (Resilience) allows Human Psychological Maturation to develop. Resilience (Psychological buoyancy) is a characteristic of Psychological Maturation

History of Defenses Used

- Psychological Defenses (**Coping Strategies)** range from extremely dysfunctional to highly functional. And although much has been written concerning making choices for successfully **coping** with every day types of problematic situations, few equate this advice with opportunity for development of potential strength to deal with devastating types of life tragedy.
- Unwillingness (or less often inability[2]) to accept the truth of objective reality lies at the core of much of the stress and anxiety surrounding human situational problems and relationships conflicts

---

[2]   Psychosis or other symptoms of serious Mental Illness

Developing Functional Coping Strategies

- The value of Functional (pragmatic) Coping Strategies within our <u>personal **and** relationship</u> situations may be more objectively perceived in the context of consideration of the cause and effect within the Reality of our situation. For example how may my behavior have effected the behavior of the other or what have I been thinking or feeling that keeps me from learning to deal with the reality of my present situation.
- It is important we don't misunderstand what we can change and what we can't., What is fair and what isn't. Drop your expectations, shoulds, oughts, perceptions of fairness, etc. because they do not reflect reality
- Realize no one can tell another "how" to face reality and accept the truth" of their own particular tragic situation because learning to cope with reality is an individual psychological developmental process.
- To solve the question of "How" to face reality and accept the truth of a situation that seems impossible to deal with, we have to understand what we may have been doing or thinking that stands in our way of successfully coping. It is important to understand what types of Defenses we have learned to use in the past and why or why not they have worked well or not at all.
- Objective reality is truth and must be dealt with. Bitterness and resentment concerning reality is a waste of time. Face reality and accept the truth of your situation because you have no choice
- Resignation to tragedy is not the answer. The alternative is tantamount to saying "Life is too hard to deal with" because my personal life (or what's left of it) is not worth the effort of trying to understand my situation and successfully coping with it. Learning to live with tragedy by not wasting the life you have is the answer.
- Techniques for <u>living without loved ones</u> lost to tragedy may include 1) taking the hand of the departed and walking thru life with the memories of the loved one that are now part of my personal essence, 2) knowledge of growth and lessons learned from the relationship and 3) giving thanks to the Universe for

the Gift of having had the other for the time of their lives. Techniques for <u>living without aspects of my former self</u> (eyesight, hearing, limbs, home, etc) may include realizing that what is past will never be lost b/c it is part of who I am today. Realize that you may not know why you are still alive but the fact that you are presents the possibility there must be a reason for it.

- Try to plan a new way of life
- Use primary process (cognition) to accept and walk through the Pain (emotional or physical)
- Make a list of things that must be done and force yourself to walk through the pain in order to get things accomplished
- Visualize cognition rising above the pain and looking at it from a great distance. I will then deal with it for as long as I can. When I can no longer deal with it, I will stop trying for the day and try again tomorrow. In this way, I will help myself live with it for longer and longer periods of time.
- Learn to value the life you have been given even though at this time, the emotional or physical pain is so great it is hard to do.
- Realize that if you are still alive your work on earth is not over. You may still have lessons to learn or your earthy Mission of helping others is not finished yet